LED TO
SLAUGHTER

LED TO SLAUGHTER

Shawna Deliah

To order additional copies of this book, contact:
Xlibris Corporation
1-888-795-4274
www.Xlibris.com
Orders@Xlibris.com
17826

Cover illustration courtesy of Jim H. Lee, Sr.

CONTENTS

CHAPTER 1

THE BABY

I lay here talking to this stupid machine. I've been doing that a lot lately. Most of my friends have stopped coming to see me anymore. Maybe they're really as busy as they say . . . or maybe they're just afraid. Dying can have that effect on people. It has only been about three months since I learned the fact that I was dying of AIDS. Good bye pain. So long humiliation, fear, anger, loneliness forever! The end of my life is my beacon of hope and my only relief from this torturous illness. The 80's will always be remembered as the decade of the AIDS epidemic; I will be remembered, albeit for a short time as one of its victims.

It is still very difficult for me to admit that sexual activity led directly to my fate. I seldom considered myself as anything more than a girl with a healthy sexual appetite. By the tender age of three, I had already discovered that some places were more fun to touch than others. This was especially true if someone could find the "magic spots".

Old Bill could always find mine. He always had candy for me, too. My older brother, David, first introduced me to Bill. The old man only lived three doors down and since I was already three, I was allowed to visit all by myself. Bill and his daughter, Kate, lived in the house on the corner. They were always so very nice to me. I liked visiting them. I especially liked it when Kate wasn't there. I visited the green house on the corner a lot.

Mom said that Bill was a sad, lonely person and we kids should be nice to him. It was easy to be nice to someone who could give you as much candy as you wanted and could always find your "magic spots".

I first met Old Bill on a lazy spring day. David was dragging me to the park so he could play ball. As we walked past the bright green house, I noticed an old man kneeling on the ground, playing in the dirt. Rather than hurrying after my brother, I slowed my pace so I could watch what he was doing. Intrigued, I finally stopped . . . heedless of my brother's urging to hurry up.

"Well, hello there little one," came the raspy reaction. "What's your name"?

"Tarah! That's my brother, David. He calls me Rah. Watcha doing?" I asked.

That was the innocent beginning of a mutually fulfilling relationship. For the rest of that day and during our entire time together, Old Bill shared with me the everyday miracles of the world in which we lived. Many hours were spent planting seeds, watching for new sprouts, nourishing the young plants, weeding and marveling at the beauty of our blooms.

Many warm nights were spent on the porch while Old Bill pointed out different stars and the astrological pictures in the skies. He showed me how to find The Big Dipper and The Little Dipper, Orion's Belt and other vistas in the skies. Together, we admired God's artistry.

Old Bill never seemed too busy to answer my endless stream of questions.

When I asked him about Vietnam (something on TV a lot) he tried to put the horrible carnage into language that a small child could comprehend. He spoke of his military experience during World War I. How he and so many others had been injured. This led to a discussion of another war that brought to light the fact that his only son lost his life when his "boat" sank. Shortly after that, his wife died from what the doctors called T.B. Old Bill knew that she had died from her broken heart. It was fatally damaged on the day the soldiers told her that her boy would not be returning from The Pacific. This left him a grieving widower to care for his teenage daughter alone. Since then, they had taken care of each other.

The time we spent together was filled with laughter and learning and maybe even a slanted, yet unique, kind of love. He answered all my questions with patience and understanding, always stressing the goodness of mankind. He tried to minimize the mistakes and cruelty that humans aimed at one another. He spoke with wisdom that taught and touched an insecure, curious little toddler with an enlightenment that far surpassed her gentle years.

Old Bill seemed so nice to me and his attention was special. No topic was left unspoken. From space to race, he explained the situations of our world. He spoke openly and honestly with me. He never spoke down to me or ignored me even though I was only three and a half. My memories of this time are amazingly vivid.

Old Bill and I shared lots of secrets. Especially on lazy summer afternoons when we would have special, quiet time . . . just the two of us. He would take me upstairs to his magical room and let me play on the snuggly, fluffy comforter. Sometimes we would wrestle around or he would tickle me a little.

Each shared afternoon was special and surprising. His attention took many turns but he always managed to make me feel so special. I was shown the differences of our bodies through simple games and mild deception. His seduction during one such moment was so complete that, despite my natural inclination to resist, he cajoled me into "tasting" each other in different places. I really didn't want to kiss, taste or even look at his big, long thing . . . it frightened me, but Old Bill did not! He gently allayed my fears.

It really felt very nice when he kissed me down there. Sometimes it felt so good that I'd wish he'd never stop. Old Bill always found my "magic spots" during these sessions. He would rub "magic lotion" all over me, making sure all my special parts were covered. He said these special parts needed more magic . . . then he would make me feel magical.

Some part of me will always remember that old man as a gentle, generous friend who made a shy little girl feel important and understood. Be assured that many lessons were learned by that toddler that would play an important part in her future (even though I would be unaware of their significance until much later). Children are often much more sensitive to the causes and effects of controlling influences in their lives than adults. They can readily incorporate these influences into their specific domains and thereby extend the limits of their own power. Only after I grew older did I come to understand the disturbing aspects of childhood sexual molestation. Yet some child-like part of me still clings to the memories of those special moments. No shadow was ever cast over these adventures. No one ever interrupted us. No pall of child exploitation ever soured the sweetness that glazed these special moments in my mind. I filed them under tenderness and smiles!

CHAPTER 2

THE CHILD

I have been remiss up to this point in failing to properly introduce myself. My name is Tarah. I am 26 years old and the odds dictate that I shall not celebrate another birthday. My discomfort is almost constant and increases on a regular basis. The diarrhea is a bitch! Being nearly continuous, it necessitates my wearing a diaper. In the last three months, I have lost 47 pounds . . . bringing my weight to a grand total of 93. When I am able to stand I measure 5 foot nine. My emaciation leads to problems that are commensurate with being bed-ridden; namely, grotesque contractual deformities and bedsores. My butt looks like a rump roast (excuse the pun). Also due to my limited mobility, I am susceptible to frequent bouts of a very rare form of pneumonia that is called Pneumocystic Carinii or PCP, for short. As time progresses, the antibiotics that the doctors are using to fight this infection become less and less effective as my immune system becomes more compromised. This pneumonia, or any one of the opportunistic infections, will eventually take my life. I'm not crying, not really . . . because "I LIVED"!

I'm not very comfortable talking to a machine but at least you don't talk back, you can't interrupt and you remain non-judgmental. I like that!

My experiences with Old Bill lasted about two years. At about the time he died, I started school. Almost immediately, I felt a certain inexplicable longing. I knew I wanted and needed something or someone but at the age of five, I was not clear about just what that could be. Then, as if by magic, I ran into a very special crossing guard . . . literally. He was a big bear of a guy named Gus. I was running to school one morning when my progress was cut short instantly. It felt like I had run into a brick wall. The unyielding structure turned out to be my newly found friend in a uniform. He picked me up in his burly arms as easily as if I was a feather and laughed. His bulging belly shook. I shook. I believed at that moment the whole world shook. As our mutual giggling subsided, I remember feeling at peace. The longing, which had gnawed at me since Old Bill's death, had vanished.

I liked this person called Gus. It soon became apparent that he liked me, too. Every morning he would take my hand as we crossed the busy intersection and, when we were safely on the curb in front of the school, he would slip two or three chocolate kisses into my hand. He never did this for any of the other kids. He said I was his "special girl".

At the time, I thought that Gus should have been a teacher instead of a crossing guard. He seemed so smart and so eager to share his wisdom with me . . . especially about kissing.

Oh! I know! You're thinking, "what's a kid of five know about kissing? Right?" Well, I knew quite a bit. Watching TV could be very enlightening to a kid. When big people kissed on TV, it lasted a long time. So far, no one had ever kissed me for a long time. I guess you could say that Gus was like a kissing teacher. I used to wait for him and he'd walk me most of the way home after school. One afternoon he showed me the shortcut along the railroad tracks. Naturally, we checked for oncoming trains first. These tracks ran between the schoolyard and my neighborhood. As we scurried along, Gus stopped suddenly and whispered, "You wanna see my secret place?"

"You bet!" I chirped almost immediately.

Gus took my hand and helped me cross over the big metal rails. Bending a bit, he guided me through some thick sticker bushes. I didn't even get scratched. We soon came to a small clump of trees that seemed to he hiding an old, vacant factory . . . what was left of it, anyway.

While I was looking around, Gus had settled himself on the dried leaves and was motioning for me to come join him. Noticing my hesitation, he assured me that I would not get my dress dirty. To make certain, he suggested that I sit on his lap. Overjoyed, I leaped into his large, outstretched arms. For a while we just sat there without saying anything. I felt so comfortable and safe . . . like a baby in its mother's arms. When I looked up, Gus was looking at me and smiling.

"Can I give you a kiss?" he asked.

"Sure, Gus!" I replied as I threw my arms around his neck. His large hands engulfed my frail shoulders and, like a gentle giant, he dissolved my embrace by extending his arms to full-length, only to pull me back against him. He paused just long enough to say, "Kiss me on my lips, my little Tarah Doll".

Tilting my neck upward towards his face, I offered to him my puckered lips that he smothered with his own. I noticed how warm his lips were . . . almost hot. Suddenly, there was more than just our lips touching. His tongue was licking my lips, searching for a way into my mouth. When he slipped it between my lips, I sort of liked it. It made me feel warm inside. It danced around in my mouth and suddenly I realized something. This was the reason big people kissed for a long time. They were kissing with their tongues, too.

All too soon, the outside world intruded on us and we started on our way, once again. We retraced our steps and soon reached the railroad tracks. I knew I was gonna be late getting home, but if I showed up before dinner started, nobody would even notice. As we neared my house, Gus bade me goodbye in his usual manner. He'd lift my hand to his lips, plant a tender kiss on my fingers and bow like a gallant knight. Then he'd tip his hat and silently walk away.

"Let's keep that adventure our little secret," he whispered the next day. "If you tell anyone, then they will want to come to the secret place, too. Pretty soon it would get crowded and noisy and wouldn't be secret anymore. Where would I take my girlfriend, then?"

"Am I really your girlfriend, Gus?" I questioned excitedly.

"My one and only," he answered.

Our rendezvous continued throughout kindergarten. Nobody ever found out about our secret place or our secret adventures. As our exchanges progressed, so did my pleasure. I shared some secrets that Old Bill had taught me. Gus taught me things, too. He was always gentle and kind and always explained each new dimension added to our secret kissing game. It was special having a pal who could make you feel so special . . . especially for a kid. I would continue to search for someone who could make me feel like that for the rest of my life.

CHAPTER 3

THE EDUCATION

I lay here thinking how nice it would be to have one of Gus' kisses . . . or anyone's for that matter, right now. Most people are reluctant to even hug me or shake my hand. God forbid that they should kiss me. AIDS has been called by many the "epidemic of fear". How well I know! They're not talking about the victim's fear, either (although terror overwhelms you from the moment the diagnosis is established). No! The fear alluded to in the expression refers to the near-paranoia associated with the transmission of the AIDS virus.

By now I hope that most people know that the deadly HIV (the virus that causes AIDS) is predictably transferred from one person to the other through the blood and semen. It should be obvious to all how one could contract this disease through sexual practices commonly experienced today. Where blood and semen mix, the environment is conducive to the establishment of the virus that causes "Acquired Immune Deficiency Syndrome". For all the information that scientists have been able to assimilate about this new disease, there is still so much more to learn. Someday, they may actually find a cure or possibly even a vaccine. Until that time comes, I am forced to lie here in bed, usually afraid and alone, sharing my innermost thoughts with an insensitive machine. No offense! The self-control that I learned in Catholic School has really been effective.

After kindergarten, I was to attend the local parochial school as my siblings did.

This meant that I would get to wear a uniform everyday and be taught by the mysterious nuns. I was so excited until David started telling me horror stories about the way the nuns beat the students. One day, Mom caught him saying it and sent him off to bed without his dinner. David did not really mind since he didn't like what we were having that night. Anyway, I sneaked him up some peanut butter and jelly sandwiches when I went up to bed. We lay under the blankets and ate those sandwiches like we were having a picnic.

I was telling you about my attendance at the new school. I really liked Catholic School. There was never any confusion or excessive noise. The nuns almost always spoke in tones barely above a whisper. I tried to pay attention in class. Sometimes I'd get caught talking while the sister was teaching. At this point she'd interrupt her lecture and ask me if I wanted to take over teaching the class. The entire class would laugh and I would turn crimson. This experience would make me try even harder to listen to what the teacher was saying.

There was a time during my years at Catholic School when I gave serious consideration to entering the convent. I shared my thoughts about entering the sisterhood with a very special nun who evolved as my mentor during those formative years. She shared with me an insightful look at life behind the crucifix. She compared her life to any happily married person with the distinction that she was "married to Christ".

Entering the convent seemed like an easy, acceptable way to leave home as soon as possible. From a very early age this had become my mission! Catholic school was preparing me for the bogeyman known as the "real world". In fact, the nuns used to justify some of their seemingly cruel disciplines by informing us that they were preparing us for the tough world we would enter after graduation. They had no idea!!!

During my years in Catholic School I formed no close ties with my peers, mostly due to my family's financial struggles. I had no one with whom I could share special moments, my secrets or my dreams. Mainly, I kept to myself and read anything I could get my hands on. I had to do a lot of housework, too . . .

Once while I was helping my mother strip the beds, a magazine fell from under the mattress of the bed that David and I (bed wetters) still shared. I quickly realized that this was something that I should hide from my mom's view. The single glimpse that I caught revealed a scantily clothed lady with very big titties. I stuffed the magazine into my bureau drawer and bided my time until I could retrieve the "booty" and analyze my new leverage.

My opportunity came that night after I had cleared the table and finished the dishes. Giving my usual performance of moping about with nothing to do, my father gave me his customary "kick in the pants" and sent me to my room . . . and out of his sight. When I was certain that on one followed me, I pulled the magazine from under my tee shirt and started to turn the pages. My mouth must have dropped open a foot before I had turned half a dozen. On every one, I saw the most beautiful women wearing little or nothing at all. What was my brother doing with this book? I would definitely ask him later. For now, I saw the potential for using this as a weapon against a larger, stronger opponent. It was always valuable for a little sister to have some advantage to even the odds against her older brother.

For the moment I was enjoying the pictures. The women all appeared to be touching their "magic spots" and special places that Old Bill had taught me a few years before. Without even being aware that I was doing it, I had begun touching my "magic spots". I began to feel very good, too. Suddenly, something happened. It felt like the "gigglies" exploded inside of me. I had not felt this for ever so long. It felt wonderful!!! I had forgotten how wonderful it felt! I continued to look at the pictures and touch myself . . . and pretty soon it happened, again. Suddenly, I understood that I could make this happen anytime that I wanted it to. Without my awareness, I had learned how to masturbate.

This gave me a sense of control that I never had before. Being an imaginative child, I soon developed other ways to make "the gigglies" come. This practice emerged into a ritual that I continued through most of my life.

CHAPTER 4

THE HOUSEHOLD

I t's funny to think how much we take for granted . . . like masturbating! At present, it is difficult to imagine the ease with which I could bring myself (at such a tender age) to the pinnacle of human ecstasy. I haven't been able to do so for months. This is mainly due to the lack of coordination that I am experiencing as a result of this disease. I initially noticed that I was having trouble walking. Many times it looked like I was tipsy. Later, such weakness necessitated my having to be helped to walk for even short distances. This is where I find myself today; namely, completely dependent on someone for every vital function of my body. This can be entirely unnerving!

Catholic School taught me that I should suffer my tribulations in austere silence as exemplified by Our Lord, Jesus. This takes self-discipline. I had learned my lessons well. Except when complaining aloud to you, machine, I try to suffer silently whatever AIDS . . . or life, dishes out. So far, it seems limitless in the scope and variety of misery that it is capable of inflicting on its pitiful victims.

Another doctrine that the parochial schools seemed eager to instill in our minds was the idea of purity, and the importance of one's virginity. Unfortunately, I was not as quick to comprehend this theme as I had other things that were absorbed through my education or my experience. At the age of nine, virtuosity and pleasurable gratification seemed incongruous images. Be assured that my virtue remained intact through fifth grade. Before that, only the hymen of my mind had been pierced. Only a little of my innocence had been sacrificed. However, my memory banks were continuing to retain all input and file information for future recovery . . . no matter how incomplete or unclear.

In the third grade, I met one of the few females that I ever got close to. Kari and I met during recess on a cold winter morning. She had just moved to our town this year and, being rather reserved, stayed pretty much to herself. On that particular day, the "clique" girls had grown tired of hassling me and decided to turn their hateful attention towards Kari. Being obviously terrified, she began to cry softly.

'Super Tarah' to the rescue! I faced the group of rich, spoiled brats and told them to leave her alone. I went home that night with hideable injuries and a new best friend. Kari helped me home that night and our bonding began.

She promised to come over the next day after school and stay awhile so we could play. She would have stayed then, but her mom expected her home and would worry if she was late. So we made our plans and waited.

School dragged the next day, interrupted only by my summons to Mother Superior's office. Imagine that! They had noticed my injuries and wanted to know their origin. Following the "honor among thieves" rule, I stated that I had fallen on the stairs on my return from recess. I knew that to inform the nuns of the real nature of my injuries would lock Kari and me into the grip of torment that this group of "nice girls" could inflict on two "outsiders". I never entertained thoughts of revenge against the "in crowd". Apparently, this was the work of the Lord and he would show them the error of their ways in his own time. I did not need to concern myself with revenge. After an agonizingly long time, the final bell sounded and the school day finally ended.

Kari and I walked to my house. On the way, I tried to prepare her for my home. Not that I was ashamed of it or anything like that . . . it was just that our tiny house was sparsely furnished with cheap, second-hand or discarded odds and ends. The threadbare rug in the living room was lying between a shabby, overstuffed and miserably dusty couch, and a stained, torn chair with a missing leg. Its sole purpose seemed to be drawing attention to the pine crates that served as our occasional tables. Any large remnant of material might be used as a window dressing. As always, the noxious, ever-present stench of kerosene permeated the air.

I also wanted to prepare her for my family, themselves. Bringing a new friend home to a poor family is one thing. Bringing them home to meet your personal version of "The Addam's Family" is quite another. I did not want Kari to see the strange relationship that I had with my parents . . . especially my father. Apparently, my siblings seem to have been bestowed with abundant physical and emotional nurturing. Unfortunately, I had been denied this necessary ritual of bonding with both parents. While I did not understand the reasons for this omission for many years, I was no less affected by the pain, humiliation and emptiness that it caused in my youth. To a new friend, meeting my family was something akin to facing a firing squad without a blindfold. Fortunately for me, Kari was up to the challenge.

When we entered the kitchen, I saw my mother hunched over her ironing board. She always seemed to be ironing. Hell, she ironed everything: socks, underwear, even sheets and towels. She considered permanent press clothing innately evil and ironed it anyway. (My parents had more than a few of these strange ideas). Even though she looked like a strong wind would blow her away, I never remember my mom being sick. Shit! I never saw my mother eat an entire meal without interruption until I was older. She unselfishly put her husband and children first.

My mother was a devout Catholic and practiced her faith religiously. She accepted all of her church's doctrine as if "from God's mouth to their ears". Throughout my childhood and early adolescence, I truly considered her to be a saint who walked amongst us. She was a quiet, humble and obedient wife without question. She was a devoted mother and a dutiful homemaker. She was charitable, forgiving and the epitome of the peacemaker. She was always praying or going to church. She was an exemplary

Catholic. She never seemed very conscious of her physical appearance. Oh, she kept herself well-groomed but she never wore any make-up. She kept her hair cut short and allowed the grayness to add unattractive years to her all-too-apparent age. She was able to maintain a stoic demeanor under any and all circumstances. She was not the buddy/mom that so many of the other kids had during those years. I was never able to think of her as "my friend". No! She was always "my mother".

Likewise, my father was always the parental figure . . . a strict disciplinarian who tolerated no shenanigans. He made the rules. He interpreted the rules. He enforced the rules. Frequently, he also broke many of them. Having never finished grammar school, he had to work very hard to support his family . . . a fact that he never let us forget. He did instill in us a deep appreciation of music and education. He scoffed at religion and God. He was blatantly prejudice against a wide range of groups including, but not limited to the following: Blacks, Orientals, Jews, communists, hippies, politicians, the rich, the poor and the noisy. He was against all causes of change including civil rights, urban renewal and women's lib. He appreciated male supremacy, white supremacy and the American Dream. He had a sharp tongue, a sharp wit and could cut any man down to size with words. He was strong and hard working and despised anything or anybody that was not. He was, above all, the head of his family. And what a family it was!

Peter and Wendy were the older siblings. They were as close to perfect as you could find. Their lives seemed perfect, as well. Both were very handsome individuals. They were both excellent students and superb athletes. Peter was Student Body President and Valedictorian of his senior class. Wendy was head cheerleader and was chosen Homecoming Queen by her peers. Needless to say, my parents were quite proud of these two offspring. Neither lived home. They both left immediately after graduation.

I turn my attention now to David . . . the other imperfect child in the family. I thought he was wonderful . . . still do! He had a terrific sense of humor and could always make me laugh, even when things were horrible in our lives. He was an average student, only because he really didn't give a rat's ass about it. I thought he was real smart about things that weren't necessarily taught in school, but were just as important to learn. I don't know how I would have survived my childhood if he had not been there for me so many times. Don't misunderstand me. This was no fairytale relationship. We had our usual squabbles that are likely to arise between siblings. Yet, even at those times, we understood that we had to take care of each other to insure our mutual survival.

These, then, were the principle players on stage when Kari first met my family. Somehow everyone was in his or her "best behavior mode" that particular evening. No major altercations occurred while she was there. Dinner went surprisingly well and even as she was preparing to leave, we were planning our next encounter.

Eventually, her presence in our home became accepted and expected. This allowed us to be more autonomous and away from the watchful eyes of nosey siblings. One fine spring afternoon, Kari and I were pitching in with the major house cleaning. We were really working hard with the wiping and scrubbing and mopping. When it was time for a break, we decided to lay down and rest for awhile. We fell exhaustedly on the bed on top of the bedspread. While we lay next to each other huffing and puffing, our legs touched and we pulled apart as if we had both been electrocuted. I noticed her disquieting reaction and explained to her that everything was all right. Hell, anything was okay as long as it did not hurt anyone! She eventually came to grips with this concept.

I told her how my brother and I would tickle each other on those nights when it was difficult to fall asleep. I told her how I used to trick him . . . which was never easy. I'd say "tkl u tkl me tkl mefst!" Translation: I'll tickle you if you tickle me but you have to tickle me first! So David would tickle my back or my feet for the count of 100. He would then inform me that it was my turn but would get no response from my quiet, unmoving body . . . I had supposedly fallen asleep. Soon there would ensue a brawl of mammoth proportions to which my parents would respond with due haste and severity.

Kari giggled for a long time when I finished the story. I watched and listened to her for a bit, then I started to giggle, too. We couldn't stop laughing for quite a while. Eventually, we righted ourselves and returned to our propriety as befitting two such obvious ladies.

We played pretend a lot during our friendship. We probably took shelter in the pretense as a refuge from the cruelty of the real world. There were many afternoons when two shy, quiet little girls allowed free reign to their imaginations. For hours we would spin tales of romance and adventure . . . the likes of which the world seems in need of today. In our daydreams we could squash all the "prickly people" who adversely affected our lives; the deceptive "nice little girls" at school, a short-tempered clerk at the corner store, and (our all-time favorite) our nagging parents. These mental exercises kept us entertained for hours . . . spinning macabre tales for each other.

One day, while frolicking about, we touched. This time, however, we did not pull away. The energy flowed between us. As if rehearsed, we looked into the other's eyes and things just happened. Our respirations deepened along with our taboo thoughts. The magic feelings of comfort and calmness settled over us and we wallowed in our mutual bliss. We began to stroke each other and I made my way to her "magic spots". I wanted to see if I could give her the "gigglies". I found out soon enough. I had just started to rub her when she convulsed explosively. I knew she had just discovered the magic, too.

Each private session got more intense as we became more familiar with our individual preferences. It was all so terrific that we just assumed that we would go on like that, forever. Our paradise was to end all too soon.

The news hit me like a shotgun blast. She had moved far away and I would be alone again . . . miserably alone. I never even got a chance to tell her goodbye in person. When Kari had called to tell me about her immediate relocation, Mom decided that it would be better if I was not told until after the fact. She lied and told her I wasn't there. She assured Kari that she would have me call her. The hurt of losing my best friend seemed endless. The depths of my sorrow would fill an abyss. How would I ever recover from this atrocious sadness?

CHAPTER 5

THE WRONGS

It's funny what thoughts enter your mind while you're waiting, in agony and terror, to die. Some give you comfort; others give you joy and still others may even offer elusive sanity. In Catholic School they stressed the value of the virtue of purity. They insisted that you had to obey the commandments if you wanted to go to heaven. By now, I have broken every commandment at least once and have probably fractured a few "suggestions". If I had remained "pure of body and soul", I would not have been cursed with this devastating affliction. Some morons have suggested that AIDS is "the wrath of God" disease. This encompasses the belief that an angry God is punishing me for my past sins. Since homosexual men and IV drug users accounted for most of the earliest cases, it is easy to understand how the holy rollers came up with this theory. However, I feel I must say that there were an awful lot of sacrificial lambs with this curse from the Almighty Creator. You'd think that a Supreme Being with awesome power would be able to single out its target with stunning accuracy. Oh! That I should even entertain such thoughts is surely another sin for which I must account.

During the time following Kari's departure, David tried to be almost civil to me. At night, we'd lay in bed for hours talking. He understood how much I missed her. No!!! I never told him about the touchy feely stuff, but he was perceptive enough to realize that I was hurting. He tried to comfort me as only a brother could do. He told me scary stories. He'd play stupid practical jokes. He'd race me to school. He'd even ask me if I wanted to go to the ballpark with him and his friends. He really tried to cheer me up. I would be brave for awhile but I would soon squirm over and nestle against his chest. I would cry until my eyes had no more tears. As my tears abated, the rhythmic sound of his heartbeat would lull me to sleep.

I remember one time when we got punished for arguing. We were sent to bed early and without dinner. Had our parents forgotten that David and I still shared the same room? Hell, we still shared the same bed. After all, David was 13 and I was ten years old. No one voiced opposition to our sleeping arrangements. We could have easily resumed our squabble on the other side of the door but we were too angry with our parents. We plotted potential vengeful strategies in the darkness. Leaning on pillows with our hands propped behind our heads, we dreamed of schemes that would render our parents powerless. Showing no mercy, we chopped off heads, imprisoned in squalor and banished to deserted islands, where the only other inhabitants were the hungry crocodiles. Suddenly, my brother stopped his musings and turned towards me.

"You're changing, Rah!" He remarked quite seriously. "I've noticed. I see your chest stretching your T-shirts. Can I see? Please? . . . Just for a second? Lift up your nightgown so I can just look at you."

I obediently raised the garment up to my shoulders. After all, I trusted him and he wouldn't tell me to do something if it was wrong. Besides, I was fascinated. I could tell that David was, too.

"Can I just touch them . . . just once," he begged as he stared into the depths of my eyes. "Just for one second . . . I promise!" he pleaded intensely.

I nodded my consent and he lightly touched my naked breast with his fingertips. After a few seconds of tenderness, he waited for my reaction. My resultant smile made him continue, as I knew it would. I wanted him to keep touching me. It made me feel warm and good all over. He continued. He guided his hands expertly over my nipples until they formed tender peaks.

"Do they hurt, Rah?"

I explained that some days they were more sensitive. I told him that if I got hit there, it hurt really bad.

"I won't hurt them, RahRah! Watch! You won't even feel this . . . don't worry. I won't hurt you."

He lowered his face over me and planted a single, birdie kiss on each taut nipple. He teased them with his limber tongue. I learned how to tease him with my touch, as well.

These touching sessions became almost a nightly event. We both knew instinctively to keep these adventures our secret. Not that we thought what we were doing was wrong, we just did not see the need to explain anything to anybody . . . since we weren't hurting anybody. These sessions proved to be an invaluable educational opportunity for me. Through my brother, I learned as much as a curious, prepubescent girl could about the male anatomy. One night, he tricked me into jerking him off and almost put an end to our escapades at the same time.

He suggested that I grab hold of his wiener and it would do a trick

"Now move your hand up and down real fast and you might get him to sing. Faster . . . real fast. Yeah, that's it, Babe. Yeah . . . ooh, yeah! That's nice . . . real gentle. Gently . . . Oh, be careful. Be gentle or he might throw up on you," he chuckled.

No sooner had he spoken the words when this warm, slimy liquid squirted out, all over my hand. The scream escaped my lips before I was aware of it and before David could muffle the sound with a blanket. It also brought the expected immediate response from our parents. They arrived simultaneously at our bedroom door. We managed to keep our composure when they demanded to know "what the hell is going on in here?". David and I feigned sleepiness and, with heavy eyelids, murmured our innocence and ignorance as to the origin of any commotion.

We continued to share a room for two more years. More accurately, we continued to share a bed for two more years. Now many people, upon hearing this recording, may be tempted to blame my brother. If you are one that feels this way, try to understand that this young man was trying to deal with the ordinary perplexities of adolescence in the framework of a partially dysfunctional family. He was accumulating his feelings about love . . . and lust, and adjusting them to accommodate the structured world that structured his life.

A major turning point began one afternoon with my late arrival home from school. I had been helping the nuns with odd jobs to help defray the cost of my piano lessons. My father insisted that these were too expensive but I wanted to learn how to play with all my heart and soul (and my fingers, too).

Anyway, that is why I was late that day. I could not have foreseen the turbulence that would result from my tardiness. When I did not get home on time, my evening chores were delegated to my other siblings. Even with the shifting of responsibility, or perhaps because of it, dinner was late getting to the table that night. Unfortunately, my father was not!

He demanded to know the reason for the disorganization in his home at his mealtime. When he found out that I was the culprit, he flew into a blind rage. He threw the entrée across the room, at the wall. He then told the family that there would be no dinner for anyone that night. With eyes blazing with fury, he turned his attention towards me. He ordered me to clean up the mess that he had just made. While my attention was diverted by the task at hand, he had loosened his belt and swatted my backside. I continued to kneel over the ruined meal. He raised the belt and brought it again across my butt. I tried to keep quiet even as I felt the first welt spring from my flesh. He continued to thrash me until I had completely gathered the pieces of the shattered serving dish and all remnants of the ruined meal. As I tried to stand up on my wobbly legs, he grabbed my hair and literally dragged me from the room and away from the watchful, albeit helpless eyes of the family. I was on my own.

Still holding my hair, he ascended the steps three at a time and upon reaching my bedroom door, hurled me bodily inside. In one movement he kicked the door closed, reached his powerful arm towards me, grabbed at my clothing and tore the worn cotton dress from my body in one motion. With no cessation of movement, he brought the leather belt down across my bared back with a fury that I had not witnessed before in my father. I was paralyzed with fear and the searing pain that was emitted with each blow. As I began to shrink away from him in desperation, he became even angrier and ordered me out of the rest of my clothing. I was petrified but did as he said.

He reeked of alcohol and this pungent odor was clouding my thought processes, too. It had certainly had an effect on his. I was in the throws of the worst beating of my life and I really did not know what I had done to merit such severe punishment. Since it was my father . . . somewhere in the dark recesses of my mind . . . I deduced that I must have deserved it. He was a good father . . . at least to my brothers and sister. Tiring of the strap, he soon just started to hit me with his fists. He tagged me good a few times before my eyes swelled shut, leaving me helplessly unable to escape from his brutality. His threat to kill me if I made a sound was enough to insure my absolute silence throughout the ordeal.

Sometime later, I was aware of being lifted onto my bed and being covered with blankets, but I was unwilling to surrender the comfort and security afforded me by my unconsciousness. Only after hearing by brother's soothing voice did I allow myself to let go of the darkness and respond to the discernable concern in his voice and in his unseen eyes.

"Rah, are you all right?" he queried softly with a compassion that was all too obvious.

I attempted to reply but found the effort too painful. So I simply nodded weakly.

"He beat you bad, Rah. He beat you real bad this time."

I felt something cool and pleasant on my forehead. My brother wiped my face with a gentleness borne out of desperation. I felt the coolness, again. This time on my neck . . . then on my shoulders and down my arms.

The initially pleasant sensation soon gave way to the severe stinging that seemed to come from everywhere, at once. The pain seared its way into my brain. It seemed that nowhere on my body was left unhurt. David turned me over to minister to my back. What he saw there made him curse and renew his vow for revenge.

With the utmost care, he applied the cool cloth to my wounds and bruises. As before, this brought the agony into focus with such clarity as to take my breath away. He spoke softly throughout the ordeal so as to console me in my misery. I was so grateful to him for his kindness and love.

After he did what he could to ease my suffering, he laid down next to me, being careful not to disturb me. He began to touch me gently. He pressed his lips to my nipple and took it into his mouth. He sucked it gently for a few seconds before turning his attention to the other one. Awkwardly, as was befitting a young, inexperienced kid, he moved his mouth upward along the lines of my neck, over my lower jaw and settled them upon my waiting lips. He was kissing me. My brother was actually kissing me and I was finding it very stimulating. Sensing my reaction, his lips became slightly more possessive. He took me into his arms in a comforting, reassuring way. His hug filled me with contentment.

Due to the proximity of our bodies, I could feel his erection. He slid one hand down to my stomach and beyond that to the newly acquired patch of pubic hair that was evolving between my thighs. Sliding further still, between my open legs, he began to gently stoke my "private area". His stirring movements caused a desire to burn deeply within me, possibly radiating from my very soul. I yearned for more . . . of what? . . . I was not sure. David seemed to realize my unspoken desire even as I was becoming aware of my excitement. My body was gyrating with unspent emotion in spite of my physical discomfort.

"I don't want to hurt you more, Rah," he sighed and began to pull away. Struggling to gather my strength, I reached out for him and begged him not to stop.

"Don't leave me like this, David. Please don't stop," I pleaded. "Teach me about these feelings and my body's response to them."

He regained his embrace and began to kiss and caress me with a tenderness so unusual in a vibrant teenage boy. His timid attention was definitely feeling better with each passing moment. His hand moved skillfully to my most sensitive areas and he was able to evoke a powerful hunger in a young girl's sexual appetite. He continued to whisper tender thoughts to me, which forced an air of utter calmness to wash over me. This peace allowed me to experience the pleasure that was flowing from him to me without fear or guilt or pain. He guided his moistened fingers through my narrow opening but stopped when he discovered my virginity.

"I'm so sorry, Rah. I shouldn't be doing this," he lamented. The agony on his face was more than I could bear. I shook my head almost imperceptibly. Throwing my arms around his neck, I hugged him.

"It feels wonderful! Please, don't stop. I'll try to be brave," I promised.

With evident reluctance, he started his seduction again, with much patience and control. This time, when his wet fingers began their penetration, I tried to relax and allow it to happen. It still hurt a little, but there were other feelings emerging from our activities that I began to enjoy.

This seemed to please David, as he became noticeably more excited himself. My heart had begun to race and this was intensified with each new sensation that he elicited. A lust had formed within my soul and cried out for satisfaction. David understood what I was experiencing without the need to exchange any words.

"Can I make love to you, Tarah? Can I put myself inside you? Please . . . I promise . . . I'll be gentle and I'll stop anytime that you tell me to".

He looked up expectantly into my eyes. My gentle nod seemed to be adequate reply to his request. He rolled over so as not to put any pressure on my brutalized body and rested his weight entirely on his arms. Slowly, he lowered himself so that he could maneuver more effectively. He aimed his penis at the mysteries hidden deep within my cavity and guided it with gentleness and guarded determination.

The initial pain shot through me with burning intensity. I paid for the intrusion with my blood, sweat and silent tears. Eventually, the discomfort subsided, which allowed me to enjoy the more pleasurable aspects of our encounter. His motions were sending signals of a different nature to my brain and seconds later I experienced the "gigglies". It was my first and most memorable climax via intercourse. Shortly thereafter, David's excitement culminated in his own orgasm, requiring a good deal of control on his part, refraining from making all the noise that he wanted.

Following our interaction, he gently cleaned me up and made sure that I was as comfortable as possible. Then he quietly slid from between the sheets and rested beside me. He offered me his hand, which I readily accepted. I held on to his hand until I fell asleep, drawing from him the security and contentment that I had been searching for all my life.

When I woke up the next morning, I was so stiff and sore that I could hardly drag myself out of bed but it was time for school. Since David had already left, I knew that I was running late and hurriedly selected a uniform from the closet. Turning towards the bureau with the sole intention of gathering my clean undergarments, I unexpectedly caught my reflection in the mirror and gasped. My face was swollen grotesquely out of proportion. Both of my eyes were blackened and nearly swollen shut. My mouth did not look like my mouth much less work like it. Small, uneven projectiles of white enamel occupied the spaces formally filled by my teeth. My entire body was a mass of lesions and welts; yet I felt no pain. I reasoned that my own father had inflicted these injuries on me, therefore I must have deserved it. I felt no animosity towards him whatsoever. I simply felt quite alone.

I began to cry quietly. I did not want to go to school looking as I did. The intensity of my weeping increased but still, I made no sound. What was I gonna do? As if in answer to my unvoiced question, my father pushed open the door and entered my room. This time there was no fury in his eyes . . . only resignation.

"You are to stay home from school until I give you my permission to return," he announced forcefully. "You are to stay here and help your mother. You are restricted to the house and there will be no TV or radio . . . understand? After dinner, you will go straight up to your room and stay there unless I send for you. The phone is strictly off limits! Stay away from it or I'll break your fucking hands. Don't give your mother any trouble or I'll kill you when I find out about it."

As abruptly as he had come, he left. I was to be a virtual prisoner in my own house. My mother was to be my warden. Since my mother was a good Christian wife, I knew that she would do nothing to thwart her husband's authority . . . she would follow his instructions to the letter. I rolled over onto my tear-stained pillow and continued to cry.

CHAPTER 6

THE VIOLENCE

As I lay here talking to a machine, I realize that I never considered myself much of a crybaby. Occasionally, lately the pain will make me cry. More often, the fear would make me cry. When the doctors told me that I had developed skin cancer, I cried. This seems to be an additional curse for some AIDS' victims. It is a rare form of skin cancer called Kaposi's Sarcoma. It presents itself as ugly purple/brown patches on your skin that don't go away. More than likely, an infection will enter my body via one of these minute openings in the cancerous lesion. This can make me so sick that even the "big-time, big city doctors" won't be able to do anything but watch me die. So far I've pulled myself through this course of the disease. If you survived, there were numerous other maladies that were eager to replace it.

Come to think of it, there are different kinds of "cancer" and one that will never be described as such in any medical journals. It is, however, just as deadly. Until recently, most forms of cancer were synonymous with doom. This diagnosis in any form could tender terror in even the hardest hearts. Lately, AIDS has made cancer take a back seat on the morbidity scale. Yet, the cancer that I'm referring to remains an unspoken entity except for the victims of its destruction. Strangely enough, its victims are not the hosts for this disruptive pathogen. Its name is hatred and its malicious power is widely known. The number of its casualties is incalculable.

I've been a victim of this cruel ailment since early childhood.

The source of this malicious destroyer whittled away at my confidence and self-esteem almost continually throughout the first half of my life. The carrier was my father. Whereas he was a generally loving, giving person to the other members of our family, his interactions with me were overflowing with undisguised disgust and contempt. His beatings and other severe punishments were an incomprehensible chapter of my life. They assumed a major role in the memories of my life in his house.

What was more disheartening to me was the fact that I had no understanding about the origins of his malevolence. If I had had an inkling of what caused him to despise me so much, I would have tried anything to change his attitude about me and make him love me. My attempts to discover even a clue proved futile. When I questioned my mother about his handling of me as compared to my siblings, she brushed it aside lightly as standard sibling rivalry. Come on, Lady! The hatred that he directed towards me oozed from his very pores.

The worst part of all this was the fact that at one point I loved and respected my father more than any other human being on the face of the earth. To my blindly adoring eyes, he was a prince among men and a warrior of the gods. He was my father in the eyes of God and therefore if he meted out severe punishments or administered painful whippings, it must have been because I deserved it. I spent a major part of my pre-adult life trying to win his acceptance and his love. It pains me to admit that I have failed miserably. I have not seen that man since I was 15 years old.

My mother became aware of my diagnosis soon after I did. She still tends to think of it as proper atonement for my sins. She dutifully stops by regularly to see how I'm doing. She still remains ambivalent in her feelings towards me, but as my mother she assumes some responsibility for my care. Also, David stops by once in awhile or phones to check on my condition and my situation. For these kindnesses I am truly grateful.

Sorry! Some days I get to ramblin'. I'll try to stay focused. As I had previously described, the morning following my father's atrocious beating began as any school day with one noticeable exception. I did not go to school. Little did I know that by the end of that day, my champion would have emerged to vindicate my suffering. It began so insidiously. My father had decided to rid himself of the vile contempt that he experienced in my presence. He deduced that this would best be accomplished at the corner taproom.

While walking home, his path was blocked by a group of hooded youths demanding his wallet. Considering his level of intoxication, it was not surprising that he refused to relinquish the pittance that he had in his possession at that moment. The gang started to taunt him but soon their mood became more assertive and their attack, more aggressive. My father was a strong, vibrant man but he was no match for the band of healthy young hoodlums that confronted him. The injuries he sustained from the ensuing assault were serious enough to keep him hospitalized for several weeks.

Later that same night, I became aware of tapping on the bedroom window. I was alone in the room since David had not returned yet from the basketball game he was attending with his friends. I was reluctant to respond to the sound until I heard my brother's muffled voice affirm his identity. I assisted him through the small opening that the dilapidated window casing afforded him. I tried to keep the noise to a minimum since I knew that he had broken his curfew. He was quick to inform me that it did not matter since Dad wouldn't be coming home for quite some time. My throat constricted fiercely as I tried to ascertain the meaning behind his simple statement. One look into his eyes told me there was more to this discussion than what was being said.

David related the occurrences of that evening. He and his friends had not attended any game. Instead, they contrived a scheme to retaliate for the horrendous cruelty inflicted on me by my father, so recently and so ruthlessly. He had been one of the hooded assailants that had sent my father to the hospital. How sad! It seemed that the sins of the father were becoming the sins of the son. It was always my belief that you could not rid the world of violence with violence.

On that night my brother and I took an oath never to refer to the incident again. I also extracted his promise to refrain from all acts of violence in the future unless his life, or the lives of his loved-ones were in jeopardy. To my knowledge, David has remained a man of his word.

CHAPTER 7

THE TAKEN

To some people the incestuous activities that occurred between my brother and me were abominable. To me they were a lifeline to sanity. His genuine affection and complete tenderness served as a barrier against the cruelties of our world. The concept of love and sex were intertwined in my mind and intermingled easily with other concepts such as gentleness and caring. This illusion was soon to be shattered.

The entire episode began innocuously enough. My brother and I had gone to our secret clubhouse. In actuality, it was a lean-to attached to a repair shop in our neighborhood. Inside were the towering stacks of unfolded cardboard boxes and miscellaneous packing supplies. We had obtained the owner's permission to use this tiny hide-away as our meeting place. Prior to taking up permanent residence there, we had firmly established a pleasant atmosphere. There was little in the way of furniture but the boxes were useful for any number of purposes and we used our imaginations to create our private empire.

That particular day we convened our meeting with the five necessary members to fulfill the requirements of the bylaws. David was the president. Johnny and Georgey Green, our vice-president and our treasurer, respectively, and Timmy Sharp, our sergeant-with-arms were also present. Last, and certainly least, I was present as well. Being that I was the only member who paid dues on a regular basis, my presence was paramount to the continued survival of our club. Shortly after the minutes were read and old business was shelved until the next meeting, we heard our mother's voice cut across the backyards and demand my brother's return home immediately. Father O'Brien had phoned with his urgent need for a server to assist at a funeral mass. Since this meant an easy ten dollars in his pockets, David was off like a shot.

I decided to stay at the clubhouse after the meeting was adjourned. I liked hanging out with these guys. It feels like I'd been doing it all my life. It was also a ploy to delay my return to a house where I felt like an intruder. Stretched out on the clean, dry, flattened boxes, we talked and told jokes and ragged on each other. Soon, however, our barbs and jabs exploded into a wrestling match. The twirling, twisted mass of sweaty bodies rolling around on the floor were soon claimed by exhaustion. We laid there, an intertwined form of humanity, puffing and panting. Suddenly, Timmy disengaged himself from the tangled mess and commanded our attention with his shout.

"Hey, look what I can see!" he squealed and pointed in my direction.

All eyes turned my way and focused on my chest. During the tussle, my shirt had been tugged out of my waistband and had worked up far enough to expose my breast. I blushed deeply as I reached for my shirt to pull it down. Georgey had grabbed my hand before I was even aware of it and his strong grasp prevented any further movement of that hand. Before I could swat him with my other hand I discovered that it too, had been snagged and was being held in captivity.

Sensing a quickly changing atmosphere, I became more aggressive in my struggle to free myself. I also tried to see what had become of Johnny. I found out soon enough when he made a grab for my ankles. He only caught hold of one. The other was my only defense. Since David and I did a lot of wrestling, I held my own for an admirable length of time. I quickly realized that these three older boys were in no serious danger of losing this match. I, however, refused to go down without a proper fight. Mustering all my strength, I swung my free leg around and nailed Johnny flush on the chin. Lifted him clear off his feet, I did!

In their surprise the other two loosened their hold on my wrist, allowing me an opportunity to attempt a getaway. This was not to be. During the passage of vital seconds, Johnny had regained his composure and, with a satanic glint in his eyes, he yelled.

"Get her, you assholes. Now bring that fucking little bitch back over here to me. I think she needs to be taught some manners".

"Leave me alone! You better all just leave me alone right now! I mean it . . . or I'll tell David and he'll fuck you up," I retorted as bravely as I could.

"All three of us?" countered Johnny. "I don't hardly think so. We'd make mincemeat out of him and feed him to the dogs. Hell! I could handle that punk with no sweat. Now, about those manners . . . no time like the present, Angel.

"Secure the cunt, you wussies. We wouldn't want her to miss this etiquette lesson. She'd miss all the fun. Today, we're gonna teach her how to play nicely with us dirty gentlemen," he snarled to his cohorts.

Johnny pointed to the floor and his stooges lowered me to the floor per his silent instruction. The hopelessness of my situation began to flood through my brain with the intensity of a tidal wave. I struggled in spite of my fatigue. Finally, in desperation, I screamed for help. I knew almost before the sound escaped my lips that I had made a mistake, but I saw no other options. Someone quickly stuffed a rag into my mouth. I fought the nausea and hysteria as I watched while Johnny secured my gag. His eyes darted around the shelter as if searching for something specific. He located what he wanted and reached over some boxes and displayed a handful of rope pieces. He tossed several to his cohorts, and commanded them to tie me down by my wrists. They both did what they were told. When they were finished, my wrists were spread wide above my head and secured fast by the ropes. Seeing the uselessness of struggling against these tenacious bonds, I turned my attention back to Johnny. Without my awareness, he had already undone my snap and was working on lowering the zipper on my jeans. I began to tremble.

Without further instructions, Georgey and Timmy were securing my ankles as they had my wrists. I barely realized they were doing so, since all my attention remained focused on Johnny. He had succeeded in pulling my jeans as far down my legs as logistics allowed. He freed his penis from the captivity of his trousers and aimed it in my direction.

"This ramrod is gonna teach you who not to kick in the future, Slut."

With a snarl pulling his lips away from his teeth, he advanced towards me. I was terrified by what he held out for display and dramatic effect. His penis loomed above me appearing precariously huge.

"Dear God, please make him stop," I whispered to myself.

He did not! Leaning over me and smirking, he roughly pushed my knees apart and wedged his muscled physique between them. He eyed his conquered, frightened prey and made ready for the kill. Without further preparation, he punched his formidable weapon into my painfully dry cavity. I felt my skin rip. I felt the blood trickling down. He still did not stop. In fact, he became more insistent and aggressive. There was no tenderness here . . . only pain and fear.

Not wanting to be overlooked, the other two requested equal time . . . but Johnny informed them that I needed additional niceness tutelage.

"Stick your cock in her mouth, Timmy and we'll let her give you a nice blowjob," he ordered without missing a stroke.

Timmy came around and straddled my neck. After unzipping his pants, he pulled his wiener out and shook it at my face, imitating Johnny's earlier antics. With tears burning my eyes, I silently pleaded with him to stop this cruel game but to no avail. He undid the gag that insured my silence and immediately replaced it with his cock. I began to choke but he made no move to remove the rotten thing from my mouth. He kept thrusting his pelvis forward in the same pumping action that Johnny was imposing on my tortured vagina. I tried to twist my head away from his savagery but he told

Georgey to hold my head still. Grabbing a handful of my hair with each hand did the trick.

Johnny's movements were becoming more urgent and sporadic. He came, in a violent spasm of energy and sweat. I felt his hot liquid filling my insides. The thought was repulsive. Seconds later, Timmy ejaculated his sticky cum into my mouth, I refused to swallow it after tasting its bitterness. I waited until he had removed his disgusting cock from my mouth, then I pursed my lips and attempted to spit his load back at him. Unfortunately, my lips were virtually numb from his brutal assault. Besides, spitting while lying flat on your back is no easy task. Most of the cum sprayed over my exposed flesh.

Georgey, realizing that he had not yet had a major portion of the fun, demanded his fair share. Johnny noticed that I had spit out the semen and decided that I still wasn't very nice. He bet Georgey that he didn't have the balls to jerk off in my face. The three of them broke up at this suggestion and Georgey gleefully accepted the challenge. Despite his initial embarrassment, he started to whack-off mere inches from my face. As he got into it he rubbed his cock across my cheeks and over my bruised lips. He stabbed it into my eye socket hard enough to make me afraid. Even though my mouth was empty I had no intention of screaming. I feared that if I opened my mouth he would poke his penis inside. Besides, at this point, what difference would a bit more humiliation make. Noticing his increasing excitement, I closed my eyes and waited for the inevitable. I hadn't waited long before the warm, thick liquid splashed my face and cascaded down my cheeks and neck. They smeared the gooey stuff all over my partially disrobed body.

"Ain't that nice, Sugar?"

"Yeah, little tag-a-long. You feel so pretty when you're slippery . . . so smooth and creamy . . . ooh, Sweet Tarah Baby. You're so nice, you're making my cock throb again. What say you be really nice to Johnny and suck my cock real nice . . . then maybe we'll let you go. Real nice, Sugar, or I'll stick my big hard rod so far up your asshole that you'll choke on it. Is your asshole as tight as a pinched faced motherfucker like you should be? Yeah, I bet that's real tiny, huh? Open up that pretty pink mouth of yours and see if you like the way my "baby juice" goes down, Sugar. Let me see if you can be nice, yet."

The ugly vision of him sodomizing me made me quickly acquiesce to his demand. I accepted his offering quietly. Watching our activities had had a hormonal reaction on the other two. Since my mouth was occupied, they agreed to take their individual turns fucking me. Finally, the three of them had spent their loads and they prepared to leave. I realized that I had better do something fast, since there was no way that I was gonna be able to free myself if left in my present state.

"You were right, Johnny. I needed to learn everything you taught me today. Thank you! I promise I'll be nicer from now on. Before you leave do you think one of you nice guys could untie me?"

After a brief, secluded meeting, they agreed to untie my legs and one of my hands so that I could eventually free myself after they left. Securing their zippers and righting their appearance, they prepared to leave without a look back.

However, a few seconds later, Johnny reentered the shack and reminded me that if I told anybody about anything that happened, he'd take immediate action. Knowing my weak spot, he suggested that some night David might be very late getting home . . . very, very late . . . maybe too late. I understood the threat behind his words. With that, he left.

. . . And I was left alone. My breathing was the only sound I heard as I lay on those scattered pieces of cardboard . . . all alone. The rapid steady beating of my heart seemed to keep pace with the flashing visions in my mind. My breathing was becoming more rapid. There was just too much to think about right now. Hell, I was only 12. What a mess I found my way into this time. I hurt everywhere and I felt so ashamed. The shuddering sigh escaped before I could prevent it. It was quickly followed by another and another, until my anguish consumed me and racked my body with convulsive sobs.

Eventually, I pulled myself together. I tried to make myself look decent before I left the shelter of the clubhouse. I knew I'd never return and I felt a twinge of regret in losing this part of my childhood. However, I felt no sadness in leaving the scene of my initiation into the "real world".

The walk home was a torment at every step. Decisions had to be made right away and no one could make the choices but me. Yet, in reality, the decisions had already been made for me. I wasn't going to tell anyone what had happened today . . . ever! David's life was at stake here. I couldn't risk that! No! This entire episode would remain locked in my subconscious mind for a very long time. Besides, I was also too ashamed to tell anybody what happened. If my mother knew, she would only cry about my lost soul. If my father found out, he would surely find a way to blame me and beat me up again. So I said nothing.

Fortunately, no one was about when I reached home. I hurried upstairs and got a hot bath. No amount of washing or soaking, however, was going to make me feel clean. I scrubbed until my skin was raw before I realized that fact. I felt so totally violated . . . like I'd never be clean again!

CHAPTER 8

THE SCOUTS

Sometimes it seems that the more things change, the more they stay the same. Almost fourteen years have passed since the episode in the clubhouse transpired yet I remain a victim. There are weeks at a time when the only time another human being touches me is during the never-ending physical assessments that I endure, or when someone lifts me into my chair or puts me back into bed. No caresses! No Hugs! No kisses . . . not even a peck on the cheek! Some days I could just scream for some human warmth and compassion. A smile on a friendly face would be so nice! A mischievous wink would be akin to Christmas Morning! I'm lonely right now! Putting my thoughts into this machine may help someone deal with similar problems someday, but for myself . . . I think I may just be doing it to keep my life in prospective and keep some semblance of sanity, at least in view of the public's eye.

Maybe I'd feel better if I talked about happier times . . . like when I was a Girl Scout. Gee, they were the greatest days of my childhood. The local troop met in the clubrooms of a local factory and it was close enough for me to walk to the meetings on Wednesdays, after school. This particular troop was very active since the same factory that lent free use of the facilities amply sponsored it. The financial assistance contributed to the troop promoted good public relations for the company and we couldn't have cared less where the money came from, as long as we were able to continue with our various projects.

One such project was a memorable Halloween party that my troop hosted for our brother Eagle Scouts from a neighboring town. Our combined troops were having a weekend campout on Halloween weekend and Saturday night we planned a gala Halloween Party. We were sure to play all the corny games which we, secretly, all enjoyed.

We spent the better part of the time before the party preparing for it. We cooked a large kettleful of baked beans . . . for an entire day. When we got ready to stir them, we discovered that the spoon stood straight up in the gloppy mess and made a unique sucking sound when we tried to pull it out. Despite all this, they ended up tasting great, as did all the "mystery foods" that we conjured up.

Naturally, we all donned appropriate costumes and our guests started to arrive. This was my first real boy/girl mixer and I was a little nervous. However, my sister scouts really helped me feel comfortable and everyone seemed to be having a good time.

Mrs. Parker, our leader, was a terrific lady who really enjoyed being around young people and we enjoyed being around her. She kept the party jumping with the best "oldies but goodies" and she introduced us to a very new, very different dance/music called "disco". We twisted with Chubby Checker and bumped with the Beegees and she even managed to slip a slow song occasionally, to allow the opportunity for the Eagle Scouts to crush our toes.

I was slow-dancing with a very nice, if slightly unattractive scout named Leroy when the pretty ballad ended and it was followed by a jumping, gyrating new song that was becoming very popular. Unconsciously, I started tapping my toes to the pulsating rhythm of the song. With obvious reserve, Leroy tentatively asked if I wanted to "Hustle". I assumed he was talking about the newest dance craze and not the art of ripping people off. I had watched the sinewy couples' fluid movements and intricate intertwining on TV. I was dying to give it a try. I nodded with the proper amount of shyness and allowed him to take my arm and lead me towards the center of the dance floor.

Space was at a premium at the onset of the music, since every couple there was tempted to try their hand (or should I say feet) at the skillful execution of one of the oldest artforms . . . dance. Initially, the crowded conditions hampered our attempts to express our creative styling but we soon alerted those in our immediate vicinity to our need for a bit more "elbow room". Slowly, almost imperceptibly, the narrow circle that encompassed the limits of our available space began to expand. The tide of attention started to veer from several different focal points to a central area of interest . . . namely, to the shy but proficient couple occupying the limelight.

Hearing only the music, and feeling only my partner's very skillful, confident arms guiding our energies, I found myself flowing on the vaporous fumes of self-expression. The music dictated my actions as my partner determined our direction. We whirled and twirled and curled our way around the dance floor and into the hearts of the appreciative spectators. At the conclusion of our memorable performance, with all the skill and aplomb of true professionals, we exchanged mischievous secret winks, pompously smiled to the crowd and each other and bowed to our "adoring fans".

The exhilaration experienced from our moment in the sunny rays of peer approval and acceptance was to remain deeply buried in my subconscience for a long time, but there was definitely a link between my moment of adolescent glory and the exuberance elicited from the freedom of dancing. This link would later become a cohesive force in an otherwise shattered existence.

Girl Scouting offered me the opportunity to experience many unique types of activities to which I may otherwise never have been exposed. I had a chance to work on an assortment of merit badges from a wide range of interests. Mrs. Parker was pleased with my enthusiasm and welcomed the time we spent together, while applying our energies to the completion of the requirements for each decoration to be earned. At the end of my scouting involvement, I was the proud owner of two full sashes of hard-earned awards; the variety of which ran the gamut of artistic, creative and practical skills and interests including: drama, music, homemaking talents, sports and athletic prowess, and community service achievements.

The preceding list is not to be considered an inclusive listing of every experience gleaned from my scouting days. After the camping trip and the Halloween social, my self-confidence began to surface again. At least, I could stand to look at myself in the mirror. I also began to like myself again. My attitude about guys was changing rather rapidly at the same time. Since the situation in the clubhouse, I had been making a concerted effort to avoid any unnecessary contact with them. I took great pains to make certain that I was not alone with a member of the opposite sex for even the briefest period.

The young men that I met through scouting were gentlemen, who managed to erase, or at least minimize, any discomfort that I may have felt in the initial phases of our encounters. As a matter of fact, I became quite friendly with a number of the Eagle Scouts and wanted to get to know some of them better. It was probably simple, harmless adolescent curiosity. My opportunity to intensify my budding relationship with Paul, one of the older members, presented itself sooner than expected.

Our two troops planned a joint venture to visit a large amusement park. We chartered a luxurious bus and had a real party just getting there. Being little more than country bumpkins, we were quite impressed with the glitter and glamour of the whole scene. Most of the exhibitions were very enjoyable but I especially gravitated towards those with a futuristic theme. There was a lot of promise to behold in their future. As a group we rode every ride and some of the more exciting ones, I elected to repeat . . . a few times. Having never been any place like this, I was in my glory. More often than not Paul was my brave companion on each one. I had met him on the camping trip already. He was so handsome that I never dreamed that shortly we would be riding The Scream Machine ride together . . . not to mention all the other rides. We even took a slow, relaxing boat ride through the "Tunnel of Love". It seemed such a short ride and yet, even in that brief passage of time, our sweet, tender kisses became more exciting and passionate. When the ride was over we both knew that we each craved more and we schemed and planned for the bus trip home. Our strategy was simple. We would just make certain that we got dibs on the back seat.

We returned to the bus in plenty of time to beat the others so we scattered our jackets and packages of souvenirs across the length of the bench seat and claimed it as our own. There was plenty of extra space on the bus, so there was no need for anyone to insist that we share our territory. Paul explained our early return by informing the bus driver that I was not feeling too well and thought that it might help if I could rest in the comfort of the bus. The driver agreed.

The news of my unhealthy condition was made known to Mrs. Parker immediately upon her arrival and she commended us on using good judgement in seeking out the shelter of the bus. She decided that it might be a good idea if Paul stayed near and kind of kept his eye on me to see if there would be any changes. This was even better than anything we could have imagined!

Slowly, the others began meandering back to our designated area in the parking lot and the bus was gradually filling up. Each new arrival, eager to share their experiences with the others, contributed to the decibel level until the din reached ear-splitting proportions. In record time all bodies were present and accounted for and the journey home commenced. The atmosphere on the return trip was entirely different from the exuberance of the ride up to the "Big Apple". In fact, it could be argued that the "big apple" had taken a "bite" out of my fellow scouts. Almost immediately, they started to drift off to sleep . . . one by one.

Paul and I were very patient. Besides, we were having a most enjoyable time in our own private world. In a valiant display of gallantry, Paul covered me with his long, bulky coat; to the occasional "nibshit's" eyes it would appear that he had done this to keep me comfortable. Little did they know that I was feeling pretty comfortable as it was and that my internal temperature was being affected more by what was occurring under that coat. My nipples were already taut projectiles as they responded to the skillful maneuverings of his educated hands and fingers. In the silent darkness, his mouth possessed mine, as his kisses became more devouring and demanding. My own desire was rapidly approaching the limits of my control. A quick survey of the other passengers easily verified our hopes and suspicions that slumber had taken the lot of them as its victims, leaving only the driver unaffected. Fortunately, he seemed content in his capacity of transporting his cargo back to the point of origin safely.

With minimal effort, Paul positioned himself behind me on the rear benchseat. I felt his warmth and desire along the entire length of my body and this only enhanced my excitement. Silently he extracted his penis from his unzipped fly while I managed to avail myself to his proximity by hiking up my skirt and exposing my awaiting "vessel" to him. Since neither of us were strong advocates for underwear, our efforts were not seriously hampered by intricate undergarments.

With skill and care, he guided his ready shaft into my warm, moist vagina. It accepted it greedily. I positioned my legs until I found a comfortable position that allowed maximum penetration. His body warmth and generalized excitation was able to penetrate the clothing between the rest of our bodies and my response to his sexcited state caused his emotions to soar to new heights. My own inner feelings were transcending spheres of unexplored territories. With each passage of his hand over a part of my body, my desire only mounted; with each touch of his lips to the nape of my neck, my need of him became more evident. I had lost all control over rational thought . . . knowing only that I wanted and needed him just that way, at just that moment. His reaction to my sensations dispelled any doubt that I may have been harboring in regards to the sincerity of his desire for me. Our passion culminated in our achieving simultaneous orgasms. It was almost impossible for me to contain my urgent desire to yell out how wonderful it felt and how wonderful he felt and how wonderful I felt!

We remained cuddled together for awhile to savor the delicious joy and serenity that we were sharing. Eventually, we righted ourselves and re-examined our appearance. No one traveling on that bus that night was ever to discover what transpired between the two young scouts on the back seat. Somehow we knew that this would, in all likelihood, never happen again.

I never saw Paul again after we returned from the trip. I believe someone told me that his father had inherited some valuable property in Arizona. It really did not matter to me. Those special moments we shared were very important to me and very much needed at the time. Paul made me aware that I was a reasonably attractive and desirable young woman with whom a worthy young man could find happiness and fulfillment . . . if only for a few minutes . . . on the back seat of a chartered bus.

My home life remained virtually unchanged during this time. One significant difference was the fact that I no longer shared sleeping space with my brother. Finally, someone noticed that we had stopped wetting the bed! Hooray! David and I had already come to the realization that what we were doing was wrong. Although we both somewhat regretted our separation, we knew that it was time to move ahead with our lives.

I moved into my sister Wendy's room. I invaded her "private sanctuary". Needless to say, she was not thrilled by my intrusion. Hey! Being shoved into the marked territory of my older sister was not high up on my list of life's dreams and aspirations . . . I can assure you! I was, however, intrigued with the idea of spending hours chatting with her about every subject from men to moonwalks. I imagined myself watching her prepare for an evening at the theatre or for dinner at some fancy restaurant. This fantasy never materialized. Besides the vast age difference, we had nothing in common, except that we did not really like each other very much.

I became little more that a scullery maid for the prissy poop. She constantly ordered me about, until she had no more use for me, then she'd order me out of the room like a dog. Wendy was, after all, 22 years old. She resented having a 12 year old crowding her and she never let me forget it. I was not thrilled either and tried to avoid her and "our" room whenever possible. Besides, who cared? It would only be for a few more years . . . right? Hell, she had to leave home sometime. Didn't she?

CHAPTER 9

THE MOVIE

Boy, have I got privacy now! I have uninterrupted privacy for weeks on end. If silence is golden, then I've turned into King Midas. At first, I thought I'd like being left alone for long periods of time, but it soon became apparent that being alone was not the same as being lonely. This feeling of isolation that I experience constantly, even when I am with other people, can be stifling. I am acutely aware of my visitor's hesitancy to approach me too closely or to touch me. However, I do understand. Sometimes I don't even like having to be trapped inside my own body.

David was the one who thought that it might be a good idea for me to record my thoughts on this machine. He thought that it would be a positive diversion to which I could direct at least part of my abundant free time and teach the world about AIDS.

He said, "Who knows? You might even learn something in the process".

I already had learned something. I've learned that it's most difficult to talk to a cold, mindless, unemotional machine. Once again, Catholic School discipline claims another victory! Hey! It beats talking to yourself. Right?

Catholic School played a significant role in my life. It was through my Catholic education that I was taught values and beliefs that were to sustain me during my tempestuous life.

The deep-rooted religious beliefs, the Christian ethics and the self-discipline that were instilled in me by the nuns during my grammar-school years helped me keep focused . . . most of the time. While I occasionally lost sight of these concepts they were, nevertheless, available to me as a source of strength and understanding. The major drawback with attending a parochial school was the constant interjection of the importance of virtuosity and virginity into our class work. My guilty conscience worked overtime to impale me with the knowledge of my impurity, but I was able to acknowledge the fact that I did find some interaction with the opposite sex most enjoyable.

In truth, I was sort of confused about love and sex and pain and affection and how they were divided . . . or how they were supposed to fit together.

During one "purity push" lecture, as I pondered a certain bus ride home, I actually blushed. The "penguin" noticed my redness and asked if I needed to leave the room. I could see by the look of concern on her wrinkled face that she thought I was ill. I simply nodded and made my exit. I "goofed off" in the lavatory for awhile then returned to class . . . assuring my teacher that I was okay.

When I was in the seventh grade, I snuck out of the house one evening to go to the movies. I was going to walk there and back. I had no fear whatsoever in regards to walking home after nightfall. I only had to go about two miles and these across city sidewalks. It wasn't like I had to skulk through spooky, deserted wooded lanes. Somehow, I ended up alone and bored. I am still uncertain about the sequence of events. The movie had been a bomb and, if I had met anyone there that evening, he also must have been a bomb.

I was rather enjoying the walk home in the brisk night air. My feeling of tranquility was due, in major part, to the fact that my father wasn't supposed to be there. It was less nerve-racking to sneak in with only Mom to bust me. Don't misunderstand! No less preparation or thought went into the planning and activating phases of the final triumphant scheme. It was simply that the terror was missing. That made a "Mom only" encounter infinitely superior.

I was more than halfway home before I noticed the sensation.

I was not alone on the "deserted" street. I could feel that I was not alone. Inevitably, the answering echo to the sound of my footfalls on the pavement confirmed my instincts. The increase in volume of his crunching footsteps indicated that he was decreasing the distance between us. I was not ecstatic over this discovery. I did not want to turn around. That would have been too obvious. I simply quickened my pace. So, too, did the echo. Oh Lord! What was I gonna do? What could I do? I knew I could not run the rest of the way home. He was right behind me. I could hear his labored breathing. In mere seconds he would be able to reach out and grab me. A biting cold chill ran down my back as the icy sound of his raspy voice whispered my name.

"Tarah!" he quietly yelled.

Wait a minute, lunkhead! If he called you by name then he couldn't possibly be a murderous stranger. Murderous . . . maybe, but no stranger. Turning slowly, I confronted my would-be assailant. Hell, he went to my school. He was a year ahead of me. Jamie Something . . . I think. Yeah! He was one of the upper-crust crowd . . . from a real nice family. Lots of money there!

"What the hell are you trying to do besides scare the dickens out of me?" I snarled, my fear entirely forgotten.

"I was just gonna walk you home. I saw you walking all by yourself. It's really not safe for a pretty girl to be out alone at night. There are some crazy people out here in the real world." He oozed sincerity and charm.

Ignoring the compliment, I informed him that I was quite capable of finding my way back to the nest without any assistance from him, and proceeded on my way. As expected, he fell in step at my side. I really did not mind his company since his scaring tactics had left a strange, lingering doubt in my mind as to the wisdom of this sojourn through the darkness. As we walked, we chatted easily. Along with his vicious good looks, he was also witty and a natural conversationalist. The verbiage rolled between us with the fluid motion of a babbling brook; broken only by the waves of laughter skimming across the waters of our mirth. Without effort, he slid his arm around my waist . . . seeming to sense my disquieting fear . . . experienced at his hands, I might add.

A shiver ran through me and he pulled me closer, believing it to be from the chilled night air. The warmth of his body penetrated the shirt and sweater that he wore. I wondered if he had any chest hair and if he was a good kisser. That's not as strange as it sounds. You see, I like to rub my hands on a guy's chest while we're kissing. Okay, maybe that was as strange as it sounded.

By this time we were approaching my house. I was about to thank him for seeing me safely home and being so nice, when he interrupted my attempt.

"Would you like to go for a short walk before you go home? It's still pretty early," he asked politely.

I nodded demurely. Hot dog! I was going to get a chance to try out his kisser after all. I knew what the intentions were behind his invitation. I decided to play along. Who knows? Maybe I'd even find out about the quantity and quality of his chest hair. Man, would I have something to contribute to the bathroom scuttlebutt tomorrow! Better yet, maybe I'd just keep this a private, personal moment.

We had only strolled a short distance when he guided me with his strong arm to a secluded area behind an old shed. A yellow full moon shone down on us as he gently tilted my chin up to meet his warm and waiting lips. His aftershave filled the night air with a heady scent, which was having an incredibly intoxicating effect on me. With his anxious tongue he was eagerly seeking entry into my mouth. I parted my lips and teeth slightly but was totally unprepared for the assault of that busy tongue, having found its admittance unbarred. Possibly, I also detected a hint of alcohol on his breath. No problem! He had been every inch the gentleman on the way home and I wanted to continue kissing him just a little longer.

Quite unnoticed until now, his hands had become busy, too. I ignored the almost inaudible gasp as he managed to get under my sweater and blouse and encountered my undershirt. Almost without hesitation, he continued until he finally reached skin.

After stroking my accessible back and butt for a few seconds, be brought his hands around and made a valiant effort to stimulate my breasts, under an enormous burden of clothing. He began to tug at my blouse and sweater to free them from my skirt's waistband and expose my breast.

At this point I informed him that it was time I was getting home. I began to straighten my clothing and therefore had not witnessed the hint of his displeasure in response to my request, until I felt myself crashing to the ground. Before I had even touched down, he had already ripped my sweater and blouse asunder. Another quick yank easily tore my undershirt. Still swimming in the wake of the shock of hitting the ground, I was easy prey for this ruthless animal. Pulling my skirt up to my waist, he tore the dainty panties loose with one rip. He readied himself for his prize.

My senses were returning, slowly. I began to wiggle and flap my arms and I was about to scream. Jamie's perception was again keen and, with amazing swiftness, he pulled my head up by the hair; grabbed the back part of my dangling blouse and quickly twisted it up over my head ensnaring both hands and eliminating the use of my arms. Simultaneously, he stuffed his handkerchief into my mouth and finally secured it with my own scarf. I took that to mean that there would be no more kissing tonight.

"Now shut up and lie still or I'll fuck you up so bad your own momma won't be able to identify your body," he hissed

I relented without further struggle. What was to be gained by trying to prevent the inevitable? . . . except a few broken bones or a squashed face, and I'd have a hard time explaining them to my parents and teachers. Jamie made a perfunctory attempt to arouse me, or maybe himself, again by nibbling my nipples and breasts but he soon tired of that and went for the main gain. His impatience and my tension made entry painful.

I started to cry. His rough humping seemed to go on forever. Just when I thought that I couldn't tolerate another plunge of his weapon into my aching damaged vaginal canal, he exploded into orgasm. He gave a mighty jerk and came crashing down on my agonized body in a series of spasms. His giant bulk crushed the air out of my lungs and my stuffy nose (from crying) hampered inspiration even more. My desperate struggle went unheeded until I was afraid I was gonna suffocate. Suddenly, the beast rolled over, growling like an animal. At least I could breathe again. I had been spared a crushing defeat. My tears continued to fall, silently.

Finally, he turned towards me and said: "I'll see you in school tomorrow".

"What makes you think I won't tell on you for this?" I asked hesitantly.

He paused only momentarily as he shot a non-committal glance in my direction. With the arrogance of a jackal, which he so much duplicated, he simply said: "You won't! You won't or I'll kill you".

My heart fell to my feet. He was correct, after all. He would not hesitate to do as he threatened and I knew this. If need be, he would hunt me down like a dog and I was sure that his execution would be slow and painful . . . just like his rape. This was surely to remain another memory buried deep in my subconscience. It would remain there forever, so long, unable to rise to the surface. There, they would lie dormant along with so many other thoughts, feelings, and memories, where they could no longer impose their own specific terror into my already screwed-up reality.

I can remember it all, now. As silent tears rolled down my face, Jamie walked away, laughing that maniacal giggle, and slipped into the night. I walked back to the house and slithered through the quiet corners of my home to the sanctuary of that room that I shared. That night, the room was the only thing I shared, as I curled up under the blankets and secretly cried the tears of a young girl . . . hurting and alone.

It is so easy to lay here and ponder the wickedness that we humans expose ourselves and each other to, throughout the course of a lifetime. With HIV infection, this is even more prevalent. In fact, upon learning of their positive HIV status, some individuals feel justified in spreading the infection. These morbid pieces of humanity will direct their energies into trying to infect as many other people as possible before they die. How much more diabolical can a soul get than to wish this hellish infirmity on any non-suspecting victim? It seems to me that there ought to be a special place in hell for these demons in human guise.

CHAPTER 10

THE CHANGE

Remembering back to that time in my life reminds me of the lack of family in my life, right now. I have lived alone since I first became aware of my infection. At that point my health had been good and the Activities of Daily Living (ADLs) were no problem for me to handle independently. However, as my health degenerates, more and more of my ADLs begin to require the joining of forces, as any one of a number of helpers perform the duties that I can no longer accomplish successfully, unassisted. At least this affords me the opportunity to converse with these kind and generous people (many of whom were total strangers before they found out that I had become a victim of AIDS' special path of destruction). I can't imagine how I would survive without their love.

About this time in my homelife small, almost insignificant, changes were in the wind. My mother seemed to be changing imperceptibly, but to this child's eyes a metamorphosis was taking place. Not too long ago, my mother wore only shabby clothes and no make-up. She seemed to have little regard for the way she presented herself to the public-at-large. Most of her energies went to assessing the needs of her children and husband, and on this she concentrated her efforts. Things were about to change.

Soon after my graduation from Catholic School and subsequent entrance into high school, I began to see a difference in the way she addressed my father and the way she looked when I was leaving for school in the mornings. Before this, it seemed that my mother would no more raise her voice to my father than I would. She had accepted his brashness and bitching all through my childhood. She even told me that it was a wife's responsibility to accept the word of her husband as the language of God, and to do as he commanded in all things pertaining to the family. This was the way Jesus had instructed and this was the prescribed way to fulfill the vows Christian women took on their wedding day. For too many years, my mother subscribed to this archaic doctrine.

Eventually, an erosion began to take place. At first, it was just the shift of her glance or the tilt of her head that seemed to have changed. Gradually, her whole demeanor changed, as well as her position that she had assumed of subservient underling. The strength of her personal convictions began to erode upon the stony barricades of my father's tyranny. They actually started to have loud battles where they would be shouting and yelling their abuses to each other with little regard as to who may be listening.

My mother's appearance began to change, too. The roomy moo-moos were replaced by form-fitting dresses that flattered the here-to-fore unnoticeable curves of her sweeping silhouette. With the flair of an artist, she painted her face with the colors of Spring . . . just the hint of color to evoke the whisper of a blush on her cheeks and to enhance the watery softness of her shimmering blue eyes. Many afternoons, upon arriving home from school, I would come home to an empty house, instead of having a home with the ever-present mother in the doorway . . . greeting the returning school children with the proverbial "milk and cookies".

I could not fathom what was taking place in my home and between my parents. Sure, there were still those times when they ventured behind locked doors, under the guise of going over the monthly bills, but these peaceful moments were few and far between and there was an increasing amount of turmoil between these scattered events. At times, the tranquility of our home was shattered for long periods of time. Occasionally, I prayed to God to intervene in our family's situation. I wanted everything all right again. Be careful what you pray for . . . He might just be listening!

One afternoon upon my return from school, I knew immediately that something was amiss. I was just adjusting to the idea that Wendy had left home to find herself. This left me pretty much to my own devices. Now I was being told that we (my mother and I, that is) would be leaving.

"Where are we going?" I inquired. "And when are we coming back. Do I need to take anything?"

"Bring everything that you want to have with you. We will not be coming back," Mother replied with no further explanation.

Thus we left my father's house. David was staring through the upstairs' window; watching us walk away. He felt as helpless as I did. He had already been informed that he was to remain in Father's charge. I assumed this meant that I was being remanded to the custody of my mom. Our future loomed ahead of us, and yet we knew precious little of the tangled web that had been spun about our family and which now threatened to ensnare all but the most agile among us.

Mother and I moved into a small apartment with a man that I had never met before, but with whom Mother seemed very enchanted and familiar. I found it very difficult to adjust to those first few weeks of sharing my living quarters with this unfamiliar male being in such close proximity to me. However, I said nothing to my mother about my discomfort, since she seemed to be having enough trouble herself. Eventually, things settled into a comfortable groove. Little did I suspect that the gates of hell were about to open up and dump a full measure of its satanic weight on my naïve shoulders. This happened at the time when Mother sought to advance her skills and become a contributing member to our newly formed "family". She had been hired as a cocktail waitress in a local tavern. She did well with her easy smile and charming, winning ways of dealing with other's tribulations. She never noticed the subtle change in the way her paramour began to express himself to his new stepdaughter while she was hard at work.

Before setting up house in the new place (sans Father), Mother introduced me to the man with whom we would be living. The first thing I noticed about him was how he seemed to adore my mother and the feeling was obviously very mutual. He was really a very nice guy! He was always charming and made us both laugh quite often with his silly and endearing antics. His manner was in no way like that of my cruel, crude father. He accepted my mother and me into what had to have been his bachelor pad before our invasion. Yet, he never complained. He treated me as any child would have wanted her own father to and I valued the friendship that I shared with this man.

One evening while we were waiting for Mom to finish yet another late shift, we decided that there was plenty of time to watch a movie or even some cartoons, without cheating on my predetermined bedtime. I was overjoyed to have some quiet time with this very special man who had suddenly come into my life. As we watched the shifting forms of the caricatures on the screen, we snuggled together on the couch for warmth and comfort. We often did this and Mom never complained. In fact, sometimes when she was home, she would join us. This was, therefore accepted by both of us as appropriate behavior.

What happened after that seemed to have converged on us without warning and neither of us was aware, at the time, of the ramifications of our actions on that day or the days to follow. Our hearts guided us to that island in our subconscience that allows us to accept and be comfortable with situations that would otherwise prove to be uncomfortable and unacceptable.

I felt his warmth and was aware of his scent as we reclined together on that old, musty sofa that evening. We were alone and feeling happy and I only wanted to make these moments last. We were forging a partnership in a new relationship of our family dynamics.

My stepfather was also eager to have me feel happy and comfortable with him as well. He was generous with his paternal-type hugs and kisses. Teasingly, he called me his new little daughter. At fifteen, it was reassuring to have a good male role model. I would seek him out frequently for advice or reassurance. He became the much-needed father figure in my life.

Cliff realized pronto that some of my patterns for displaying my affections towards him were simply inappropriate. Cautiously, he tried to explain some of the subtle taboos, while considerately accepting my overt demonstrations of sincere joy that he had rescued me from being "fatherless".

Routinely, he would mention that I was rather advanced in the "language of seduction" for a mere girl. Thinking that this impressed him led me to try even harder to seduce him verbally. So insidious was its beginning that I was unaware of the subtle and, eventually, not so subtle change that was occurring between us. Our acquaintance turned into association, which increased to friendship, which developed into a comfortable companionship, which blossomed into a relationship of intimacy. The way we both figured it . . . our ship had come in!

Never during our early meetings did the idea strike me that what was passing between us was in any way wrong or against my Christianity. Surely, we had become the epitome of the loving, wholesome Christian family. We were trying to keep the home that was shared with the "stepfather" full of peace, love and happiness. This is precisely what I was trying to do! Having never had a simple homelife or a normal relationship with my father, I had little with which to compare my current situation. Even when some of the things that Cliff suggested seemed somewhat awkward, considering that all these actions evolved so gradually, there was no way that at any specific moment I could have viewed them as bizarre. They gradually molded themselves from what had transpired before.

During the many evenings that we waited for Mother to finish work, Cliff would teach me about myself: body and soul. His leathery hands glided over my skin with the slipperiness of quicksilver. He always made our adventures culminate with my body being overcome with wave after wave of the "gigglies".

SHAWNA DELIAH

In retrospect, it seemed to me that my stepfather started to make his moves on me almost as soon as my mother sought employment outside of the home. Cliff had been in favor of Mom's working from the very beginning. In fact, he suggested it the day we moved into his apartment . . . right after he met me for the first time.

As I recall, Cliff never had a steady job. He always seemed to manage to arrange employment for a few days whenever he needed a few extra bucks for which he did not have to account.

We settled into a ritual. Mom would leave for work, then Cliff would make a grandiose presentation of a new trinket that he had procured specifically for his "chosen" daughter. I would be only too eager to show him how grateful I was for his thoughtful gift. His gentleness belied his intent. Eventually, he became more demanding in his request for my displays of affection for him. Upon his subtle insistence, our "love games" became more involved. In answer to his incessant pleading, I reluctantly agreed to allow him to penetrate my flesh with his masculinity. I had no awareness of the potential consequence of our exploits, but I was happy to see that these shared times seemed to please him immeasurably.

This time was good for my mother, too. Cliff was a model husband in her presence. He showered her with tenderness and encouraged her in her attempts to face the big, bad world into which she had recently ventured. She did not seem to pay much attention to me after she started working. She definitely had no notion that I had been experiencing severe nausea for much of the last few weeks.

The nausea seemed to be without end and the odor of almost anything would send me scurrying for the bathroom. I would frequently be assaulted by wave after wave of nausea from which there seemed no escape. I fell asleep feeling sick to my stomach and I woke up the same way. Cliff had no idea when I came to him before school one morning and informed him that I was not feeling very well. He smiled his charming smile and told me to relax next to him on the couch and he would make me all better. He tried, too . . . but to no avail. I was just too sick.

I probably would have continued to suffer had it not been for the school's mandate to investigate prolonged absenteeism. After about a month, the vice-principal's secretary discovered my lack of attendance and made the mandatory phone call to my home. Somehow, she managed to reach my mother at work who was, needless to say, totally unaware of my truancy and the reason behind it. She promised the school authorities to check it out and straighten out any difficulties. She had no idea what she was getting herself into. No idea at all!

CHAPTER 11

THE QUESTION

My mother walked out onto the balcony where I was "catching some rays". She knew that I had stayed home on that particular day but prior to the phone call, she had been unaware that I had not been to classes for over a month. Ironically, I felt totally confident in my deception. In her usual direct approach, she assailed me with the interrogation.

"Tarah. I had a phone call from the school today. Would you mind telling me what the hell you think you are doing? Why haven't you been going to school? Are you in some kind of trouble? Have you been fighting? I thought you liked your classes and your teachers this year. You seem to be doing very well . . ."

"Whoa, Mom! Wait a minute! I do like school . . . but you don't understand. I've been really sick. I haven't said anything before this because you've been too busy to notice, but that's not your fault. I thought that with a little time it would pass, but it doesn't seem to be getting any better. Don't worry about school . . . you know I'll make it up . . . no sweat! Nothing I've done so far has helped. I'm kinda getting a bit scared."

My mother's face softened a bit at this.

"Don't worry another second, sweetheart. Tomorrow we will pay old Doctor Holladay a visit. He will probably prescribe a tonic and you will be "fit as a fiddle" in no time."

With those encouraging words, I retired that night at peace with the world. Mom was on top of things and she would see me through this difficulty. Whatever the outcome of the doctor visit, I rested securely in the knowledge that my mother would be there for me and extend to me the comfort and support that was never extended to me while we were living under my father's reign. Nothing was gonna impede my newfound family from coping with any situation that presented itself to us. . . . Almost nothing, anyway.

The following morning found us waiting in the crowded vestibule of the doctor's office. I had already had blood drawn for a variety of lab tests. I was simply waiting for my turn to be seen, examined and educated by this wise physician.

"Tarah, the doctor will see you now," squeaked the skinny receptionist.

I was promptly ushered into a small dressing room where the nurse instructed me to disrobe and put on the paper gown provided. I was helped up onto a long, hard table that felt as though they used the lower compartment for storing their ice. Of course, throughout this whole humbling experience, my mother remained diligently at my side. She offered me steady encouragement and tried to allay my fears of the exam to come.

Doc began his assessment at my head and proceeded in an orderly manner down to my toes. Just as I was about to leap off that uncomfortable slab, I was instructed by this gentle healer to lay back and relax. He then lifted my feet and placed them into metal brackets that were attached to the side of the table. Again, I obeyed.

I was quite afraid and, at that moment, ashamed considering my mother was witnessing this entire ordeal and had yet to offer me any solace. Now, this man in the white professional coat was instructing me to spread my knees wide open. How could I? If I did, I would be exposing my most private parts to him, right in front of my mother.

"It's alright Tarah, Darling. Do as he tells you. He's just trying to find out why you are sick . . . then he'll fix you up, good as new," Mother said as if suddenly sensing her young daughter's turmoil.

I tried to relax.

"Let your knees fall outward . . . that's good. Try to relax."

I felt his hands touching my inner thighs.

"You're getting very thin, young lady."

Something touched my special place down there . . . it was cold. It felt wet. It was starting to invade my inner sanctum . . . going up inside of me. At the same time I felt something find my bung hole . . .

"Relax, Tarah. You're doing very well . . . "

. . . The white voice droned on and on. The unseen thing found the exact center of my anus and seemed determined to gain entry into its tiny cavity . . .

"Relax. That's good. We won't be too much longer."

The pain shot through me like a knife that was intent on carving its way into my body. Did he have even an inkling of how much he was hurting me?

"Great! Now bear down, child. You're doing very well! Isn't she, Mother?"

. . . Now he was putting something else in to my vagina . . . but I was full. It could not possibly hold anything else. Please, someone stop this torture . . . please, someone . . . stop him . . . please . . . stop this . . .

"Tarah," my mother crooned. Wake up, Tarah. You're okay! Wake up, Honey. The doctor is finished with you. I guess you sort of passed out, but the doctor assures me that you're just so weak. Try to get up. Here, I'll help you. Try to get dressed and then we can go home."

Gradually, I emerged from the murky grayness. The darkness had shrouded me at some time during the exam. Now it was over and I could leave. Mother explained to me as I was getting dressed that the doctor would contact us within a few days with the results of the lab work and his interpretation of his physical assessment.

Two days later the telephone rang. Cliff answered it on the second ring, since Mother had worked the late shift last night and was still sleeping.

"Hello? . . . Yes it is. This is her father speaking. . . . Yes. . . .

Yes . . . I understand. Oh! I see! Yes, ma'am . . . I understand. I'll be sure to relay this information as soon as possible. Thank you for calling. Goodbye!"

It was a stranger who turned to look towards me from across the room. There was a cold glint in those familiar eyes that was anything but familiar.

"Oh, Baby, Baby, Baby! You and me may have big trouble on our hands, soon! Just remember that I love you very much and will do everything in my power to protect you from her wrath."

"Whose wrath?" I questioned, not knowing whether he was playing one of his mind games with me or not.

"Never mind, kiddo. Why don't you just come over here and give your steppappy a smooch," he whispered. He implored me, not only with his voice but also with his gentle, coaxing eyes as well.

Without thinking, I flew into the remembered security of his strong embrace and within moments, we were exploring each other with a renewed intensity as if each minute was sure to be our last one together. We both were oblivious to our surroundings, having gotten swept away by our passion. Therefore, neither of us was aware of any other activity until the screech penetrated our feverish concentration and alerted us simultaneously to the impending disaster. Mother was standing there in the doorway of the bedroom and was staring at the sight before her, with eyes bulging and mouth agape. As we disentangled ourselves from each other's embrace, the groaning assaulted our senses and invaded our joy. Mother was screaming and began to fly towards us. Her hatred and disbelief erupted spontaneously and her awesome anger was directed to me, alone.

"You slut. You filthy little whore . . . with my husband. I'll kill you right here and now with my bare hands," and with the utterance of those words, she catapulted across the room and attempted to wrap her hands around my neck.

At the last possible moment, Cliff was able to intervene for my sake and managed to get my mother quiet enough to listen to him.

"You can't hurt her. Not now! She's pregnant! If you kill her, you will be guilty of murdering two . . . her and the baby."

After a short pause to allow this information to be processed, she turned her venomous eyes to me. There was no affection in those eyes now. They were hard and cold . . . like shards of glass. Behind the glass, there was a raging fire . . . fueled by her anger, muffled only slightly by her surprise.

"Whose the bastard's father? Do you even know, Slut? I don't care anyway. I'll make all the arrangements for the abortion! Right away."

My mind was racing. I was pregnant! What a mixture of emotions churned inside of me! What a terrible way to find out! Hey! I was going to have a baby. The images were a mixture of ecstasy and terror. However, the thought of doing away with the baby was not part of any of the scenarios in my head. 'My abortion'? I thought . . . No! No . . . I want my baby. I cannot destroy this life within me. How could she even think such a horrible thought?

"No, Mother!" I yelled desperately. "I could never do anything that would hurt an unborn child. I won't! And I won't let you, either."

"You will do as I say or I will kill you both, here and now as I was determined to before I was so rudely interrupted . . . And you . . . !" She suddenly turned her venom on Cliff. "How could you do anything as perverted as what I watched you doing with my daughter? I thought you loved me. What were you thinking?"

As gradual as the ebbing tide, the current shifted. With all the cunning of the great oracles of mythology, Cliff began to weave a thread of words out of which he constructed a web of deception that encased my mother like a tomb. He explained to his distraught wife that what she thought she witnessed was actually a poor interpretation of the events that she had discovered unfolding before her eyes. She had mistaken our innocent "wrastlin'" for demonic carrying on. He assured my mother that neither he nor I were capable of the type of activities of which we were unfairly being accused. Gradually, his whipped cream narration softened her heart and dissipated her anger. We were then able to turn my mother's energies away from the negative and realign her towards the more positive aspects of my predicament. More quickly than imaginable, she became quite interested in readying me for motherhood. She wanted me to feel confident about my abilities to provide all the necessary aspects of motherhood. The question of paternity seemed forgotten. With great patience, she explained that the nausea that had ravaged my very soul for the past six weeks was a common problem during early pregnancy. She assured me that these symptoms would ultimately subside and I would begin experiencing the joys of carrying a tiny life inside of me.

Approximately one week later, my mother and I were having the sort of conversation that had the innate potential for growing ugly. All that week, she had been trying to coerce me into revealing the name of the scum that had defiled my assmed virginity and abandoned me in my delicate condition. Out of absolute frustration, I ran from the room in tears. What could I say that would not open up many newly healed wounds? I snuck out of the apartment to secretly keep my appointment with Doc Holladay. He had told me very discreetly at that last visit to contact his secretary at my earliest convenience to set up my next appointment. It seemed that there were many issues that needed to be addressed and he thought that a few of these could best be handled without the omnipresent figure of my mother lurking in the background.

I found myself back in the torture chamber. I was greeted pleasantly enough by the skinny receptionist and ushered immediately into the inner serenity of my doctor's private office. It was spacious, comfortable, cozy and masculine . . . just like old Doc Holladay, himself. This man had been my doctor since forever. In his presence I had always been comfortable. He was an old-fashion, no nonsense kind of person, but he was fair. If you obeyed and were "a good girl" he was fine. I had never challenged him because I could sense a fire in his soul. He was a religious man and greatly respected my mother's devotion. He smiled easily when I entered and proceeded to insist that I sit down in the chair across from his desk. When he looked deeply into my eyes, a coldness engulfed my spine.

He had something to tell me and it was of a serious nature, judging from the concerned expression of his countenance. He told me he needed more information about the paternity of my child. There were genetic questions that needed to be answered. There were too many questions to which I had no answers. There were questions about chromosomes and issues of deformed babies.

"Is there something wrong with the baby I'm carrying," I queried.

He simply repeated that he needed more information . . . about the father. He was asking me if I knew who the father was. This could be serious and he needed that information . . . to protect the fetus. I had to tell him or my baby could die. It might be too sick, too deformed to survive.

"It was my stepfather," I whispered.

"I'm sorry. I didn't quite hear what you just said. I know this is difficult and uncomfortable for you, but I'm simply trying to understand the entire situation. Armed with all the available information, I will attempt to advise you of all your options and offer suggestions on how to proceed. Now, Tarah, I need to know who the father of this child is." The good doctor was sorely aware of my discomfort and shame, but he insisted on my repeating those notorious words.

"It has to be my stepfather's child. I have not been with anyone for almost a year," I responded louder this time. In fact, it felt like I was screaming this unfortunate information for the entire world to hear. "Please, Doctor Holladay," I begged. "Please don't tell anyone about this secret . . . especially my mother. Not yet! I promise I will tell her. Just let me do it in my own way at the right time."

My tears were falling helplessly from my eyes. Sensing my anxiety and possibly understanding the added stress that this difficult situation would impose on our unique family structure, the doctor acquiesced to my pleas and assured me that he would allow me to handle this delicate matter.

As I plodded homeward, I contemplated the precarious events that had led up to this dilemma. Somehow, I would make my mother understand that I would not . . . could not, put my conception at risk. I had to make her understand that I considered this God's will. She had to believe that the child developing inside of my womb was his creation and that by his command, I must see this pregnancy through to the end. I was certain that I would need The Almighty's intervention to make my mother see this as my personal cross to bear . . . a cross that I would carry with personal satisfaction and absolute joy.

Okay, Mr. Recorder! I'm kind of worn out. It's a good thing that I have no social life, since I don't have enough energy to sit up for more than an hour at a time to do this dictation. I'll get back to you as soon as I can. By the way, I think maybe David was right. Although I know that you're just a machine, saying these things to you is helping me gain a unique understanding of my past. I'll talk at you later!

CHAPTER 12

THE IRONY

After my arrival home, I made a quick assessment of the temperament of the household. Miraculously, my mother seemed to have forgotten about our last conversation and my disquieted spirit before I left the room. She greeted me with her warm smile and our conversation flowed easily into a comfortable outpouring of verbiage that seemed to caress my confounded soul.

"You know, Tarah. I am so pleased that you and Cliff are getting along so well in so short a time. I'm sure that this has been a difficult adjustment for you. I pulled you away so abruptly from that other house, but rest assured that I did this for your safety as well as my own personal reasons.

"As you well know, there was so much animosity and even hatred in your father's heart that was so often directed towards you, Baby. I think that the time has come for me to dispel some of the mystique surrounding these overtones that have confused you so much.

"This is so difficult for me but I feel that you are now old enough to understand some of the complexities of the adult world. Listen carefully and try to keep an open mind until you have heard my entire story.

"One night over 16 years ago, I returned home to your father in quite a state of disarray. Thinking quickly, I convulsed into a fit of body-wracking sobs and informed my husband that I had been raped on my way home from the confession that evening. It would seem that my appearance substantiated my story and he immediately insisted that I seek medical attention at the local emergency room. There I was carefully examined by a physician and referred to the local police for further questioning. Of course, you understand that I had not been raped, but had secretly spent the earlier part of the evening in the arms of my secret lover. Does that shock you? Well, it shouldn't! Your father and I were having trouble even then.

"Within a month, I made an appointment with my own doctor and he confirmed my suspicions that I was pregnant. With all due haste, I informed your father of my condition. He accepted it for the moment with resignation. Later, however, he began to question the timing of my conception and eventually determined for himself that it was the result of my rape. He was insistent that I terminate my pregnancy immediately. I was crushed.

"I informed him that I had no intention of ending my child's life. I continued to argue with him long into the night that it was against all my religious convictions. It was murder, pure and simple, and nothing he could say was going to alter my perception. Eventually, he reluctantly acquiesced and my pregnancy ended with the birth of a girl child who would be named "Tarah".

After an unmistakable pause I choked, "Then it was me?"

"Yes, my child. God blessed my life with you. You were a beautiful baby , , , so happy and playful. You made me as happy as any mother has ever been. Unfortunately, my husband was never able to accept you as his. That was why he was so hurtful towards you, while being so loving and generous to your brothers and sisters."

Suddenly, so many aspects of my life began to make sense. As I continued to assimilate this new information, my mother dropped another bomb in my lap.

"Isn't it funny. To think that after all these years, Cliff and I would somehow manage to end up together and even be allowed to raise our wonderful daughter together. You see, Darling, Cliff is really your biological father. That actually explains your easy, natural affinity for each other. You were drawn together by your mutual bloodlines. He has certainly proven to me that he loves you as well as any man has ever loved a daughter of his own."

What was this woman saying. He could not possibly be my father. After all, he was the father of the baby that I was carrying. That would mean that . . . no! I couldn't even bring myself to form the thought. My baby . . . my poor little unborn baby was not going to get a chance to experience life. How cruel! No . . . no! I had to figure something out. I needed a little time to form a plan. I had to think of some way to save my little baby from their destruction.

I began to send my silent prayers heavenward. Oh, merciful and all-powerful God. Please help me! Help me to save this child. Why would you plant this tiny life inside of me, only to have me allow these brutal people to rip it from my loins before it is wholly formed?

No! I would refuse to do this. I swear to you, Baby, that I will do all that I can to insure you a safe and happy entrance into this world. At that moment, I resolved to go see Doctor Holladay first thing in the morning. I was sure that he would know how to advise me of my options . . . given this new information.

Options. Now there's a powerful word. Alternatives has a nice ring to it. Doesn't it? And choices . . . what a marvelous sound. The possibilities seem endless. How wonderful to be allowed the opportunity to select from a virtual smorgasbord of options that life usually offers for the taking! Thinking back, it seems to me that I wasted too many of these opportunities for adventure. Too often, I chose the easy way out, or the most secure route in the end. What was I afraid of losing? Whatever it was, it appears as though I lost! Dying from AIDS, or any other illness that drags its victims through a quagmire so revolting that even the very demons of hell avoid its depths of despair, tends to make them more introspective, which is the main reason I am ramblin' on and on as I am now.

I talk to this unsympathetic machine about my innermost

thoughts; my fears, hopes, beliefs and secrets. In return, I get no response at all. Maybe an occasional beep . . . to let me know that it is time to change the tape. Other than that, it offers me no consolation whatsoever.

Some days, I feel so weak that even breathing seems to be more trouble than it is worth. My appetite dwindles with every passing day. Of course, the aforementioned diarrhea does not help anything. My weight seems to be melting away daily. Sometimes I think that some of the copious amounts of medicine I gobble down several times each day only adds to my problems. Other days I'm too weak to care.

I digress. Yes, yes, yes! I was talking about options . . . specifically, the options that my doctor was to relay to me during my appointment that day. I was up early and managed to get ready quickly and quietly. Soon, I was silently closing the big front door of our apartment and was hurrying to his office, which was located in a large office building on the other side of town. Fortunately for me, it wasn't a very big town and I managed to arrive safely and was just about to sit down in the waiting room when the skinny receptionist called my name. Hesitantly, I stood up and somehow willed my legs to carry me through the door and down the hall. I soon found myself inside one of the tiny cubicles that served as his exam rooms, again.

As soon as the doctor stuck his head through the doorway, I began to extol the new intimacies that surrounded my situation. With the revelation that my biological father had sired this child, the developing entity within my womb, he stood up to his full height, took a deep breath and proceeded to eliminate all of my options with a single sentence.

"This evil thing must die! It is documented in the Bible. This creature is devil-spawned and it must never be allowed to be born. God will mightily curse those who attempt to save this vile monster. No! It must surely be ripped from your belly before it contaminates life." The good doctor continued as if nothing strange was going on. "I will, however, need parental consent before I perform the abortion. You are to tell no one except your parents what is about to transpire. There could be serious repercussions. I will discuss the financial aspects with them when next I see them. I'm sorry, Tarah. There is really nothing else to do. Hurry now. Go home quickly and explain the situation to your mother. I'm sure she will be in full agreement with me on this. It is imperative that we waste no time in ending this foul and evil conception. I only pray that we are in time to kill the beast".

I began gathering my coat and purse as I tried to gather my thoughts. I could not tear them away from the black abyss of those merciless eyes of the doctor. No options were left available to me. He had commanded that it be so. The beast must die . . . the beast . . . the baby . . . my baby must die. It is God's will . . . I must obey. I always obey.

Somehow, I managed to steady myself. I knew I had to get out of this place. On shaky legs, I maneuvered my way through the reception area, along the corridor and by some miracle was able to create a path which sliced through the sea of humanity in the crowded waiting room. Not one of the people waiting took any notice of the obviously distraught creature leaving the premises.

The cool blast of early morning mist struck me soundly as I began my return trek across this little city. I began to fully realize what was expected of me. They wanted me to sacrifice my baby. They wanted me to offer this innocent lamb up as atonement for some atrocious, heinous sin. But it was my sin, not the sin of my child. I should be the one to pay. I would gladly pay with my own flesh and blood, if only the new life forming within the confines of my uterus could be spared. I could not let them destroy the only blessing that had ever been handed to me by the fingers of God. I would run far away and not return until I decided that it would be safe for my child and me to return.

Without my awareness, I had entered the business district. My thoughts were far away. My body carried on in the intermittent reality. For some reason, I was running . . . running along on the sidelines of my memories. My immediate surroundings went unnoticed. From somewhere, the fog was rolling along in thick gray sheets, like the sails of a hundred invisible ships. The sounds of the awakening city melted together and molded itself into a whirlpool of noise that closely resembled the cries of dirges being sung by faceless mourners in the obscurity of darkness.

CHAPTER 13

THE BUS

Suddenly my machine has stopped. The beep tells me that the tape has reached the end. Putting a new tape in is quite simple and, even in my weakened condition, I accomplish this task without too much difficulty. There now! I am ready to continue. It may be easier for me to take a few minutes here, for clarity's sake, to describe to you what happened that morning in the center of the business district as I ran blindly to an unknown destination. I was desperate to put as much space as possible between the doctor's office building and me.

What you are about to hear is strictly hearsay. I will probably never know exactly what happened but, through the years, I have been able to piece together a scenario from news clippings and rumors. According to most of the witnesses at the scene, the bus was traveling towards the busy intersection at a pretty good clip. A crowd had gathered on the corner while waiting for the light to change. Although a few of the passersby had even noticed the young lady running into the crowded area, fewer could have imagined what would occur in the next split seconds.

With complete disregard for the other pedestrians and traffic signals, the obviously frazzled young woman dashed into the busy intersection. The petite figure hit the midsection of the huge windshield, directly in line with the terrified eyes of the driver and the startled passengers. A loud, dull thud was heard just before the screams of the onlookers. Miraculously, despite the pandemonium, someone summoned emergency services and the ambulance arrived quickly. The paramedics were led to the scene while a team of mounted policemen made a valiant attempt to disperse the crowd of gaping spectators.

While I struggled for breath, the EMTs ripped the blood-drenched clothing out of their way and attached some electrodes to my chest, started an IV and made an initial assessment of the extent of my injuries. Throughout the ordeal, great care was taken by everyone to avoid any unnecessary movement of my body to prevent further accidental complications. The decision was made to transport me to the nearest hospital as soon as the appropriate field preparations were completed. St Luke's was our destination after I was carefully loaded into the ambulance.

Our arrival in the emergency room caused quite a stir and the white-clad figures of the medical personnel began to scurry to and fro in a dizzying fray of activity. Assorted lab tests were conducted along with a barrage of x-rays. Several doctors examined me to assist in determining the extent and severity of my injuries. The first major discovery was the pneumothorax. This life-threatening injury was caused by the impact of the bus busting several of my ribs which, in turn, punctured my lung, causing the negative pressure needed within the pleural cavity to be eliminated. I was scheduled for immediate surgery, even though they only had the information that was obtainable from my purse. The surgeon inserted tubes into my chest and reestablished the correct pressure. Having saved me from immediate demise, the medical team turned their attention to my other varied injuries. I had suffered numerous broken bones including complex fractures of all extremities, a fractured scull, cracked vertebras and ribs and contusions. Countless hours of therapy would be required to rehabilitate myself if I was strong enough to live through the critical period. After the consulting physicians agreed that everything feasible had been attempted and my vital signs were reasonably stable, I transferred out of recovery and into the Intensive Care Unit.

At some point during this frenzy of activity, someone had the sensitivity to contact my family. Of course, I was completely oblivious to all these proceedings. I was entirely submerged in fighting my own "demon" that had caused me to plunge headlong into the path of the oncoming bus.

CHAPTER14

THE BLACKNESS

My senses were useless. My eyes were unable to distinguish shapes or colors. My ears heard no clear sound, only the blending of indeterminable noise swirling into a whirlpool which formed a cacophonic, maniacal din with slippery abandon. For some unknown reason, I was running. I knew that running was the fastest way to get away from here and I wanted to get away from here as quickly as possible. Why did it seem as if everyone was moving at once . . . moving towards me? There was so much commotion here. There were too many sounds: The eerie squeal of tires trying to stop, a scream, footsteps . . . many footsteps, many voices. Somewhere, far away, there was the unmistakable sound of a siren . . . its woeful whine growing with intensity. Figures were scurrying in the dazed scamperings in unconscious imitation of frantic squirrels. A short blast from a car horn . . . someone offering a prayer to God requesting his mercy. It all seemed so far away. I couldn't breathe . . . gasping . . . no air . . . no air to breathe.

Until now, the blackness had been content to remain in the background . . . unnoticed by all . . . deciding when the inevitable bondage would transpire. It began its approach . . . silently it floated towards me . . . silently gliding . . . unassuming . . . unnoticed . . . slowly, stealthily wending its way through the unwary crowd . . . coming closer . . . wrapping its tentacles of darkness around me as if to offer me protection from some hideous fate. As it got closer I could share its emotions and thoughts . . . pity . . . too much blood . . . peace . . . quiet peace. The sights and sounds and smells of the city were fading steadily. The blackness continued its steady progress towards my crumpled figure. Its sole intention was to sojourn within the victim until she became uninhabitable. Total blackness arrived moments ahead of the ambulance.

Movement

Cold noise

Featureless faces

. . . but mostly just blackness.

Later there would be pain. Pain and tears! So much pain and so many tears! For now, there was only the darkness, the numbing emptiness where anger and fear and hope and joy merged together into a concoction so bland it swelled up in my throat threatening to choke off the air that kept life in my body. This place was devoid of emotions and thoughts. Blackness rules here. It dictated all thought processes. It controlled movement and the rhythm of tides and the gyrations of celestial orbs. There are no survivors in the blackness. It conquers all invaders. It dominates absolutely. There is no mercy or kindness or affection. There is only darkness. You are powerless against this indestructible foe. It, alone, can decide to relinquish its prey to the world of light. It has decided to release me to seek the light, but not until it takes the opportunity to suck as much of my life out of me as possible. So the darkness grows deeper . . . always deeper . . . seemingly, through the very bowels of Hell.

CHAPTER15

THE NIGHTMARE

I find myself sitting bolt upright in bed. I notice that the machine is still running. I had been recording. I must have fallen asleep and the dream came. The same dream that began in the blackness. My hair and bedclothes are damp with the sweat that also covers my body. My heart is racing like a drum inside my chest and my breath is coming in short, sporadic gulps. Oh, yeah. I'm beginning to remember it more now. I wish I could forget the overwhelming desperation that seems to plague the very fiber of my being in that nightmare.

The grotesque figure always pursuing the dark shadow of the small female form carrying the bundle through the blackness. A steely glint of light from some unknown source reflected on a sliver of metal and cast its glimmer of doom upon both the hunter and his prey. Later, as the recurring vision continued, the flight seemed to have ended, at least temporarily. For the shadow with the bundle can be observed hiding behind some old cartons in a dark, deserted alley. Deep gulps of air were being sucked into flared nostrils while sweat mixed with the grime on exposed skin to form an unsavory muck that clung tenaciously to its unsuspecting host.

A shamefully pathetic token of light fell from a single exposed lightbulb above and only a narrow slice of the figure's face was visible. The contours and the softness were unmistakably that of a woman, or perhaps even that of a girl. Suddenly, there was movement from inside the parcel. For Heaven's sake, it was alive. The bundle was alive.

With obvious love and gentleness, the girl's figure began to unwrap the bundle, lifting off layer after layer of grungy fabric to slowly reveal a small, white hand. Even from a distance, one could see the five perfect fingers, stroking the air and grasping at unseen objects. Another hand soon joins its twin and takes up the rhythm of the dance. Two perfect little hands waving on the end of two tiny white arms that seemed happy to be freed from the confines of the bundle.

. . . Then the sound begins . . . quietly at first, like a breathless whisper. Slowly, the tone begins to form into a drone like that of distant bees. Gradually, it ripens into a sound so ungodly that it sends terror coursing through your blood vessels, which carry it back to the pounding heart that seems like it will rip open from the pressure. Only it does not rip apart: there is no turning back now. The hooded figure is about to uncover the bundle.

She screams as she eyes the monstrosity in her arms. The large bulging, bloodshot eyes peer out from sockets gouged out of the waxy, scaly, slimy skull. The reptilian projection from the oral cavity recoils at the initial sound of her screams, but quickly begins to slither out a few inches and resumes its frantic flapping and sweeping movements as before. It leaves gooey threads of slime dripping off its edges and dangling from its chin. The demonic face gazes back at the hooded figure who unwrapped it from the bondage that had made even the slightest movements impossible.

Suddenly, another figure moved into view and again the night was sliced by a flicker of light gleaming off the slivery blade of the dagger poised about the demon child's form. The hooded figure seemed paralyzed and made no effort to escape or fend off the attacker. Therefore, the weapon slashed through the space unhindered and found its target. As it dug into the scalp of the tiny creature, a foul-smelling gelatinous, green goo began to ooze from the wound. Other swipes of the blade into the face and neck of the bundle yielded more grisly fluids which gushed out of the gaping holes left by its sharp edges.

The two shadowy figures tilted their heads until their eyes met. Both seemed incapable of looking away. The smaller from, still holding the soggy, dripping package, saw a proud smile on the lips of the assailant as he clung to the slime-smeared weapon. The larger figure held his head high and with dignity as would be befitting a brave and dutiful warrior. She knew him! She knew this figure standing over her! She knew that he had driven her away and caused her to run with the little bundle that now sagged limply in her arms. This was Doctor Holladay. He spoke only a single sentence.

"Tarah, you may come home, now," he whispered softly and extended his hand to her in a warm and welcoming gesture.

Finally, I understood. It was me who wore the hooded garment and carried the sacrificial bundle in my arms. It was me who had done nothing to protect it from the unmerciful horror of this evil medicine man. It was me, alone, who heard the maniacal screams of laughter emerging from its bowels . . . a cackling so vile and disgusting that it could only have been uttered by Satan, himself. . . . Then the blackness returned and fully engulfed another helpless victim.

CHAPTER 16

THE REEMERGENCE

I remained unconscious for nearly eight months. Doctor Holladay was my attending physician. Specialists had been called in from all areas of professional expertise. It was later revealed to me that my mother had been a constant fixture at my bedside during this entire period. Cliff had also taken his turn at the bedside vigil and shared the worry and grief with my mother. Together, they pooled their strengths and their prayers and waited for my recovery. Apparently, Doctor Holladay had not revealed to them the discussion that had transpired between us at his office just prior to the accident. It had not been necessary.

The blackness receded as gradually as it had entered. My senses slowly began to assimilate the information coming through the blackness to the respective receptors. The process was garbled for awhile. My eyes heard the vibrations of the mystical hospital protocol. My ears were able to see the colors of my environment. My nose tasted the sourness of my situation long before my mind was fully able to comprehend what that situation really was. My fingers were able to distinguish the various odors in my immediate surroundings. My throat could feel the complicated textures of my life. The grayness fought for control and eventually was victorious over the blackness. With the grayness came more coherency in the interpretation of my sensory exploration.

First, the sounds were able to penetrate through the gray opacity that surrounded me. At last, my ears attempted to sort and differentiate the varied noises that constantly bombarded them and tried to make meaning out of the din. Quick to follow was the realization that the selection of scents that invaded my nostrils was slowly being sorted by my olfactory system and filed within the data-processing portion of my brain. That system was retrieving the correct identifying label for each odor: Alcohol, antiseptic, roast beef, someone's perfume, soap, freshly-laundered linen and a man's pungent aftershave lotion.

Soon the clatter of dishes and utensils was distinguishable from the chatter of my caregivers. Some of these voices seemed to be vaguely familiar to me, but many were not. Some of these overheard conversations were punctuated with laughter and expressive exclamations. Others were simply the mindless droning of those engaged in menial tasks that required little brain activity but endless patience and an appropriate amount of technical training.

My sense of feeling was returning much more slowly, and for this I was unwittingly grateful. There was so much pain. It felt like every part of my body hurt. Sharp objects were frequently being stuck into my flesh and every available orifice invaded by unseen phantoms. I sensed, rather than felt, the tubes that protruded from these same openings. Soon, I could tell the difference between the rough, inquisitive and hurried hands of the doctors from the slower, gentler, more compassionate hands of the nurses who washed and massaged my much-abused body.

I remember thinking . . . why are they talking to me? Surely they did not expect any response from the heap of motionless humanity that they so tenderly cared for. But talk they did! Throughout the entire ordeal of any procedure, these dedicated professionals kept up a flowing conversation: About any interesting current events in the recent headlines, about the unpredictable weather, about the latest fashion trends, about the juiciest gossip, about the various clandestine affairs of their co-workers or anything else that could possibly interest a seriously injured teenage girl in their ICU.

It seems that no one expected me to survive the devastating injuries when they brought me into the emergency room so many,

many months ago. It had been a bus that had knocked the life out of me and left me in this comatose state. On initial assessment of my condition, the doctors quickly ascertained the punctured lung and the resulting hemothorax. They immediately set about to correct this life-threatening problem and saved my life. Next, a tracheotomy was performed and I was placed on a ventilator that mechanically controlled my respiratory process. In an amazingly short amount of time, all biological functions that were required to maintain homeostasis, were being controlled and monitored by a virtual army of men and machines.

It is quite evident to me that it was due to my mother's strong insistence that these life-support measures had not been rescinded prior to my emergence from the grayness. I could hear her arguments now. With a complete disregard for the professional opinions of the medical staff and various social advisors, I am quite certain that my mother insisted that life-support be continued until "the Good Lord called his child back to Him in Heaven". Euthanasia was not a doctrine that the Catholic Church or my mother accepted. It was looked upon as humanity playing God and I am certain that she would fight the very demons from Hell before allowing even the suggestion of this possibility. Therefore, I am still alive and I do conquer the grayness that followed the blackness. I do recover!

The morning of my emergence was no different from any that preceded it. The clicking, beeping, ticking, and buzzing that flowed from the menagerie of mechanical watchdogs furnished the background noise. The regular players knew their cues and delivered their well-rehearsed lines, as usual. The script had not changed for months, so everyone was comfortable with his or her roles. The props were appropriately placed for the solitary scene. Costuming was kept simple and was mandatory for all but the most minor characters. Prompting was neither allowed nor necessary. The lighting remained constant throughout the production. No Oscars or other accolades were ever to be bestowed on the players, but truly brilliant and heroic performances were a daily ritual. Oddly enough, the leading lady had not uttered a syllable or made the slightest hint of a spontaneous movement since opening night. She was about to deliver the performance of her life!!!

What was that? Something was touching me . . . touching my hand. Warm. Soft. Stroking my hand. Holding it. Squeezing it gently. More holding. Lifting it. Something else was touching my hand, now. Something even warmer and softer than before. There were noises, too. Familiar sounds. Voices. Well, a voice anyway. I knew the voice . . . or at least I thought I did. It was a woman's voice. Yes! Now I remember . . . it was my mother's voice.

The grayness was evaporating more rapidly, now. There were shadows and areas of blinding lightness. As I concentrated, these overlapping fields began to emerge as two separate entities. These blurred visionary blotches gained substance and form. They took on assorted shapes. There remained, however, a large blob of blueness ahead. Suddenly, the blueness shifted and I recognized my mother as she turned her body towards me. Instantly, a gasp escaped her lips and then she was gone. No! Come back!! Please don't leave me!!!

As quickly as she vanished, she reappeared. She had simply gone to summon a nurse. Almost immediately, a small group had assembled around my hospital bed and all eyes were riveted on my face.

"Tarah . . . can you hear me? Do you know where you are? How are you feeling? Tell me how you're feeling," pleaded the small oriental nurse with jet-black hair.

"Are you comfortable, Tarah? Tell me if you're not and I can give you something to help you deal with it," offered the nurse with flaming red hair and an impressive overbite.

"Mommy's here, Darling. Everything is just fine. Talk to me, Sweetheart. Tell Mommy what hurts and I'll make it all better. Why doesn't she answer me? What's wrong? Dear God! Won't someone tell me why she doesn't answer my questions. She's awake! I know she is. Won't someone please help my little girl. She's alive and I love her so much. Please!" begged my mother as she teetered on the brink of hysteria. Her tears continued to flow down her already streaked cheeks.

With that scenario began my recuperation. I had to start at the beginning. I had to learn to walk and talk all over again. It was like being a newborn at the age of sixteen. There would also be physical therapy and rehabilitative training that were both grueling and exhausting . . . to say nothing of the pain. My mother and Cliff were very supportive of my efforts during my long convalescence. Their love and encouragement made me strive even harder and push myself to the limits of my endurance. Eventually, I recovered. To the utter amazement of the team of doctors who had structured my course of treatment, to the nurses who ministered to my needs and monitored my progress, and even to the auxiliary personnel on staff, it was like a miracle.

Between ICU and the step-down unit at St. Luke's Hospital and rehab, almost five months of my life had been accounted for. Amid a massive outpouring of tearful farewells and wishes for my continued recovery, I left the hospital with the assistance of my mother and Cliff. They drove the short distance to our apartment handily and guided me to my bedroom where I promptly fell asleep. The excitement of my departure from the hospital and my subsequent return home after so long, had left me exhausted . . . as the nurses had predicted.

Time passed quickly and my strength slowly, but steadily returned. It dawned on me that I had been injured when an early autumnal wind blew the brittle, fallen leaves into wisps of heady dust. Now the clean, fresh fragrance of late spring lingered lazily in my nostrils and the sun tried to coax the dormant shoots under layers of soil to punch their way up through the earthen barricade and enjoy the radiant warmth. Winter had completely passed me by this year. Come to think of it, that was no great loss.

Before I knew it, I had begun to think about returning to school in the fall. Of course, I would have to repeat my sophomore year, but considering the alternative, I could not complain. My mother excitedly swept me off to the various department stores and proceeded to outfit me in the latest fashion. These extravagant spending binges were something to which I was quite unaccustomed, and yet I was not about to look the proverbial gift horse in the mouth. After each of these outings, we carried an unbelievable assortment of dresses, skirts and blouses, sweaters and scarves, undergarments, shoes, purses and other accessories into the apartment. Folding everything neatly, we dispersed the individual items to their proper places.

No one ever considered the possibility that I would not be attending classes in the fall. We just assumed that this would be the scenario. Something unexpected happened that would alter my future for years to come . . . and it involved Cliff.

CHAPTER 17

THE LESSON

The summer seemed to fly by on wings of desperation. For the first time in my life, I felt like part of a complete family. My mother and I shared precious golden hours together in the sun and warm breezes of those lazy, crazy weeks. We literally shopped 'til we dropped . . . dropped a surprising amount of money, that is. We drove to Philadelphia and enjoyed the museums, The Franklin Institute with its planetarium, the marvelous zoo and, of course, we each wolfed down world-renowned Philly Cheese Steaks.

We spent carefree days lounging on the sun-drenched beach at Cape May, rejuvenating our tans and our relationship. Later, in the early evenings, we would walk through the beautifully restored Victorian neighborhoods and admire the gingerbread houses with their perfectly manicured gardens. One of our favorite restaurants there offered seating on the veranda, which allowed the guests to feast on the view of the compelling Atlantic Ocean, while supping on the delicacies prepared by the talented chef. On several occasions during this memorable time we just talked. No subject seemed awkward or improper. We shared special memories and sacred secrets and grew closer to each other than either of us had ever imagined.

Frequently, Cliff would join us on our various escapades. Sometimes he would even think up his own personal adventure to share with us. Either way, all three of us delighted in the joy of simply being together and, as Cliff was so fond of saying, "having the time of our lives". Even the smallest errand we undertook as a family could wind up as a crusade. Any chore at which we aimed our combined efforts became a game . . . even yard work!

During the last week of August, Cliff and I were outside of the apartment building, planting some saplings that one of his "work buddies" had given him. After getting the owner's permission, we mapped out our strategy and set about planting these little promises of tomorrow. I unloaded the smaller trees from the truck while Cliff prepared the sites. Upon hearing the phone ringing, Cliff excused himself with an exaggerated bow and ran to answer it, while I continued to carry the saplings to their new beds. Cliff came through the door wiping the sweat and grime from his brow. He smiled and resumed the work of positioning the trees upright in the neat row of holes that we had already dug.

"That was Mom on the phone, calling to tell us that she was gonna be late. One of the girls got sick, so she's taking over her station. Says she's been really busy tonight and the tipsters have been busy, too. She said all we have to do is heat up the casserole in the refrigerator for dinner".

I avoided any response and continued my task. Cliff resumed his duties of chief gardener and, before we knew it, all the trees were stretching their roots in the fresh, sweet soil of their new and permanent locations. Feeling the justified pride for a job well done, we brushed the dirt from our hands and our clothing, and went inside to clean up and have dinner. We were famished.

Cliff suggested that I take my shower first, to give him time to pop the food in the oven and set the table. I went to my room to gather the things I would need for my bath (I never took showers), dashed into the bathroom and turned on the spigots. I carefully poured a measured portion of my favorite bath crystals under the teeming flow from the faucet, which immediately exploded into billowy mountains of softness. While waiting for the tub to fill, I brushed my hair and my teeth, tuned the radio to a classical music station and grabbed a clean towel from the closet.

When the water level and temperature finally suited my fancy, I submerged myself into the hot, invigorating puffs of silky, fragrant bubbles and allowed them to perform their unique dance of titillation against every cell in the skin, from my neck to my toes and back again. After shampooing my hair, I sank back into the hypnotic tranquility, closed my eyes and listened to the beautiful music. The stirring strains of the violins wafted through the air, bestowing upon the universe their unique message of love and beauty. With eyes closed, the harshness and pressures of this world gently slopped away into a state of limbo. The effect was so calming. Tensions melted beneath the water's steamy surface, leaving me mesmerized within the web of musical splendor.

With a slight stretch of my long arm, I picked up the lighter on the nearby cabinet and lit the scented candle. The flame flickered at first, but soon burned brightly . . . casting macabre shadows in all directions. The fragrance started to linger in the warm moist evening air and mixed with the intoxicating vapors of the scented bath.

At first, I thought I had fallen asleep, but my barely audible gasp assured me that this was not the case. Something had startled me. Something had brought an abrupt end to my sabbatical. The ambience of the bathroom actually seemed to have changed. An eerie, sinister feeling permeated through my flesh and engulfed my heart with an undeniable dread.

Checking the maze of shimmering images that skittered across all visible surfaces, my gaze was drawn to movement in the far corner of the room. Out of the shadows stepped Cliff. He wore nothing but a snicker. My heart kicked into overdrive, beating out a distress signal against my ribcage. I was uncertain how to handle this situation. Since nothing untoward had transpired between us since my release from the hospital, I had failed to prepare myself for anything along these lines.

Quickly checking to assure myself that no part of my anatomy showed above the waterline, I swung my attention to the man standing there, looking down at me; passion masking any resemblance of the devoted father who shared his home and his heart with me. The same person who diligently assisted in my rehabilitation and kept my spirits up with his humor throughout my long convalescence now wanted to start anew. He seemed to expect our relationship to degenerate into the vile, incestuous tangle that had led to the conception of misfortune that was terminated by the bus. In fact, no one had broached the subject of my interrupted pregnancy at all. I was certain that Mother had also informed him of our true relationship . . . if he hadn't known it all along.

Now he wanted to experience the craziness all over again. How could I stop him? I wanted to stop him. I knew that nothing like that could ever happen again but here, in the security of my home, I was about to learn a great deal about life and trust. The lesson would forever alter my ability to differentiate between deception and sincerity, thus lessening any intuitive tendencies that may have been harbored deeply into my sub-consciousness.

As he stepped forward, the candle's glow illuminated his nakedness and his furrowed brow. His scent carried on the slight breeze that his movement created. There was no doubt in my mind that I was in a precarious situation . . . nothing to gain and everything to lose. This man who stood over me was my father, my true biological father. Yet, he glared lecherously at my submerged body as if his stare could actually penetrate the murky liquid that concealed its delights. Without a word, he extended his hand towards me and beckoned me to stand. His staring eyes were riveted to mine, almost hypnotically. I was unable to pull my eyes away from his piercing, demanding ones.

Obediently, I began to rise. On unsteady legs I stood up and Cliff noticed the droplets of water cascading over the curves of my torso and landing in the entangled pubic hair that already glistened with moisture. Disregarding my subdued but persistent objections, he reached over with his still-extended hand and took hold of mine. Gently, silently, he maneuvered me out of the tub.

In whispered pleas, I begged him to stop. Out of total frustration, I threatened to scream my lungs out in an attempt to alert the neighbors. With a sadistic smile and effortless motion, he reached for the volume control knob on the radio and, gave it a quick twist. The beautiful offerings of classical composers, being swelled to exaggerated decibel levels, grew to become a strange, maniacal cacophony that would easily muffle any noise I might create.

With his other hand he cupped my chin and pulled me towards him. Our eyes were still locked in the non-disruptable stare when our lips touched. Now, both hands were holding my head, keeping my lips firmly pressed against his. His excited tongue waited impatiently for my lips to part, but I kept my jaws firmly locked. I knew, without a doubt, this if this man somehow managed to sneak any part of his body past my teeth, this scenario would suddenly turn a whole lot uglier for him.

Fortunately, I was spared this decision. Cliff's attention was filtering down to my neck. I could feel his hot breath and the slippery trail that his tongue was leaving on my skin. I could hardly breathe. I remembered where this was heading. I continued my pathetic cries but Cliff acted as though his ears had been closed and he was unable to hear. Either that or he was simply ignoring me.

By this time, he was rubbing his hands up and down my back as he maintained enough pressure to prevent my maneuvering out of his grasp. His hungry mouth found my breast. Expertly finding my nipple, his tongue took lashing swipes across my sensitive areola. I just wanted him to stop. God forgive me, but his sensual prowess was igniting the embers and stirring the fire of my own human passion.

"Please stop, Cliff. Please! I'm begging you as your daughter. You are my father! For Christ's sake, you must stop this before it goes any further. Mother will be furious . . . and it's wrong! So terribly wrong! If you stop now, I promise you that I'll never say anything about this to her or anybody . . . ever!"

The tears, that I had been holding back since he had stepped out of the shadows and exposed himself to me, finally brimmed over my lashes and fell onto my cheeks. Suddenly, I felt sick to my stomach and dizzy. It felt as if my legs would give out and my knees had the consistency of jelly. Cliff must have sensed this because he shifted his weight and lowered me to the floor. Sensing the inevitability of my situation, I thought about fighting back . . . saving my "virtue" . . . preserving my visceral integrity. Then I thought again!

Cliff was not a large man, but he was well proportioned, and all of his proportions were well built. What was to be gained by fighting his advances and possibly getting hurt in the process? Besides, I remember reading somewhere that sex crimes such as rape were motivated more by violence than by sexual drive. By returning the attackers aggression, you could actually be adding to his level of enjoyment that he gets from the assault. That particular article went on to say that the best way to deal with aggressive, undesired sexual behavior was passively . . . non-threatening, non-combative, passive acceptance.

I did as he told me without question. I allowed him freedom for his depravity. While he satisfied his biological urges, I formulated my plan. Even though the nature of the lesson was not apparent at this moment, I knew that I had grown up today. Cliff's collapse into a fit of spasmodic, jerking movements alerted me to the finale in this criminal drama. I feigned my own explosive, orgasmic gyrations. I panted theatrically, while praying that the curtain would fall and the players would make their exits. I would be ready to execute my scheme.

Cliff, himself, could not explain his strong desire for me since I was little more that a child . . . his child, no less! Even now, having just spent his energy, among other things, he continued to touch and stroke me. In an amazingly short time, his lust returned and he took me again, against my wishes. Surely, his appetite would soon be satiated. After the third time, the natural fluids of my vagina, having long since dried, made every thrust of his penis a painful stab, sending waves of agonizing torture shooting through my body. At long last, he stood up, shot a momentary glance in my direction and announced that dinner was probably burnt to a crisp.

How could he even think about food? I remained quite nauseated after what happened. For an undeterminable amount of time, I just laid there on the bathroom floor. I felt naked, dirty and used. This could never happen again. Somehow, I would get away. I knew I had to leave this place. As I continued to concentrate on the idea of leaving, some of my strength returned. I managed to grab hold of the tub and pulled myself up. Stepping into the cold, murky water in which I had been bathing, my immediate thought was to wash off the evidence of my victimization.

Looking down, I noticed a large glob of Cliff's semen clinging to my inner thigh. At first, the sight of it almost made me sick. It reminded me of so much that I just wanted to forget. Yet, I could not forget how I felt and my resolve dictated that I never be made to suffer like this again. I had to remember the smell of my own fear and the feeling of my trust being sacrificed by someone I had trusted. I gathered the vile fluid into my hand and looked at it. I could smell the stench that filled my pelvic cavity. Suddenly something went click in my head . . . something having to do with the smell of the cum in my hand. I placed my hand flat against the skin between my breast, smearing the gooey mess from there, down to my stomach. With my other hand, I reached under and inserted two fingers into my vagina and allowed another dollop of juice to drain down into my palm. Without hesitation, I smeared this across my breasts. Unintentionally, I had made the sign of the Cross, even as I was praying that God would show me what I should do now. I decided not to wash after all. The stickiness would serve as a reminder to me that men needed sex and they did not seem to set any particular limits regarding its acquisition.

All I wanted to do was survive, and if this meant I had to go through some changes, then so be it. With God's protection, I had nothing to fear. I began musing over my plan. To be successful, it had to be implemented tonight. I had to be gone before my mother finished work. This meant that I had to work fast.

CHAPTER 18

THE FLIGHT

Hello, Mr. Machine. Sorry about being gone so long; I had to spend two weeks in the hospital. Some opportunistic infection or other got me. As you should be comprehending by now, AIDS' victims never know for how long they will remain healthy. However, I am feeling so much better now and I've really missed talking with you. Sometimes I think I might be getting just a little bit "under-swabbed on the upper deck". You know . . . kinda losing it.

Truth be known, that's really how I deal with the loneliness and fear . . . by venting my thoughts and memories to you . . . hoping to make some sense of this bizarre twist of fate. By saying these words aloud to you, even though you are simply a machine, I am able to express my innermost thoughts and feelings without employing defense mechanisms and other rational, psychological protective devices to insure my mental stability. Bet you can't guess who's been to some "therapy sessions". Probably not as many as I could have, or should have attended but enough to learn some of the jargon tossed around just to maintain a suitable atmosphere. Anyway, it's nice to talk to you after all the time away.

It's really a shame I wasn't away on an adventure or even a lazy vacation in some tropical paradise, where they serve you sweet, colorful drinks in frosted tumblers . . . where only the sparse shade provided by the palm trees protects your lean, bronzed body from the scorching midday sun. Tropical trade winds laded the air with moisture, heavy with the aromatic treasures from the generous blooms of exotic wildflowers. A choir of songbirds would harmonize their individualized fantasies. Whew!!! I just realized how much I needed a vacation. Sure . . . it was only a verbal vacation, but it works for a little while and the price is right. Well, enough chitchat!

I was telling you about the night Cliff taught me a lesson and a woman was born. Trying to remain calm, I collected my thoughts. Thinking discretion was the better part of valor I would only take the essentials. What I took I would have to carry. This meant that every article finally chosen had to pass numerous eligibility tests before being selected. Since I was already in the bathroom, it seemed like the logical place to start. I picked up my natural-bristle hairbrush but immediately opted for a smaller plastic one. Of course, I would need a toothbrush. In girl scouts, I had learned about the many uses of baking soda, therefore I would not have to take additional soap, toothpaste or deodorant. I carefully placed the box of baking soda into my bag. I found three washcloths and added these to the contents of my traveling bag. I chose a single tube of my favorite lipstick, flipped it into the bag and secured it all into a very small package.

Realizing that precious time was ticking away, I hastily grabbed my bathrobe and tugged my arms through the sleeves as I made my way to the kitchen. I did not want to risk Cliff's becoming suspicious were I to take too long. Nor did I want any altercation with him at this point so I took my lead from his attitude as I surveyed his last-minute preparations for dinner. He acted as if nothing had happened less than twenty minutes ago, not more than a hundred yards from where we stood.

Dinner passed pleasantly enough but I found it difficult to concentrate on our polite conversation. My mind was racing ahead to the next several steps of my plan. Through sheer strength of will, I managed to keep up my end of the spirited dialogue until the agony of the meal came to a natural end. With my most winning smile, I volunteered to do the dishes. With enough sweetness to choke a horse, I suggested that after doing all his exhaustive chores, he deserved some quiet time to rest. I encouraged him to watch some TV until I finished squaring up the kitchen then I would join him on the couch.

Flashing him my most seductive smile and a quick, flirtatious wink, I strolled into the kitchen and made the appropriate noises for the task. In reality, I was searching for something in the way of munchies that I could take along with me in case I got hungry before reaching my destination. With little trouble, I located a tube of crackers and several pouches of processed cheese. These would suffice nicely as treatment for any hunger pangs that might attack me at an inopportune moment.

From the livingroom came the sound that I had literally been praying for. He had begun to snore. With that sound came the imagined clanging of a large, rusty-hinged door being flung open. Now, the only obstacle between me and the successful completion of my plan was . . . time. I was in control. As I made my way to my bedroom carrying my goodies, I plucked my other bundle from the bathroom without breaking stride. Tossing these gingerly on the bed, I began to think about my required wardrobe. I again took careful consideration of each article to be taken. I could only take the basics.

Carefully, I chose what I thought I would need. I took none of the new clothes that my mother and I had recently bought on our many excursions to the malls. One thing that seemed to be universal criteria for selection was comfort. Much too rapidly my satchel was filling up: Two pairs of shoes, a pair of jeans, two pair of shorts, my favorite short skirt, two pairs of stockings, two pairs of socks and two summer tops. As I dressed I layered my clothes, allowing me to take a few extra garments. There was only one more thing that I had to do before I could execute my escape.

Moving as silently as a cat, I crossed the hallway and entered my parents' bedroom. I went directly to my mother's dresser, opened up the smallest drawer and retrieved an envelope from under her pink, lacy negligee. Hurriedly, I counted the crisp bills tucked inside. There were 18 twenty-dollar bills. I was painfully aware that this stash represented almost all of my mother's tips for the last two months. This was supposed to be their getaway fund. They were planning to go on a cruise. It now represented my getaway money. I regretted having to steal it, especially from my mom, but I appeased my conscience by rationalization. Since I had not worn any of the clothes that overflowed from my closet, I knew that she could return them for a full refund. This would more than cover the amount taken.

I was ready to hit the road. There was still a shock of sunlight streaming from the western sky so there was no need for me to rush to the station. I had plenty of time before it grew dark and by then I hoped to be on a bus bound for elsewhere. I tried to look inconspicuous in the terminal. I wanted nothing of my actions to attract any attention from the gathering crowd. I had to consider the possibility that Cliff and my mother would become concerned about my sudden departure. I wanted no witnesses to remember me and accommodate their inquiries. I tried to blend into the background.

Clutching my bulging satchel, I waited my turn in the depot. With unfelt confidence, I requested a one-way ticket to Philadelphia. Since this was the last scheduled stop on this specific route, I could disembark at any stop along the way without notice. Sitting quietly in the terminal, I waited for my departure time.

Finally it was time to board the bus. I opted for a window seat in the center of the bus and encouraged myself to relax. We were scheduled to arrive in Philly in about an hour and, since I wasn't planning to go that far, I anticipated an ETA of less time. I settled myself comfortably in an attempt to crystallize the final aspects of my escape.

I hoped the note left on my mother's dresser was convincing enough. I had propped it against a bottle of exotic perfume. On the envelope I had written MOTHER. The note was brief out of necessity . . . I did not know quite what to say. Time had continued to tick away. I finally scribbled that since my accident, I began to realize how little I knew about life. I wrote that I wanted to experience the spectrum of its choices. To accomplish this, I needed freedom. I informed her that while I appreciated the beautiful new clothes, I had left them all behind so that she could return them and use the money as retribution for the tip money taken. With promises to take care of myself and sincere expressions of my love, I signed the note, folded it and slipped it into the matching envelope. I labeled it as described and placed it on her bureau like a sentinel at its post.

My mind drifted back to the imagery passing within my field of sightless vision, as I peered thoughtfully through the window. Night's darkness had completely encompassed my world. Out of the shadowy film of grayness, figures gracefully emerged. These figures took the shape of Victorian homes within the murkiness. As the struggling bus came upon a red light, the pause gave me the chance to get a better view of the buildings lining the street. The lighted sign above a busy store informed me that the establishment was the Collingswood Pharmacy, therefore this town must be Collingswood. I knew from my recent ventures into Philadelphia that we were just outside of Camden. It was then that I suddenly noticed the slow, gradual deterioration of the scenery. The pretty suburbs were quickly replaced with the menacing decay of the inner city. Large gutted structures lined the nearly abandoned streets. I saw the victims of poverty anguishing in their personal battlefields, in full view of the apathetic public.

The flashing lights on the bridge that linked New Jersey to Pennsylvania jerked me back to the present and the realization that I had missed my intended stop. By this time, we had reached the pinnacle of the bridge and began our descent towards The City of Brotherly Love. Especially at this time of evening, the city was abuzz with scurrying pedestrians and vehicular congestion. The obvious pace was staggering for someone like me from a more sequestered, more serene, more rural area. My despair was increasing at an alarming rate as we made our way through the city towards the bus depot.

I started to question the wisdom of this whole scheme. Was I crazy? . . . Leaving my comfortable home in exchange for the complete emptiness of my future seemed incredibly stupid at the moment. Did I really think that I would be able to survive all alone in the real world . . . a world of which I knew precious little? It dawned on me in this vulnerable pause that the money that I had in my possession would not be enough to sustain me for long even on the most frugal budget. My confidence started to fade. I envisioned myself slinking back to the apartment with my tail tucked between my legs like a beaten dog.

The thought of Cliff's lecherous, leering eyes and the memory of his hands manipulating my flesh as he willed interrupted my reverie. My resolve returned with a vengeance. Living on the street was preferable to the pressures of sharing living space with him and his perverted sexual games and the deceit. Starving to death was an acceptable alternative to the heavy guilt that fed upon my soul alone.

The lights of the terminal heralded our impending arrival and I readied myself along with my few belongings to expedite my getaway from the terminal. I climbed down from the bus, checked out the immediate vicinity and decided to find somewhere in the neighborhood to have a cup of coffee and clear my head. There were major decisions to be made and time was of the essence. The imposing city beckoned from all sides. I had no idea which direction to take to begin my new life.

I retraced my last few steps to question a security guard about the location of a convenient eatery. He offered me a quick list of local options and even suggested his favorite place. Following the advice of this amiable stranger, I took off into the darkness. My footsteps echoed in the night air as I took my first steps towards my own personal tomorrow.

CHAPTER 19

THE CORNERSTONE

As I walked through the late summer breeze that Friday evening I was overwhelmed by the perplexity of my feelings. Mostly I was swept along on the wave of exhilaration that accompanied my newly found freedom. On the other hand, I was completely aware of how absolutely alone I was and this led to an enormous amount of fear. It was a fear that I was willing to accept as part of my maturation process. This growth would greatly aid me in finding my niche in this big, wide, impersonal world. This was my world now . . . or at least I hoped it soon would be mine.

The warm night breezes were filled with the sounds and smells of this amazing city. The splashing waters from the majestic fountains, enmeshed into the architecture of the local square, gave the illusion of natural peacefulness. Surrounded by the lushness of indigenous flora, the scents of bountiful blooms mingled with the fragrance of freshly mowed grass and rode on the droplets of moisture being emitted by the cascading fountains. The effect was intoxicating but my high lasted only a few, brief moments.

Quick to smother my tranquility was the sobering realization of my immediate situation. I had nowhere to go and no one that I knew that I could turn to in this city . . . or anywhere in the whole world, at this point in my life. I had no job, no skills and no education. I had only enough money to exist for who knows how long. I simply had to! I had to make it on my own. What other choices did I have? I could not go back and live with my mother. There was simply too much there that would be impossible to explain . . . to anyone's satisfaction. Even if I could, I had no desire to once again become Cliff's sexual toy. I just wanted to forget and go on with my life, if possible. My life! I liked the sound of that. I quickened my pace. I had to be getting close to the place that the guard suggested.

The sounds of the place reached me long before I caught sight of it. It was music, to be sure! Lively happy music filled my ears and my soul. Oh, my goodness! It was a Polka! I could not believe my ears. They were playing a polka record on the jukebox. The bouncy sound seemed to pull me into the café. The place was jumping. Every table and booth in the house was packed with happy, smiling people. All available counter space seemed likewise "ocupado". The sounds of clinking glasses and clanging pots mixed discreetly with the music and the patron's chatting. It almost seemed like a welcome that was directed at me.

Without my awareness, a woman was leading me to an unseen seat. She guided me through the sea of humanity and showed me to a heretofore-unnoticed vacant seat. The "leading lady" reminded me of someone . . . but who? Suddenly, it dawned on me! She looked just like "The Old Woman in the Shoe". She was large, round and visibly soft. That phraseology described not only her person but her persona as well. She extended a warm smile to me while inquiring if I would like a cup of coffee. I simply nodded and continued to watch her as she proceeded with her duties. Despite her sizable frame, she glided between the tables and among the customers with the grace of an empress. Not surprising, those same patrons treated her like a queen.

The genuine affection I saw being passed around lavishly that night in that warm and welcoming café seemed unlimited. I found myself wishing that I could partake of some of that caring. I continued to watch as she readied my coffee. This woman somehow managed to get my coffee while sliding a piece of apple pie to a bulky guy with a long beard sitting at the far end of the counter. She simultaneously slipped menus, napkins and appropriate eating utensils to two other patrons, directed more new arrivals towards available spaces, squawked orders back to the cook and made it all seem so effortless. She set my coffee down on my table and, in a flurry of ruffling petticoats and another warm smile, she was off in a flash.

I sipped my coffee slowly. I did enjoy the taste of coffee and this was fresh and good. I began to realize that I was getting a little hungry. I had been too keyed-up during my dinner with Cliff to eat very much. I had simply appeared to do justice to the meal and now my stomach was talking to me. I remembered the cheese and crackers in my purse, but I decided to save them for later. Since I was here, I decided to get some real food. It might give me the strength that I would need to face my uncertain future. Besides, I really wanted to extend my visit to this charming spot with all the interesting customers. In truth, I just wanted that lady to smile at me again. That smile seemed to radiate the warmth of the sun.

Out of the blue, it occurred to me that there was no one else in the place that seemed to be helping with this sizable crowd. The large woman seemed to be doing everything at once, all by herself. I noticed at one point a young man not much older than myself, who cleared a few tables and carried a heavy tray out to a crowded table. He seemed to be putting more effort into staying out of earshot than helping with all the obvious chores that needed to be done.

Upon closer scrutiny, the woman showed signs of fatigue. There was a thin layer of sweat across her brow and strands of her hair had come unfurled from the neatly wrapped bun perched high on her head. She seemed to be having a bit of difficulty breathing with all the rushing back and forth from the kitchen. She was, remember, a good-sized woman.

After watching her for awhile, I realized that she was approaching my table. Before she was able to reach me, at least three customers requested refills of their coffees, to place or change their orders. As busy as she was, there was nothing hurried or unpleasant about her mannerisms or treatment of the diners. Each person was greeted warmly and jokes were exchanged without any disruption of services. As she turned her attention to me, I looked into her weary eyes and asked, "Are you always this busy?".

She nodded and replied, "yep! This normal crowd for Friday night. Only me to vork tables though. Pauline, my vaitress broke leg . . . so now only Gerta can serve all the nice peoples. Everybody so nice. Nobody get angry if Gerta slow too much. We like family".

Her German accent was soft and subtle as if much effort had been spent trying to lessen it. Only when she was excited or in a hurry did it become noticeable . . . like now. I found it delightful. As a matter of fact, I found myself drawn to this lady in the colorful, full skirts. Without a moment's hesitation, I asked if I could help her refill the empty cups of several patrons. She was obviously pleased with my offer and quickly retrieved a fresh pot from behind the counter.

"You be my guest, Libchen."

So began a very special time in my life. As I poured cup after cup of the steaming fluid into those unceasingly empty vessels, I felt wanted and needed. The various patrons were ready to share their smiles and warmth with me without asking questions of the new "waitress". As I went about with coffee refills, I tried to gather some of the unneeded dirty dishes that were accumulating everywhere. With relative ease, I managed to clear most of the tables and keep the customers content until the German lady got caught up. I was really enjoying the interaction with this friendly crowd and actually lost track of the time. To my surprise, Gerta came out of the kitchen carrying a well-rounded plateful of delicious-looking food. She sat the abundant meal down . . . in front of me. She sat in the opposite seat taking my hands into hers and thanked me profusely for my assist.

"You no can know how much you help Gerta, tonight," she said. "Friday nights are always busy but since Pauline broke leg only last night, there no time to find somebody to fill spot. You did good job, tonight. You been vaitress before?"

I could have lied and said that I had, but I wanted to start my new life on the right foot, so I shook my head.

"Not really . . . but I used to help out in the school cafeteria. I sort of traded that for piano lessons when I was younger."

Suddenly, this large, gregarious woman shook with laughter.

"I didn't know they came more young than you, Libchen." She continued to laugh heartily as she said, "You talk like you hundred years old, child! I have dishcloths older than you. You are sad maybe little bit, too? Sometime tonight I see your face is so serious like you have problem. Eat your food . . . uh . . . what is your name child?"

I told her my name and she sat and chatted with me while I ate. The food was plentiful and delicious. She soon got around to asking me if I could remain until closing to help with the workload. She assured me that I would be well paid for lending a hand. I was planning on doing it for nothing. Suddenly her face lit up like a firecracker on the fourth of July.

"Heck! If you vant you could have job here. We already vere short one full-time vaitress before Pauline's accident. Ve vere considering making less the hours that ve stay open, but many of our customers are regulars and depend on us from early in the morning. We also have our steady crowd for lunch and dinner. The local students often choose our place to gather. Our friends and neighbors often come here in the evening for dessert and coffee. Vhen could ve close our doors on people who keep us open?"

She paused as if waiting for an answer. I think I might have been in shock. Had I heard her right? Had she just offered me a job? Was my future unfolding right in front of my eyes? Oh, thank you, Jesus, was my silent whisper as I readily accepted her offer of employment. I felt so fortunate at that moment. My first night in the big, bad city and I lucked out to the max. I found a job where I could do something that I could do and be working for this special lady with the intermittent accent.

After finishing my meal, I began my first real job. It was a wonderful feeling. As per her instructions, I stashed my satchel in the small room that led into the walk-in (a real big fridge that you . . . walk into! Right?) After rechecking the contents, I tucked my small purse into the bulky satchel then I spun into my new duties. It was almost six hours later when we finally got a chance to sit down, again. The last patron had just left. Since I had been keeping up with clearing the tables as I went along, the bulk of the heavy work was done. For the most part, the remaining side-work could wait until tomorrow.

Gerta and I sat down wearily but feeling fulfilled. As we shared another cup of coffee, we finally got a chance to extend our introduction beyond the rudimentary exchange of names. She, along with her husband, Frank, owned and operated this establishment. As she spoke, a tall, thin man approached our table and, even before being introduced, I instinctively knew that this was her spouse. His rugged face broke into a warm smile as he eyed his bride and the stranger sharing coffee with her in a booth in the corner.

After our initial amenities were exchanged, Gerta informed Frank that I had accepted the position as the new waitress. He was obviously pleased that Gerta would have some help. He told her that he had been growing concerned as the evening progressed about the amount of work that his poor wife had to handle, virtually unassisted. He had been kept quite busy himself in the kitchen and felt uneasy about the overload this caused for her. My acceptance of the position permitted the blessed relief to permeate his being.

It was Gerta who remembered my overnight satchel that I had stashed earlier in the anteroom. She asked me if I needed a ride home or something. She quickly detected the unrest that stirred up in response to her question. Here, again, I decided to be honest with these wonderful new friends. Keeping my head bowed and my eyes averted from theirs, I whispered, "I'm running away".

Instead of angry outburst or inane lectures, they showed only concern and compassion. Frank sliced through my discomfort by saying, "It must be our lucky day! Ve get a new vaitress and you get to stop running. Our little place here would definitely be considered away from almost everyvhere."

Somehow I knew in my heart that they did understand my situation. Through the course of our conversation as we lingered over our quickly emptying cups, I tried to explain my precarious situation at home without giving too many details. It was quite sufficient to tell them that I could not get along with my stepfather and felt that the time had come for me to leave.

Gerta smiled her heart-warmingest smile and reached over to grasp my hand. As she patted it gently she related a story about her daughter, Greta. It seems she left home without permission when she was my age. She said she had to find herself! There had been a lot of bickering before her abrupt departure, mostly involving her need for more independence and her parents' refusal to cooperate. I had a hard time imagining how anyone could have trouble interacting with this loving, caring couple.

They both agreed, however, that the time their daughter had spent "on the lam" had probably been a better education than they could have provided for their headstrong offspring. When the "prodigal daughter" returned on her own, they found her to be more mature and aware of the importance of finishing her education (the most common argument that had contributed to her initial desire to flee). With obvious pride, they explained to me that after her return, she completed high school with honors, and was awarded a scholarship to the Academy of Music in Salzburg, Austria.

Although they both missed their daughter a great deal, it was evident that they were very pleased with the way she turned her life around. They insisted that I would also find my way to the path that my life was destined to take.

Suddenly, a giant yawn escaped me. It was after 2:00 a.m. and it had been quite a day. Even in my exhaustion I realized that I had no idea where I was going to sleep in this big city and the thought was almost paralyzing in its magnitude. As if sensing my dilemma and shooting a pleading glance to her husband, Gerta suggested that I could sleep in the room vacated by Greta. I sensed rather than saw the reaction that Frank had difficulty hiding. I graciously declined their kind offer and tried to assure them and myself that everything would be fine.

Gerta was not taking "no" for an answer. Almost immediately, she came up with a viable alternative. She just remembered the small room behind the restaurant that her daughter had sectioned off as her "private place". Frank also became enthusiastic about the idea. They agreed that it was the perfect solution. Before I knew what was happening, these two amazing people were ushering me, a perfect stranger, through the kitchen, past the walk-in, around a tower of shipping crates and into a cubbyhole that contained a bed, a dresser with a mirror, a table and two chairs.

Despite its relatively small area, I felt drawn to the place right away. It was . . . cozy. Yes. That was the perfect word. Cozy! I was overwhelmed by a sudden wave of fatigue. I collapsed on the inviting bed as my new bosses were discussing this being part of my work agreement. Since they could not possibly be worrying about which park bench their new waitress would be sleeping on, my staying here would be part of the deal. With murmured thanks to these friendly, loving people and to God for guiding me to these new friends, I fell asleep.

Sorry for the interruption but there was someone at the door. A lab technician from the local laboratory comes here periodically to take blood for the various lab tests that are done on me. They even draw extra vials of the contaminated fluid for the researchers that are working on AIDS projects. Unfortunately, no one had discovered much of anything about the disease except how you get it and that it is fatal. This was information that I was already privy to, in the most personal and unforgettable way.

Sometimes it's funny to watch the different lab techs that come here. They are informed of my diagnosis before they are sent here. Since the introduction of the universal precaution advisory, issued from the office of the Surgeon General, most are aware of the importance of wearing latex gloves when drawing blood, as a way of protecting themselves from exposure to HIV, the virus that causes AIDS. Some let their fear get the better of them and walk in here garbed in an outfit that might protect them from a nuclear attack.

How they are attired is of little importance to me. What does interest me is their ability to obtain the necessary specimens with the minimum of pain. Some manage to be civil despite their vaguely disguised disgust. Others brighten my day with their quiet acceptance of both my diagnosis and me as a living human being. To all of them I give my heartfelt thanks since, without them, I would have had to make numerous trips to the hospital just for routine lab work. This disease's utter depletion of my strength has made short trips in the car around town exhausting. It is impossible for me to do it without assistance from others.

Today my favorite techie, Sandy, came for my "donation". She always seems like a ray of sunshine when she visits. Her smile could brighten up the gloomiest day. She always comes prepared with a joke that she knows I will enjoy. She can make me laugh, but Sandy has a serious side, too. I feel that I can talk to her about anything and everything. She listens to my fears and hopes, my dreads and my dreams, all without any hint of judgement or prejudice.

Today, she brought me a bouquet of fresh springtime flowers, which cheers my disposition with both their exquisite beauty and their intoxicating fragrance. Sandy knows that I am making this recording of my memoirs and she asked me if I could somehow mention her in it. I promised her when she left to consider it done.

This brief mention could, in no way, do justice to my feelings for this funny, fearless friend who has come into my life at such a bleak time. She has, on many occasions, been my inspiration, especially when I'm going through the many difficult experiences associated with this horrible illness. For her kindness and humanity I will always be grateful.

Now, to return to the scene of the aforementioned eatery. "The Cornerstone" was the name of the establishment owned by

Frank and Gerta. If this very sweet couple had not befriended me, I have no idea what would have happened to me in that strange city.

As I woke up Saturday morning, I was well aware of the sound of rattling dishes from the kitchen. I jumped out of my new bed and began to prepare myself to begin my new duties in this restaurant. I was their new waitress. Isn't that what Gerta said last night before I fell asleep? More than anything, I wanted to do a good job for them so that I could repay their kindness in some tangible way. As I completed my daily grooming, I was struck by the thought of having nothing appropriate to wear for my first day as a waitress. I could have saved myself a lot of needless aggravation. Sometime during the night, Gerta must have hunted through Greta's stuff and came up with a white uniform that was almost my exact size.

When I entered the kitchen, Frank was quick to tell me how professional I looked, then he directed me to the list of specials for the day. He also told me that I would find Gerta already at work in the serving area. He said that she was waiting anxiously to explain my duties and he assured me that both of them would be available to help me or answer any questions that may arise.

Having never been a waitress before, I had little working knowledge of my responsibilities but I was eager to please and I learned quickly. I began taking orders immediately from the early regulars. At this ungodly hour, they were waiting to be served breakfast. Afterwards, they would traipse off to work at the local factories and various plants in the neighborhood.

Other regulars included truckers passing through Philly with their big rigs loaded with various commodities. In the early morning hours, many local business people stop into "The Cornerstone" for some of Frank's famous German sausage that he made every month. Cute, perky secretaries strolled in after the breakfast crowd left, specifically for their daily ration of Gerta's homemade strudel that had a texture so light and flaky, these intelligent, working girls had literally duped themselves into believing that they had relatively few calories.

Afternoons were heavy with gray-haired women on shopping excursions and matinee aficionados. Frequently, visitors to the several local hospitals would stop in for a light snack to tide them over until they got home. Some came here simply to pass the time while a relative or loved one was undergoing surgery at one of the many hospitals. Some of these people only stop in here once, for their own convenience, but many return anytime they find themselves here in the city. The regulars enjoy the atmosphere and the company almost as much as the delicious food that is served here daily.

I enjoyed working there from the very beginning. The regulars seemed only too happy to welcome a new member into their exclusive club, and I was equally willing to join their special group. Before I knew it, the Weber's (Frank and Gerta) were extending more and more of the responsibilities for the smooth operation of the restaurant to me. Many nights I locked up the place after everyone else had left. I was so encouraged by such demonstrations of their absolute trust in me that I worked even harder to please these wonderful people who helped me out when I most needed a helping hand.

After working for them about a month, Gerta approached me about continuing my schooling. Before I was given a chance to express my doubts about this, Gerta was detailing her idea of how I could best accomplish this feat. It seemed like she had done her homework. There were several schools in the area that offered night classes to area residents at reduced tuition cost. By using their address, I would be eligible for participation in the city's new literacy programs, too. She had really left no excuses uncrushed. She had even arranged my schedule so that I was not on duty on the nights that I had classes.

The following Monday night, I felt like the schoolgirl that I was as I walked the short distance to night school. Since it was the middle of the semester, I had to contend with a battery of tests to determine my class standing and my knowledge base. There were no actual grades for these tests. They were simply to ascertain how much you know and your ability to assimilate information. I must have done pretty well on them because in a few days, my counselor called me into her office and told me that I should be eligible to take my high school equivalency test in about three months. If I passed that, it would mean that I would actually be graduating before my former classmates.

I was very grateful to Gerta for having the kind of faith in me that I had always wanted to find in the adults to whom I had looked for support in the past. When I got back to the restaurant with my results from the tests, Frank and Gerta were so elated that they chased everyone home a little earlier than usual. The three of us and a few close friends had a party to celebrate my "victory". I knew I had a lot of hard work ahead of me but, with the support of these two wonderful people, I was determined to live up to their expectations.

The next five months passed almost in a blur. Attending classes took up most of my time off. Luckily, learning has always been easy for me, but I still spent the rest of my free time studying and reading. The teachers at the adult learning center were, without exception, very conscientious volunteers. The only payment they received for the many hours of their time that they contributed to the program was the understanding that they were improving the plight of humanity . . . one young brain at a time.

I religiously handed in all my assignments, took solid notes in class by being particularly attentive, attempted to participate in class discussions when feasible and studied into the wee hours of the morning just before any major test. I was working for my high school diploma and this elating thought sustained me when my body and my spirit began to weaken.

My skills as a waitress began to emerge as I continued to work at "The Cornerstone". I just had to tune into the proper headset. Imagining myself sitting down in this busy eatery as hungry as a man-eating alligator at a skinny-dipping party did the trick. In this way I could anticipate the customer's needs and thus be better organized, more efficient and better tipped.

It felt like I divided all my waking hours between my schoolwork and serving meals. Hey! Please don't think I'm complaining. I was ecstatic, if not somewhat exhausted, to discover that I had such stamina. I was extremely grateful for this amazing opportunity to finish my education. With Frau Weber's steady encouragement, I managed to intertwine my two basic responsibilities without shortchanging either.

As a waitress I worked every afternoon after school and all day Saturday and Sunday. Understand both Frank and Gerta suggested that I not work so many hours, at least until I finished my classes. However, to me that reeked of charity. I intended to work to support myself and attempt to repay, in some small part anyway, the tremendous debt of gratitude that I owed to the Webers. The fifty dollars that they withheld from my paycheck every week could not recover the cost of our meals, most of which I ate with them. Yet, they insisted that it abundantly covered both room and board. Some paydays, I questioned if they even took any money out of my check, at all.

I remember I had such a voracious appetite during that time. Frank's cooking was the best and I never skipped seconds. I did not need to worry about my weight because I was careful to eat good, healthy foods and I was simply too busy to gain any excess baggage. I could eat anything I wanted and I tried everything.

I have always subscribed to the theory that food is one of life's greatest pleasures. Today, as I lay here recording these thoughts on you, Mr. Machine, I am also enjoying my Pulmocare feedings. Continuously, between the hours of 7am and 11pm, I infuse can after can of this thick, nourishing formula through a tube that the public health nurse inserted into my nose a few days ago. Since my acquisition of AIDS, my appetite has been diminishing steadily. This tube, which passes down my throat and goes into my stomach, is my basic source of nutrients. Add to the problem of my poor appetite the loose and painful teeth in my mouth and it compounds my dietary problems.

I miss eating real food, but going to the dentist is impossible. The bill is usually steep and must be paid at the time of service.

Since I have no money, I get no service . . . except maybe lip service. Besides, once I informed the health care provider of my HIV status, it is amazing how quickly their receptionist realizes a scheduling error and apologizes for any inconvenience. She offers to reschedule but I decline, realizing that I would run into another snag if I had the audacity to show up. Considering the trouble involved in keeping these bogus appointments, I've learned to live with the pain. My teeth will probably start to fall out one by one, anyway. There doesn't seem to be much I can do to prevent this without professional dental care.

Some people would question my decision to be so honest about my HIV status, but I know for a fact that the most important single issue about AIDS is understanding the facts of the disease and dispelling the myths. This is a case of what you don't know can kill you. I could not live with myself if I thought that I had intentionally infected another human being with this dreadful virus.

Well, there I go, off on another tangent. I was recalling my experiences at "The Cornerstone". This inevitably leads me to think about the wonderful owners, The Webers. They met each other for the first time in this country after they had both fled from their homeland, Germany, during the reign of terror that was inflicted by Adolph Hitler. With little more than their hope and their belief in God's love, they came to America to be free. With much hard work and prayer, they were able to build a new life in this country and provide for their family.

It seems ironic to me that both of their children returned to Germany. Their only son, Eric, is serving his country in the United States Army as an MP. He is stationed on a base somewhere in Germany. After graduating from the music academy, Greta accepted a position as a professor at a major university and remains there even today. From their letters we know that the two sibs get together periodically and keep in touch with each other by phone. The Webers are as proud of their son as they are of their daughter and rightfully so of both.

They were truly a Christian couple who lived their faith every day of their lives, every hour of the day. We always attended Mass together and during this time, my belief in God developed into the faith that continues to sustain me even through the brutality of AIDS. Chiefly through their outstanding example, I learned to recognize and develop the virtues that complement a Christian's life: Honesty, forgiveness, understanding, generosity and fortitude to name a few. From that period in my life to the present, I have tried to cultivate these virtues into my lifestyle. I will always remember the Webers with love and gratitude for enabling me to participate in my faith and follow its doctrine.

Before I could even imagine, I was able to graduate from night school. My teachers were all very happy for me and proud of me, too. They knew how hard I worked and I received a special award for my grades and my perfect attendance. These were presented to me, along with awards to other deserving graduates, with much pomp and circumstance at a special ceremony held in our honor in the school auditorium.

Everyone's family was there on that very special evening and, needless to say, the Webers were there to cheer me on. I was so happy when I looked out into the sea of faces to see these two important friends acknowledging my success. Since they had been so instrumental in my endeavors, it seemed appropriate to me that they should share the glory.

After the beautiful ceremony and the distribution of the diplomas, the adult education graduating class was gathered for a class photo. When this was done, the photographer announced that individual photos could be obtained for a nominal fee. Frank and Gerta insisted that I have my photograph taken. I tried to dissuade them as I mentally calculated the extra cost, but they would hear none of my protests. They told me that it would mean so much to them if they had a nice picture of me for their living room wall. How could I object? It was so little to ask after all they had done for me. So I stood tall and proud in my cap and gown and I smiled easily for the camera. After the financial arrangements and mailing data had been secured, my happy little party left the school and returned to the restaurant.

We had shut down early so that everybody could get ready for my graduation. Therefore, since the building was completely dark, Frank insisted on going first to make sure that everything was safe. While we waited under the bright street light, Gerta and I passed the time with an easy exchange of chitchat. She could tell that I was very excited and she joined in with her own enthusiasm.

Frank soon reappeared in the doorway and beckoned for us to come in. I followed Gerta into the dimly lit restaurant and was totally unprepared for what happened next. Suddenly, the bright lights came on and a large group of people shouted, "Surprise!" I was! There were presents and ice cream and even a cake decorated with a figurine of a girl in a cap and gown. The Webers gave me a beautiful gold cross that came in a velvet box.

Needless to say, I was overwhelmed. Everyone seemed to have a marvelous time and it was quite late when I finally fell asleep. Just before I did, however, I said my nightly prayers as always except that I whispered my special thank you to God for all the blessings that he had bestowed on me that day. I especially wanted to thank him for guiding me to the Webers on that summer night that suddenly seemed so long ago. I touched the golden crucifix that hung daintily around my neck. I whispered my thanks again and fell asleep.

CHAPTER 20

THE EXPANSION

Welcome to my real world. My home health aide just handed me a pile of mail. The look on her face told me that there were a number of bills before I even began to sift through it. Nothing new here. Since I have been unemployable for two years, I am eligible for social security. The bad news is that since I am only 26 years old, I do not have much money in my fund. Fortunately, they accepted my request for SSI payments and this helps a little. Honestly, however, I would not be able to survive financially without the large amounts of help from volunteer groups, religious organizations and private individuals who contribute money for medical expenses that are not covered by public assistance insurance. These same generous people also contribute food, clothing and various sundries that make my life a little more tolerable.

It is difficult enough to deal with the physical and emotional hardships of this morbid entity, but the pressure of the financial incongruities often imposes as much stress and mental suffering as the other two combined. At times, usually when dealing with a stack of new bills such as now, my thoughts tend to drift into a macabre spiral, spinning my spirits downward. This leaves me feeling utterly empty except for the realization that at least when I die, I won't have to worry about the bills anymore. Nobody will have to worry about the bills because no one is really responsible for me . . . but me. Oh, wow! I did not mean to be such a downer. Sorry! Let me try to remember other times before I work myself into a self-pitying jag.

Back to the time following my graduation . . . I began to work more at the restaurant. Shortly after my graduation, Frank and Gerta started to develop plans to enlarge their business. For many years they had dreamed about building a banquet room, which would enable them to cater special events for the people in the neighborhood, such as weddings, christenings, birthday parties and even a graduation celebration. Recently, the adjoining property went on the market and Frank had investigated and realized that since the asking price was more than reasonable, this could be the springboard for their lifelong dream of the banquet room.

Once the legalities were worked out and the property was actually in their possession, Frank and Gerta wasted no time in beginning the task of renovating the area to be used. Every moment of their spare time was spent tearing down unnecessary walls, replacing the worn out carpeting, rejuvenating the usable furniture and sanding and painting ad infinitum. Their excitement was contagious and I volunteered my services as much as possible. However, during this time I was helping out more and more with the routine operations of the restaurant. I attempted to assume some of the mundane duties in order to relieve the Webers, so that they could have more time and energy to work on their dream.

It was during this time that I became more aware of another group of regulars that, until now, had escaped my attention. Around one o'clock each afternoon, a select bevy of young women sauntered into our eatery. To look at them, you knew that food intake was not high on their priority list. Most were extremely thin but all seemed to be in real good shape physically. As a rule, their orders consisted of lots of liquids and low-calorie, high nutrition foods . . . salads, cottage cheese, yogurt and gallons of coffee with sweet and low. Occasionally, one of the lesser healthy specimens would just drink the coffee.

As I spent more time in their midst, I began to understand these young women and where they were "coming from". Most would have been labeled "bad girls' in practically all social circles. As for intelligence, they ran the gamut from ignorant, illiterate high school dropouts, to women who were attending classes in very prestigious facilities of higher learning in Philadelphia. For the most part, they seemed happy, ambitious people with high hopes for their futures. What they were doing now was simply a means to an end.

What they were doing now was go-go dancing. There were several local bars that hired these girls by the hour to be the entertainment at their places of business. Clad in very skimpy costumes, the girls would dance on platforms in front of the patrons and during their breaks would circulate through the crowd and through bouts of conversation and flirting could effectively increase their income by 100 percent or more.

It seemed to me that most of these girls had pretty low moral values. As I got to know some of them better, it only served to confirm my suspicions. As we became more comfortable with each other, they would expound on some of their after-hours antics with owners and patrons of the places where they danced.

Many of these girls would think nothing of sleeping with these same people after stimulating their carnal desires. Some of these alliances would only last a day or two, then the girls would move on to the next conquest. This was actually how some of these women survived on a day-to-day basis.

It was inconceivable to me that any decent girl would, of her own volition, give herself to any man that she did not love. Even after all that I had experienced, or maybe because of it, I had promised myself that I would not give that special part of me to any man unless I was in love with him. With no idea what it was like to be in love, I figured that I had plenty of time to worry about that in the future. Until then, I continued to hold fast to my own private concepts of love, which were cloaked in fantasy and romance. Even Gerta shared my vision of the romantic knight in shining armor, who would carry me off to his castle and make me his queen. Meanwhile, Frank and Gerta were working feverishly on the new banquet facility. In fact, several months after my graduation, they were putting the finishing touches on the whole operation. They were very proud if not a little fatigued, and the staff of the restaurant was planning a small celebration to surprise them on the timely accomplishment of their lifelong goal. Unknown to me, this party was also being planned to celebrate my upcoming 18th birthday, as well.

The entire staff of "The Cornerstone", as well as many of the regular patrons, were on hand when the Webers entered the front door for what they thought was simply a routine inspection by the board of health. Of course, this was truly a ruse to simplify the logistics for the party . . . getting everyone here together without telling them why. As they were assaulted by a resounding "surprise!", the smiles that stretched across their faces were repayment in full for all the sacrifices and hard work of the last few months. The new banquet room was filled to overflowing with potted plants and floral arrangements that had been arriving all day, as many local merchants were eager to share with these fine neighbors on this happy occasion.

It wasn't until one of the busboys made the official announcement of the arrival of the cake that I was given any inkling of my part in this affair. After ceremoniously congratulating the Webers on the completion of their new banquet hall, he suddenly requested that I come forward. With so many preparations for this fiesta, I had actually forgotten that my birthday was so near and, therefore, had no clue what the kid had in mind. Once I was up on the newly constructed stage in the amphitheater portion of the facilities, he signaled for the cake to be brought in. Simultaneously, the crowd began to serenade me with their boisterous rendition of "Happy Birthday" and presents were emerging from every nook and cranny in the place. Their spirit of generosity and love overwhelmed me.

Afterwards, we toasted the Webers' future and, by the time we were ready to part, everyone seemed happy and tired. As we bid adieu to the last of the guests, we fell into the nearest booth, filled with joy and prostate with fatigue.

The next year passed quickly. The new banquet facilities enabled Frank and Gerta to expand their business, and within a few weeks of the official opening, many of the available slots on the calendar had already been reserved for a special event. Both individual families and local businesses had chosen this spot for various activities. Not only were they using the new facilities, but they were also quite impressed with the quality and care that went into the banquet menu planning. Needless to say, this venture was a huge financial success and the Webers were quick to share the wealth with their employees, commensurate with our degree of involvement in the project. It was such a happy time for us all.

It was also a very busy time for us all. Gradually, I had been assuming more and more of the responsibility for the daily duties of the entire establishment. This meant contacting our suppliers with the request for commodities that we would be using in the upcoming days. It also meant planning the menus for both the diner and the banquet hall events. More recently, I began scheduling the rentals of the facilities, which often meant presenting the package to perspective clients and going over a pricing list and available menus to best accommodate their specific requirements. I enjoyed my new responsibilities, but it left very little time for socialization in my life. This worried Gerta and frequently she would broach the subject as we were working side-by-side shredding cheese or chopping vegetables or any of the hundreds of little chores that we did each day.

During one of these workfests, Gerta expressed her concern over my lack of contact with my family. This certainly caught me off-guard, since I had said very little about my family since my arrival. No one had ever prodded me for more information and I never brought up the subject. Now, suddenly, I was overcome with a deep longing to hear from my brother, David. Oh, how I missed him! My emotions must have shown all over my face, for Gerta suggested that I should try to get in touch with someone. She probably assumed that I was thinking about my parents. In truth, I had no desire to get involved with anyone but my brother . . . only I was not sure how to go about it.

Eventually, I did manage to force myself to contact my mother by phone. I made it a point to keep it short and impersonal. In reality, it was wonderful to hear her voice and I admitted secretly that I missed her very much, too. I resolved that in the future, I would try to set things right by her. After all, she had not really done anything wrong.

For the moment, however, I simply asked her if she had heard from David and, if so could she tell me how to get in touch with him. Delightedly, she relayed the fact that they corresponded every week and she gave me his address. After only a few seconds hesitation I whispered, "Goodbye. I love you, Mother". Without further ado, I replaced the receiver and ended our first encounter in almost two years.

At least I had David's address. I looked at the address that my mother had given me. It was not your typical street or mailbox number. It sort of looked like an address to which Gerta sent her son's mail since he went into the service. Almost immediately, I decided to quit analyzing and simply chose to write to the address and wait for a reply. I said nothing to anyone about this familial encounter. I always kept my personal life separate from my business life and seldom did the two meet during my lifetime. However, I knew that getting back in regular communication with David would mean so much to me and I was very grateful to Gerta for her gentle insistence that I make the first move.

David's life had taken on as many twists of fate as mine had. Unbeknownst to me, after Mother and I had left the home of his father to move in with Cliff, he had decided to join the Marines. The next day he had hitched to the recruiting office and had never looked back. He had done his basic training out in San Diego, then had been stationed at the military base in North Carolina, Camp Lejeune.

From the first letter that my brother had ever written to me, I also found out that he had put in for overseas assignment and was just waiting to see if his request would be approved. He wrote many questions about my whereabouts. He had tried to contact me right after I had run away, but since no one in the family was aware of what was happening in my life, my mother had to tell him that she had no information regarding my location. He wrote that he had worried a great deal about me since our separation but that deep down inside, he knew that I was a survivor.

At Gerta's suggestion, I obtained a mail box at the local branch of the post office. In this way, I kept my living arrangements to myself. At this point in my life, I still felt the need to maintain an insulating barrier between me and the world of my family. Since David was "on the move" so to speak, he did not press for more specific data. He was only interested in my general well being and, since my letters to him conveyed my contentment with my life, he was willing to accept my need for privacy.

He had no idea why I had left Mom's apartment in such a hurry without so much as a word of goodbye. I still had not divulged the secret reason of my flight to anyone. Now it seemed senseless to open up that stinking can of worms. At this point, there was nothing for David to do. In fact, there was nothing left to be done by anyone. In my mind, it was a case of "case closed". My new life was filling out very nicely, thank you, and I felt that for the first time in my life, I was controlling my destiny.

Time was passing quickly. The new banquet room had been in operation for a year and it was proving to be the financial bonanza that Frank had been hoping it would be. I was achieving a certain degree of skill in my dealings concerning my ever-increasing responsibilities at the restaurant and I was enjoying the chance to increase my business prowess in the process.

Tonight, the staff was planning my 19th birthday party. I had a showing on the premises scheduled later this evening after dinner, then it was "party time". I was hoping to secure the booking of the room rental for the upcoming wedding reception before I locked up for the night and transformed myself into the guest of honor at my party.

At 7:00 p.m. I locked the outer door and waited for my anticipated clients to arrive. If memory served me right, Mr.

Handy and his son, Rob were searching out a place to hold the younger man's wedding reception. Mrs. Handy had sounded very enthusiastic on her initial inquiry. She had located our phone number in our ad in the telephone book (my idea!) and when I discussed the various menu items available and our prices, she had a hard time hiding her excitement. We made tonight's appointment during that initial telephone call.

I noticed how quiet it was in the restaurant when there were no people around. The Webers had stated earlier that they would be gone until about 9:00 p.m. They had some last minute errands to run prior to my party. In truth, they usually made themselves scarce whenever I had a showing. They thought that their presence might make me nervous so they always busied themselves elsewhere when prospective clients were expected.

The quiet knocking brought me out of my reverie. Mr. Handy and son were prompt. They were also forms from the same mold. Both men were tall, although the senior was slightly stouter. Both had thick shocks of hair that looked like spun gold; the younger's fell to his shoulders. Both men strolled into the vestibule of the banquet room with quiet assurance.

I plunged into my spiel, which flowed with little effort on my part. As I showed off the cozy loveliness of the actual reception area, I outlined the different entrees that our menu featured. The Handys were polite and attentive as I described the numerous choices they faced: appetizers, soups, salad ingredients, side dishes, and desserts. After covering every imaginable aspect of the contractual arrangement, we walked back to the small office that Frank had built off the side of the building right after the acquisition of the property. I seated myself behind the small desk and gestured towards the two upholstered chairs that faced me. Neither men took any notice of my suggestion that they be seated so we could work out the final details.

Rob walked over to the door, quietly pushed it closed and turned the lock. With that sickening click, my stomach tightened. Mr. Handy had surreptitiously positioned himself behind my chair and was weaving his fingers through my hair. Rob turned to face us with a look of eager anticipation on his youthful face. He watched as his father spun my chair around and pulled me to a standing position in front of him. With the fingers of his left hand still entwined in my hair, he began to undo the buttons on my uniform with the fingers of the other. I knew that if I was going to do anything to help myself that it would have to be done quickly. The problem was that I had no idea what to do. There was certainly no way that I was going to overpower these two sizable men. There seemed no visible escape.

As I fought to keep my emotions in check, I tried to reason with them. When that approach proved futile, I began to plead with them but to no avail. As I searched their eyes for any signs of weakening, I recognized the sinister gleam that radiated from them. I had seen that look before. It was in the eyes of the young boys in the clubhouse so long ago. It was in the eyes of that older student, Jamie something . . . after the movies. It had been in Cliff's eyes the night I left home. Now it was in the eyes of these two men and that realization brought tears to mine.

They seemed to be progressing in this rape in a most unique, calculated manner. The men proceeded in the most methodical style from one phase to the other. As the father undid the top buttons of my uniform, his son stood by as if waiting for instructions. His father beckoned for him to approach us. When he got closer his father told him to remove my uniform from my shoulders. I could contain myself no longer. I prepared myself for the yell of my life. As if sensing my intention, Mr. Handy jerked my head back smartly with his left hand. I am not sure which hurt more . . . the unnatural snapping of my cervical vertebrae or the force of pull on the roots of my hair. Either way he silenced my impending scream for help.

"If you want us to fuck you up real bad, you're making all the right moves. We can do this neatly or we can get messy, if that's what you prefer," Mr. Handy whispered in my ear and the stench of alcohol almost made me gag.

Meanwhile, his son had slid the top part of my uniform so that it hung around my waist. His father directed him to remove my bra. He obeyed without hesitation. Next, his father ordered him to step out of the way and watch. As I stood there half-naked, he studied my body with a sardonic smile.

"You picked a winner, kid. She's perfect," his father said as he shot his son a wink. "I'm sure she won't mind if Daddy shows his little boy about the birds and the bees . . . using her as the container of honey. You are sweet! My God, what a body! Today, Son, you will become a man watching this lucky lady become the lucky recipient of all my expertise."

With those words, the die was cast. He began to rub his hands from my neck to my waist, paying particular attention to my breast along the way. He cupped one in each hand and massaged and kneaded them into arousal. He was quick to point this out to his observant son before he sucked one of my hardened nipples into his mouth.

We all heard the distant sound at the same time. The Handys froze. The sound of jingling keys snapped their attention for a fraction of a second. In the next moments I spun myself out of Mr. Handy's grasp. His son raced to the door and unlocked it. The sound of a door opening permeated the silence. Without a hint of hesitation Mr. Handy followed his son out into the darkness. I quickly gathered myself together and returned to my tiny room.

Within a few moments Frank Weber knocked on the door.

"Tarah ve forgot the money. It good thing my head is tight on my neck otherwise I may leave it home, too"

Having quickly jumped under the covers of my bed, I was feigning sleep as he peaked into my room . . . He dropped his voice instinctively when he saw me curled up under the blankets. He silently closed the door. I heard him whisper to his wife, who was apparently waiting for him "She's taking a nap . . . she needs to take it easy. Tonight vill be special. Let me just grab the money and we can be on our vay. We should be back in plenty of time to vake her."

I heard the front door close and the lock snap back into its secure position. I was alone again. I got out of the bed and readied myself for the impending celebration.

CHAPTER 21

THE GLITTER

I'm back! There was someone at the door and the doorbell interrupted my train of thoughts. I am glad I stopped, though. It was my "buddie" from the AIDS Task Force in this county. At essentially the start of the AIDS epidemic, the task force set up this system of support between victims of this disease and people who cared enough about other people to learn the facts. These same loving people go out and help those who suffer from its effects anyway they can.

For me, it's the fellowship and company that mean so much. My buddie, Amy has listened to me cry and curse, spit and scream and she always allowed me to do so openly . . . without guilt or embarrassment. Without passing judgement on my lifestyle or on me, she offers not only an outlet for my tangled emotions but she also gives unconditional love and unparalleled support. Her visits make me strong enough to suffer through the devastation that follows this diagnosis.

At the party after my run-in with Mr. Handy and his son, I had to make it appear that everything was copesthetic. The party went off without a hitch. Gerta gave me a beautiful gold locket in the shape of a heart that I was to add to the cross on the chain around my neck. She said that it represented the three cardinal virtues . . . at least, two of them. The crucifix symbolized faith and the heart: love. She told me that the hope should always be in my soul. Frank attached it to the chain around my neck as I marveled at the loveliness and thoughtfulness of the gift. Inside the locket, there is a small oval picture of Gerta and I, taken only a few days after my initial arrival at "The Cornerstone". With tear-filled eyes, I bade goodnight to these wonderful people. Goodnight, . . . and goodbye.

Gerta promised to wake me up in the morning to go to the bank. I told her that I wanted to deposit the money that I received at my party. In reality, I intended to withdraw all the money in my account and leave this city and these nice friends. There was no way I could stay here any longer after what happened. Yet there was no way I could force myself to tell the Webers what had transpired. They would want me to go to the police with the information. I could not bring that kind of disgrace to this family and business that meant so much to me. My mind was made up and I lay awake all night planning the beginning of my new life. There were major decisions to be made. The real problem lay in the fact that these decisions had to be made in a very short time.

The next morning when I woke up, while having my coffee, I composed a short letter to the Webers that I hoped would express my sincere appreciation for their hospitality and their love, which they so generously shared with me. I told them that I just felt a deep, almost haunting desire to make a change in my life and I felt that now was as good a time as any, to make the necessary adjustments. I promised to keep in touch . . . a promise that I could not keep. I never saw Frank or Gerta again, but I never forgot them. Many nights, I remember these loving, Christian people in my prayers.

I left the note propped up on the counter along with the gold heart locket. Earlier, I had quietly packed my belongings into my overnight bags. I straightened the little room that had been my safe and private domain for over two years of my life . . . until the unfortunate events of the night before. I did not want the Webers to find out about anything that had happened. If I wasn't around, they couldn't ask me a lot of questions that I did not want to answer. Without a sound, I slipped out the rear door carrying all my worldly possessions over my shoulder. I went to the bank, withdrew my entire life's savings and decided to head to the Jersey Shore.

Two hours later, I was in Wildwood. In New Jersey, the legal drinking age had been lowered to 19. Since it was now perfectly legal, I had an early morning "strong one" in a bar that seemed to cater to nightshift workers. I was sipping on a pina colada when I noticed the sign on the wall. It was advertising their annual bathing suit contest that was to be held that evening. I asked the barmaid what the eligibility requirements were. Since there were really just a few formalities, I gave my name and the five-dollar entrance fee.

Afterwards, I finished my drink and decided to walk along the boardwalk. Wildwood was delightful on this early summer morning. I had five hours to kill before the competition. The soothing sound of the surf pounding the turf under the boardwalk had a calming effect on my jangled nerves. I grabbed some grub from one of the many food vendors tucked in the tiny shops that lined the oceanfront. Continuing my sojourn down the "boards", I heard the shrill screams of terror and delight coming from the amusement pier on the next block.

With a mind of their own, my feet meandered into the midst of the chaotic joy of the other patrons enjoying the sights, sounds and smells of the attractions. I ventured through the haunted house. I rode the roller coaster, and even dared to tempt fate by riding the giant Ferris wheel. Yeah, I know . . . big deal! Right? If you knew how terrified I am of heights, you'd understand that this was a major victory in my daily attempt to conquer my fears. Even though some years have passed since that ride, I can still vividly recall that it scared the bejessus out of me. The terror became part of the excitement of the ride.

After two hours, I had the bright idea. I had enough money to last for a while if I budgeted it wisely. I wanted to splurge tonight. I could rent a room for a day or two. This would give me an opportunity to relax a little, spruce up and get ready for the contest. I headed inland knowing that the further from the beach you go the lower the prices for lodging.

I was looking for a reasonably clean, affordable and safe motel when I spotted a large seaside resort-type cottage that announced a vacancy. When I went in to ask about renting for only a day or two, they assured me that this would be fine. We quickly worked out the details to the transaction and they ushered me into a cute, cozy nook on the third floor. They also assured me that they lived on the premises and had an impressive security system keeping their home safe. They seemed comfortable with the idea of renting to someone as safe as I was and wanted me to be comfortable in their home . . . as if sensing my unrest.

As soon as they went downstairs I began unpacking my cosmetics and the new red bathing suit that one of the other waitresses had just given me for my birthday last night. Gee! That already seems like such a long time ago. I filled the tub in the bathroom on the second floor with scented beads and enjoyed my newly found luxury. After toweling off, I primped with exceptional care to details. My hair hung in shiny cascades down my back and my eyes appeared to sparkle with mischief. The sleek, silky red bathing suit hugged the curves of my body like a 1960 MGA Mark II Roadster hugs the road. My upper body had filled out from lugging heavy trays everyday. My legs were long, lean and powerful. They were the legs of a dancer. Tonight, I would get my chance to dance.

Suddenly, another memory beamed into my head from out of the blue. It was a night long ago, when I was a Girl Scout and we were having a party with the Eagle Scouts. At one point, my young partner and I cleared the floor . . . I think we were doing "The Hustle". I could still remember the excitement of the moment, when I realized that all eyes were focused on us. It was delicious! I anticipated that same feeling of exaltation to engulf me later, when I competed in the contest.

I turned my attention back to my appearance. With exceptional care, I applied my make-up using techniques learned from magazine articles that I had read at the restaurant. From eyeliner to finishing powder, great care was taken to insure uniformity in color and proper blending of the delicate hues. My lipstick and blush were the same fire engine red as my bathing suit. Next, I slipped a white wrap-around dress over my swimsuit, slipped my feet into a pair of bright red heels, slipped a red patent leather belt around my waist and slipped my dark silky tresses under a large, red sunhat.

I looked like a college girl going to a cotillion as I made my way through the charming vacation cottage that was now my home. The stroll along the beach, on my way back to the lounge, did much to calm the butterflies that had begun to gather somewhere beneath my diaphragm. The rhythmic pulsations of the tide against the turf made all troubles seem insignificant in the total scheme of things. A pair of seagulls, as if sensing my pensive mood, trailed me silently as if hoping to transcend the bridge imposed by the language barrier between humans and other species. I approached my destination with a powerful, new freshness of spirit and a determination that was rooted deeply; As a newly sprouted seed, it would need tender, loving care to bloom.

Upon entering "The Lazy Boy Lounge" I headed straight for the sign up desk and penned my dancing name brazenly across the paper:

GLITTER!

There was an empty booth across the room and I hurried over before anyone else could get there first. When the barmaid came over I ordered a Pina Colada. There had been four names on the list before mine, so I knew that I had some time to relax and check out the competition. My drink came just as the festivities began.

I was glad that I had not been the first contestant. At least this way I could get an idea for my time in the spotlight, as I watched the reaction of the crowd to the other participants. With each sip of that cool, creamy liquid from my glass, my nerves loosened considerably. Watching my competition soon gave me to know that I had nothing to dread. There was no originality in their moves and very little skill. Worse still, there was no heart in their dancing.

While the contestant before me was performing . . . and I use that term loosely . . . the DJ approached my booth and asked if I had any special record that I wanted him to play while I danced.

"'I Will Survive' by Gloria Gaynor," I replied without hesitation.

"Can do," he responded, smiled, nodded and walked away.

I took my place behind the curtain and waited for the fourth contestant to finish. To the polite applause of the cheerful crowd, she made her way to where I was standing. She bade me good luck as she hurried past. Taking slow, deep breaths as I waited for my introduction, I attempted to collect my thoughts. My only expectation tonight was to enjoy myself and get a chance to experience something that I always thought I wanted to do. Ever since talking to the dancers at "The Cornerstone" I wanted a chance to try. Now, I wanted to savor every moment of my metamorphosis into my alterego . . . Glitter.

The first few strains of my music permeated the room and the slow, languishing melody created the perfect atmosphere for my entrance. With deliberate shyness, I emerged from the shadows into the spotlight and surveyed my audience. They were already mine! As the music continued, I swirled around in graceful circles while holding the full skirt of my white dress, and allowed the silky folds to billow around the provocative curves of my lower body.

As the song started to build some intensity, so did my dancing. With teasing playfulness, I discarded my red hat and engaged a patron in some mild flirtation. The cheers from the crowd added fuel to the fire that was burning within me. The driving rhythm of the music pulsated through me and the natural movements flowed to my extremities, pulling me along in a powerful, exciting, almost spiritual dance of suggested sensuality.

Slowly, and with painstaking deliberateness, I unhooked the red belt that held my dress together. The crowd reacted immediately with a resounding shout and a chorus of whistles. All eyes watched as the belt glided to the floor. The music had returned to the initial slower, headier refrain. This allowed me ample opportunity to torture the audience about what goodies could be hidden under the purity frock. One thin layer of material prevented their eyes from feasting on the obscured delicacies of my flesh. Even as high kicks revealed my thighs, they begged for more. As I revealed my naked back, they begged for more. They were, however, unprepared for my next move.

As the song reached a crescendo, I grabbed my dress while slipping it from my body and proceeded to wave it like a banner around my body and over my head. The bright spotlight reflected off the shiny red material of the revealing suit and ignited the crowd. They seemed particularly pleased with my abundant bosom and the inadequacy of the suit to properly harness the firmness of their peaks. As the last penetrating bars of the song announced the approaching finale, something totally unplanned happened. The snap that held the straps of my suit together, behind my neck, came apart. The audience assumed that it was part of my act as I sprang into the air with jubilation, then fell into an exhausted heap on the floor. With that leap into the air, as I reached the pinnacle of my ascent, the front of my suit fell away from my body. For the briefest moment my breasts were bathed in the hot spotlight and then, just as quickly, disappeared beneath my torso as I scrunched on the stage in a tight, heavily breathing ball of sweating flesh.

The applause was thunderous. As I waited for the techie to dim the spotlight, I wallowed in the sound of clapping hands, stamping feet and an assortment of hoots, hollers and wolf whistles . . . all for my benefit. Only after the lights went down did I stand up and begin to gather my hat and dress from the pre-selected spot where I had tossed them . . . seemingly, with utter abandon.

Now all I had to do was watch while the remaining girls

competed and the judges picked the winners. I ordered another drink and literally glowed when the barmaid congratulated me on my performance. Having redonned my white dress with the bright red accessories once again, I looked like a quiet, sedate debutante. The façade went deeper than mere appearances. Even my mannerisms and body language spoke of a gentler lifestyle than I had ever been permitted to experience.

The owner, Mr. Landis approached the small podium and requested silence from the exuberant crowd that now filled the lounge to overflowing. He was ready to reveal the two runner-ups and then he would announce the winner. The second runner-up was a tall, thin girl with red hair who wore a baby blue bikini and danced to some country ballad. The first runner-up looked like a brunette body-builder with abundant athletic finesse. Her modern dance number was quite a hit with the patrons and she received an enthusiastic round of applause as she made her way through the audience to accept her prize.

The redhead was presented with a bouquet of fresh flowers, a bottle of wine and a fifty-dollar savings bond. The brunette had reached the stage and was holding her bouquet, her wine and a one hundred-dollar gift certificate from a local merchant. It was now time to announce the winner.

Even though I knew that I had danced rather well, I also knew that I had no experience at this type of thing. It began to dawn on me that I had "a snowball's chance in hell" of winning and I began to pick up my things and head back to my rented room. As I stood up to leave, the sound finally penetrated my foggy consciousness. The owner and most of the customers were looking in my direction. Once again, he spoke the words, " . . . and the winner is . . . Glitter!"

I won! I won! I could hardly believe it. My legs felt like rubber and my hands were trembling as I advanced towards the stage. When I reached the podium, Mr. Landis shook my hand, offered me a bouquet of long-stemmed, red roses, a bottle of champagne and a check for five hundred dollars. The audience had not stopped their ovation and, as I attempted to return to my table after the presentation, the din became deafening. The patrons increased the intensity of their show of appreciation.

When I finally reached the booth, I had every intention of finishing my drink and going home. Moments later, I saw the owner walking towards me. With a gracious smile, he asked me for permission to sit down.

"Sure," I said and gestured towards the seat across from me. I was still in shock after being awarded the top prize and the owner was about to shock me more.

"You were delightful tonight. The crowd loves you. I have a proposition for you. Interested?"

"In hearing your proposition? Yes," I replied with more maturity than I actually felt.

"How would you like to work here on a permanent basis. You could work any hours you wanted and the money would be befitting a woman of your obvious talents."

Looking at him, there were no discernible traits that would lead me to believe that he harbored any ulterior motives. Upon further conversation, I learned that this idiot was willing to pay me handsomely for a minimal amount of time and energy on my part. We worked out a deal where I would work every weekend evening for at least four hours. During the week, I could choose to work either in the evening or during the very busy lunchhour. I would be paid in cash, under the table, so no deductions would reduce my net income.

His offer took me by surprise but I tried to analyze the options. If I accepted his offer, I could be independent. I could continue to stay in the nice home that I had been lucky enough to find. I was sure that the owners would be happy to extend the terms of our verbal agreement. If I did not accept the offer, I would just have to look elsewhere for a job . . . probably a waitress position, since that was my only area of any expertise at present. Waitressing held no real thrill for me, so within a few moments I had made a monumental decision.

"I accept your offer, Mr. Landis. You seem like an honorable man and honor is a very important characteristic in any person with whom I have to deal. If it suits you, I could begin this weekend. I will, however, need some assistance acquiring a few costumes. If I draw up some sketches and submit them for your approval, could you put together the people who could do the work." I hoped that I sounded more confident than I felt inside.

"Of course. That's wonderful, Glitter. No problems with costuming, I assure you. I know great, talented artists who can create any look you desire. With you wearing it, any outfit would become a work of art." His casual charm came easily and I found myself blushing. I already liked this guy.

After finalizing our agreement, I promised to drop off my sketches tomorrow afternoon. Mr. Landis shook hands firmly when he said goodbye. He seemed to be quite pleased with himself for thinking of offering me a job and pleased with me for being smart enough to accept it. In truth, I was pretty pleased with myself, too. What had initially been a stab at a chance for some excitement turned out to be an opportunity of a lifetime. I was anxious only to begin my new career.

That night, I walked along the beach in the direction of my attic room with the sounds of the ocean surrounding me. I felt so happy inside, but I also felt so lonely. I had no one in this whole wide world with whom I could share this new development in my life. So that night I shared it with the moon, the sand, the waves and the tides.

The next afternoon, as promised, I returned to "The Lazy Boy Lounge" and left sample sketches of the type of outfits I might prefer when I danced. I also left my vital statistics and other measurements, along with the drawings to expedite the process. I was eager to begin this phase of my work experience.

I had three days before I was scheduled to start dancing. This gave me time to think about the journey on which I had decided to embark. Never in my life would I have ever imagined that I would become a go-go dancer. On the surface, it would seem to be a decision that was sure to compromise my Christian values. However, I was determined to keep my dancing elevated to an artform and, in this way, actually please God. Yeah, Right!

I had always been very proud of my body and I worked hard at keeping it toned by various workouts, on a regular basis. As long as I kept my distance from the clientele who frequented these so-called "shaker bars" I could eliminate the possibility of these activities leading me "into temptation". My motto would become "I tease . . . I don't please". I intended to live by that motto.

The next few days were a maze of recreational splendor. I sat on the sandy, sun-drenched beach and stared out over the Atlantic Ocean for hours at a time. I shopped for a bright, sunny, new wardrobe. I jogged along the ebbing tides and climbed the ever-changing sand dunes. Reaching deep into my inner self, I tried to discover my identity and judge for myself if this was the *me* that I wanted to be.

At some point each day I would make the time to practice my dancing. My preferences in music ran along the heavy metal, hard rock lines. Although I could dance to any kind of music, the hard, driving rhythms and angst-filled lyrics appealed to the underlying rebel that I was becoming. I dialed my radio to an appropriate station and stretched out my muscles. Working certain moves over and over until the movements of my gyrating body mimicked the sounds of the instruments and voices of the song playing at the time. Dancing seemed to be self-supporting. This meant that the more I danced, the more energy I seemed to have. I instinctively knew how to move the various parts of my body to acknowledge certain feelings that always seem to well up inside my very soul whenever I heard music that appealed to me. Finally I felt ready, both physically and emotionally, to tackle the next agenda that life had thrown my way. I was ready to dance.

My living accommodations had already been cemented after speaking with The Warners . . . the owners of the beachhouse that I shared. They agreed to lease me the "penthouse" on a monthly basis. My lease even included meals. Mrs. Warner was a wonderful cook. I would have to guard against any untimely weight gain.

Friday evening, I walked towards "The Lazy Boy Lounge".

It was barely 5:00 p.m. I wanted plenty of time to check out my new costumes and evaluate the area where I would be working. Mr. Landis was not there but a nice barmaid showed me where the dressing room was located and assured me that the owner was intent on witnessing my debut in his club.

Fortunately, I had the presence of mind to bring a temporary costume to my debut in case the new ones didn't fit or hadn't arrived. The roughly cut jeans fit my slender rump to perfection. My top was simply a tube top with a few minor alterations. Applying make-up in the small, dimly lit room was a challenge . . . to say the least. A single oblong window opened minimally and permitted very little air exchange. A single light bulb, hanging high overhead, was suspended from a globeless fixture.

A good feature about the room was that it was located right next to the employee's bathroom. Little more than a dirty hole in the wall, this area held the only semblance of privacy in the joint. I made it a policy to use this facility only when absolutely necessary. The lighting was better so I could put my make-up on faster and easier; I just stayed away from the filthy toilet. Many nights to follow had me rushing back to my attic aviary, praying that no one was occupying the first floor bathroom.

By 6:00 p.m., I was ready to hit the stage. Someone should have told me to break a leg or something but, as usual, I was alone in my corner. Just as these dismal thoughts raced through my head, I saw Mr. Landis walking towards me. His warm smile told me that he had not reconsidered and thought that hiring me had been a major mistake. He introduced me to Judy and Sandy, two of his best bartenders, and encouraged me to check out his place a little . . . to get the feel of it before I "punched the clock".

The red and walnut motif was easy on the eyes, especially in the dusky bar. The smoothness of it glistened from hours of loving attention. The hanging lamps, spread casually around the large rooms, lent a Casa *Blanca* ambiance to the surroundings. The stage was lit by a variety of lighting techniques that were managed by skilled technicians during busy hours or during special events, like the contest. Otherwise, the dancers managed the lights via toggle switches to the side of the stage.

The jukebox is always of special interest to the dancers. I perused the offerings and was pleased to see quite an assortment from which to choose. This would make selecting the music for my set so much easier. There were only a few patrons on the premises at this time, so I could continue my meandering in reasonable obscurity.

Soon I had made my way back to the dressing room to find another dancer had arrived. She introduced herself as "Cranky" and later I would learn that this name had nothing to do with her disposition. She assumed that this was my first time dancing here. She would have fainted if she knew that this was my first dancing gig ever!

She explained how the dancers worked here. The jukebox was rigged so that during the hours that the dancers were working, no money was necessary to make your selections. Since I was going to go first tonight, I just had to go to the jukebox when ready and punch in the numbers for the four songs that I wanted to dance to during my time on stage. After this, "Cranky" would choose her four songs. While she was dancing, I was supposed to circulate through the crowd. She had informed me that this crowd was easy with tips. I also understood that during these breaks I could opt for a costume change. I wondered where my costumes could be!

I guess I thought I was as ready as I'd ever be. I signaled to the barmaid that I was prepared to start my block, chose my songs and made my way to the stage. Remember the butterflies that I had earlier . . . well, now it felt like I had giant condors swooping through my bowels. Then the music started. I remember how everything else faded into the background. I was left alone with the music. Everyone there could hear and see and feel the music as I danced.

Before I knew it, my turn had ended and the small crowd went wild. As I tried to navigate around the floor, it seemed that each person there, whether male or female, wanted to shake my hand and offer their own brand of welcome. It truly amazed me how kind these strangers could be. I felt very welcomed here. I wanted to dance here for the rest of my life.

As "Cranky" had said, the tips were great. Of course, I assumed that some of this was due to the novelty of a new dancer here and the tips would drop off dramatically after the newness wore off. So I decided to enjoy it while it lasted. I danced two more blocks before I even took time out for a costume change. When I finally took a few minutes to prepare myself for this switch, I realized that I did not even have another costume in my possession. At that moment, a knock came on the dressing room door. As I cautiously opened it, one of the bouncers handed me a large, impressive box through the narrow opening.

My costumes! My new costumes from Mr. Landis. I was so excited I could not help shaking as I opened the box. What a smorgasbord of class, taste and originality I found inside! Five costumes . . . each a masterpiece of color and texture. One had a long satin-lined, velvet cape. Another sported a parody of southern charm. My favorite was a Victorian, lace-drenched corset with authentic whalebone stays and pull-tie laces in front. Enclosed with the costumes was a card that read:

> Glitter,
> May you always shine. May these Rags be ennobled by your touch. They are Yours!
>> Good Luck,
>> Mr. James T. Landis

I quickly slipped into a hot pink outfit complete with matching gloves and sweat band, freshened my make-up and made my way to select my songs. The growing crowd enthusiastically greeted me when they saw the view that I presented, even before I got on stage. By the time I began my block, I felt and looked radiant. Inwardly I knew that I was having too much fun to consider what I was doing work. Yet, I was making four times the salary I did as a waitress. God! Wasn't America great!

By the end of my shift, I was hungry, tired sweaty and one hundred and sixty dollars richer. That total did not even include my tips. Only after I showered, ate and sat down in my new favorite chair to relax did I count my tips. I almost fainted when I realized that, after uncrumpling all those bills, my tips totaled more than two hundred dollars. The combined wages and tips came to almost four hundred dollars. This represented more money than I earned in a month at the restaurant.

I was beginning to like dancing more and more. Besides all the obvious benefits, it enabled me to meet new and, often, interesting people. I met one of these people the second night that I danced at "The LBL". His name was Derek Steele.

CHAPTER 22

THE GLITCH

Oh, Mr. Machine. What are we gonna do with me today? It has been a strange one. Worst of all, it has been totally my fault. It had to have begun before I woke up this morning. If the truth be known, I woke up in a despicable mood. I was an argument waiting to happen! I squabbled with every person with whom I had contact today. I even managed to alienate the two sweetest, most endearing people in the world. I believe I mentioned them both before in my musings.

Sandy, my lab technician and I exchanged words earlier today over nothing. Later, my mood erupted during a visit with Amy, my "buddie". It was the briefest of encounters, but it was the first time that we ever had harsh words pass between us. Fortunately, I had enough sense to apologize to each of them before their visits ended. Fortunate also for me was the fact that both women found it in their hearts to forgive me.

Now what, you may ask, has brought on this horrendous behavior? Hey, I'm dying here . . . so cut me a small break, please! Occasionally, I can't maintain my Pollyanna façade. Today, however, there is another force behind my foul disposition. Today is the day that I am going to open up the can of worms in my life that took the form of Derek Steele. It was such a confusing time for me. My emotions rode a nightmarish roller coaster. I was learning about life and love. At least, I was trying to learn.

In all honesty, I don't exactly remember the first time I met Derek . . . or at least became aware of him as an individual. He frequently came to the lounge. Initially, I became aware of him as a tipper. Quickly, I knew that I could count on him for several dollars during the course of any given shift. What next attracted me to him was his sense of humor. Our relationship evolved so naturally and quietly that neither one of us noticed.

During my breaks, when I chose to mingle with the crowd for tips and absurd conversations, I frequently found myself sharing quips with this delightful little man. Even though he was just my height, he presented himself as one cocky little dude.

It was several weeks later that I allowed myself the luxury of agreeing to meet Derek outside of the security of the bar. Amazingly enough, one of my neighbors, who I met in the yard while helping with the yard work, was a mutual friend. As a matter of fact, these two young men grew up together, went through school together and have been best friends since early childhood. This afforded Derek and me an easy way to break the ice. Brian, my neighbor and his best friend, invited us to a bar-b-que. We both accepted and agreed to go together.

From the very first encounter between us, there was definitely a strong chemistry. The space between us seemed suddenly charged with energy of unusual strength. His winning smile and easy charm had impressed me when I was working. At the bar-b-que, I was able to relax and enjoy the comfortable conversation and whimsical exchange that we shared.

Since I had just met Derek, I was a bit hesitant to divulge too much information about myself. He, on the other hand, seemed to enjoy sharing his story with me. He was the only child of aging parents. Even though his arrival was unexpected and occurred later than usual, it was well received. No parents could have loved a son more. Understandably, his parents were not very strict in their child rearing, and Derek admitted he was somewhat spoiled. Their way of dealing with any unpleasantness that included their precious son was to overlook his imperfections. If this proved to be impossible, then they would simply seek out someone else to blame. Their leniency was helpful during the early, formative period of our developing relationship. His parents actually allowed me to stay overnight with Derek. No! I don't mean that they let me stay in the guestroom. I was permitted to share Derek's bed!

During our first few encounters, Derek and I shared numerous conversations. He told me about his disastrous, short-lived marriage. He openly explained that his inane violent streak had destroyed it soon after the vows were exchanged. After severely damaging both of his parent's vehicles in the same week, and being arrested for driving under the influence, he was finally forced to admit to a cross-addiction to alcohol, cocaine and amphetamines.

As part of his probation, he agreed to attend a residential recovery program. This universally accepted twelve-step program was designed to help the self-admitted addict to change their lives. Derek readily admits that this rehabilitation effort probably saved his life.

Being the curious type, I had to ask him why he drank beer when he came to the bar and watched me dance. Wasn't this against the rules? Wasn't he supposed to call somebody whenever his desire for a drink became overwhelming?

Derek confided in me that the program had not been as successful as everyone had hoped. He continued to drink but he no longer drove home afterwards. He also stated that he enjoyed smoking pot on a fairly regular basis, too. He said that he was proud of the way he had dramatically reduced his use of coke and speed. He no longer required these substances on a regular basis, but rather he allowed himself only the occasional freedom of participation in these forbidden fruits, with the rationalization that occasionally was better than everyday.

Our developing relationship was based on many levels, not the least of which was the physical aspect. As mentioned before, there was some type of chemical/energy connection between us almost immediately. This bond seemed to heighten as our physical attraction grew. It was evident the first time we touched . . . a modest handshake. As our fingers met and our palms touched for the first time, it felt like some strange and wonderful flame raced through my blood vessels and flooded my brain and my heart with overwhelming emotional explosions. It was surely a spiritual phenomenon, which transcended time and space.

Despite our mutual efforts to proceed slowly, the attraction was too strong for much of a delay. During a shared slow dance, as we stood close to each other on the dance floor and allowed our bodies to move together as a single entity, we both noticed how nicely we fit together. I noticed how firm his chest felt as it pressed against mine in rhythmic gyrations. With his strong arms wrapped around me, I felt protected. When he smiled as he peered into my eyes, I could feel my resolve to maintain a comfortable distance slipping away. I also knew that I would give myself completely to this man before the night turned into tomorrow.

Later that evening, we entered Derek's parents' home. He greeted his folks in his usual casual, chipper tone, then he introduced me as a new friend that he had met that day. He told them we were going into his room for awhile and play video games. With knowing smiles, they both told us to have fun before resuming their television viewing.

We ran like children through the house and into his room. Derek did not even pretend to set up the Nintendo. After closing the door, he turned around and took both of my hands into his slightly larger ones. For a time, we just stood there watching each other, wanting each other. In unison, as if rehearsed, we moved as a couple to the end of the bed and sat down without giving up each other's hands.

The heat had already started to rise in me just because I was so close to this sexy little man. It was apparent that his emotions were riding the tides as well, when he gently bent forward to place his warm lips softly on mine. Almost immediately, my lips responded to his attention. As the tip of his tongue moistened my lower lip, mine parted slightly as if with a mind of their own. His eager tongue soon noticed the enticing opening and began to explore, with deliberate slowness and surprising gentleness, the sensitive, moist and waiting areas to which he had just gained access.

How I wanted him at that moment! However, I was rushing nothing. We began to explore the exposed surfaces with sensitive fingers. Every part of my body seemed to be reacting at once to his exciting touch. With coordinated motions, he began to move his lips to my neck while his nimble fingers unceremoniously undid the top button of my blouse. As he nibbled his way to the other side of my neck, the second button was undone. As he lowered his head to my breasts, my blouse floated effortlessly off my slender shoulders. Since I was not being the passive participant in the experience, his shirt soon followed. After a few more moments of tantalizing each other, we abandoned our other clothing and quietly molded our bodies together on the freshly-made bed.

We wanted each other with equal intensity. First though, we wanted to know the other completely. We took our time exploring each other and exchanging indescribable pleasures. Finally, just when I thought my excitement would cause my body to explode, Derek took me. With tenderness, he penetrated me and my desire for him increased. I pulled him towards me and raised my pelvis to accommodate him. With each plunge, he dipped deeper into my feminine cavity, exciting me to new heights and, eventually, causing me to climax at the moment of his healthy ejaculation. With the hot, liquid evidence of his love shooting inside me and his hot, whispered words of desire floating in my mind, we became one.

Thus, Derek and I became a hot item that summer for the romantic gossips. We went everywhere together when I wasn't working. We made love anywhere and anytime during the next several months. My desire for him and his for me seemed to increase every time we touched. We could not seem to get enough of each other. It appeared that when we found each other, we found paradise.

Even paradise can have bad days, however. The first problem we encountered was Derek's lack of a work ethic. The last job that he held had been on the night shift. He had somehow convinced his parents that this had been the underlying cause of his problematic drinking. He continually assured them that he was constantly seeking employment but he was not about to settle for just any job.

I could not imagine when he sought out these jobs, since when he was not watching me dance, we were hanging out together. I figured he knew what he was doing and it became apparent early in the relationship that he did not appreciate other people's interference into his life . . . not even mine.

The second and biggest problem was Derek, himself. He was certainly the most regimented person that I had ever met. His existence seemed comprised of a series of habits. His elderly parents handed down most of these habits. They always ate dinner at the same time each day. No matter what! At any time of day or night, they knew with absolute certainty what TV show they would watch and that never changed. No matter what!

Once, when Derek's mother took ill, I volunteered to help out with the household chores, until she was back on her feet. Neither Derek nor his parents ever told me thanks, but they let me know that I had not wrapped the coffee grounds properly before disposing of them in the trash. After they had instructed me in the correct procedure for throwing away their used coffee grounds, I had the audacity to ask them why they did it that way. Their condescending attitudes were suffocating as they explained in glib phrases that it was to control the odor. Oh yeah, right!

Since Derek was the only child of elderly parents, he was used to getting his own way about everything. He had surely never accepted the idea of compromise. Needless to say, given the circumstances, Derek was the apple of his parents' eyes. Their household revolved around him.

Even though both parents had serious health problems, Derek insisted on keeping two of the most wild, vicious dogs right inside the house. They had full run of his bedroom when he was out, but when Derek came home, those dogs understood that the whole house was their personal domain. They deposited large clumps of dog hair on furniture and rugs. The stinking dog hair was everywhere. They could just as easily drop their load on the living room carpet. During the time when I was helping out the ailing Mrs. Steele, I also assisted with the family's laundry. After washing a load of clothes, I would hang it out on the clothesline in the sunny-fresh breeze. If they were dry before I left for work, I would fold them and place each person's pile on their respective beds. As I hung out the wet laundry and again when I took the dry clothes down, it made me nauseous to see how much dog hair remained on these supposedly clean articles. Even the dish towels and bed linen were covered with it. Yuck! I thought to myself, "How can these anal-compulsive people put up with this filth?" . . . Like I said, "Derek always got things his way at home and he wanted those dogs".

Derek managed to carry this powerplay over into our relationship. He managed this by subliminally injecting his rules into the workings of our affair. There appeared to be two major rules that evolved soon after we became involved. The first law stated universally that Derek was always right . . . in all things . . . at all times . . . by all standards. There were no justifiable arguments. There were no allowable questions. Derek Steele was always right . . . end of discussion. The second law emphatically exclaimed that Derek was not confined by rules. This enabled him to get away with the times when he was not dependable and made deadlines and time frames meaningless.

"Where was your head?" You may well ask. In a sentence, I was in love with this little man. He was the first man to treat me like a woman. He was the first man, not a boy, who made me laugh as a woman laughs. He showed me at least once a day how much of a woman I could be. I just enjoyed being around him and fully expected to spend the rest of my life with him. This meant that I would have plenty of time to work on those tiny, little imperfections in his disposition. For the time being, I was enjoying life. I finally had someone important in my life. It soon became evident that my world seemed to revolve around Derek. That was just fine with me. So what if he sometimes did not show up for a prearranged event like a picnic or movie date. I understood that sometimes, after helping one or the other of his parents with some chore around the house, he was so exhausted that he fell asleep. I also understood I was not supposed to call his house in case his parents were sleeping. Derek said that he felt the shock might aggravate his father's heart condition. Even though this made it difficult for me to get in touch with him, I understood the reasoning behind it and actually admired him for being so considerate of his aging parents. The fact that he made these same parents cry with his moody tantrums and insufferable inconsideration when it suited him was beside the point.

As our sexual awareness of each other increased, so did Derek's possessiveness. This became a problem, immediately, at work. He was intolerant of my mingling with any other male customers during my off-stage time. When he was in the audience watching me, it seemed natural to spend break time with him. My boss, on the other hand, saw things differently. He explained that my duties included playing the role of "hostess" during my non-dancing time when I was not changing costumes. This meant that I was supposed to circulate among the clients, spreading cheer and making them stay in the lounge longer, spending more money on drinks and food.

This eventually led to our first official break-up. I did not see Derek for almost a week and I was broken-hearted for the entire time. It seems, amazingly enough, that Derek missed me a lot, too. Naturally, during the separation period we were not intimate with each other. Heck, we didn't even see one another.

I was continually depressed during that time. Just because I knew I would not be seeing Derek, simple tasks like getting up in the morning were very difficult. On several of those days, I just stayed in bed until it was time to go to work. After work, I would go straight home and instinctively go to the security of my nice warm bed. If it had not been for my job, I might not have ever gotten out of the rack at all.

A week to the day after our first fight, I found my body would not allow me to spend another minute in my bed. I had to get up and do something. Since it had rained the day before and the sun was shining brilliantly on a totally beautiful day, I decided to do a little early morning weeding.

It felt wonderful to be outside in the cooler morning air. Suddenly, I heard voices next door. I looked over the fence, prepared to give a friendly greeting to Brian. I was not prepared to come face to face with Derek. Yet, there I was, staring into his mischievous baby blues. Brian and I exchanged casual greetings.

Suddenly, Brian had something to do elsewhere and he hurried away, leaving the two of us there with only the silence between us. The conversation was difficult at first, but we both seemed anxious to keep it going after it began. Derek soon took the initiative and inched his way closer to me. I read this as a positive sign and told him that I missed him. He took hold of my hand and gave it a meaningful squeeze. That was all it took. No apologies. No discussion. No real solutions to the problems that had instigated the disagreement. We were a couple again.

There was one small bit of information that was not made known to me until much, much later. Had I been armed with this information sooner, it might have . . . no . . . probably would have, changed the course of both of our lives.

During our break-up, I had not even considered going out with someone else. I guess deep down inside, I knew that Derek and I would get back together. This, however, had not been the case with Derek. He had, in fact, been out with several different girls and he did not try to hide the fact from anyone other than me. Later, I learned that several times during that week he brought those trollops to The Lounge when he knew that I would not be there. Of course, no one told me about this until it did not make a difference anyway. I was glad that he had the decency not to come there with anyone else when I was there. I was so vulnerable then that I don't think I would have been able to handle it.

Well, we finally got back together and life was as it had been before. We laughed, we talked, and we made love. Often we made love two or three times a day. Even this often, it was wonderful each and every time. In fact, it actually seemed to get better, the more we did it. Derek was always up for it (excuse the pun). It was obvious that my body turned him on.

It was lucky for me that he demonstrated his appreciation of my body in such an obvious way, because that was the only way I would have ever known that he liked the way I looked. Derek never gave me compliments. He never told me that I looked nice or smelled good. He never told me that he thought I was beautiful or pretty or cute. He never even told me that he loved me. He once explained that I should know how he felt about me by how he treated me. At the time, I chalked it up to another one of "Derek's Rules". I had yet to chalk up how Derek Steele really felt about me.

By the end of that summer, Derek had yet to find suitable employment. Since his unemployment compensation had run out, he was surviving on what his parents gave him, and the money that I "lent" him. I was very generous with him because I loved him so much and because he was always in a good mood after I gave him some money. We always had such a good time, at least until the money ran out.

By this time, Derek had turned me on to smoking marijuana. This was an experience I thoroughly enjoyed from the very first time that I tried it. Therefore, it was never a problem that I ended up paying for all the pot. That was the only reason that I was allowed to continue dancing. Even Derek knew that I could not make the same kind of money with any other job that I was qualified to do. During this time, he promised that when he found a job, he would insist that I get a different line of work. Until then, he tolerated it. I had to contend with his sarcasm, rude remarks and evolving cruelty.

I don't remember the first time that he struck me. I do know that it was when we were alone. The public humiliation and abuse did not happen right away. We slowly worked ourselves up to that. I am certain that when we made up afterwards, he promised that he would never do it again. Of course, he did, and it tended to escalate.

After the first few slaps in the face, I tried to put up some type of defense, but this only made Derek angrier. The first time I actually struck out and hit him, I had to call off work for three days so that I could let the bruises heal enough for make-up to cover them. Still, I continued to accept his excuses and believe him when he insisted that I had forced him into doing it. After apologizing to him, I would promise to avoid upsetting him anymore. Then we would go make love.

By the end of the month, we were inseparable again. Our luck began to change, too. Derek obtained a position at a local factory. The starting salary wasn't too shabby and there was room for quick advancement. With the new job, his temperament improved somewhat and he became violent less frequently. We began to discuss moving in together. He could not understand my reluctance to move into his parents' home with him. I could not make him understand that I wanted to take care of him. I wanted to cook his meals and do his laundry and make the bed that we shared. I wanted to be able to scream and shriek in delight when we made love. Having to silence my cries of passion so as not to disturb his parents was disturbing to me!

He told me all that responsibility made him nervous. I pointed out that I would be sharing the responsibility with him. In truth, I felt that this little man was not quite ready to leave the security of his parent' wings. I felt that we were ready. I was not prepared, however, for what was to transpire the next day.

For the past several weeks, I had not been feeling too well. I figured I had some kind of flu because I was sick to my stomach and felt so dizzy all the time. Derek noticed that I was under the weather and tried to joke me into feeling better. Even though my period was late, I was not concerned because I had never been regular and did not really keep much of a record of it. The only reason I knew something was different was the fact that I had not needed to purchase sanitary needs for a while and I was enjoying the savings. Derek had agreed to borrow his parents' car and take me to my appointment at a local health clinic. However, that morning, we had another argument and he had stormed out of the house and took off, squealing tires for two blocks. We had argued about moving in together. Oh, we both wanted to live together. We just disagreed on where.

I believed that we should hunt for a small apartment and, with our combined incomes, we would be able to handle the financial requirements for our freedom. He insisted that now that he had a job, I could quit dancing. If I moved in with him at his parents' home, I would not need to work at all. Derek was not comfortable with the idea of his woman commanding a larger salary than his.

After his quick exit, I cried for hours. I knew that he would end up getting his way again. At this point, I did not feel well enough to put up much of a fight . . . Besides, I rationalized that it would not be for very long and at least Derek and I would be together.

Since Derek had not returned to my room by the time of my appointment, I had to call the health center and reschedule for later in the week. When Derek finally returned, it was like nothing had transpired that morning. He was in a jovial mood and even seemed playful. There was no mention of our fight and, of course, he offered no apology for making me miss my appointment. As a matter of fact, he had not even bothered to inquire about my present state of health.

That evening, without any further discussion between us, Derek told his parents that I would be moving into their home. He told them that I had recently lost my job and could no longer stay where I was. Without a struggle, they acquiesced to his demands. There was little enthusiasm in their reception of me, but I supposed this was due to the suddenness of their son's newest proposition.

The next morning, with no assistance, I assembled my personal possessions into a neat pile on the porch and waited for Derek to pick me up. It pained me to say goodbye to the Warners. There was also the matter of my work. Since I had plenty of time before he got off work, I decided to walk to "The Lazy Boy Lounge" and give Mr. Landis my notice in person.

Naturally, he was disappointed but he graciously consented to my departure. He even wrote me a check for a week's salary as severance pay, and extracted my promise that if I ever changed my mind I would come back and dance in his club. With a heart-felt embrace, I assured him I would do so and before my tears started, I turned and walked away.

Mr. Landis had to have been aware that Derek's insistence was the real reason I gave up my dancing. He had seen numerous displays of his disapproval of my line of work in the Lounge. I understood now that it was because of concern for me that he never had Derek thrown out of the bar during one of his tirades. I knew I was walking away from a very important friend.

For the next month I became little more than a slave. I did all the household chores around the house as his mother presided over all aspects of each separate duty. She was like a slavedriver. Even his kind and quiet father left a list before he left for work, odd jobs around the yard that I could do for him. After doing all these tasks, I had very little energy by the end of the day. No one in the house had any idea how weak and sick I felt almost constantly. I did my best to hide my illness from these people. I was grateful for their hospitality and made every effort to live up to their expectations.

Of course, Derek expected us to be intimate when he got ready for bed. Luckily for me, even in my weakened state, he was capable of exciting me and I always tried to make these encounters special for him. He was ever increasing in his sexual demands and, after each session, I found myself completely spent both physically and mentally.

By dawn's first light, he was always ready to go for it again and, of course, I complied. He took each hesitation on my part to engage in sex as an affront to his manhood or even a lack of fidelity on my part. With this in mind, I never denied him when he gave any indication that he wanted to make love.

After all this time, I still did not feel any better. Finally, I convinced Derek that I should keep my appointment at the health center. I told him I probably just needed some vitamins or something and I would be as good as new. I assured him that it would not cost him anything since it was a free clinic. My appointment was for that evening. I needed to keep this appointment, otherwise I would have to wait almost another week before I could see the doctor.

I was flabbergasted when I asked Derek, after his long workday had ended, if he could take me over to the clinic and he consented. He waited in his mom's car while I went in. I prayed silently that he would come in and sit with me while I waited. Even though he stayed in the car, I was still very grateful that he drove me there. I walked in slowly and gave my name to the receptionist. She handed me some standard forms to fill out and I carried them over to a nearby chair, removed my coat and sat down.

While I completed the paperwork, my nervousness increased. So, too, did my nausea and dizziness. I took several deep breaths to keep me steady. Before too long, I had the questionnaires done. As I handed them to the receptionist, she informed me that the doctor could see me now. On wobbly knees, I followed her into an examination room. She instructed me in the normal routine and within minutes I was sitting on the exam table waiting for the doctor.

When he arrived, it was a pleasant surprise that Dr. Lacey turned out to be a woman. For some reason, most of my apprehension left immediately. She was kind and gentle and thorough. After my check-up, she instructed me to wait in her office and she would come back shortly and review the available lab results and clinical findings with me.

The minutes slithered by like hours as the fancy timepiece on the doctor's desk ticked the seconds away. Even in the air-conditioned office, the sweat flowed down my sides from my armpits on that summer afternoon. Nervous fingers fidgeted with the knots on the strap of my purse. I took a couple of deep breaths and tried to reassure myself. What did I have to be nervous about, anyway? I needed some vitamins and maybe something to control the nausea and dizziness . . . maybe a shot of B-12.

When Dr. Lacey walked into her office, she was smiling. I immediately relaxed a little. I reasoned that she would not be smiling if I were dying of cancer or some other fatal disease.

"Well, Tarah Lindsay, let's see what is going on with you," she began with genuine concern in her voice.

She opened the file that she had been carrying when she entered the room. She silently reviewed the information for a bit. At one point, she glanced up and studied me rather pensively. Without a word she returned her attention back to the file.

After a few more minutes, Dr. Lacey looked up to me and said, "except for the fact that you are somewhat underweight at this point, I see no reason why you won't be able to deliver a healthy, happy baby in six or seven months".

I sat there dumbfounded. Pregnant? Me? Now? Why? Meanwhile, the doctor continued her spiel, " . . . Of course, we will need to run a few more tests but there seems to be nothing out of the ordinary at work here. I can give you some medicine for the nausea, but that should disappear shortly on its own. Do you have any questions, Tarah?

From what time warp had she materialized? Did I have any questions? Yeah! 'What was I gonna do' seemed like a good place to start. I had so many notions floating around in my head that I could do nothing but lower it and give her a negative shake.

"I'll give you some prenatal vitamins and you must become more aware of your nutritional needs", she continued. "I'm sure most of your recent weight loss is due to your morning sickness, but it is important to take in suitable nutrition during your gestation period. Speaking of period, it would help us pinpoint your due date more accurately if you had a better idea of the timing of your last one. Well, when you're feeling better and are further along in this pregnancy, we'll send you for an ultrasound to determine the age of the fetus. Until then, my receptionist can give you another appointment. I'll see you in about a month and we'll see how you're doing at that time."

With that, I knew that I was being dismissed. She had said what any good doctor should have said during an initial visit. I got up and walked to the door as I murmured my appreciation.

How should I break the news to Derek and his parents? I wondered how he would react to the idea of becoming a father. Amazingly enough, as much as we made love, we never discussed the possibility of making a baby. I had no idea how he felt about having children. We just never discussed any of this. Now, we would have to discuss it. However, now it would not be just speculation. We were going to have a baby! With the unexpected jolt of excitement, I crossed the torrid parking lot and slid into the front seat, next to an obviously angry Derek. His sweat-drenched shirt was proof enough to me that he had waited too long in the heat.

"Sorry for taking so long. They were sort of busy," I offered.

"Yeah, yeah, yeah, . . . so what the fuck's wrong with ya, Bitch. You better not have given me nothin'," he snarled.

"I haven't given you anything yet, but give me time," I quipped.

'Derek was in no mood for my levity.

"Now what's that supposed to mean, you goofy bitch? I ain't got no time for none of your stupid, fucking games. What the fuck took ya so long? You and the doctor playing some kinda hanky-panky in there   thinking it's funny that I'm out here sweating my ass off?"

By this time, he had worked himself into an irrational frenzy. He grabbed a handful of my hair and, with a quick and furious tug, my head went crashing backwards into the window and then forward into the gearshift. My nose began to bleed.

"No, Baby! I love you. I will always love you. Please, just listen to me for a minute. I want to show you how much I really love you," I cooed.

At least he had stopped momentarily, so I continued in a soft, soothing voice, "I love you so much that I don't know what I'd do if you did not want to see me anymore. You have to know that I would do anything for you, Derek."

I reached over and began stroking the wisps of hair behind his ears and added quietly, "I'm pregnant, Derek."

After a noticable pause, he asked, "Whose is it? Do you know?"

I felt like I was undergoing open-heart surgery without benefit of anesthesia. With tears spilling over my lower lashes, I queried, "How could you even think of asking me that? I've been with no one since our first time together. You know that! I fell in love with you the first time we met and I want to spend the rest of my life with you. How could you possibly ask me if I knew whose baby this is?"

"Hey, slut! You weren't no virgin or nothin' the first time we met and you weren't too tough to coax into my rack. So I figured you never was too tough when a healthy cock was around . . . and seeing how I got a pretty healthy cock, I figured you might not be too tough to have around for a while."

This verbal assault left me stunned. Nonetheless I knew that he would eventually come around. I pleaded with him to believe me when I vowed that this child that had already formed inside me had been conceived in love . . . the love that we shared. It was just a lot for him to accept at the moment, but I knew that he would warm up to the idea of fatherhood, once he had time to consider it. We rode home in silence. My nose still hurt but the bleeding had stopped, so I tried to make myself more presentable before we got to the house. When we got to the house, Derek ushered me quickly into his room and told me to wait there until he came back.

"Where are you going?" I asked.

"I'm gonna tell them, you asshole. Where the fuck you think I'm going?"

"Don't you think I should be there when they find out that they are going to be grandparents?" I thought of that as a family moment and I wanted to be part of it.

Suddenly, Derek wrapped his arms around me in a tender embrace and whispered, "This is for real, right? You're being straight with me about this baby thing, right? There is a living baby inside you that is my son or little girl. Tell me the truth, Tarah. That's all I want is the truth."

"Oh, Derek, darling! I love you so much that now I can offer you my most precious gift . . . your very own child. Our child! Don't you see that this child is a product of this special love that we share? Soon, we will be able to share our love with our wonderful, new baby."

Before I knew what was happening, we were under the sheets sharing more of our love. I was deliriously happy. Derek had accepted the pregnancy. He was showing me how happy he was and how much he loved me with each thrust of his savage member. As always, his lovemaking was hard and furious. I found myself completely spent after such sexual fulfillment. I must have dozed off. The next thing I remember was Derek taking me again.

From the shadows on the wall, I knew that it was almost sunset. I must have slept for hours. I knew that dinner was over. What a shame! For the first time in weeks I felt hungry. As usual, when Derek touched me, my body responded. I fell back limp and quivering after my climax, just in time to appreciate Derek's moment of ecstasy inside of me. Afterwards, I relaxed for a while, appreciating his nearness. I was so utterly exhausted that I probably would have fallen asleep again if I hadn't been so damn hungry.

As if reading my mind, Derek said, "Let's go get something to eat, I'm a starvin' Marvin".

"Good idea! I'm hungry, too."

"This will give us a chance to talk," he added.

I got the feeling that there had already been a lot of talking done on the very subject that we were about to tackle.

"I take it you already told your parents. How did they react?" I asked cautiously.

"Not too bad. Dad wants me to do the right thing. Mom thinks you should have an abortion. How would you feel about that?"

For the first time in a long time I was angry, and I fired back, "An abortion? Are you nuts? Even if you don't choose to believe it, this is our baby! Yours and mine! Now your mom wants us to kill it . . . just murder our wonderful baby. I can't believe you even thought about it for one moment."

I was absolutely livid. I really could not believe that Derek would have even contemplated such a heinous idea. He was suggesting ending the life our love had created before it even had a chance to live.

With his usual cavalier attitude, Derek interjected, "Yeah, Dad didn't like that idea much, either".

"What about you, Derek? How do you feel about all this? Knowing in your heart that this child has your blood flowing through its tiny veins, what do you think about it? What do you think about us having a baby? What do you think about me?"

At this point, my rage turned into pain and fear. What if Derek could not accept the baby as his, or did not wish to take the responsibilities? This simple question caused my heart to hurt . . . like being pierced with an ice pick! What if I had to raise this child all by myself? I knew how tough the world could be on someone who was vulnerable. I trembled at the thought of how very vulnerable this baby would be with me as its only parent.

Once again, Derek broke through my reverie with his response. With characteristic nonchalance he crooned, "Baby, baby, baby! Take a chill pill and cool it. Nobody's gonna hurt the baby. Now, nothing's definite yet, but we might have a place to live . . . on our own. When Grandpop died last year, it seems he left my dad a house down in the boonies. It needs some work but Pop said we could stay there for nothing, if we were willing to fix up the place. So, see? We have somewhere to be together . . . like a family. You and me . . . and baby makes three," he giggled.

I did not know what to say. Here I was going on and on in my mind about Derek not wanting this baby and here he was getting us a place to live. He had called us a family! My heart began to sing.

Derek walked over to me and held me close. "Relax, Baby! Things always work out for me. Just trust me!"

"Oh, Derek! I do trust you. Honestly, I do. I love you so

much! I'm so sorry about earlier . . . for yelling and getting myself so upset. Please forgive me. I'm really sorry," I cried.

"No problemo! Mom told me that pregnant women act nuts sometimes. It has something to do with their hormones," he laughed.

I capitalized on his good humor. "Oh, so now I'm nuts, am I?"

I turned around and pushed him backwards. We tumbled onto the bed together and rolled around and giggled and tickled each other. Here I had a definite advantage over Derek since tickling was second nature to me. Derek, on the other hand, was as ticklish as sin. As our bodies writhed among the bedspread and pillows, the proximity made us both aware of the heat flowing between us. Once again, we enjoyed the physical aspects of our relationship. Afterwards, while panting in each other's arms, we casually agreed to go get something to eat and off we rode "into the sunset".

The next two months were spent at Derek's parents' house. I still did all the cooking and cleaning and laundry for the family. Under the watchful eyes of his mother, I kept the house clean and the family well fed.

Without exception, Derek and I made love every night. Sometimes on his days off, and even when he worked, like during his lunch hour, we could easily entice each other between the sheets in the middle of the day. His lovemaking was as demanding and furious as ever. I thought, maybe I was becoming addicted to his sexual appetite. Oh, well! At least it was free and legal. So where was the problem with that?

While we stayed with his parents, Derek's treatment of me improved. His father would not tolerate any physical demonstrations of anger. He really wasn't thrilled about it when Derek and I exchanged heated barbs at the top of our lungs. I was always blamed for these loud encounters. However, during these passing months, we tried to settle our differences in a more amiable manner.

My appointments at the health center were important to me. The doctors there kept records of my weight gain and did blood work to keep tabs on my health. Dr. Lacey was still concerned after my third visit, because my due date was still up in the air. She estimated that I was almost five months along and she recommended that I get an ultrasound before my next scheduled appointment, to pinpoint my date of confinement. Otherwise, I was progressing well in this pregnancy. Although my weight was below the norms set by the American Medical Association, since my morning sickness had subsided, the doctor assured me that this would no longer be a problem.

Since I had no medical insurance, I was constantly worried about the costs of various aspects of my care. Dr. Lacey informed me that all tests ordered by the staff of the clinic would be paid in full. She ordered me to stop worrying and enjoy this special time in my life.

That night, Derek and I shared the news of the day. I related the occurrences of my clinic visit. He seemed as anxious as I felt about the need to have an ultrasound, but he shared my happiness with the doctor's report that my health, and that of the baby, was good.

He was absolutely bubbling when he told me that we could probably move into the "hut" by this weekend. Even though I had never seen it, I was also quite excited about the move. This would allow me to become the woman of my house. I was anxious to begin my duties of playing "wife" to Derek. I would be able to clean the house the way I wanted and even be able to rearrange the furniture without getting permission from every person in the house, in triplicate. I could plant flowers and shrubs in my yard anywhere I wanted. I would finally be able to walk around the house without dressing like a monk.

The following Saturday, I caught my first glimpse of the hut. I was totally unprepared for the reality. I had envisioned a cozy, serene cottage on the edge of the woodlands with flowered paths and a white picket fence. Wrong!!! The picket fence of my fantasy was, in actuality, an eight-foot high cyclone fence with barbed wire encircling the top perimeter . . . like a prison.

The cottage was even more of a disappointment. It was little more than a shack. There was only cold running water and it dribbled out of the faucet, a murky, odorous liquid that required boiling before consumption. The toilet worked by pulling a rope attached to the tank above the bowl. This allowed the water to flush the system. There had been nothing done to modernize the kitchen for more than thirty years. At least, everything worked, including the wood-burning stove that was the focal point of the kitchen. This should prove interesting since I had never even cooked on the bar-be-que grill before, let alone over a wood fire.

Derek assured me that we could get this rattrap fixed up and it would make a nice home for us. At least his enthusiasm was contagious. Soon, we were picturing our little castle with a new coat of paint and some "minor" repairs. We decided to move in tomorrow.

The next day, I got up early and started getting my meager possessions packed into boxes. Derek joined me a bit later and began sorting through his stuff. He was only going to take his clothes and a few sundries. This eventually turned into a mile-high mountain of junk, packed into what looked like three hundred boxes.

Brian had borrowed his father's truck for our move, and was waiting for us when the packing was done. The only furniture we had to take was Derek's bedroom set and a couch and an old dinette set from the basement. While I started to carry the boxes out to the truck, Derek and Brian made a beer run. Two and one-half hours later, they returned to see that all the boxes had been loaded onto the truck and all they had to do was plop the large, heavy items on top. After lunch, we made off to our chalet.

By 4:00 p.m., the truck was unloaded and both guys were not. I encouraged Brian not to drink too much before driving home, and this sent Derek into a frenzy after Brian left. He told me to mind my own business and stop telling his friends what to do. When I tried to explain that I did not want his friend to get into an accident, it simply made him madder. Since he was heavily intoxicated anyway, he went off into one of his tirades and slapped me hard.

He made the situation clearer by adding, "Now that we're in my home, I don't have to put up with my dad's bullshit . . . or yours. If you get out of line around here, I'll do what I have to, to keep you in your place. So watch your mouth, Baby, or I'll watch it for you! Now go get me another beer . . . please!"

I decided not to argue with him while he was like this. I was exhausted from all the lifting and carrying and had not had anything to eat since lunch. I just wanted to go lie down. I started walking to the bedroom, when suddenly I was being pulled back by my hair. Losing my balance, I fell to the floor. Derek grabbed me up and slapped me around until my head was spinning.

"Now go get me my beer, Sweetheart," he ordered.

The truculent sneer that I saw on his face stopped any further dissension on my part. He ordered me to lie on the couch next to him while he drank it. He told me to play with his cock and make him feel like a man in his new home. I did as I was told. Soon we went into the bedroom and, as always, we had sex. I fell asleep with tears falling from my eyes on the first night in our new home. "Home Sweet Home!"

CHAPTER 23

THE GLOOM

Hey, Mr. Machine! Did you miss me? Well, I was in the hospital again. I try not to complain too much. It just seems to make me more miserable and upsets everybody else. Besides, before this bout, it had been slightly over a month since my last admission. I was gonna have David bring you in so that I would be able to "discuss" different things with you.

At first, I was too sick to discuss anything. As my strength returned, I kept assuming that I would be discharged within a day or two. It would have been a lot of trouble to go through for so short a time. So I kept delaying David from bringing you in here until I got discharged . . . and here I am. Before I got sick, I was telling you of my intriguing relationship with Derek Steele.

The months that followed that first night in our home became a confusing web of cruelty and fear and attention and remoteness and pain. My life had become a fragmentation of reality and nightmares, and often the reality was worse.

I became increasingly aware of Derek's uncontrolled hostility during this time. His demonstrations of his absolute power over me escalated in frequency and intensity. What made it even more frightening to me was the randomness of their occurrence. Derek's moods became more sporadic and less predictable. Sometimes, the slightest thing could provoke his tantrums and it was me who suffered the physical and verbal abuse.

Fortunately for me, the bruises were easily hidden by a bit of make-up. Some of the emotional scars were to last for the rest of my life . . . at least, up to now. The mental cruelty that I endured throughout much of this time did indeed twist my outlook on life and my own self-image. This led to some significant changes in my future behavior, and in the general direction my life took. During this time, however, most of this cerebral stuff was clouded from my view, by a few scattered moments of tenderness, and many episodes of unlimited, unbridled sexuality.

It seemed from early on that Derek was awed by the idea of becoming a father. When the ultrasound revealed that I was carrying his son, Derek's boundless happiness was obvious and genuine. I actually found him reading an article about the importance of the development of a child's potential during early childhood. Occasionally, he would even hold me tenderly in his arms and shared his hopes and dreams of his son's future with me.

When he returned from the supermarket with the week's groceries, there was always adequate fresh fruits and vegetables and plenty of milk. He understood the importance of proper nutrition during pregnancy.

He also understood the dangers of my smoking and my pot use during pregnancy and quickly forbade me to indulge in either activity. This was easily accomplished, since he controlled all the money and decided how it was spent. While I realized his motives behind his edicts during my pregnancy, I thought him insensitive for continuing to smoke pot and do crank with his friends in our home . . . right in front of me. He even teased me about it in front of his friends.

During my second trimester, Derek began to drink heavily on a regular basis. When he reached a certain intoxication level, he seemed to lose any and all inhibitions and made crucial errors in judgement. He frequently missed days from his job and went to work with a severe hangover on more than one occasion. It did not surprise me when he came home one afternoon and announced that he had been laid off due to absenteeism.

"This could be what we need . . . a time to get to know each other again."

Derek's sincerity poured over me. There was definitely something about this little man that sparked some simmering embers under the surface of my consciousness. When he pulled me towards him, he simply touched my hand and caused a pulsation that erupted from my midsection and spread in every direction at once. The gentle touch of his lips against mine melted away the bad memories and allotted room for the marvelous new ones that we were on the verge of making. These memories took the sting out of his attacks and made me reassess my conception of reality.

Our passion was genuine and homespun. Each time was a tapestry of sexual exploration and love giving. Both partners giving completely of themselves to make the other most fulfilled. Each chance we took in the arms, and at the feet of the other, cemented between the sheets of our bed, made it unthinkable that there could be any challenge that we could not overcome.

Eventually Derek seemed to be drinking all the time. Money was scarce since his job "snafu" but somehow he always seemed to have enough cash for beer and pot. He told me often that he made extra cash when the guys came over for poker. This was also occurring more frequently. During these poker sessions, Derek expected me to keep the cold beers and sandwiches coming. I generally paid little attention to the conversation at the table. My job was to keep the complaints down to a minimum.

It took me by surprise, then, to lift my eyes while doling out vittles and find myself the focus of their collected attention.

"Tell ya what, Derek! If you lose, I get to bite the buttons off of Tarah's blouse and taste the spoils while you hungrily watch me feast."

This good ol' boy had his lecherous eyes riveted on my bosom.

"For you to call would be one hundred dollars . . . And all I want is a taste."

Without hesitation Derek nodded his consent, "I'll see you and I'll raise you double or everything! If you beat my hand, as your hand is right now, you can have her to yourself for one hour."

I could not believe my ears. Here was the man of my dreams and he was betting his obviously pregnant lady in a card game. I watched, transfixed as his opponent stood in disbelief and pulled from his wallet two hundred dollar bills to cover his wager and began to make his way to my side while informing us that he had covered his bet.

"Wha'cha got, Mr. Steele?"

With appropriate smugness, Derek showed his cards, declaring, "My three queens are taking great care of their two kings. So I'll just gather up some of these presidential bookmarkers lying on the table and take my fourth queen and celebrate my victory!"

Before his fingertips had a chance to light on the pile of money before him, a swift hand prevented any contact and a spine-tingling chill blew through me as his voice broke the silence.

"With the four 7's dealt to me, I built the foundation for a tower, and now it serves as a temple to my new queen. For one hour, I transgress the limits of heaven and hell. I taste the nectar of the gods. All power over love and hatred are mine!"

With this simple prose having been spoken, he grabbed my hand and proceeded towards the front door. Instantly, I knew that we were heading to the cabin that this group used for a hunting lodge in the winter. Out of honor, the others would not follow. This left me the helpless prize in their insufferable games.

When I opened my mouth to try to ascertain his commitment to this fiasco, he ordered me to shut up. He said that it was part of his fantasy. For one hour, I was expected to endure the harsh treatment during the most humiliating experience one could imagine . . . and I was expected to endure it in silence. The only existing rule ensured that the baby's life would not, and could not be endangered. Other than that, anything goes.

The slimy trickster set his watch's timer as we entered the lodge. He tried the light switch but nothing happened. I silently thanked God for the darkness . . . and the imposed silence. I only had to endure sixty minutes of whatever and then it would be over.

He began to undo the buttons on my blouse, but he seemed to be extremely awkward. It was quite a long time, perhaps the blink of an eye, before I realized what was causing such clumsiness. He was biting the buttons off my blouse just like the original wager dictated. When these obstacles were no more, he began to investigate his booty.

His lips moved in an orderly and provocative trail over my breasts and there was no way that I could impede their reaction. His warm, wet tongue tasted my nipples and worked its way slowly up my neck. Following a carefully-planned blueprint, his tongue erotically explored my highly-sensitive ears. Soon, it hijacked my mouth.

I simply allowed all this to happen as I concentrated on the fact that Derek had sanctioned this from the very start. If I enjoyed any part of it, it would serve him right. After all, he was supposed to love me. How could he have offered me up like so much cattle?

The trickster continued his exploration of his conquest in the darkness. He slid his plump hand down my belly and rested in the thick, dark hair. With trained movements, he investigated my inner thighs and tickled my pubic area. Methodically, he repositioned himself and began sniffing my exposed genitalia. The sound of wanton passion escaped his throat and slowly he approached his waiting, quivering prey. He relished in his victory and quickly brought me to my climax. As he lowered his massive frame gently into position, he assaulted my feminine cavity until his own passion was spent. He then tumbled off the couch and glanced unceremoniously at the illuminated hands on his watch.

"Great! We still got some time left. Get up!" he ordered as he grabbed my arm roughly and pulled me to my feet. As he kicked the door open with his foot, the streetlight's powerful beam flooded that part of the room.

"You sure are a pretty little thing. Even in the darkness, I could tell how wonderful you are . . . and you smell good and you do what your man tells you. Yeah, Derek is a lucky man to have you for his squeeze."

During this smarmy speech, his hands were on my skin again. He cupped my breast and sucked my nipples with ferocity that gained their undivided attention once again. With controlled, rhythmic gyrations, he pressed his hips against mine and enticed his own desires up to the surface. He slipped his arms around my shoulders and lowered me to my knees.

Instinctively, I opened my mouth just as his penis touched my lips. With warm, salty tears coursing down my cheeks, I sucked his cock with an intensity that came from somewhere so deeply hidden inside us, that few ever gain access to that level of consciousness. The hot liquid from his orgasm announced the end of this nightmare. I swallowed the substance of his ejaculation along with the memory of the events in the darkness.

We dressed in silence and within minutes were rejoining the poker players once more. As I entered the room, a chorus of laughter broke out as the occupants of the room noticed the lack of fasteners on the front of my blouse.

"Did he bite 'em off, Honey?"

"Did he bite anything else off, like maybe a nipple or two . . . no wait . . . I see them! You still have your headlights on high beam, Toots."

I shook my head in disgust and walked over to Derek where I expected a warmer greeting than what I received.

"Go put something else on, Slut. We've got some talking to do later."

Without a backward glance, I turned and went to the bedroom. When changed I rejoined the crowd seated around the card table and remained their attentive hostess until the last loser left.

Derek's mood was nothing like I expected. His treatment of me when I came from paying off his gaming marker had led me to believe that he was somehow miffed at me. Knowing Derek as well as I did, this was not only possible . . . it was probable. However, here he was now, being sweet and gentle and funny.

We were walking towards the bedroom, arm in arm, like school kids. His words of love were like honey flowing to my heart. His sincerity caressed my emotions in a loving embrace and his body tempted mine. We exploded into jubilant convulsions of our passions until I lay passively in his arms.

Without preamble he began, "we gotta talk".

"I'm listening, Babe. What's on your mind?"

"You know when you were gone, the guys kept saying what a good woman you were to get me out of that jam I was in tonight. They think you're great . . . and they think you're great looking, too.

"Well, the guys know that money is hard to come by for us right now. And they've offered a way to help. I let them know that we wouldn't be accepting no charity. They suggested a way to get a little cash flow happening around here. We have the potential of raking in some pretty good capital, too. If I did not love you so much I wouldn't even consider letting you do something like this. I trust you or else I would never be able to ask you what I'm about to ask of you."

I felt like I was strangling . . . gasping for air. My lungs felt paralyzed. I was certain that my heart had stopped. Derek continued without noticing.

" . . . And they're willing to pay buku bucks just to touch you, and I'll be there, and you'll see, everything will work out fine."

In my shock, I nodded. My eyes were fixed on his and they gave no clue that there was anything amiss with his newest proposal. He intended to pimp me out and I knew that I would go along with his wishes. Don't you understand? I really loved this little man and nothing that he asked was I empowered to deny. Maybe I was addicted to him or something nutty like that, but I just wanted to make him happy in any way I could. He tried to convince me this could ultimately help us grow stronger in our relationship and make us appreciate our love for each other even more.

I had no idea what I was getting into. At any hour of the day or night, one of Derek's friends could breeze in with a fistful of cash and be allocated a portion of time in which I was designated a "toy". I never even saw any shortage of interested clients.

The one bright spot of this arrangement was that during this time, Derek was less likely to strike me with force and possibly leave a mark or bruise on me. Damaged goods did not bring in top dollar on any marketplace. This led him to come up with creative methods of punishment when I did not live up to his expectations.

At this point, Derek became enamored of bondage. I never had a clue as to where this interest originated, but whenever Derek deemed it necessary, he would tie me up somehow and leave me there alone to contemplate my sinfulness. At one time, I was left alone in restraints, fed nothing and allowed to remain in my own excrement for three day.

Derek had been prepared for the difficulties that this session would impose. My lower body had been encased in a large, plastic sack when I was first confined. This had been a novel embellishment to his previous bondage episodes. It did, indeed, lessen the mess that would have resulted without this precaution. When Derek finally returned, he dragged me outside, cut the stinking plastic away from my body and "hosed me down" with cold water. Almost as soon as I had been ushered back into the house, Derek informed me of the impending arrival of an important client and urged me to clean myself up quickly.

He made special chains that he inserted into my pierced ears and secured to various hooks that he had installed throughout the house to prevent my escape from his ruthless cruelty. He must have forgotten about the vicious dogs in the yard that prevented my going outside at all. Their gnashing teeth insured my imprisonment in my own home. Inside my home they posed no problem so long as I did not attempt to leave, or if Derek was there.

One evening, with pride he showed me the collar that he had formed with his own hands and he slipped it tenderly around my neck, fastened it to the bedposts and proceeded to make me his again. All through the night, he kept taking me and telling me how much he needed me. It became a real power trip for him.

When there was alcohol involved, his demands and ideation took a more bizarre twist. One night, during a poker game, it seemed like everyone came over half lit. Since the booze flowed freely at all these games, the players were quite inebriated early on. I tried to slip away quietly and unnoticed, but Derek noticed. He jumped up and grabbed my arm and pulled me into his lap as he sat back down.

"Where you going, Face? I got a present for you. I made them for you but I'll have to prepare you for the honor of wearing them."

In his outstretched hand I saw two dangling earrings. They were a lot larger than I would have chosen but they looked beautiful . . . like silver. There was a sturdy matching chain attached to each piece. I lifted my hands to my ears to remove the earrings that were in place, but two of his friends grabbed my arms. I was gently lowered to the floor and the pressure continued to hold my upper body pinned snugly to the worn carpet. I had no idea what was going on. Suddenly, Derek's face was above me and I instinctively relaxed. His friends continued to hold me fast.

"Baby, I'm doing this for us, forever. I'll try not to hurt you but if I do, it will only be for a few minutes then you will be mine forever."

The relief that had momentarily calmed me now gave way to true terror. My heartbeat was so rapid that I thought it would explode. Derek kept his eyes fixed to my face. Perhaps seeing my fear enhanced his experience.

He lovingly caressed my right breast with his left hand and brought his warm mouth down to my taunt nipple. He licked and sucked and teased it into a hardened, pointed pinnacle . . . a testament to his lovemaking skill. His sensuality almost neutralized the acrid situation in which I found myself. When he reluctantly pulled his mouth away he slid his right hand towards my captive breast. I noticed the shiny thing held tightly in his hand. The long thin piercing tool reflected eerily in the light. Suddenly I became aware of his intentions. My mind was racing . . . and unbelievably so were the dogs. They had been watching the foray unnoticed until this point. To them this appeared to be a giant wrestling match. They wanted some of that action. As they sprung onto the backs of my two assailants, Derek lost his balance and fell backwards. Using this heaven-sent interruption, I made my getaway. I quickly dodged into the bathroom, locked the door, dropped to the floor panting and began to cry. The sounds from outside the door continued for a long time, but eventually things quieted. Derek came to the door soon after that. His demeanor was drunk but repentant.

"I'm so sorry, Tarah," he sobbed. "I was only trying to complete our bond to each other. To my soggy, soaked brain this seemed like a good idea. To me this would have represented our becoming one."

At this point my terror had not quite abated and Derek's drunken state did nothing to dissuade my fears.

"Go away, Derek. Leave me be! You scared me tonight. Go away! Please! We'll discuss this tomorrow. Please go to bed and sleep it off. I promise you we will talk in the morning."

Through the door he consented, "I understand. I am so sorry, baby. Sometimes I am a big, stupid jerk. I'll see you in the morning. Please don't be too mad at me."

Resisting all temptations to race into his arms were repressed by my fear. That night spent on the bathroom floor was spent pensively contemplating my situation with Derek and my future. I felt trapped right now, but I knew that by the morning light things would return to normal.

Following this bizarre episode, Derek continued to be emotionally abusive but the physical cruelty noticeably lessened. Meanwhile, my time of confinement was fast approaching. As suggested by my obstetrician, I had had an ultra sound in my eighth month so we knew that our little bundle would be a male. Finally, it seemed that my delivery date was near. I was certain that Derek would react well to the birth of his son and I was ready for this pregnancy to end. I would soon become a mother!

That Friday, I became aware of some lower abdominal discomfort while I was preparing Derek's breakfast. He was up early as usual and was heading out. I did not see any need to worry him with my common complaints. Promising to be home before dark, he strolled out into the world while I remained trapped within a barricade . . . complete with guard dogs and chains. By this time the "savior" dogs were just a memory.

Early that afternoon, the discomfort shifted into pain. Intermittently, I walked or rested but no position allayed the agony that was growing within me. I was going into labor. A chilling terror gripped my heart. A wave of pain divided my thoughts, which cleared my head somewhat and brought logic into a leading role.

Since this was my first delivery, I could expect to spend several hours in labor. Derek was expected home in several hours, so I urged myself to relax. I tried to putz around and straighten up, but I soon gave in to the contractions and tried to appreciate what they were able to tell me about the progression of my labor.

I knew that frequency was important and mine seemed to be fairly frequent. One seemed to begin before I had a chance to forget the one that went before. By checking the clock at the start of each contraction, I was able to determine that my labor pains were occurring every ten minutes like (if you'll excuse the pun) clockwork.

There was really no reason for panic. This meant that I had plenty of time before I would have to take drastic action. Suddenly, I realized that I could not call the ambulance. The dogs would prevent anyone from infringing on their territory. The authorities would have to shoot the dogs in order to rescue me. I was sure Derek would not be happy about losing his dogs. No! I'd just wait for him to come home and then he'd take me to the hospital.

Miraculously, he called around six o'clock and said he'd be home shortly. I could tell that he had tipped a few, so I handled him carefully. The abundant background noise on his end made conversation difficult, but I let him know that I was in labor and he would probably have to get me to the hospital as soon as possible.

Our call was somehow disconnected then, so I replaced the phone in its cradle. I sat down and focused on the events about to transpire. Significant moments of a lifetime unfolded before my eyes in an effortless wave. I was thrilled that I was a catalyst in that tide of events and proud to share them with Derek. I was certain that he would return in time.

I soon learned that was not to be the case. Sometime after dark, Derek stumbled through the front door and tumbled into a heap on the bed. He never even noticed me or checked to see if I was all right. He headed straight to the bedroom. Slowly I made my way to the bedroom. He was sprawled out on the bed. He reeked of liquor.

"Derek. Derek," I whispered quietly. I gently touched his shoulder. "Wake up, baby!"

There was no response.

"Derek. Baby, please wake up. I've got to get to the hospital. I'm in labor," I whispered a little louder and gently shook his shoulder. "Derek, get up. Please! Get up. This is IT! Your son is coming."

Still no response.

I knew from experience that Derek was lost to the world. In this condition he was able to sleep through anything. I knew better than to waste my time and energy. Besides I seemed better able to cope with the progression of my labor, and to me this signified that all was well.

"I've waited this long," I thought aloud. "I'll be fine until he gets his head together a little bit, then he can get me to the hospital."

After a cup of hot tea, I made my way back towards the bedroom. As I passed the couch, I heard the splash. As I lowered myself to the couch, I felt the wetness. I knew that my water had broken and that all I could do was wait there and silently endure the pain until he woke up. At least Derek was a morning person. I fell into a fitful sleep while waiting for him to get up. My labor steadily progressed through the early morning hours.

Just after dawn, Derek got up and immediately knew that something was going down. He helped get me ready for my trip to the hospital. My pain was almost constant. I was barely conscious. He kept trying to apologize on the drive to town. Finally, I told him that if he didn't forget what happened right now, I would ban him from the delivery room.

"What happened?" He joked.

I loved this little man so much and it thrilled me to know that I was about to present him with a son. When we arrived at the emergency room, they immediately directed me up to the maternity floor while Derek went to the admissions office.

By the time I saw Derek again, my recently donned hospital gown was drenched with sweat. My contractions had increased in frequency, duration and intensity. That had to mean something. Right? I couldn't wait for the fucking pain to stop. Doctors, nurses and lab techs flitted in and out. Under their pleasant façade, I detected traces of worry and fear.

When Derek found his way up to the "birthing room," I was in a panic. I had no idea what was going on but something was definitely wrong. I sensed that they had turned off the alarms on the machines. When they fastened the wires to my swollen abdomen, I was unable to hear the expected heartbeat of my son. It was probably just the stupid machine not working. Maybe the heart rate was too fast and they did not want me to worry about it. I could handle that. Derek went in search of the clinic doctor, promising to return with some good news.

After three serious contractions had passed, Derek entered the room. The doctor and nurse closely followed him. Doctor Lacey reached for my hand and I noticed the tears in her eyes before she jerked her face away. Oh, God! Derek had tears in his eyes, too. What was wrong? Before I could formulate this question in my mind, a searing pain bore through my stomach. My focus returned. My thoughts raced even faster than my heartbeat. Had

they forgotten about the baby? Hey, I could take a little pain. I'd
be okay! Hang in there with me, you guys!

"Tarah, the nurse has to give you a little medicine, but she
can put it in your IV. This way, we can save a little wear and tear
on your butt," stated Dr. Lacey even as she nodded her go-ahead
to the attentive nurse.

Within seconds, calmness overtook me. Although not strong
enough to eradicate the pain, it managed to make it less of a focal
point. Why were they giving me pain medicine, anyway? After all,
wasn't the pain just a natural part of labor? I wanted to experience the
pain. I did not want anything to hurt my baby. Wasn't it better to
have my baby naturally if at all possible? Then I heard . . .

" . . . We are unable to detect fetal heart sounds or movement,
Doctor. There appears to be meconium in the fluid. This doesn't
look good. Watch her vitals! There's little doubt as to . . . "

Too soon, it became all too clear. They were discussing my
baby. My baby had died before I could give him life. I could
almost hear my dreams shatter as they fell from my heart. My
belly still held my dead baby. I would have to deliver my dead
baby. Once again, I tasted the salt of my tears. Now, more than
ever, I needed Derek's strength and his protective love. In my
weariness, I searched the room for his face. I found only emptiness.

"Where's Derek," I croaked.

"I sent him to the visitor's lounge because you both need
some rest. I'll have the nurse give you some additional Valium so
we can get through this with as little anxiety as possible," Dr
Lacey replied.

"I don't want any more medicine. I want to be aware of what
is going on. And I want to be here for Derek," I insisted.

"Tarah, there is no need for you to endure the pain. There is
no way to predict how long this will take. I don't want to do a
C-section at this time since you are so young. If we proceed
cautiously, there is no reason why you won't be able to deliver
dozens of healthy infants naturally."

"This is our son, Doctor. I will deliver him with dignity and
love," I pleaded with unspilled tears in my eyes. "Finally, I will

have to give him back to God, but these precious moments will be ours, forever. No one will rob me of them."

Six excruciating hours later, I delivered my eight and one-half pound son. He was a beautiful child even in death. Doctor Lacey allowed me time alone with my baby. She explained that this would engrain the fact that my baby was dead, and thus help me in dealing with the resultant grief.

I had to endure all this alone. Derek had left hours before, even though he had been told of my decision to tolerate the experience of delivery without narcotics . . . just so I could be there for him . . . in case he needed me. He left a message for me that he would see to my impending discharge in the morning. The doctor felt that I would be better able to grieve outside the confines of the hospital setting.

So I sat and held my dead baby in my arms. I held his little head carefully cradled safely in my palm. I cried as I whispered my broken dreams to him. I prayed that God would protect my baby until we were reunited for eternity. I trusted in his love and his mercy. I memorized his features and kissed him gently on his tiny lips before handing him over to the nurse who waited unobtrusively nearby. This same nurse returned to my room later and suggested that I allow her to give me something to help me sleep. I readily accepted her offer.

By 10:00 a.m. the next morning, I was up and ready to go home. I patiently awaited Derek's arrival. Meanwhile, the nurses were at their station, drawing straws to determine who would break the latest round of devastating information to me.

It seemed that Derek had returned during the night and left two large boxes at the nurses' station. Inside these cartons he had hastily thrown all of my clothes and personal items. He informed the nurses that he never wanted to see me again and that I should stay away from him and his family. He blamed me for getting his hopes up, only to dash them into bits when the baby died. He promised them that if I tried to contact him he would involve the authorities. He told them that he thought I was evil . . . possibly possessed.

My nurse, Miss Chris, reassured me and vowed to have a social worker stop by to help me sort through what was left of my life. She was a tower of strength as she attended to the torturous task of finalizing the arrangements for my son's funeral. She was my sole source of comfort as we stood in the dreary drizzle and witnessed by final goodbye to the little boy that was to have been my son. Her understanding and compassion guided me through the sorrow that threatened to overwhelm me. On our ride back to the hospital, she allowed me to cry without interference. It felt so good to cry openly for my dead baby. When we got back to the hospital, she gave me my discharge instructions and kept everything progressing smoothly.

Within an hour after the ceremony, she had arranged temporary shelter for me, a ride there and enough foodstuffs to ensure my survival for several days. She had also made an appointment for me to talk to a therapist in the area. She said that she knew that I had a lot of grief to resolve and believed that a therapist could make it a little bit easier. Despite her valiant effort to maintain her normal professionalism, I noticed the tears in her eyes as she bade me goodbye and good luck. Before my tears started to fall again, I headed for the cab that would take me to the women's shelter.

After about a week, I left the shelter without leaving a forwarding address. On my own, I decided to skip the therapy bullshit and face reality. I re-entered the world with a new perspective and a new attitude. From now on, it was my life. My way or the hiway! If men became entwined in my life, I would control the situation. They would exist solely for entertainment purposes. They were here simply to be used in any way necessary and discarded when no longer wanted or required. That was how I was planning to operate. I liked the stronger, new improved me. I knew that I was beginning a brand new life, again, and I wanted to get everything that was coming to me . . . any way that I could.

CHAPTER 24

THE FANTASY

As I lay on this daybed suffering, mere months away from my own demise, I focus on that time in my life that it all began. If this virus is transmitted through the semen (so say the experts!) then I *should* have this disease. Christ! I'd fuck anything in pants for money and some pot. I may be paying for it now, but they sure paid for it then. They all paid!

Before I left the shelter, my counselor insisted that I take a few bucks "for a rainy day". She pressed five crumpled twenties into my hand, wished me well and left the room. I got up and moved to the front door, confronted with the sudden realization that a new life existed for me on the other side of that door. As I opened it, I knew that I would meet the challenge head-on. Using my God-given talents, I would create my own empire. I would have lots of nice things, quickly.

During the ride on the bus to a suburb of Camden, the fantasy evolved in my mind. I wanted to dance, again. There was just no way that I could return to "The Lazy Boy Lounge". I did not want to risk running into Derek. I had no idea what I would say to him if I did. I hated him with such a passion for abandoning me. I hated him in proportion to the level of passion that we had shared.

There was a rooming house a short distance from the bus stop, with a sign in the front window advertising a vacancy. As I entered the front door, a mousy girl who was on the verge of becoming a mousy woman greeted me. In a quiet monotone, she related the rates and the rules of the house. She ushered me through her lovely home and showed me the two available rooms. Both were nice but I opted for the ground floor site with the deck.

She introduced herself as Virginia. She told me that she had inherited her beautiful, cozy home from her mother when she died. She explained her need to rent out rooms to allay the expenses that home-ownership produced. She accepted my good jewelry in lieu of my security deposit and promised to return them when I would one day leave. I paid cash for the first week in advance. I explained that I would begin looking for employment first thing in the morning, pursuing several leads. After thanking her, I inquired about the name of a good eatery in the area. She rattled off a half-dozen locales in an unintelligible gush of info then suggested that she had plenty and would be pleased if I joined her. It was the first of many dinners that we were to share. Sometimes we ordered take-out and sometimes she cooked. We always had a good time when we dined together. Before she left me to unpack that first day, she told me to feel free to use the phone book in the hall. She thought it was a great source of useful information. She said, "You can use the phone, too. You can make as many local calls as you need to, for nothing". We made an arrangement for any other expenses that may arise. She gave me a set of keys and our conversation ended.

I began my attempt to seek employment the very next morning. I looked under "entertainment" in the yellow pages and found an agency nearby. When I called the number, a man who called himself Slim answered the phone. We arranged an interview for later that afternoon. I told him that I had some experience as a dancer in clubs down by the shore and he seemed anxious to meet with me as soon as possible.

Having spent extra time on my hair and make-up, I headed out the door with plenty of time to walk to the office complex where the agency was located. The large neon sign over the door announced the fact that I had arrived at The Studio Guild. Another sign directed clients to wait for the receptionist, who would be with them shortly.

I chose a stylish modern chair facing the window and tried to relax and make myself comfortable. Before too long, a young girl approached my seat and requested my name. I informed her that I had an appointment with Slim. She nodded her understanding and disappeared behind the wooden door from which she had just entered the lobby. Presently, she returned and ushered me into one of the inner offices.

"Slim will be with you in a few minutes," she said and closed the door behind her as she left.

I found myself seated in a small office without windows or fresh air. It had recently had an occupant who indulged in smelly smoking . . . maybe a pipe. The stagnant air hung in a murky gloom in the room. The carpeting was dirty and worn. The large desk was littered with papers and flyers and other "desk stuff" in disorganized clumps. Intermingled with that clutter were scraps of material, yards of assorted trimmings and scattered amongst it all were the various tools of the sewing trade. I had just started my observation of the exotic and invariably naked collection of artifacts around the room when one of the doors opened and in walked the person that I just knew had to be "Slim".

"Hi, Sweetheart. I'm Slim even though I don't look it. Welcome to Studio Guild. If you're looking to make a lot of money, you've come to the right place. Just looking at you, I can tell that there is definitely a market out there for your talents. Of course, I'll have to observe those talents and meter them out to the most lucrative markets. Can you dance?"

"I'd say so," I responded with more bravado than I felt.

"Come back here and I'll let you know," he countered as he headed for yet another door.

'This one led into a large room filled with boxes and racks of costumes. To one side was a large platform surrounded on three walls by mirrored walls. My entire being was drawn to the stage area. In the back of my mind, I heard him ask me what kind of music I liked and I replied airily that it did not matter . . . I could dance to anything. The sound started to fill the room and without realizing my movement, I headed to the stage. I began to dance!

The music flooded over me. The rhythm dripped of shades of disco. The floor reverberated with the steady, pulsating beats and my heart became a member of that percussive ensemble. Everything else faded. The dance became it all . . . to claim it all. I forgot about Slim. I forgot about my shyness. I forgot about everything except the dance, the music and me.

All too soon, it was over and the expression on Slim's face told me that he had not been disappointed by what he had seen. I was now, officially, a Studio Guild Dancer.

If I could make it, there was a shift available at a lounge up on "The Boulevard" this afternoon. Since it was within walking distance, I took the gig.

Slim asked me about costuming and I admitted that I had no dancing clothes with me. He said he could make me a costume right then and there. He directed me to a small cubicle that the girls used for changing when they came here to practice. I went in and removed my clothes. I came out of the "closet" and simply stood next to the stool on which Slim sat until he acknowledged my presence.

With a concerted effort, he slowly allowed himself to stare at my nakedness. His eyes drifted over my body as if he were trying to memorize the sections. At the touch of his fingers, my flesh crawled . . . and he knew it. He worked meticulously and in utter silence. Within ten minutes, however, I had quite an erotic outfit in my hands. Slim was, if nothing else, a consummate professional.

We quickly worked out the details of an informal contract and laid down a few basic ground rules. I was now officially a go-go dancer! My introductory charge was mutually agreed upon, at twenty-five dollars an hour, with a three to one split with the agency. If I counted tips, I could easily make over one hundred dollars, cold cash. For dancing?!? God, I loved this country!

I thanked Slim and rushed back to my room to get ready. I

spent the next two hours getting groomed. I washed and perfumed all of me and shaved everywhere except my eyebrows. I painted my nails and took particular care with my make-up. I was ready to rumble. My muscles ached to roar into action. My soul waited to escape. My emotions yearned to soar beyond the limits of reason. I wanted to dance!

I arrived early at the club to allow time to introduce myself to the owner, the bartenders and the other dancers. I was to dance through happy hour. This was sure to be lucrative in the tips department, too. Since this was to be my "premier" at this club, it was decided that I should perform last. While waiting for the other two girls to do their twenty minutes each, I got into the rhythm of the crowd and the beat of the music.

At the first strains of my favorite song at that time, "Every breath she takes", I made my way up onto the stage from the darkness of the wings. Slowly I began the *un*hostile take-over of my potential prisoners. With subtle and limited eye contact, I set the snares and with exuberant passion, I offered myself as both bait and coveted prize.

The music became my master. I could dance to any kind of music because I could feel and hear the rhythm, the melody and the words. Instantly, my mind would translate these images of light and sound and time into my particular body language. As the tempo of my songs increased, so, too, did my non-verbally diffused passion. The crowd watched in appreciative silence while I danced and thunderously showed their pleasure when each song ended. By the time my twenty minutes came to an end, they were mine!

For the next half-hour, I strolled through the crowd, savoring the adulation and garnishing a healthy collection of tips . . . small tokens of esteem that I could "take to the bank". I seemed to have some need for such incredible amounts of positive and pleasant attention. I was almost a bit sad when my shift ended, but I knew I had a new career. For the next eight months, I danced regularly at several of the nicer clubs and lounges in the area. I followed the rules and never caused any trouble. By adhering to strict, self-imposed budgetary limitations, I was able to purchase a used car. It was certainly no Mercedes, but for almost two years, it served as dependable, affordable transportation.

There were several ways to increase my fiscal potential if I used a little creative imagination. My friendliness could be encouraged in different ways. Since Derek's departure, my attitude about men had taken a turn for the despicable. They were a commodity to be used for whatever purpose one deemed necessary and then discarded like a used tissue. I thought that I finally understood what men wanted and, for a price, I was ready, willing and able to anticipate and accommodate these.

For almost four years, I shared all of me with these faceless men . . . all of me except my heart. This precious and vulnerable organ I kept tucked safely away in the recesses of my consciousness. I could share sweat and tears, affection and anger, teasing and comfort. I would offer anything but my love. These predetermined boundaries were known and understood by all participants.

Some of these sexual and profitable interludes lasted for weeks. Most, however, ended after an evening of teasing and pleasing. Throughout either, the principle priority was the acquisition of the almighty dollar. Each victim was siphoned in every overt and covert manner, to the level that would not raise any suspicion when the hour of my departure arrived. In return for the monetary contribution, these clients purchased my company and undivided attention for a given timespan.

Keep in mind that both my specific partner and I appreciated the mutual attention. Throughout our lovemaking, we were certain to exchange verbal pleasantries and these exchanges became subconsciously important to me. With both my dancing and my affairs, I became the recipient of many compliments relating to my body and my personality. While taking these verbal niceties with a grain of salt, I was able to plant in my mind the qualities and attributes that were important to men. If ever I were to align myself with only one special man again, I would use this ill-gotten data to keep him happy.

Without warning, my dancing career took an unforeseeable twist. Slim had decided to branch out his exotic gigs and he felt that Glitter was a natural. Tarah was the one he was worried about. She held a rather tight hold of her purse strings. Some capital would have to be invested for this venture to work. I knew that Slim was dying to be given reign to his creative talents. Working together, he and I were to put together one of the most happening exotic shows ever. By untightening the fiscal flow, I was able to give Slim a marked advantage in his search for an exciting and titillating costume that would match the adventurous nature of my dance choreography.

Since most of my gigs were bachelor parties, my dance was geared to that atmosphere. Trying to blend the right combination of erotica and sensuality in my dancing with a special mix of contemporary music and the magical, mysterious throws of my costuming, was a challenge that I thrived on. Each moment that I was "on stage" was meant to be exciting and provocative without degenerating into the slutty, dim-witted samplings of my competitors.

Special pains were taken to accommodate the bachelor party crowd. My agency's rates were kept sufficiently high to insure the proper clientele. Some of the most beautiful homes in Philadelphia, Cherry Hill and the surrounding areas were places where I was the entertainment. Always accompanied by a personal bodyguard (arranged by the agency), all financial transactions were completed prior to my appearance, which was usually a well-kept surprise. While I was cloistered in the most convenient waiting area, my escort would reinforce the ground rules and make the necessary arrangement for my pre-recorded music, as he tried to blend into the crowd.

To initiate the "show", the guy in charge, usually the best man, would isolate the bachelor, then get him to sit in a conspicuously-placed chair, facing his friends who had arranged for this. They were as anxious as he was to share in whatever was to come. The flames of lust and passion were being fueled by anticipation.

Softly, almost imperceptibly, the strains of music swirled up from out of the noise and excitement. The sweet melody began to take shape. Slowly, their attention was drawn towards the portal from which I was to make my entrance. The open staircase was the epitome of distinction and grace.

As Lionel Richie serenaded the crowd with his unforgettable "Hello", I made my appearance from the shadows, dressed in a long, flowing gown of yellow. Resplendent with a matching picture hat and gloves, I captured the bachelor's heart and hormones with a shy wave of greeting . . . "Hello".

This special joining of words and music lent itself deliciously to this type of gathering. To the endearing words of love, I lavished the bachelor with measured doses of flirtation and suggestive touching. Simultaneously, I would ensnare the curious crowd with my alluring, almost hesitant glances.

By concentrating my attentions on the single important individual, I actually increased their level of excitement. By the conclusion of the song, I had positioned myself at the knees of the betrothed, looked deeply into his eyes and whispered "it may start getting a little harder . . . to take".

Song number two was generally faster and hotter. I was still completely attired in my costume sans hat. Time to start "taking it off". One of my favorites for this portion of my show was "We Ain't Gonna Take It" by Twisted Sister. At this point in my show, I got my first chance to demonstrate my athletic dancing abilities and my seductive disrobing techniques. Through a languishingly long siege, I eventually stepped out of my "overgown". Naturally, beneath this I had layer upon layer of gradually decreasing material. Without the encumbrance of the long gown, I had the freedom to dance!

The next three songs afforded me the opportunity to get to know the crowd, while I peeled off various lingerie apparel. Alternating between fast and slow songs greatly enhanced my performance by allowing me a breather. "Alone", by Heart and "Girls Just Want To Have Fun", by Cindi Lauper were often included. If my gig was to be held down at the Jersey Shore, which was often the case, I would seductively instruct the boys in the special appeals of a "Jersey Girl" with Bruce Springsteen's help. By the beginning of the sixth and final song, I was still wearing pasties and a G-string. By then, the crowd was appropriately stimulated. On any given night, their teeth would be sweating!

My last song was always soft and gentle. "Lady, Lady, Lady" from the soundtrack of Flashdance, was a favorite. Eventually, attired only in my birthday suit, I would literally float through the crowd and around the room, trailing my yellow boa behind me as I made my exit. That was my gig!

While I was gathering up my carefully scattered articles of costuming, I graciously accepted the accolades from the appreciative spectators. Meanwhile, my bodyguard was arranging for the collection of tips and the possibility that additional services might be required. Most people would be amazed at the amount of money average guys are willing to dole out to obtain a quickie or blowjob in the name of friendship. My bodyguards kept any additional activities between him and me.

I'd wait a few minutes to see what offer my escort would propose, then I would simply decide if it would be worth my time and effort. More often then not, I would perform the requested service, for which I was well paid, and accepted their suggestion that I partake of the bounty of their table. There was always an assortment of good food, a variety of alcoholic beverages and an impressive sampling of controlled dangerous substances. Needless to say, I was receptive to all of the above in generous proportions.

Occasionally, I would do other types of gigs, such as birthday parties, graduations, or any special event. My show could be modified to any level of respectability, on a moment's notice. At a mixed party, I would seldom go past my G-string. It was a riot watching the reaction of those rich, uptight socialites to my body and the effect it was having on their menfolk.

I was so greedy then. Nothing meant more to me than money. With enough money, I understood that you could buy anything you needed or wanted . . . except what I wanted. The Beatles sang the truth years ago when they told the world that "Money Can't Buy You Love". Love was really what I wanted . . . to love and to be loved. Love was the only thing I needed. I yearned for that one-on-one kind of love that lasted forever. Love was what I sought but I ended up with money instead . . . a poor substitute.

Like I said before, at this stage of my life, I would have done anything for money. Hiding behind the security of my alterego, Glitter, I coasted through the facade of this vile direction my life had taken.

I can barely remember the blowjobs in some closet-sized storage room to some nameless, faceless jerk with a permanent hard-on. Almost totally forgotten are the quick fucks for the bucks with an inebriated, baby-faced bachelor who would not remember anything but the legend come tomorrow. Perhaps, I had only imagined the torrid glances, the drooling tongues and the bulging trousers. Maybe for Tarah . . . for me, none of it ever happened. Yeah, and maybe I'm not dying!

Hey, partner. There's the phone so I gotta go! Later, Dude!

CHAPTER 25

THE KNIGHT

Sorry for the interruption, Mr. Machine. That was a bill collector. Some eager beaver in the accounting department at the hospital came across an old bill with a balance that they thought I should take care of immediately. Yeah, right! I can barely afford a can of soup for dinner and I'm gonna worry about a bill from some institution. I really wish I could. I wish that I could just write them a check to cover the balance and be done with it. Hopefully, Charity Care will make this bill paid in full like they have done so often this past year.

The money that I *was* able to accumulate during that deplorable time in my life of whoring around lasted less time that it took to earn it. Who knows what would have happened if I had not gotten so devastating an ailment as AIDS? The acquisition of wealth had become of paramount importance to me. In my mind, the end justified the means.

Maybe no one can understand my need for the almighty buck. Maybe you won't be able to understand it unless you've been hungry before . . . I mean *really* hungry! I felt as if I'd been hungry all my life. Not simply a hunger for food, but an insatiable desire for a relationship that was mutually pleasant and redeemable. No one had really ever given me his heart or his soul. I wanted so desperately to love another as I wanted to be loved. Instead, I found comfort in comfort. My material possessions afforded me a cushion against the unholy, unkind world beyond my walls of protection. If I was going to live alone, I was going to be comfortable.

Working hard would ensure that I would never experience hunger again. There was serenity in knowing that I had a secure homestead where I could retreat whenever the world became too cruel for me. The most infectious bliss overwhelmed me upon realizing that I would never have to be dependent on anyone again. I could not imagine anyone who could lure me out of my web of solace. Then again, I could never have imagined anyone like Kevin Rhodes.

Slim had arranged for Kevin to be my bodyguard one night for a high-society gig in the Chestnut Hill area. The client had booked two exotic shows for some fancy affair and I was to share the bill with a new girl, Gem. We each had our own bodyguard and Kevin was to be mine.

Gem's bodyguard opted to drive, thereby relegating us to the back seat of the car. For the first few miles, I quietly assessed the man sitting purposely on the seat next to me.

If I had to choose one word to describe him, it would have to be burly. His thick crop of dark auburn hair rested comfortably on his broad shoulders. The lower half of his impressive face was covered with a close-cropped beard of the same coppery hue. His bright smile showed through when he grinned. Above it, his sensitive blue eyes remained fixed on something ahead and he continued to scrutinize his prey, undaunted by my visual investigation.

A strong, ruddy neck held his head high and proud. His shoulders were wide and seemed to pull at the seams of the well-made overcoat he wore. His chest seemed massive as it heaved rhythmically as he breathed. His waist had a tucked and tight appearance and his muscular thighs stretched the linen of his fitted pants to the limits. He seemed so serene in his stateliness.

When I had asked Slim who my bodyguard would be for the night, he told me precious little about Kevin. He assured me that he was a real nice guy. He explained that Kevin produced and directed shows for the local public station and had even done some TV work during the winter Olympics that were held the year before in upstate New York.

He had endured a painful divorce a few years ago in which he had lost almost all tangible assets. He now lived alone in a comfortable cabin on the banks of a tranquil lake. He had a college education and he liked to sail.

"So, you like to sail, huh? I asked in an attempt to start a conversation.

"Slim's been talking," he retorted with not even a sideward glance.

"I think I have a right to ask a few questions about the person in charge of protecting me."

"So you have, Miss," he stated as he turned his eyes towards me. Those eyes were so blue that it was certain that angels had selected small portions of a summer's sky specifically for that purpose. "But since I'm sitting right next to you now, you can ask me anything you deem necessary."

The darkness hid the sudden blush of embarrassment that his words caused. He caught me off guard with his polite bluntness. I was actually at a loss for words. As if sensing my discomfort, he discreetly changed the subject.

"So how long have you been a dancer, Glitter?"

The slight infliction when he stated my name had not gone unnoticed. Inexplicably, I felt slightly ashamed of my chosen profession . . . and he didn't know the half of it. Fighting hard to quell the sudden rush of uneasiness that I was experiencing, I quietly responded, "Ah . . . the exotic stuff . . . a couple of years. Before that, I go-go'd for a while".

Hoping that that would be the end of it, I feigned astonishing interest in the buckle of my coat. Kevin, however, continued unabashed.

"Do you enjoy it?"

"It pays the bills."

"How often do you work?"

How long would I have to continue to endure this inquisition? Why was he so curious and why were his innocent questions making me so uncomfortable.

"Often enough to pay the bills."

"Okay, you're right! It's really none of my business. Would you take it the wrong way if I told you that you look very nice?"

"How could I possibly take that the wrong way? Thank you kindly, M' Lord," I replied with exaggerated courtesy.

The faintest hint of a smile formed on Kevin's countenance. As quickly as the insidious discomfort had entered my spirit, now it was dissipating. I was beginning to relax a little bit and, who knows, maybe he was, too.

Suddenly the long ride to the gig did not seem to be quite so long. Gradually, a smooth, easy and most enjoyable conversation flowed between us. We covered quite a potpourri of subjects and found that what we were saying was not as important as to whom we were saying it.

With equal ease we imparted bits of information about ourselves. I found it so easy to share a tiny portion of myself with this sensitive, intelligent and witty person beside me. In a comparatively short period of time, we discussed literature, politics, music, sports and even the weather. We each listened intensely as the other one spoke. That back seat became a surreal setting for our banter.

Having no awareness of the passage of time, we suddenly found ourselves at our destination. The show went smoothly and the crowd proved to be quite the generous tippers. After the completion of my dance, I returned to the secluded area of the house where I had waited while Gem had performed earlier. I was somewhat surprised to discover that she was nowhere to be seen. Shortly thereafter, Kevin knocked softly on the door and called my name.

I opened the door slightly and inquired as to Gem's whereabouts. A curious expression flashed momentarily across his face. His total attention was directed towards me and he searched my face thoroughly for a reaction as he spoke.

"She's in the back with the best man. You're being saved for the bachelor."

His casual delivery of this message sliced through me like a sword. His casual acceptance of his perception of the situation stung deeply and left my insides in turmoil. Not understanding my own reaction, I felt a sudden need to blow his perception of the situation to smithereens.

"In that case, the lucky bachelor better not mind getting "sloppy seconds" because that's all that's available. Those little creeps couldn't borrow enough money in a lifetime to afford me."

"Could I?"

I was about to explode with conflicting emotions. Part of me wanted to laugh aloud at his apparent audacity. Another part wanted to lash out at his cruel attempt at humor. A third portion wanted to cry as a result of the pain that his remark caused me. Yet, a small inner voice wanted to simply say yes. The strangest thing was that I had no idea why his words had such an effect on me.

"Maybe." Wow! What a retort!

"Maybe?"

"Maybe you'd have to pay . . . and maybe . . . not." My voice trailed off to a whisper.

With astonishing speed for a man of his girth, he took my hand and gently pulled me towards him.

"Maybe?" he repeated more softly and continued to draw me closer.

I was mere inches from him. I could feel his body heat. I inhaled the scent of his cologne and his strength. With each step I took in his direction, my anticipation increased. Almost imperceptibly, our bodies touched. Without realizing it, I lifted my face to his and peered deeply into his captivating blue eyes. He lowered his head until our lips met. His kiss was gentle, warm and undemanding. I savored the moment. I also knew I wanted more, but was not about to break the spell. We both seemed reluctant to pull ourselves apart but the sound of Gem's approach made it mandatory.

I hurried back into the dressing room, gathered my personal gear, got redressed and before long, we were heading back to the agency. Kevin seemed involved in his own silent musings and I was dog-tired. Just as I laid my head back on the seat and allowed relaxation to engulf my body, Kevin started to speak.

"It was magic watching you dance. It was as if the music carried you away, and you allowed us to watch. I thought you were wonderful."

"Thank you, Sir! However, you were not supposed to be watching me dance. You were supposed to be observing the crowd. You know . . . anticipating problems and preventing them from occurring," I teased.

"I assure you, Dear Lady, that protecting you was always my highest priority. Surely though, you would not fault a person for marveling at the splendor of the Grand Canyon or puzzling over the mysterious smile on Mona Lisa. When a work of art and a natural wonder of the world merge their greatness, the result is spectacular in its beauty and depth. That is how your dancing affected me, Glitter."

I was shocked at the depth of his sincerity and the height of his praise. This dashing, sophisticated man was pouring his honest emotions out to me and I found myself speechless. Even as he looked at me as if awaiting my response, I was numb with ecstasy. I was aware of the yearning within me. My lips remembered his. They were hoping for an encore performance.

I remained silent, however. Afraid of breaking the moment, my thoughts remained unspoken. My hunger remained unsatisfied and my hopes remained unfulfilled. The oppressive silence was ear splitting.

By this time, we had arrived back at the studio. Slim was standing by the door and greeted us as we entered the office. It seemed that the client had already called him and thanked him for sending such a terrific, classy pair of dancers. After the social formalities were finished, I prepared to leave. Bidding them goodnight, I reached for the doorknob. Kevin's hand landed on top of mine and prevented my quick exit.

"Can I give you a lift, Glitter?" he asked demurely.

"No, thank you, Mr. Rhodes. I'll be fine. I appreciate your offer," I replied with equal deportment.

I walked out of the stuffy office and into the clear night air. Up until then, I had not noticed what a beautiful evening it was. The walk home was both invigorating and relaxing. My mind was spinning with thoughts and memories of the night . . . of the gig . . . of the dance . . . and of Kevin Rhodes.

The next morning, Virginia, my mousy landlady, awakened me with a message to call the agency. When I did, Slim informed me that he needed to talk to me ASAP. I hurriedly got dressed and started on my way. My thoughts were racing wildly. What was wrong? Had I messed up somehow? Maybe Kevin had mistaken my silence for nonchalance. Maybe he even thought that I had been intentionally rude. Well, we'd know soon enough since I was fast approaching my destination. Walking into the building, my thoughts were heavy with trepidation.

As I opened the door to his office, Slim greeted me warmly. His use of his pet name for me eased some of my tension.

"Come in, my little glitterbug. Sit down. I want to talk to you."

I took the proffered chair and a deep breath as I waited for some indication of what was to come. Slim's smile took on what could only be described as an angelic air.

"Well, well, well! Seems we have a gentleman in our midst," he purred.

I was totally confused and replied, "What are you talking about?"

"Kevin asked me if it would cause you any trouble with me if he asked you out to dinner."

"Why would that cause me any trouble"?

I was still totally unprepared to react to the question at hand. I needed time to think and, as expected, Slim was rattling on in his usual way.

"So he's asking me out to dinner," I interrupted. "What do you think, Slim? Think I ought to go out with him? You know him better than I do. You'd tell me if there was anything maniacal about him . . . wouldn't you, Slim?"

"Hey, I've known Kevin over twenty years. Every once in a

while, when he's bored, he'll call me and see if there are any exotic shows in the area that night. If there were he'd go as a bodyguard. He always does a fine job and usually leaves his percentage of the take with me for the dancer, since he certainly doesn't need it. Here's yours from last night. I must admit that this was the first time that he has ever shown the slightest interest in any of the dancers.

"I think you ought to go out with the poor devil. He really is an impressive guy. He said that he enjoyed talking to you, last night. You attracted him with your gift for stating the obvious in the most intriguing manner."

Arrangements were finalized and three nights later, I was preparing for my first date since . . . anyway, my first date in a long time, and the nerves were already wearing thin. Virginia was helping me dress, since I had suddenly become all thumbs. She seemed more excited than I did about meeting this Kevin Rhodes.

After our last meeting, I had confided in her about my intense feelings for this knight of my fantasies. Her quiet company helped allay some of the churning fear that was pulling at my emotional integrity. Her nimble fingers drew my hair up into the most enchanting style and after affixing the barrette amongst the shiny curls, she stood back to admire her handiwork. We were both so pleased with the outcome that we almost missed the ringing of the doorbell.

Virginia hurried to answer the door. When Kevin entered, you could hear an audible gasp of appreciation escape her lips. As I entered from the hallway, they turned in unison in my direction. Kevin looked marvelous in a dark blue suit with a white kerchief fastened handsomely around his neck. He looked like a modern-day captain of some Viking vessel. After the introductions and subsequent farewells, we departed.

We had dinner at an incredible restaurant in Center City, Philadelphia. The food was exquisite and the service was above reproach. Kevin ordered for me since I was unfamiliar with many of the items on the menu. We enjoyed a delicious red wine which he explained was made in Germany and which complimented the various courses with dignity and grace. I was too full to order anything from the bountiful dessert cart, but Kevin insisted that I choose something to take home.

As we slowly sipped our expresso and reveled in the sweet strains of the music, we settled into the easy conversation that had surfaced on that first ride to my gig. Through our discussions, he allowed me a glimpse of his sensitive and compassionate nature. I shared the depths of his feelings and the madness of his sense of humor. By the end of the evening, there was a definite bond that was forming between this Nordic adventurer and I. After walking me to the door, he gently pulled me close and touched my lips with his. The warmth of his lips drew me closer still and I threw my arms around his neck and insisted on more.

With obvious reluctance, he withdrew from my embrace and mumbled his goodbye. All at once, he turned to me and he whispered into the night air that he had had a wonderful time and, if I did not object, he would call me in the morning. After witnessing my nod of acceptance, he turned and walked into the night.

Upon entering the house, I was immediately aware that Virginia had waited up for my return. Even as I was removing my coat, she pressed me for details of my date.

"I can tell by your eyes that it went well. Did you enjoy yourself?"

I proceeded to tell her every tidbit of information that she requested. By the end of my monologue, we were both exhausted and headed for our rooms.

"You know what, Tarah?" She added before she entered her room. "I think you fell in love tonight!" She closed the door and left me alone with my thoughts. Of course, she was right but I could not allow myself the luxury of admitting that . . . at least, not yet.

The next several months passed in a dizzying whirl of unique and intriguing experiences. Kevin had the capacity to share his wealth of knowledge without assuming a superior air or talking down to his listener. We shared the museums of Philadelphia and the sunrise off Atlantic City with equal ease. He was a graphic encyclopedia of local trivia and yet never seemed staunch or stuffy. We played baseball at bar-be-cues and ate grilled chicken till we could barely walk. We took quiet evening strolls along the beach in Cape May after enjoying a relaxing walk through the Victorian offerings of this quaint, picturesque seaside resort. We paddled our canoe through the majestic scenery along the banks of the Maurice River. Even when we toppled our vessel and landed upon the jagged rocks on the bottom with our bare feet, our spirits were unflappable. Kevin took me to a professional hockey game and did his best to explain what appeared to be "lunacy on skates". He took me fishing and it was with Kevin Rhodes that I experienced catching my first fish. Naturally, I threw it back, but the fight was a thing of beauty.

Occasionally, we would spend quiet hours with Virginia, playing parlor games and musing over the world's situation. Frequently, one of us would have to play the role of devil's advocate, since we generally shared the same political views. This made for stimulating conversation in which we each contributed various perspectives on a number of topics.

Since our relationship was building in such a pleasant crescendo, I considered arranging a meeting between Kevin and my brother, David. Along with Virginia, we spent an entire evening with him dining on good food, drinking fine wine (thanks to Kevin) and talking up a storm. As David was preparing to leave, during his goodbye hug, he whispered how pleased he was to see me so evidently happy. I quickly assured him that my apparent happiness was genuine and that Kevin was my source of joy. He seemed quite impressed with Kevin and wished me luck before he left. After his departure, I was sure that it was right to allow Kevin to nudge deeper into my life.

Each passing week brought new surprises. We swam in the lake behind his home. One sultry summer night, we decided to go skinny-dipping. To feel the cool water against my body was intoxicating. The full moon lent an air of unrealism to our aquatic antics. We splashed about like carefree children and chased each other in wild abandon. We laughed and yelled and enjoyed ourselves that evening. Suddenly in the darkening world of water, our bodies touched and the spark that had ignited initially on the ride home from our first gig was rekindled in the tranquil embrace of the lake. The flame of our passion was about to engulf us and we were about to let it happen. Having kept our emotions to ourselves up to this point, we were ready to transcend previously set barricades and allow our passions to take over.

Kevin picked me up effortlessly in his arms and carried me into the house and into his bed. We spent the remainder of the night entwined in each other's arms, discovering the depths of our feelings towards each other. Kevin's body was as fit as my imagination had deduced long ago. His Viking image remained intact. Our lovemaking was natural and mutually satisfying. He made me feel beautiful and sensual. His skill and delicacy were obvious and well defined. He repeatedly took me to the heights of ecstasy. As I finally lay panting in his strong arms, he whispered, "I love you, Tarah. I've known it almost from the first moment I met you, but haven't had the nerve to openly admit it . . . even to myself, until this moment".

Without hesitation I cooed, "I love you, too, Kevin."

Through the darkness my lips sought his and, upon finding them waiting hungrily, began the passion once again. I felt no dread about admitting the obvious. I did love him and had since our first meeting. I was so pleased that these feelings were reciprocated. I was immediately able to offer a special place to him in my life and my heart. This was the man with whom I wanted to spend the rest of my life.

Over the next several months, we cemented our relationship. Kevin was awesome. He never had any problem with me dancing and he frequently accompanied me to various functions as my bodyguard. Naturally, my extra-curricular activities had stopped the moment of our first encounter. Shortly thereafter, we decided to move in together and he welcomed me into his home. My joy was boundless. I looked forward to sharing every aspect of my life with this surprising gentleman.

This pseudo-honeymoon atmosphere continued and even survived the arrival of my mother on the scene. After careful deliberation, we agreed that it was time to introduce her to the man in my life. As stipulated, Mother arrived without her husband since I had no desire to see him . . . my father. The evening passed without incident and my mother seemed happy that I had landed such a fine "catch". Since it had been years since we had seen each other, we both felt awkward. It had been David who made this meeting happen. It would take us time to repair our relationship. I never did tell her what occurred the night I left.

My life seemed destined to merge with Kevin's and we were both overjoyed at the prospect. However, I should have been more prepared for the forthcoming snafu. For as long as I could remember, whenever I was really happy, something always came along that had the potential to destroy my joy. This was to be no exception. Just after we moved in together, something developed that threatened the very essence of our unconfining union.

By now, I knew the initial signs and symptoms in a heartbeat. The nausea, the fatigue and the dizziness were undeniable and, without a doubt, heralded my pregnancy. Damn it! Just when I found myself in a meaningful entanglement with a one-in-a-million kind of guy, I found myself faced with yet another unplanned pregnancy. More remarkable still was the fact that I was happy about it. I was thrilled with the idea of having another child, especially after losing my baby a few years before. Besides, Kevin would make a wonderful father. Of that, I was certain. Now, the only difficult part was breaking the news to him. I confirmed my suspicion two days later after visiting a local doctor under a fictitious name. Later that evening Kevin and I were preparing for a romantic dinner. I felt that this would be an appropriate setting to inform him of my condition and check out his reaction.

"Kevin, . . . er . . . There's something that . . . ah . . . I . . . I need to tell you."

"Tell me anything, Sweetheart. I just like the sound of your voice in the candlelight," He replied.

"Baby, this is serious . . . "

"I can tell that by your beautiful face, Tarah. What's making you look so worried?" He stroked my face from across the table. "Tell me what's troubling you so that I can erase that frown and enjoy your smile instead. I know that you haven't been feeling well. Is that what's worrying you?"

"Well, sort of." I tried to control myself and plunged into it head-on. "Kevin, I went to the doctor's today. I may be . . . no, . . . um . . . that is . . . " I took a deep breath as I prayed in desperation. "Kevin, I'm pregnant!"

He seemed stunned by the news although we had used no type of contraception whatsoever at any time during our intimate moments. He simply said that he needed a little time to digest the whole concept of becoming a parent. Regrettably, he picked that moment to inform me that he had to take a short trip to Las Vegas on business, but he assured me that we would discuss this in great detail upon his return. How convenient!

As he kissed me passionately goodbye, he sauntered into the night air and was "Sin City" bound. A part of my heart was seized by anguish. What would I do if he refused to have anything to do with this child that our love had created?

In the past forty-eight hours, I had already grown quite fond of the idea of our expected blessing. Perhaps I had misread his signals. I hoped with all my heart that he would eventually become as enamored with the prospect of bringing our child into the world as I was. Relying on my intuition, I believed that deep down inside he would be thrilled by this new direction that our relationship was about to take. His unexpected, undefinable reaction was most certainly due to the suddenness with which he had had the entire situation "dumped" on him.

I waited anxiously for his thought-out response while he was away. It seemed like an eternity. What would I do if he was upset even after he had had time to get used to the idea? What if he could not imagine someone like me as the mother of his children? What if he did not really love me as he had professed? Yeah! I know . . . what if? . . . What if? . . . What if?!! I have such a knack for being a pessimist.

I knew what we shared was real. What I felt when we were together was exactly what I had always imagined true love would be like. Every moment was special and cherished. I knew, deep in my heart, that Kevin felt the same way, too. There was no way that he had duped me into a false security. The roots of this relationship were woven too deeply. Our passions, emotions and intimacy were intertwined and formed the tapestry of our mutual devotion. Thus was formed our "product of conception". A new life created by our love . . . a true legacy of who we were and what we could become.

In that instant, I decided something that was to effect the rest of my life. There was no way that I would do anything to jeopardize the life of the miracle growing inside. It seemed that I had waited far too long for "my baby". The memory of that nearly fatal bus accident flooded through me. The decision of its life or death ripped from my frail shoulders even as the fetus was severed from my nurturing womb by cold metal and unyielding momentum. Quick to follow was the tearful recollection of a small, quiet bundle held gently in my arms. So lifeless, yet so loved.

I wanted this baby so badly . . . needed it so desperately. At twenty-three, I felt that I was thoroughly capable of bringing a child into this world. I wanted to shower my baby with the love and affection that I had always been denied. With Kevin at my side, our love would blossom into a garden of wishes that would always come true. We would become a family. What had been my lifelong prayer would become our reality.

The doorbell interrupted my silent, cerebral reverie. I knew immediately who had to be on the other side of the front door. One look at his face and I would be able to predict his response. With both trepidation and delirious excitement, I ran towards the foyer and threw the door wide open.

The face that awaited me was not Kevin's. It was the face of a stranger . . . a stranger hidden behind the largest bouquet of blue-tipped carnations that I had ever seen.

"Where would you like me to place these, Ma'am?" the unfamiliar face inquired.

"There must be some mistake. I certainly did not order any flowers," I replied more calmly than I felt.

"Beg your pardon, Ma'am. Is this 140 Madison Avenue?" he asked with quiet reassurance. This is rather heavy."

"I'm sorry. Sure. Yeah, . . . uh, I mean . . . right! This is that address."

" . . . And are you Tarah?" he continued with just a hint of teasing in his voice.

"Yes I am, but . . . "

"Then these are definitely for you. So where would you like me to place them?"

"Could you put them on the table, please?" I requested as I showed him into the foyer. "They are so beautiful! Who sent them to me?"

Already making his way to the door, he paused to look back. And replied, "There's a card".

How strange, I thought. He did not even wait to see if I was going to tip him. Turning my attention to the surprise delivery, I reached for the small white envelope almost obscured by the lush foliage and innumerable blooms. Before I could tear open the envelope, the deliveryman reappeared in the doorway. He carried another grand bouquet of fresh flowers in each hand.

Behind him, I could see several other similarly attired men, each toting various bouquets or bunches of blue, pink or white flowers . . . the traditional baby colors. They each made several trips before the original man paused for his tip. After giving him a small token of appreciation, I turned back to the makeshift greenhouse that our large livingroom had suddenly become. How beautiful it was suddenly! The fragrance was as intoxicating as the sight. Who could have done this?

Who else? This was Kevin's reaction, after the initial shock wore off, to the news of my pregnancy. Could all this mean a rejection?

With all due haste, I tore open the card. It simply read, "Read the letter that you will find with the white roses."

What white roses? There were several vases full of varying hues of pink and blue-dyed roses in the room. There were blue-flowered anemones, several species of blue and pink cornflowers, immense vases of larkspur, blue Dutch irises, towering blossoms of candle delphinium. Numerous pots of pink and blue sweetpeas were everywhere. Spiky pink and blue lupine bouquets, baskets of forget-me-nots, innumerable blue lace flowers were scattered around in matching containers and an embarrassing menagerie of bright blue vanda orchids were everywhere . . . and this was basically just the blue stuff!

Besides the pink blooms mentioned above, there were several varieties that were uniquely pink. These included: Hanging begonias, fancy chrysanthemums, giant bunches of pink carnations and freesias, daisies, gladioli and satinflowers, blushing pink tulips, miniature rosebuds and a multitude of tall pillars of snapdragons standing sentinel over this instant garden.

There were no white roses to be seen. It was during my search that I happened across the long, silver box with a white satin ribbon tied fashionably around it. Carefully releasing the ribbon, I lifted the lid. Before me sprawled three dozen perfect, long-stemmed white roses.

I gingerly picked up the gleaming white envelope discreetly placed within the folds of tissue paper. With trembling fingers, I lifted the flap and deftly persuaded the fine stationery out of its secure resting spot. With increasing nervousness, I unfolded the page and began to read:

> My Dearest Maiden of Dance,
>
> You dance like the ocean and your waves of passion crash over my body like rocks along the shore. I love you so completely that to simply think about you can bring tears of joy to my eyes. I can no longer think of my life without you in it. You make me feel alive and free . . . and happy to be both.
>
> It is with great hope in my heart that I ask you this most important question. Knowing my

unworthiness of such a rare and precious jewel, I plead for your understanding and mercy in considering my plea.

Will you give me the honor of becoming my wife? I promise to love you forever and never cause you any pain. I will protect you and try to always make you happy. No other woman has ever touched me the way you have. Your childlike innocence, in the face of such cruel harshness, makes me appreciate my life with all its niceties. Before you came into my world, I was unable to see the tranquility and considered *living* a responsibility. Suddenly, you've made it joyful and glorious.

Marry me! I am begging you, my love. Grant me this and I will always be grateful. I will become your mate for life and keep you always at my side. Silken bonds will hold our love intact throughout eternity.

I wait patiently for your answer. Take your time to consider my proposal with an open heart. I love you, Tarah Lindsay. I promise you that my love will never fade. Maybe I have always loved you.

Let me belatedly assure you that after careful consideration, I am delighted with the idea of having this baby. There is no one else on this earth that I would rather have as the mother of my child than you.

You could make me a very happy man if you give me this chance to make you my wife.

Eternally yours,

Kevin Rhodes (xxoo)

With tears of unbelievable happiness falling from my eyes, I carefully refolded the letter and slipped it back into the envelope.

Later, I would tuck it away in my treasury keepsake box. For now, I clutched it to my breast and considered its contents. Kevin loved me and had asked me to marry him. My joy knew no boundaries. A childlike giddiness flooded over me. My "knight in shining armor" had requested that I join him in Holy Matrimony. I would, of course, accept his offer of marriage without hesitation. I silently prayed that I would be able to make Kevin as happy as he had just made me. The thought of becoming his wife was like a dream come true.

Later, I'll tell you what happened when Kevin returned from his business trip. Right now, I gotta stop for a while. I feel dreadful. All I do is cough . . . cough . . . cough. I still am plagued with diarrhea and nausea which always makes me feel so lousy and weak, but now it hurts every time I try to take a deep breath. I think I have pneumonia. I have to go back into the hospital for treatments and IV antibiotics. When I get back . . . I'll get back to ya! So long, Mr. Machine. I'll talk to you later.

CHAPTER 26

THE TWILIGHT

Hi, Mr. Machine. Better yet, I'm gonna start calling you Mr. Mac. Okay? It's a little less formal. Since I talk to you about deeply personal feelings and emotions, I decided that we should be on a first-name basis. You can call me Tarah.

Aw! Come on! You remember me. It hasn't been that long. I was in the hospital . . . again. This time it was really bad and really scary. I was right about the pneumonia, only it wasn't the regular kind that can easily be treated with penicillin.

No! By the time the ambulance had arrived and everybody had donned their protective-barrier equipment, I had digressed into respiratory arrest. Fortunately for me, I had lapsed into unconsciousness and did not have to experience it when they plunged a thick, hard rubber tube down my throat and hooked me up to a ventilator.

I was kept heavily sedated with liberal IV doses of Valium, Morphine and Pavalon, a drug that evokes paralysis as the desired effect and thereby leaving its victim unable to "fight the vent". For more than a week, I lay helpless and suffering while this machine made sure that I did not stop breathing. Pooph, hiss . . . Pooph, hiss . . . Pooph, hiss . . . The only change in the sound came with an alteration in my level of consciousness.

My chest hurt like it was on fire and someone thought that putting a heavy weight there would extinguish the flames. It felt like they had stacked a huge pile of cement bricks on my chest. Needless to say, this did nothing to diminish my agony. Of course, with all the sedation, I was unaware of the discomfort most of the time . . . at least in the beginning. The unpleasant tube in my throat was awkwardly taped to the side of my mouth. Turning my head just a little bit caused a whole lot of hurt. I gradually became aware of all my distress as I regained consciousness.

At some point, a doctor came in and explained it all. He said that the pneumonia was a special kind that many AIDS patients seemed to contract. It was one of the opportunistic infections associated with this diagnosis. Pneumocystic Carinii Pneumonia (PCP, for short,) was difficult to treat and was rarely found in someone my age unless they suffered from AIDS.

During my stay in the hospital, I met a special nurse, Sylvia. She was of African persuasion and yet she was as American as apple pie. I secretly nicknamed her, "The African Queen". She had long, black braids that hung down to her waist. With a glowing sun-kissed complexion, she radiated health. She carried herself in the proud stature of a mythical warrior goddess while performing her nursing functions exuding abundant knowledge and confidence. Even more important to me, she treated me with respect, compassion and empathy. Through her efforts, I was released with the promise of hospice care and follow-up visits from the county health department's visiting nurse.

Okay, now. If I remember correctly, I was telling you how Kevin proposed to me in a love letter. Through his prose, he promised his commitment, not only to me, but to our baby as well. I recall my elation at the prospects and his impending return. Within a few days, I received word of the exact moment of his arrival via private messenger. I set about in preparation for that moment. I meticulously planned our first dinner together as the betrothed.

When it finally happened, the evening progressed even better than I had hoped. This was a time of anticipation and excitement. As most couples do, we knew that our love would last through the dawn.

That night dinner went superbly. The numerous candles glowed and perfectly illuminated the exquisite blooms on the various bunches and bouquets that graced the room. Our place settings reflected the shimmering flames and our easy conversation filled the air. Kevin uncorked the champagne that he had been thoughtful enough to bring to our reunion. The lessons learned so long ago in the Webers' kitchen now yielded a succulent feast, which we eagerly enjoyed together. Our toast simply consisted of our mutual wish for our happiness and our love.

After dinner, Kevin swept me into his arms as I began to clear the table. In a gentle motion, he pulled me towards him and tenderly kissed me. With eyes filled with anticipation, he raised his head and whispered, "I can wait no longer, Tarah. Have you considered my request? Please! If you need more time, that's fine, but allow me the luxury of knowing that a rejection is not eminent. Tell me how you feel . . . if you can."

With tears of joy spilling over my lashes, I raised my face to look into the eyes of this gentle giant. I did not know the words to express all that he instilled in my life. I could hardly believe that he really wanted me for his bride and, yet, here he was waiting for my reaction to his proposal.

"I am now and forever your humble maidservant, M' lord," I replied with medieval formality. "If it be your desire to wed such a lowly wench, then I shall not impede your progress. Under God's law I would vow to remain your mate throughout eternity . . . if that be your intentions, Kind Sir."

The tension seemed to melt away from his face. He understood my meaning to the letter. He acknowledged my acceptance with another kiss. This, more passionate than the first. Our burning desire for each other blazed furiously within each of our souls.

Silently, I offered up a secret prayer that if this were a dream I would never wake up. If it was reality, then I prayed that Kevin truly wanted to share a life with me. As if reading my thoughts, he uttered with sincerity, "You have made me so happy tonight. So deliriously happy! I promise you a full and wonderful life.

With you, I hope to raise a house full of children. I think that we are off to an amazing beginning with this special child that you are carrying and enriching even as we speak".

His left hand was reaching around to caress my still flat tummy. His right hand was reaching into his jacket pocket. It withdrew a small, velvet box. With obvious pride, he opened the lid to expose his treasure. With unbridled excitement, he slipped the gleaming ring on the trembling third finger of my left hand. The glittering diamond sent prisms of color radiating through the room as it reflected the lights from the flaming candles.

"With this ring it is official. We are engaged. Are you sure, Tarah? Are you really sure? I want you to be happy. I want you to be happy for the rest of our lives. Lives that I want to share."

I threw my arms around his powerful neck and clung to him as if for dear life. All I could do was nod my acceptance for some time. Finally, I found my voice and assured my knight of my certainty. Our very souls would be united and nothing could please me more. My next question was simple and direct.

"When?"

"Soon! The sooner the better!" he replied with similar simplicity and directness.

"I'd need to contact my brother, David. I would like him to give me away. My mother should be there, too. Is this alright with you?" I asked hesitantly.

"Anything you want is okay with me, my little Tarah Doll. My happiness is boundless because you consented to be my wife. Your wish, dear lady, is my command. It will be my delight to serve you in any way possible. Bring them to my attention and your dreams will be magically fulfilled . . . always."

Again, we embraced, and our lips met and our passions flamed. Kevin lifted me with ample arms and carried me into our bedroom. There, we quickly became embroiled in ardent lovemaking. His tongue was seeking and teasing my erogenous zones with a pleasant familiarity. I stroked his magnificent physique and quickly increased my urgent desire for him. We gave in to our desires and let our passions flow effortlessly until we were both spent completely.

As we lay there with our warm bodies entwined, we spoke of the future. We decided to get married as quickly as feasible. Kevin insisted on financing the entire occasion. Anything my heart desired was to be the order of the day. We agreed to keep it a small, intimate affair with members of our families and a handful of close friends in attendance.

The next day we had our invitations written and addressed. Together we quickly worked out every detail for our special day. Kevin was as exuberant as I was. He was also a valued member of his community. Many people were grateful for the chance to "make it happen" for a man they considered their friend. The proceedings went so smoothly that we were both surprised when all the preparations were completed.

The celebration would be held four weeks from Saturday. After our invitations were mailed, we decided on a caterer and cemented the menu. He would be responsible for many aspects of the reception and I, for one, was most grateful for his ability to lighten my load. We rented the reception hall and hired the musicians. A local florist was to supply the flowers and centerpieces and decorate the church and hall. One of Kevin's friends was delighted at the prospect of being our photographer. His only brother would serve as his best man and "Miss Vicky", a fellow dancer, would be my maid-of-honor.

When I broached the subject of my apparel, Kevin stated categorically that it would be his pleasure to procure a gown for his bride. He had it tailor-made to his exacting specifications and I was privy to not even the minutest detail. In fact, it was the day before my wedding that I got my first glimpse of his creation.

Three days before our impending nuptials Kevin left, as planned, to spend the interim at his mother's home. She was thrilled to have these precious hours with her son before we became man and wife. During this time she assured her son that she was pleased with his choice and wished us both every happiness. She had already accepted the news of the expected baby with her usual cultured dignity. Kevin thought I would be welcomed into his family with open arms and open hearts. Much later I would find out that his family was very much against our marriage. They secretly referred to me as "the gold-digger". They felt that I brought shame to the family but not a hint of this ever reached Kevin's ears.

Early that Friday afternoon, a messenger arrived delivering my wedding gown. The huge, white satin box was secured by a blue velvet ribbon, which I removed with nervous fingers. Slowly, I removed the lid, folded back the protective tissue and gazed upon the object of beauty and love that was forever imprinted in my memory. With gentle movements, I lifted my prize from the cradling box and held it against my body. It was serenely beautiful. Layers upon layers of white silk cascaded in rippling waves towards the floor. Tiny white silk rosebuds were attached to the gown as if sprinkled upon it with God's own hand. The bodice was decorated with innumerable delicate pearls, as were the neckline and cuffs.

As I stood there and stared at my reflection in the mirror, I was reminded of another time . . . when brave knights slew dragons and returned triumphantly to the waiting damsel. Even the headpiece carried out this theme. The entire ensemble including gloves, shoes, and intimate apparel was a medieval masterpiece. Tucked inside one of the gloves was a note that simply read: "To the fairest princess from a most unworthy but most admiring knight. I lay my heart at your feet hoping you will accept it happily".

My wedding day dawned bright and sunny. Even the birds of the fields joined in the festive atmosphere by lending their spirited songs to the morning. I enjoyed a relaxing soak in warm, scented water and relished in the thoughts of the man that was soon to become my husband. My total joy was explosive and contagious. The women who had joined me earlier to serve as my attendants shared my enthusiasm. One skillfully swept my hair into a style that would enhance my headpiece, which was reminiscent of the type worn by the maidens during the Middle

Ages. My mother showed up and insisted on helping me into my gown and tried to calm my nerves as she fastened my gold graduation cross, a gold bracelet and gold earrings securely in place.

Finally I was ready and, with a last reassuring glance at my reflection, I inquired about traveling arrangements to the church. No sooner had I spoken the words than the man came who was to drive me to the site. He was impeccably dressed as a liveryman and politely inquired as to my state of readiness. When I assured him that I was as ready as I would ever be, he escorted me out the door and, to my astonishment, to a waiting horse-drawn carriage . . . complete with a similarly attired driver. My escort helped me into the body of the streamlined coach then lifted himself up beside the driver. Unnoticed until now, another escort assisted my maid-of-honor into the seat opposite mine, securely closed the door and spun around to the rear of the vehicle and likewise climbed aboard.

As we made our way to the ceremony, I attempted to practice the vows that I had written. I felt certain that Kevin was, at that moment, doing much the same thing. Since I had written every word, I knew it flawlessly. However, I was nervous anyhow, envisioning saying the words in front of the invited guests. Fortunately, I remembered that I would be saying my words to Kevin Rhodes and instantly my fears vanished.

The carriage pulled up to the front of the impressive church that was nestled in this serene wooded area, replete with a babbling brook and chirping birds. On the strong arm of my escort, I mounted the pristine steps and approached the arched doorway through which I would enter the church and prepare for my final walk down the aisle and towards the man that I loved. Within minutes of my arrival, the organ rang out the familiar strains of "The Wedding March" and the small, formal procession began to make its way towards the altar.

With my beloved David at my side, I gathered my strength and slowly began my march to destiny. As we came to the predetermined place, we stopped. Whispering words of encouragement in my ear, he waited for the priest to deliver his line, "Who gives this woman today for the purpose of marriage?"

"Her mother and I do!" David answered with confidence. After a quick, affectionate hug, he placed my hand into the outstretched hand of my fiancé and made his way silently to the seat next to our mother.

I had focused my attention on Kevin since I had entered the darkened church and never had I been more aware of the depths of my feelings for him than I was at the moment he took hold of my hand and heart for all eternity. After the celebrant announced the necessary declarations, it was time for us to exchange our vows.

Kevin began. He literally oozed sincerity as he gently held my hand and peered deeply into my eyes while reciting the words that we had chosen to deliver our vows to one another.

"At this moment, on this day, and before this company I offer to you, Tarah, my everlasting love, respect and protection. I will share myself with no other woman and I will remain faithful to the vows that we are exchanging today, always and forever. With a heart overflowing with joy and excitement, I invite you to spend the rest of your life with me, as my wife. I will try unceasingly to accommodate your needs and bring all of your dreams to fruition.

"With this ring I seal our fate and our souls forever become one. All this I promise without constraints and with a free and willing spirit. With the unending help of God, our family and our friends we will unite our lives and give thanks for his blessings. Everyday, our bond will grow stronger and our lives more full. For the rest of my life, I will look to you for beauty and peace. You are the embodiment of all of my secret desires and prayers. For this and your love, I will always be grateful."

When he was done, the guests were hushed as if his words had cast a spell over them all. Only I was witness to the tears of sincerity that trickled down his ruddy cheeks and got lost in the thick, auburn beard that I loved so well.

Now it was my turn. Trying to quell the butterflies that were soaring around in my stomach, I took a deep breath and gathering courage from his proximity. I had chosen the prose with great care and with unbridled sincerity I recited my vows to this wonderful man.

"At this moment on this special day and before our friends and families, I offer to you, Kevin, my undying devotion and faithfulness. I will share myself with no other man and I promise to always keep the vows that I exchange with you today. With overwhelming joy, I agree to spend the rest of my life at your side, dear husband. I will try unceasingly to anticipate your needs and fulfill all of your desires of me.

"With this ring, I seal our fate and allow our souls to become as one, forever and throughout eternity. All this I promise without constraints and of my own freewill. Under the divine realm of God's kingdom, we will share our lives in all things and secure our future with mutual efforts. With each blessing that God bestows upon us, I will sing his praises and bless His Holy Name.

"When these blessings include children, I promise to care for them diligently and instruct them in His goodness . . . and yours. I am certain that our love will continue to grow stronger with every passing hour. At your side I will remain forever, to be your wife and offer all that I am able to your life. You are the answer to my prayers. You are kind, wise and honorable. For your offer of matrimony and your love, I will always be grateful."

Again, the crowd had drifted into a spiritual silence. The priest quoted an appropriate passage of scripture and finally pronounced us husband and wife. Declaring that man was not to defile what The Lord has blessed, he made the sign of The Cross over us and extended his hands to us in a congratulatory manner. After this brief delay, he announced to Kevin that he could kiss his bride.

Within the warm and comforting confines of his strong, protective arms, I could feel his tenderness and his excitement. Gently, he lowered his head until his lips barely touched mine. In eagerness, I stood on my toes so as to press my lips more firmly against his. The familiar heat began to stir within us. Unbeknownst to the onlookers, our passions were about to reach a heightened crescendo. Fortunately, Kevin had the wisdom and the strength to pull away before we both succumbed to our burning desires.

Finally, we turned and faced our invited guests, who seemed anxious to share in our obvious joy. There was an explosion of applause from the crowd as the priest introduced the newly-weds to the world . . . Mr. and Mrs. Kevin Rhodes. My throat caught at the sound of it. My tears, which had begun to fall as Kevin recited his vows, continued to flow down my cheeks. Again, Kevin lowered his face to mine and kissed away the salty moisture.

"You sure cry a lot," he whispered jokingly as the organ swelled with the music of the recessional.

With my arm resting on his, we made our way slowly down the aisle to greet the gathering throng of well wishers. After the perfunctory delay for photographs, we were taken to the reception in the same carriage that had transported me to the church.

Since our witnesses were traveling in a similar rig behind us, we were alone for the first time as man and wife. Before the spirited team of golden chestnut horses had transversed any sizable distance, my husband had removed most of his formal attire and was graciously helping me out of my gown.

On the rear seat of that magnificent carriage, we made love on the way to our wedding reception. Within the confines of time allotted by the distance to the hall, we enjoyed each other's tasty goodies and luxuriated in our desirous passions. We clung to each other during our feverish, mutual orgasms and continued to hold each other closely as we caught our breath. We were giggling like children as we redressed each other.

As soon as we were both properly re-attired, it seemed, our driver announced our arrival at the hall. When the carriage pulled to a halt, Kevin jumped from the seat and, placing his rugged hands around my small waist, effortlessly lifted me from the vehicle. Gently he lowered me to the ground, placed his arm around my shoulders and together we entered the reception.

The hall was beautifully decorated with an abundance of fresh flowers and a plethora of lighted candles. The music that greeted our arrival was rich and sweet. Wasting no time, Kevin gathered me into his arms and escorted me onto the dance floor. There, before our guests, we danced for the first time as a married couple. Our movements were graceful and perfectly interwoven. As we swirled our way across the floor, we received many an admiring glance from the crowd. We were so in-tuned to each other that our movements seemed almost inspired. After the music faded, we lingered in each other's arms for a few more precious moments before making our way to the table that was reserved for the bridal party.

The hastily planned reception was truly a feast fit for a king. Everyone seemed to be having a grand time and all waited for a solitary moment with the bride and groom to offer their best wishes and extend their appreciation for the welcomed invitation to attend such an auspicious occasion. Everyone was having a fun and everything proceeded without the slightest hitch. Slowly, almost imperceptibly, the crowd began to thin and my maid-of-honor set out to search for me and tell me that it was time for me to change into my traveling clothes. Kevin had made all the arrangements for the honeymoon and was keeping them to himself. He wanted to surprise me.

I must admit that I was surprised when our horse-drawn carriage deposited us at the small private airport. We were immediately transported to a private jet and were awaiting take-off instructions from the tower. Before long, we were taxiing down the runway and lifting up into the atmosphere. There was no one else in the plane except for the crew confined to the cockpit.

With obvious delight Kevin informed me that we had about a nine-hour ride ahead of us and encouraged me to make myself more comfortable. Without hesitation, I removed the fashionable jacket and matching hat and slipped my stockinged feet out of my shoes. With an unaccountable shyness, I turned my attention to my new husband. He had begun to remove his jacket as well.

I could not help but notice the muscular ripples of his abdomen and the manly configuration of his chest as he unbuttoned his nicely tailored silk shirt. The color rose suddenly to my face, and he chose that precise moment to turn his eyes in my direction. He was pleased to notice that his bride had an innocence that caused her to blush. My embarrassment increased as he continued to remove his clothing . . . piece by piece. Even though I had seen him naked numerous times, seeing him naked now made me warm with desire.

I followed his naked, masculine form towards the rear of the plane. He stopped near the rear exit and opened a concealed panel that served as a door. He bade me to enter his private sanctuary and steered me towards the bed that seemed to fill the secluded cubbyhole. He stretched his majestically svelte body across the bed and motioned silently for me to climb aboard. I was about to remove the remainder of my clothes but he prevented me from doing so. With gentle persuasion, he coaxed me into his bed and promised to undress me himself when the time was right.

On my own, I decided to become the aggressor. I climbed atop of him while fully clothed and began an exploratory tour of his natural wonders. Starting with his tempting lips, I kissed him from head to toe and back again. No portion of his anatomy went unattended. While some special areas might have been allotted more of my time and attention, all sections were tasted and savored.

While sucking the last droplets of his pleasure fluid from his tantalized penis, he began to undo the buttons that secured the front of my blouse. With nimble fingers, he released my bra and cupped my breasts in his hands. I continued my oral hold of his penis and demanded all of his seed. I knew that this was having the desired effect on my new husband. I was driving him crazy!

My continued effort was rewarded by his renewed arousal and as his steamy elixir of love filled my mouth, he pulled my face up to his, and shared in the product of my insistent seduction. As he swallowed a portion of his own sperm, he informed me that it was his turn now.

With practiced movements he twisted out from under me and covered my waiting mouth with his. An energetic tongue sought out each nook and cranny in my oral cavity from my gums to my throat. With an uncanny awareness of my erotic and sensual nature, his lips explored my body. Lingering for brief moments along the way, he had caused my desire to escalate to the point of ecstasy in record time.

When he noticed my sensual excitement, he transferred his attention and his enticing mouth to the warm, moist area between my beckoning thighs and with little effort was able to extract a generous portion of my own love juice. Without hesitation he gently guided his teasing tongue past my pulsating labia and with gentle persuasion coaxed my highly sensitive clitoris to unknown heights of pleasure. He nurtured his claim to my feminine attributes until I exploded in a wave of uninterrupted orgasms.

As I fought to regain my composure and my breath, he diverted his attention, once again, to my beloved bosom and laid claims to the taut nipples that demanded his attention. Like a tiger, he stroked my flesh with his searing tongue and propelled me to sensuality heretofore unknown to me . . . even with him. I begged him to enter me and fill me with his heat. With the rugged strength of a wild beast, he skillfully prepared for the penetration of his prey. My legs were already parting with anticipation of his projection.

As if sensing my increasing desire for him, he licked my already sensitized nipples and allowed me to aim his majestic weapon at my target. With the initial sensation of his flesh against mine, my crevice opened slightly to accept his generous offering. My vaginal muscles began to demand more of his sex tool and he willingly entered my innermost sanctums. With the combination of his rhythmic movements and the continued pulsations of my love muscles, we plunged into the arena from which there could be no return.

I knew that I was on the verge of another climax but I wanted to make certain that my husband was ready as well. Without words, this information became evident and in unison we exploded in a delicious blast of mutual satisfaction. Afterwards, we just rested in each other's arms until the pilot announced our imminent arrival on the island of Hawaii.

At the nearly deserted airport, we were greeted by a driver and limousine. Our necks were immediately draped with leis of fresh tropical flowers that scented the air with their intoxicating perfume. We were then whisked away to our secluded cottage on a large, private strip of beach that led to the Pacific Ocean. While our personal valet carried our luggage to our rooms, we strolled through the meticulously kept gardens, which boasted a wide assortment of colorful and exotic offerings. Kevin selected a perfect white orchid and tucked it behind my ear.

"You are more lovely than all of these blossoms, and you smell even sweeter. I love you so much. I am almost delirious with happiness that you consented to become my wife. You will never regret it. I promise you. I will make you so happy that you will go insane and even then, I will continue to love and protect you. You are happy, too. Aren't you, my love?"

"How could I not be happy, Husband? I love you more than I ever thought possible. You make me happy in every way. I want and need you even more than you can imagine. If your love drives me crazy, then I will accept insanity as my shelter and it will protect us both from all the destructive forces of the outside world".

In comfortable silence we finished our walk and returned to our cottage. Before leaving for dinner, we made love once more. My desire for him seemed unquenchable. His desire for me was spontaneous and natural. We gloried in our mutual desire.

Our handpicked chef prepared our sumptuous meal at our table. Under the beaming radiance of a full moon, he chopped, sautéed and served our meal. It was delicious and thoroughly enjoyed by us both. This seemed to cause our chef a great deal of satisfaction and, as he served us his specially created desserts, he bade us adieu until the morrow.

After a midnight stroll along the beach, under that same moon, we headed back to our cottage. That night we made love to each other with exuberant passion until the sun kissed the horizon in the distance. Shortly after 5 a.m., we fell asleep in our cozy bungalow entwined in our spouse's embrace. We both slept soundly.

For the next six months, my life unfolded like a charming romantic novel. Kevin's attention for me never wavered. If anything, his watchfulness over me expanded into a devotional awareness of my wants and needs. Somehow, he managed his family's estate, kept our home running smoothly and provided me with every wonderful thing this world had to offer.

Most importantly to me, he was always there for me. He even went to the doctor's with me on my check-ups. He said he found it fascinating to hear the practitioner's explanations of my level of gestation and the stages that our expected baby was experiencing while growing steadily inside my womb.

Kevin had actually selected my gynecologist for me. The man was obviously well educated but he was also compassionate and very considerate. He was well versed on the holistic approach to prenatal care, and supervised my diet and exercise regime as well as my physical development during my pregnancy. With vitamins, minerals and a carefully-controlled eating program, not only was I assured of proper nutrition for me and the baby, but I was certain to maintain the level of energy necessary to do everything that I needed and wanted to do.

Doctor Davidson was an expensive private M.D. who catered to the elite crowd to which Kevin belonged and to which I was being accepted. Kevin paid for all of my medical care and supervised all aspects of it. As a result, I had never felt better. My pregnancy evolved within me and I enjoyed every minute of it.

Kevin shared in every facet of this pregnancy as well. To insure my culinary delight, he had managed to bring home a truly valuable souvenir from the islands. Kiko had been our private chef on our honeymoon and, somehow, Kevin had enticed him away from the exotic beauty of his native land and procured his talents for exclusive use in our home. Kiko made all those fruits and vegetables taste wonderful. Under his watchful hands, our meals were not only delicious but also most healthy. I felt truly blessed.

It seemed to me that this time was one of enchantment. Not only were our sexual dreams fulfilled, but even the mundane tasks of our lives were intertwined with intimacy and affection. It was the way Kevin took my hand and held it up to his lips to plant a tender kiss in my palm "for safe-keeping". At times, I would catch him looking at me with such gentleness that it took my breath away. Even as my girth increased, we continued to do many wonderful and exciting things.

One day, Kevin breezed into our sitting room with the announcement that we were going to the circus. There, we laughed at the silly clowns, watched experienced animal trainers put their wild beasts through their paces and held our breath during the high-flying aerial acrobatics. We gorged ourselves on peanuts, popcorn and cotton candy while pledging our secrecy from the inquiring Dr. Davidson.

We went to museums and several live theatrical productions. We attended the most lavish parties and went horseback riding along the Jersey Shore. We played the slots at the casinos and stayed home and watched rented videos by the hours. No matter what we did, we were both so happy just being together.

Dammit! Oops, sorry! There's the frucking doorbell, again. It seems like we get interrupted just when I'm getting into it. Well, Mac, I'll be back!

CHAPTER 27

THE DUSK

Hey, Mac. Sorry for the interruption. Someday I'll get an intercom or something like that. That way, I would not have to go through all the trouble that is necessary to answer the doorbell. I'm glad I went through the trouble this time, though. It was Father O'Hara. He's been stopping by to hear my confession and bring me Holy Communion for the last several months. Funny thing about it is that now I have very little to confess. It's hard to break a lot of commandments when you are confined to a sickbed most of the time.

Father O'Hara is a young Irish priest who always seems to have time to share with a lonely, sick Catholic girl. Since my "reconciliation" takes very little time, we often talk about other things. Besides the forbidden topics of religion and politics, we have discussed attending a parochial school, current events, medicine, economics and even the weather. I really enjoy the shared moments of these encounters with this young, contemporary missionary.

Anyway, before the interruption I was telling you about the months spent so blissfully while awaiting the birth of my child. Months spent at the side of the most appealing man I had ever met. I thought he was simply wonderful. To be his wife was a dream come true.

At this juncture, one might argue that I spend too much of

237

my present looking back at the past. Where else can someone with no future turn? Knowing that my life could be over within a few very short months, the future holds little promise except for misery and, hopefully merciful briefness.

There are many things that I will not survive long enough to witness. There will not be a woman elected President of the United States. Sadly enough, there will not be a cure for AIDS before I die. I will never see the human residents of this planet share in its bounty while protecting all the other species and our environment. I won't get a chance to be a grandmother . . . no chance to watch my children grow into fine adults or to hold my grandchildren in my arms and spoil them rotten. Hell! Unless a miracle occurs, I will never have the pleasure of experiencing total harmony within the human race. Perhaps the future will provide mankind with the skills to live and work together without regard to a person's skin color, religious beliefs, nationality or sexual preference. Maybe, someday, individuals will be accepted for who they are rather than what they have. Yeah, maybe . . . but not in my lifetime. Right?!!

Sorry, Mac. Guess I have a pretty good case of "the poor little me's", today. At least this might give you some understanding of why I talk so often about the past.

I can remember so clearly the day of my ultrasound. As always, Kevin was right there at my side. He watched with amazement when the outline of the baby illuminated the screen. The head, the little arms and even the tiny fingers were visible on the monitor. When the doctor noted the absence of external genitalia, there was no change in Kevin's expression. The test allowed the doctor to estimate, with a fair amount of certainty that I would deliver a healthy baby girl in eight weeks.

After the ultrasound, Kevin and I went to a local bistro for lunch. He seemed genuinely pleased with the results. He showed no trace of regret that the baby was not a boy. In fact, he was thrilled with the idea of his impending fatherhood. He expressed his secret desire that his daughter would look just like her beautiful mommy. When I blushed at this remark, he laughed and told me I was adorable. My blush deepened and he continued to laugh.

During our dessert, Kevin's face grew serious, and he said he had something to tell me. He had to leave town for a few days on business. I knew that it was not a good idea for me to travel. We were being very cautious during my last trimester, due to the complications of my obstetrical history. Neither Kevin nor I wanted to take any chances with this pregnancy.

He expressed concern about leaving me in my condition, but I assured him that I felt terrific and reminded him that I respected the way in which he handled his numerous obligations. I also reminded him that I was not expected to go into labor for two months, and that he was only going to be away for a couple of days. Seemingly reassured, Kevin made arrangements for his trip. On the night before his departure, we made love with unbridled urgency.

Too soon, it was morning and the time had come for him to leave. There were tears in our eyes as we kissed each other at the front door. From outside, the blast of the cab's horn alerted us both to the inevitable.

"I'll be home soon. Take care and don't worry. You will know how much I'll be missing you while I'm gone. I promise. I love you, Tarah Rhodes. That's forever!!!

Like the true knight in shining armor that he was, he took my hand into his, raised it to his lips and gently kissed most of my anxieties away. As soon as the giant oak door closed, I began to miss him.

I was settling down to breakfast when the doorbell rang. Impatiently, I went to answer it. A deliveryman proceeded to hand over an immense vase of pink roses. The small card attached to it read simply, "To my daughter-to-be and the woman I already love".

By dinnertime, I waited with just a touch of anticipation for a phone call or some word as I began my meal. Soon enough, the doorbell rang and another three-dozen long-stemmed pink roses were delivered along with a card with this short but imaginative question.

"Do you miss me yet?"

The pink roses were delivered, again, just before I retired for the night. They continued to be delivered at the same times for the next two days. Our place started to look like a gigantic florist shop. Each time the flowers arrived, there was the same small white card with some romantic thought, precisely written in Kevin's artistic script.

With each arrival, my heart would sing, even as my heart would constrict slightly with the realization that for another night, I would not have Kevin at my side to warm, comfort and excite me. Oh, I did miss him ever so much!

When the doorbell sounded early Thursday morning, I momentarily thought that the deliveryman was slightly ahead of schedule. Usually, I was up, dressed and preparing my breakfast when the first flowers of the day arrived. That day, I had just enough time to throw a robe over my nightgown before the sound pierced the air and drew me to the door. With eager footsteps, I approached the door and bade the deliveryman to enter. He proceeded to knock louder.

Opening the door briskly, I was ready to receive my gift. Instead, there were two uniformed policemen at the door. I gathered from their uniforms that they were State Troopers. Their serious expressions caused my stomach to tighten, but assuming that Kevin had inadvertently missed paying a parking ticket, I politely gestured for them to enter.

"Are you Mrs. Kevin Rhodes, Miss?" the officer asked almost hesitantly.

"Yes, I am" I chirped brightly, my smile broadening at the sound.

"Maybe you'd like to sit down, Ma'am," the second officer suggested.

"Of course. Where are my manners this morning? Perhaps you gentlemen would enjoy a fresh cup of coffee. Or some danish? Kiko is a genius with pastry. It's no trouble, I assure you . . . "

"No, thank you, Ma'am. Ma'am . . . there's been an accident. Early this morning on the Pennsylvania Turnpike, a trucker lost control of his rig and this set up a chain reaction. There were seven vehicles involved in the incident. When the dust finally cleared, there were three fatalities. We believe your husband was one of them. Uh . . . well, we sort of need someone to positively identify the body . . . If you could, Ma'am?"

"Miss? Are you alright?"

My thought processes were not functioning properly. What was this cop trying to say? Something about my husband being dusty? A trucker rigged up some chain? . . . and now I was fighting the darkness. It threatened to swallow me whole. Their faces blurred then vanished completely. Only the black cloak of desperation remained.

Hours later I came around to find Dr. Davidson tending to me. I could tell by his expression that all was not well.

"What's wrong? Is there a problem with my baby?" I asked.

"No, Tarah. The baby's fine. Really! But we have to talk. Do you remember the officers coming here this morning?"

I nodded.

He continued, "Please try to be brave, sweetheart. This is not going to be easy. It seems that . . . uh . . . this morning it seems . . . uh . . . that, well, this truck was going too fast and well . . . you see . . . Christ! This is harder than hell." Beads of sweat trickled down the taunt muscles of his face and neck.

"I'll just have to say it outright. Honey, Kevin was killed this morning in the accident on the Pennsylvania Turnpike. It was instantaneous, I assure you. He did not suffer at all."

The darkness was infringing on my alertness, again. I struggled to keep my head clear. I took a deep breath and swallowed around the lump that had lodged in my throat. The darkness faded and I tried to focus empty eyes on his face.

The meaning of his words slowly became apparent, and I reacted instinctively. How his words hurt me, and I intended to fight back. With fists clenched, I assailed him with impotent blows.

"No, you bastard. No! No! No! How can you speak such horrible words? You beast! I hate you! Get out!" I screeched before I wilted into a sobbing heap.

Dr Davidson said nothing. With great compassion and understanding, he allowed me a brief release of the tumult inside of me.

He stooped down and embraced my sagging shoulders. There was nothing he could say . . . nothing that would soothe the ache that was building in my heart.

Eventually, I was able to get myself presentable and Dr. Davidson drove me to the morgue. The pungent smell of formaldehyde assaulted my nostrils as I passed through the bleak hall. With increasing trepidation, I watched as they opened the metal door and slid the tray out. My eyes were riveted on the still form as they pulled the drape down to reveal the body's face . . . a face with the lids closed and the soft lips peeking out between the hairs of the thick red beard. My salty tears cascaded down my cheeks as I noticed the tiny nick, almost healed, that I had caused when I playfully scared the wits out of him while he was shaving. That was the morning he left. He looked so pale, like he had not seen the light of day for months. His robust and ruddy complexion robed of its normal color by the insensitive fluorescent lights of the morgue.

"Oh, dear God," I gasped.

I sensed, rather than felt, the arm of Dr. Davidson going around my waist to offer additional support for my rubbery legs.

"Take it easy, girl. I know that this has to be difficult for you. Do you want to go sit down?"

The expression on his face conferred his enormous empathy for my situation. Realizing that I could decrease his discomfort significantly, I pulled myself together quickly.

"I'm alright. Really I am! God, this is a nightmare. I'm so glad that you are here with me. I could never have gotten this far without your being here, Dr. Davidson. I know you are aware of how painful this is for me. I still can't quite believe it is happening. But the proof is right in front of my eyes. Isn't it?" I spoke with far more composure than I felt.

"You're doing fine, Tarah. Under the circumstances, I'd say you were doing very well. Perhaps I should take you home now. I think you've had enough," he coaxed.

With all my strength I refused his offer for the moment.

"Could I possibly persuade you to give me a few moments alone with my husband? It will only take a few minutes," I promised.

With obvious hesitation he reluctantly acquiesced. Placing his hat slightly askew on top of his head, he left me alone in the cold, dreary room.

My heart was breaking as I turned my attention back to the figure on the tray in front of me. I raised my hand and gently stroked his beard. With blatant clarity, the images of our last night together swarmed through my mind. The unexplained urgency of our lovemaking suddenly became abundantly clear. Had we known? Did we have some premonition of what was to transpire? If we had, I was not conscious of it. I just knew that night that I would miss him when he was gone . . . and now he was never coming back.

Wiping my eyes and cheeks with firm resolve, I looked down at the corpse of my 'knight in shining armor' and whispered, "Goodbye, my love. I will miss you forever. How can I go on without you in my life? God! What am I going to do now? How could this have happened? How could you leave me alone like this?

"Forgive me, darling. I'm so sorry! I know that this wasn't your fault. I know in my heart that this is not the way you wanted it either. God, I'm so sorry. I love you so much. I know that I will always love you."

Suddenly I remembered my pregnancy and tears flowed again.

"I thank God for this little baby that has yet to be born. Our daughter! I promise you she will know you and someday she will appreciate what a wonderful person her father was. I will tell her all about you and how you changed my life forever."

My tears continued, flowing down my cheeks and dropping onto the sheet that covered Kevin's body. This time I made no attempts to stop them. How cruel life could be! My little girl would never be able to grab her daddy's beard or sit on his lap while he stroked her hair. She would forever be denied the sound of his voice as he tended to her lovingly. She would not be allowed the chance to hear him recite nursery rhymes while she drifted off into peaceful slumber. She would never witness the way his passionate blue eyes danced merrily when he laughed. She would never know this gentle giant who was her father except through my words. How unfair and unkind!

"Wait for me near heaven's back door," I quipped. "I'll look for you when I get there. Since they probably won't grant me free passage through the pearly gates, I'll have to rely on your assistance in getting reunited with you someday. Never forget me, Babe. Don't let this temporary separation make you forget our love. Throughout eternity I will search for you until we are able to embrace once more. 'Bye for now, Kevin. I love you . . . I always will."

I leaned over and planted a gentle kiss on the cold, hard lips that I remembered being so warm and soft and inviting. With measured steps I walked to the door. I turned my head one last time in the direction of his silent, unmoving silhouette as if trying to memorize its configuration. Then I joined Dr. Davidson and allowed him to return me to my empty home.

The next few days were a blur of activity and faceless people. There was much to be done. So many details demanded my immediate attention. At the same time, I just wanted to crawl off somewhere and cry the pain away. My mother-in-law realized my dilemma and insisted on taking care of everything. Although our relationship had always been quite strained, I gratefully accepted her offer in this time of need. Perhaps our past differences no longer mattered. Reconciliation, or even just a truce, would be a welcome change and definitely could not have come at a better time. Kevin's brother also extended his promise to assist in any way that he could. Another mountain coming to Mohammed. The only responsibility left for me was the greeting of the steady stream of friends and family who stopped by to offer their condolences.

Unfortunately, this would be the first funeral I had ever arranged. I had no idea what was involved or how I was expected to behave. The paperwork alone was very detailed and distressing. There seemed to be hundreds of papers that required the widow's signature. I was most appreciative of the help of Kevin's family. His mother made it her mission to intercept the "busy work" and rendering to me her interpretation of the various forms and applications. Many of these documents were signed without my reading them. Instead, I relied on the validity of her statements and accepted each as fact. This proved to be a costly mistake, one I was not to become aware of until later.

By the day of the funeral, our home was filled to overflowing with bouquets of every sort. Clumped between the vases of pink roses were numerous sprays from all over the world. I had no idea how many people shared my appreciation of Kevin: yet I was not surprised. The thought that so many others would dearly miss him lessened my suffering a bit.

I remember nothing of the funeral service itself. Bits and pieces of hazy recollection stir around in my thoughts, but there is no chronological order to make it seem more real. We had shared our last goodbye that night in the morgue. There was nothing more I could do. My new tears retraced the tracks of the old tears that I had shed earlier. I stood there as motionless as a statue in some surreal setting. I knew when the ceremony ended; some guiding force would encircle my waist and steer my body towards the waiting limousine.

I felt numb physically, mentally and emotionally. Feeling completely drained, my movements became mechanical . . . my actions, habitual in nature. As the agonizingly long day drew to a close, I tumbled into bed in utter exhaustion. At least I believed that the worst was over. Little did I know!!!

It has been said that it is always darkest before the dawn. Well, my world, an abyss of despair already, was about to grow even darker. The bleak information came directly from the mouth of my lawyer, Mr Warrington. After the obligatory phone call to announce his intended visit, he arrived nervous and solemn. We exchanged pleasantries then went into the adjoining parlor and sat down on the comfortable couch. He took my hand and gave it a gentle squeeze before beginning.

"Mrs. Rhodes, there's been a terrible mistake made and I'm afraid that I am the one who made it. I know that I should have checked all of those documents with a fine-tooth comb, but I was trying to expedite the legal ramifications of your husband's death. Somehow a few addendums had been insidiously added within the legal jargonese of certain documents and in my haste they were overlooked. I am in the process of trying to rectify the unfortunate situation but, so far, I haven't been having much luck. Every avenue I pick merely leads to a dead end. Please forgive me Ma'am. I sincerely regret my error and the serious problems to which it could lead."

"Calm down, Mr. Warrington," I said soothingly. "I'm afraid I don't really understand exactly what it is that you are trying to tell me. May I ask what type of documents were involved?"

"Mostly it involves your husband's will, or lack thereof, to be more precise. Lack of a new will to be even more precise. The older will stipulated that a certain percentage was to be divided among his favorite charities. The rest was to be shared equally by his mother and brother if they both survived him. There was simply no provision for you or the child in the text."

"Surely I have grounds to contest the will. Even a judge who was deaf, dumb and blind would know in his heart that this was a simple oversight. We never gave it a thought. We'd only been married a year . . . or almost anyway . . . and were looking forward to . . . so many things . . . " I was getting choked up and unshed tears filled my eyes.

"That's where the other document comes into play, Mrs. Rhodes. It seems that somewhere during your heaviest grief, you signed a waiver that virtually guaranteed refusal on your part to contest the will in return for certain stipulations: Some modest stipend for you; a meager monthly allowance for the baby's needs and an agreement to pay all doctor bills including the delivery of the baby. Medical coverage for the child would be paid until the age of twenty-one."

"Who could have done such a horrible thing?" but I knew even as the words were leaving my mouth. I knew! The plastic smile and the phony conversation had not blinded me to the true nature of my mother-in-law. How could such a witch have given birth to the man that my husband had been? It seemed impossible. Yet I recalled with astounding clarity the times when she and my deplorable brother-in-law had shoved piles of papers in front of my nose, along with a synopsis of the meaning of those papers. With pathetic gratitude I had signed every document intended, along with the legitimate collection. What a fool I had been! Now I was forced to deal with the consequences of my naïveté.

"Mr. Warrington, I am grateful for all your loyalty. Rest assured that I share the blame for all this equally with you. I, too, should have been more careful. I'm also sure that if there were anything to be done via legal channels to undo the situation, you would have seen to them prior to your visit, and traveled over here with a much lighter heart. Now then . . . what exactly are the terms of the ill-gotten agreement?"

"As I had previously mentioned, you will not have to worry about any medical expenses throughout the remainder of your pregnancy, including the delivery and hospital costs. After the birth and until the age of twenty-one years, the estate will pay the cost of health care for the child. You will be given a monthly allotment for yourself and the expected child. While it will not be on the order of your financial level during your marriage, it will allow you and your child to have a comfortable and safe environment."

I moved out of Kevin's beautiful home within two weeks. I could no longer afford the mortgage payment. Hell, I could not even afford the taxes on the place. Besides, among the papers that I unwittingly signed was one that stipulated the return of that property back to the estate. Anyway, there were too many memories in that little house and I thought I would eventually benefit from a change of scenery.

Kiko helped me pack and move into the small, shabby flat

that was more affordable. I was happy about the little park across the street, but little else. Suddenly I felt so alone. Kiko was going back to his beautiful island home, after much insistence from me. I knew that he was desperately homesick. He had been a faithful employee and a good friend. So now I was on my own.

During the day, I kept myself from thinking about the emotional turmoil on my life with a whirlwind of activity. I continued with my holistic diet with Dr. Davidson's assistance. I kept my stamina and spirits up with my program of regular exercise, plenty of rest and prayers. By continuing my involvement with the social functions of the local charities and fundraisers, I limited the hours I was alone.

Nothing helped at night. Lying silently in the darkened room left me feeling helpless and hopeless. At no other time did Kevin's absence bother me more. When my abdomen quivered with the increasing movement of our baby, I would automatically reach for his hand . . . to share the motion and the elation.

The night seemed longer and darker and colder than I remembered, too. If it had not been for the fact that I carried his child, I could have easily succumbed to my grief. Mostly I cried the long, dark hours away until the sun's brightness began to caress the world once again.

The child would be my future . . . our future . . . our child. With our daughter I would share the world in all its glory. I would show her the beauty of the land and the people who shared it. I would protect her as long as I could from the ugliness and deceit that slimed its way over the beauty. I would shield her, as much as possible, from the hate and destruction that held some people prisoners within themselves. Together we would paint our world using the cheerful colors of the rainbow and see the rain as the easel.

Well, Mac, I gotta take a break for awhile. I just dumped a full glass of juice down the front of me. Didn't mean to . . . it just got away from me. The doctors say that my illness causes some nerve degeneration, and this makes me a tad clumsy. Sometimes when I attempt to feed myself, I end up wearing more than I swallowed. So I'll turn you off for a little while and if I don't get electrocuted in the process, I'll get back to you. Bye!

CHAPTER 28

THE DAWN

Hi there, Mr. er . . . Ms. Machine. I think I'll call you "china" pronounced cheena . . . Ms. Macheena. No wait! How about Ms. Masheena? You know, like Sheena! Yeah, I like that . . . Sheena.

Well, Sheena, I know it's been a while since I talked to you last. I kept getting distracted. Actually, I kept letting myself get sidetracked. I was sort of drained when I was telling you about losing Kevin . . . it being so sudden and all.

Today you see in front of you only a fragment of the woman I used to be. Even through the funeral and the final weeks of my pregnancy, I maintained the façade of dignity and strength. With Kevin's memories I lingered in my thoughts. To the outside world I passed my days in quiet contemplation, functioning like a robot, listening to the seconds tick away on the universal timepiece.

Thus, I spent my final weeks of pregnancy reading in my bedroom, when I could not fall asleep. It proved to be time well spent. When the initial signs of labor made their appearance, I was well aware of their significance. I called the hospital and the taxi. Everything went smoothly and my arrival at the hospital was anticipated and organized. My progression through the different phases of labor passed uneventfully and I delivered a beautiful 8 pound, seven ounce baby girl on Valentine's day. I named her Erica Love Rhodes. She was not only beautiful but the doctor also pronounced her to be in perfect health.

Three days later I left the hospital carrying my infant daughter in my arms. My stinking in-laws at least had the decency to arrange for my transportation after my discharge. I don't mean to sound so bitter, but I cannot help but imagine what our lives could have been, had they not been so greedy. Surely there was enough for all of us.

Without intention, I lowered my eyes and the eyes of my adorable baby were looking intensely into mine. I suddenly appreciated my new role of motherhood. I wanted to be a mother with the ability to guide our little creation to the highest levels of integrity, grace and happiness. I had to instill in her the qualities that had initially drawn me to her father. The attributes that I knew had their seeds implanted in her genetic make-up at the moment of her glorious conception.

To begin with, her little impish face was Kevin's. It was as if some angel had chiseled her profile out of marble and used the carved features of her father for the model. Her hair tumbled in ringlets of the strawberry bronze color that I always admired on Kevin. I was soon to learn that her temperament was that of her father, too. Her pleasant smile was always close to the surface. Any playful attention caused it to bubble over into baby giggles and fill the room with joy. Erica was patient and very aware of her surroundings. She watched with brilliant intensity as the mobile over her crib floated lightly in the early spring breeze. She listened to the birds chirping melodiously and the squirrels chattering noisily in the early evening hours.

As the weather turned milder, we wandered outside. We spent hours in the park watching the squirrels scurrying about in aimless scampering. Each bird that flew over her stroller caught her attention. Her pale blue eyes caught the sunlight and reflected back to my soul the warm love that her father and I had shared.

It soon became apparent that Erica was to be the precocious member of the family. By the age of six months she had grown bored with crawling and began to investigate the advantages of standing. She was spirited and curious. With wild abandon she giggled and cooed at people and animals and even inanimate objects, like trees and cereal bowls. We went to the circus and walked through the zoo. We shared cotton candy and listened to the street people's unfamiliar ramblings.

She mimicked every word she heard and could speak in short sentences before most kids had uttered their first intelligible word. The first time she said, "Dada," I thought my heart would break. Turning away to hide the tears, I busied myself at the stove until I had regained my composure. Otherwise, these moments of quiet conversation between her and I were tender and loving.

Each day that passed brought new surprises. Looking through the eyes of my daughter made the world look challenging and inspiring. The future suddenly became bright and hopeful. Sunshine spilled into my life throughout the days of early motherhood. Erica brought a fullness into a heart that had, until her birth, been sorely empty. She was a medicinal ointment to my ailing heart and soul. When my arms felt lonely in the darkness of the night, I would gently cradle my baby in my arms until the feeling passed. I rocked her gently by the hour while nursing her. Her suckling fulfilled not only her need to bond but mine as well.

Erica was the dawn. It was always darkest right before the dawn, and losing my love had been my darkest hour. Now my life was bright again. Erica blossomed each morning like a flower, radiating happiness and love. Our playtimes were filled with learning and enjoyment. For me, just spending the time in her presence was a blessing from God. Her love held my heart together even when I knew that it was breaking. Her smile shielded my eyes from the memories and the gentle ache that they caused.

For eight months we were inseparable. We'd joke during our afternoon 'teas'. We would play hide 'n'seek and read books and we'd take turns singing songs and dancing. Most evenings, I'd sing her to sleep with one of the ditties that she professed to be her favorite. This selection varied each night but she enjoyed each one until she closed her eyes in gentle slumber. I would remain at the side of her crib and watch with devotion as she inhaled a breath and released it. I would have to fight to stop myself from picking her up again and holding her to my bosom.

Just after the day she turned a year old, I noticed that she felt a little warm. I took her temperature and when I saw that it was 103°. I ran to phone her pediatrician. Dr. Davidson had recommended her at my last prenatal check-up, and I had been pleased with our initial interview. Dr. Elly Dixon was bright and spirited and demonstrated a sensibility to my baby that rang true with sincerity. Since then, we had been keeping appointments for Erica's check-ups without fail. She was dutifully caught up on her immunizations and had experienced a normal weight and height increase at every appointment.

Dr. Dixon asked me if Erica had been experiencing any other symptoms or if her behavior had changed in any way. I told her what I knew, including the way she had grown a bit whiny and kept pulling at her ears. Dr. Dixon instructed me to meet her in the ER, and I did just that.

After her examination, she informed me that she was planning to admit Erica to the pediatric unit of the hospital. She saw my concern etch creases in my brow. My daughter had never been away from me. When I voiced my concern over this, she assured me that I could stay at Erica's bedside for as long as I wished. This calmed my fears, and the stay was only for a few days.

The diagnosis had been a middle ear infection, and it had responded nicely to the antibiotics that the doctor had chosen to use. Erica was discharged with a prescription for the same medicine in liquid form. Her health returned a bit slowly but as I watched her overcome her illness, my spirits lifted.

My joy was to be short-lived, however. Within two months she was being admitted again, for the treatment of a severe case of persistent oral thrush. She also had chronic diarrhea and her lymph glands were swollen. Dr. Dixon was admittedly perplexed by Erica's sudden turnaround and wanted to get things under control. When she was discharged, the pediatrician herself mapped out her necessary care for me. She told me not to worry but I was plenty worried.

The next several months were a nightmare. It had become almost impossible not to notice Erica's weight loss. She had become apathetic and listless. She smiled less often and, in fact, lost several developmental milestones that she had previously achieved. She no longer crawled around with enthusiasm, but seemed content to lay in her crib or in her playpen and watch the world happen around her.

One night as I watched her sleep, she suffered a seizure. Her tiny body jerked wildly in a series of spasms and a film of white foam formed between her lips. That evening the doctor admitted my baby under the diagnosis of "failure to thrive" and encephalopathy, which she explained, had led to Erica's seizures. She openly admitted that she was completely baffled by my daughter's symptoms, and had ordered a consultation from the head of Pediatrics in the hospital, Dr. Long. This esteemed colleague had recommended a barrage of lab work, and all we could do was wait for the results of those tests.

Two days later, a nurse came into the room that I shared with my baby while she remained in the hospital. The nurse said that Dr. Dixon and Dr. Long wished to see me in the conference room on that floor. After she directed me to the room, she opened the door and waited until I had walked inside before she closed it quietly behind me. Both doctors had been standing facing the windows, and when they heard the door close, they turned around in unison. They both gestured me to sit down and then they seated themselves in two adjacent chairs and affixed their worried expression on my face.

Dr. Dixon seemed to gather her thoughts first and spoke.

"Tarah, I'm sure you know by now that Erica is a very sick child. Her rather bizarre symptomatology made diagnosis of her condition difficult for me. That was the reason for my asking Dr. Long to assist me. We've been waiting for the results of the tests to be confirmed before we discussed the findings with you . . . to prevent any unnecessary anguish for you."

Her hesitation seemed like a cue for Dr. Long. One glance at his serious expression told me more than a hundred dialogues. Without raising his eyes from the floor, he began. "Mrs. Rhodes. Unfortunately, the results of the tests have confirmed my initial suspicions. Your daughter has been infected with the virus that causes AIDS . . . "

His mouth continued to move but the sounds were lost to me. Had I heard him correctly? My sweet little angel infected with the "Wrath of God" disease? How could that be?

"Looking through your file, I found no evidence that you had been tested during your prenatal care. There are several good reasons why you should be tested immediately. Even though you seem to be in general good health, we will need the results of your HIV antibody test to determine the origin of your daughter's infection.

Ah . . . Mrs. Rhodes, have you understood what we are saying to you? You seem a little dazed and . . . well I certainly can appreciate the bewilderment that you may be experiencing at this moment . . . "

"Tarah? Are you all right? Can you hear me? Is there anything I can do for you?" Dr. Dixon was unable to disguise the concern in her voice or her expression.

"Yeah, I'll be okay. This is difficult to digest. My God! I don't want her to suffer. She has already suffered enough. Please, Jesus, tell me she's going to be okay. Somebody tell me that my baby's gonna be okay . . . "

My tears and my sobs made the rest of my thoughts come out in a disorganized jumble of unintelligible words. Dr. Dixon had come up beside me and placed her hands on my shoulders. I could feel how the sobs were racking through her as well. There was some slight comfort in knowing that she cared so much.

I had so many questions. AIDS, which stands for acquired immunodeficiency syndrome, was making the nightly news. It was the hottest copy on television. Dr. Davidson and I had discussed HIV testing during one of my early prenatal visits. We had decided there was no need since the doctor had no knowledge of my promiscuity prior to finding Kevin, and I thought of AIDS as "that gay disease". Besides, even if they discovered my infection at that point, I would never have agreed to an abortion. I wanted to have my baby.

"I don't understand. Didn't we have Erica tested for AIDS? Yeah, when she was about six months old. Yeah! I remember you told me it was negative . . . remember? It was negative just like you thought it would be."

Dr. Long explained to me that HIV testing in children so young was not a reliable indication of HIV infection. It had something to do with the mother's antibodies leaving the child before the tiny body had a chance to produce its own. He told me about the incubation period of the disease. You could be infected for up to ten years and still not show any symptoms. During this whole time, you could infect others without even knowing it . . . either of you.

"How did she get it? I asked, complete bewildered by the total shock of it all.

"We are not entirely sure. We will be trying to solve that riddle as best we can. Meanwhile, we will have you tested immediately, of course. You really should have a thorough check-up. Tarah. Since your delivery, you have been looking a little haggard, but considering everything you have been through, that is certainly understandable."

I had to admit that what he was saying made sense. Since Erica's birth . . . no, even before . . . since Kevin's death, I had not been sleeping well. Some nights I would wake up after a few hours of fitful sleep covered with beads of sweat. During the day, I would struggle through the mundane activities of daily life under the weight of fatigue and general malaise. I no longer had my usual voracious appetite, and my weight loss was evident, especially in view of my pregnancy. Dr. Davidson had expressed mild concern about my anemia and seemed perplexed by my inexplicable shortness of breath but assumed that my symptoms were related to my grief.

I left the conference room numb with fear and worry. I carried the AIDS information pamphlets in my hands and would read them soon enough. I would learn that HIV could be transmitted by unprotected sexual contact. All those years ago . . . B.K . . . (Before Kevin) I hadn't even thought to ask any of those jerks to wear a rubber. Transmission was possible through "unprotected sexual contact, and I had had more partners than I could count or even wanted to. Now, my poor, precious baby was paying the highest price of all . . . for my mistakes. I felt so guilty. I immediately resolved to do everything I could to help my daughter through this . . . to whatever end was meant to be.

For the next several months, there was nothing we could do, as the three of us watched my beautiful Erica fade away from us. A week before her second birthday she passed away peacefully in my arms. As I held my sweet little girl, she took her last sip of the air on this earth and slipped into eternity. Somehow, through the veil of sorrow that engulfed me, I made the necessary arrangements for her funeral.

I had had the foresight to notify Kiko of Erica's deteriorating condition. I had kept in touch with him all along, and he was as happy as anyone when I announced her birth. He was totally stunned when I informed him of her death. Not surprisingly, he had left his paradise island to be with me during her funeral. It was this faithful friend who held my hand as I slowly approached the tiny coffin for the last time. Gathering all my strength, I walked the few steps to lay the single pink rosebud on her casket. With eyes brimming with unshed tears, I whispered my goodbye. I lightly touched the top of the heavy wooden box that would protect the soul of my baby until the angels whisked her away to heaven. There, at the pearly gates, her father would finally meet his daughter. Together they would wait for my joining them. At that time we would be together as a family for all eternity. Without thought, my hand reached for the gold crucifix hanging, as always, around my neck. With unsteady legs I turned away and began my journey into the future . . . all alone.

My daughter's death magnified my awareness of Kevin's absence in my life. At night, I would lie in the darkness and remember how it felt to have his arms wrapped securely around my waist while we slept. I remembered the moonlit walks we took when even the mundane of this world looked enchanted. The rain covered everything in its magical mist, leaving all it touched looking like it was brushed with diamonds.

Alone in my darkened room, I would converse with my departed Kevin, and share with him the events of the day. I could feel his comfort and I knew that he was steering me through the rocky seas that had invaded my life. Somehow, our love was able to transcend the barriers of life and death. In the morning, as I went about my routine, I could appreciate his immortal presence in my life. The world would have been a strange, scary place if I had to experience it alone, but through it all, I was certain that my late husband lent me his courage and strength. I quietly continued to love him.

Sorry Sheena, but I seem to be rambling. Even today, as I lay here dying . . . the thoughts of my husband and baby bring my heart some solace. I'll get back to you. I promise! I don't know how much longer I will be able to share my thoughts with you. My strength is waning everyday. I'll come back soon . . . I promise!

CHAPTER 29

THE DISCOVERY

As an AIDS victim, I suffer one symptom in utter silence. There is no medicine to lessen the heartbreak, and there is no one with whom I can share it. You see . . . the symptom is loneliness. Fear keeps most people far away.

I'm thankful to you, Sheena, for helping me kill some time. Funny thing. Time is what I have so little of. Yet, it's hard to fill the vacuous hours. Lately, I have not felt very well. It is getting more difficult to talk . . . something about nerve damage or something like that. I am glad to be able to get some of this off my chest . . . so to speak. Believe it or not, it actually helps a little. While I'm spilling my guts to you, some of my experiences take on a different form. It seems that by recalling the events that led to this stage in my life, I am able to see how they intersected and intertwined to form the basic fiber in the fabric of my existence.

Speaking of fabric . . . you remember my buddie, Amy? I'm sure I've mentioned her before. Well, she stopped over for a visit since the last time I talked to you. She brought wonderful news and a special gift. When she handed me the square piece of material, I had no idea what its significance could be. There was a delicate angel embroidered on it along with the words ERICA LOVE RHODES stitched across the bottom. Amy explained that an identical square was on its way to Washington, D.C. to be added to the AIDS quilt.

This quilt was to be a lasting memorial to those stricken

down and taken away by AIDS. The invisible thread that would hold it together was love. How cruel . . . that the only enduring part of my daughter's life was marked by a swatch of cloth on some unseen quilt in some faraway city. I guess I should not say the only enduring part . . . for me, her love will forever remain with those of us who were fortunate enough to have known her.

Amy and I had a nice visit and a good, long cry, both of which I needed desperately. We were so simpatica. She always makes me feel so much better. There had been one question nagging at me, but I had too much self-respect to ask. I just wanted to know if there would be enough space on the quilt . . . for my square. Yeah! I know. That would have really bummed her out! That's why I did not ask. Besides, maybe I did not really want to hear her answer.

It was several weeks after Erica died that I finally read the literature and had my HIV antibody test done. Before that, I considered it a waste of time. While Erica was alive it was more important for me to spend every available minute with her. After her death nothing seemed important except my grief. I had time to read later and read I did. I read everything about AIDS that I could get my hands on. I knew more than most people in the medical profession about this debilitating and demoralizing disease. I knew how it spread. I knew the symptoms and how morbid this illness could be. I also knew that I had it! I had been having signs since shortly after Kevin's death, but this syndrome is so insidious in the beginning, I had never given it a thought.

A lot can change in a few years, and by the time my results came back, I had very little doubt regarding the outcome. Dr. Davidson had related the infamous news of my seropositivity, and advised me to make an appointment with Dr. Jerrell through the AIDS Clinic at St. Michael's Hospital in Newark. Considering the fact that the effects of pregnancy on the expectant woman's immune system may cause the sudden eruption of HIV disease, I did as he suggested. Fortunately, my late husband's estate was still responsible for all my medical bills.

My care and treatment at this facility was the epitome of

professionalism. Everyone strived to treat each client with dignity and respect. I never felt like a number. The entire staff worked diligently to preserve our optimal level of health while being alert for signs of nonmedical problems that could arise. They were all truly wonderful. Even though my medical coverage would have paid for the most expensive specialists, the fact was that most were elitist and refused to treat an AIDS patient. Besides, among the staff in the clinic were the top specialists for AIDS in the country.

As you may have ascertained by now, I keep turning you off and starting again later. That is because sometimes, Sheena, I am too weak to continue talking. But this exercise in dictation has become very important to me, and I don't really understand the reason. Maybe someday, someone may learn something from my musings. If nothing else, I hope they learn to protect themselves from exposure to the virus. Remember: Sex is wonderful, but it's not to die for!

Dammit! Another interruption . . . Oh, all right . . . It's just my brother David. He has a key. He knows to just walk in. I love it when he comes to see me. He always tries so hard to cheer me up. I can see how upset he is even through his smile. I hope everything is okay at his work. He installs alarm systems in residences and businesses. He enjoys it and seems to be doing quite well. He and his family live in comfort and security. No pun intended! I'll just leave you on, Sheena. We'll check it out and see if anything develops. Don't worry. I'll edit it later if it should be necessary. You know I'll have to add my two cents to the dialogue. Shhh! Here he comes.

"Anybody home?" David called from the hall.

"No! Everybody just left."

"Yeah? So who are you? The burglar?" he kidded.

"Hey, Bro! Whatta ya know?"

"Not much as usual. So how you doing? You look sort of crappy, Rah."

"Hey, thanks for the pep talk. I must say . . . you look like the canary that swallowed the cat! What's on your mind, Punk. You cheatin' on that pretty little wife of yours . . . or what?"

"It's really nice to see that this AIDS thing is having a positive effect on your personality."

"So come on, Bro. Give your reclusive sister the scoop. What's hot? Who's not? Tell me some gossip! Let's wallow in the dirt."

"Actually I do have something to tell you. I was putting a security system in a real nice house in Germantown and the funniest thing happened. The people were real nice, and the lady offered me a cold drink. I appreciatively followed her into the kitchen. On the brief pass through the dining room, I couldn't help noticing the collection of photographs on the walls. Then, one particular picture caught my eye. It was of a young girl in a cap and gown . . . like a graduation portrait. Well, it occurred to me that something looked vaguely familiar about that picture. Do you know what it was that seemed so familiar? It was the face . . . I knew that face. In fact, it was your face, Rah."

I did the best I could to contain my impending anxiousness and consciously avoided my brother's eyes. I tried to look nonchalant as I replied tersely, "Yeah . . . and?"

"Was that when you graduated from high school?"

"Yeah, I guess it was. I'm a little surprised that they would still have that hanging on their wall. Hell, you're the only one in the family who has even seen it."

David only hesitated a moment before saying, "Well, to be honest with you, I wasn't very good at hiding my utter surprise at the discovery that these people must have played some part in your life . . . a rather important part in your life, and I did not even know them."

"It was a difficult time in my life. They gave me a job when I needed it desperately. I was getting my first whopping dose of reality, and they helped me meet it head-on. With their help . . . and yes, their love, I overcame the adversity and was, literally able to survive."

"I know, Rah. Mrs. Weber told me all about it . . . or as much as she could. You know, Rah, they have no idea why you left so suddenly . . . or how they could get in touch with you.

She told me that her husband and she used to pray every night that you would get in touch with them."

"I tried. Honestly, I did . . . but by the time I gathered up my courage to face them, they had moved. I had no idea where they had gone. Hell, for all I knew, they could have moved back to Germany."

I was suddenly deluged with memories and emotions long since repressed. I could not have imagined that the Webers still displayed my picture. I would have thought that they had put aside any affection they had felt for me, considering my abrupt and thoughtless departure. I assumed that the portrait he was referring to had hit the trash heap years ago. I certainly would have understood. As it was, I was thrilled to know that they had not forgotten me. With exaggerated calmness I continued.

"How are they? Gerta and Frank. God, you wouldn't believe how often I've thought of them. How are they, David?"

"They're fine. They were overjoyed to find a link in the chain that might lead them to you. Uh . . . They want to see you, Rah. They both want very much to see you."

Talk about your mixed feelings . . . my circuits were already on overload and this simple request created a surge that could cause me to short-circuit. I desperately wanted to see the Webers but, in truth, I did not want them to see me. Not like this! David seemed to sense the reason behind my reluctance and tried to allay my fears.

"They know that you've been sick, Rah. I had to tell them. I could tell how much these two nice people cared about you and I could think of no other way to explain my hesitation to simply tell them how to get in touch with you."

"So you just told them I was sick? . . . or what? Did you tell them what I have? Specifically?"

"I'm afraid so. You know that I could never lie to save my ass. I just told them the truth. They still want to see you. Now, more than ever!"

If I had ever entertained the thought that my heart could not possibly be injured further, I had been wrong. His words punctured it like a dagger. They knew! They knew I had AIDS! They would figure out that I was dying. Could I bear to see the grief in their eyes? I did not have much use for pity. I never saw evidence that it benefited either giver or receiver. On the other hand, I wanted to see the Webers again. I've thought about those two terrific people every single day since I left so suddenly, so long ago. In fact, I never stopped including them in my daily prayers.

Of course, I agreed to see them, but I wanted to allow myself time to get myself together. Even if I was sick, I did not want to look like I was leaning against death's door. I could get my hair done and get someone to put some make-up on me. I still probably would not win any beauty contests, but it might help . . . a little. David was receptive to all my terms. It was obvious that my agreement to allow the Webers this "audience" pleased him a great deal.

"That's terrific. I know this will please them immensely. I'll probably never be able to convince them that I was not an angel from heaven . . . sent by God's own hand to do his bidding. Don't worry! I'll learn to live with that. Thank you, Kiddo. I always knew you were terrific!" With a quick glance at his watch he made ready to fly. "Holy shit! I gotta go, Squirt. Look what f . . . ing time it is. I was supposed to be home a half-hour ago, and I still have to stop and pick up a few incidentals for dinner." David leaned over and kissed me on the tip of my nose.

"Tell your old lady there was a long line at the store and traffic was a bitch. She'll understand," I teased.

"Yeah, she'd understand if she believed my lies for even an instant, but you and I both know how well I lie, and . . . well . . . this lady reads me like a cheap novel.

"Besides she won't mind my being a little late when I tell her I came to see you. She thinks it's sweet of me to come and visit you. You know she sends her love. The kids, too. Yeah, I earn major brownie points for all this kindness. Hell, sometimes I'm tempted to tell her I'm coming to see you and then go out and get into all the trouble I could think of."

"Yeah, and she'd believe you. Right?"

"Yeah, right! When pigs fly! 'Bye, Sweetheart. Take care . . . and call me if you need anything. I mean it! Anything at all . . . anytime . . . day or night. Alright?"

When I nodded, he seemed satisfied and said, "alright! I love you, little sister. I'll see you again, soon. I'll tell the Webers that you said yes. Don't worry. 'Bye, Rah." He scooted out the door before I had a chance to say anything else.

Well, well, well. What do you think of that, Sheena? The Webers! Wow! The Webers are coming! I can hardly believe it. I can't wait. Gee, I have a lot to do before they can see me. Maybe I'll buy something special to wear. Of course, my gold cross will be hanging around my neck . . . just like every day since the day they gave it to me.

Damn! I wish I felt a little better. Lately, I've been feeling kind of poorly, to say the least. Sometimes I think that every part of my body hurts. As always, the doctors say it comes from nerve damage in my brain. Seems like there's not much they can do about it. I guess the nerves are tricky. Doctors don't know enough about the exact method of function in them to do anything. So far, nothing they've tried has helped. Sometimes, the attempted cures are worse than the disease!

I know! Bitch, bitch, bitch . . . whine, whine, whine . . . cry, cry, cry. I'm sorry. I don't mean to cry in your beer all the time. Believe it or not, I'm trying to be strong. I didn't used to be a crybaby. Sheeitt! Most of the time I not only "suffered in silence" (like catholic school taught) but I even retain my sense of humor. Hey, so I'm no comedienne! Remember, Sheena, you're not exactly George Burns. Okay you're no Jack Benny . . . Henny Youngman. Man, don't you know any comedians. How about Bob Hope. Yeah! You finally know one. Yippee! I like watching stand-ups on TV. Many of my favorites have become very famous. I've followed some since the infancy of their careers. These funny men and women have helped me through many periods of depression and turmoil. Many are among 'my most favorite people who I haven't met'. From George Carlin to John

Byner, Bill Cosby to Richard Pryor . . . Robin Williams, Johnny Carson, Jay Leno, etc. These guys have taken me to an arena without fear or pain. Where they are, laughter reins. They helped me cope.

I know you don't have a clue who any of these guys are, so I won't even bother reciting a list of my all-time favorite comediennes for you. Besides a sense of humor really isn't your strong suit, so I won't press the issue . . . just your buttons!

You know, sometimes when I get talking to you, I tend to forget that you're only a machine. Hey, no offense! You're a nice enough heap of tin. I won't argue that. Sometimes I wish you could talk, though. I get tired of doing all the yakking. Yeah, I know . . . bitch, bitch, bitch . . . whine, whine, whine . . . cry, cry, cry.

Listen up, Sheena. I'm so exhausted . . . I'm gonna need the force of the earth's gravity . . . just to fall asleep. Yuk! Yuk! Yuk! God, I hope I feel better . . . at least a little bit . . . just for a couple of days . . . just 'til after my visit with the Webers. I'd like to feel . . . a little better, at least . . . when the . . . the Webers get here. Please, God . . . please . . . zzzzzzzzz.

CHAPTER 30

THE DEPARTURE

H i. It's me. Who else . . . would it be? Whew . . . I gotta tell you . . . today I'm feeling "mighty low"! Just talking to you . . . is so hard. David thought it might . . . help a little if he turned the volume control . . . on you all the way up. That way . . . I won't have to talk . . . too loud. Maybe, If . . . I turned the switch to max . . . recording speed . . . it would come out . . . sounding more normal, too. Sounds logical . . . right? I'll try it . . . If it doesn't work . . . I'll know better . . . next time.

"CLICK."

There, that should do it. God, I'm sorry that I'm feeling so rough. Today of all days! The Webers are coming soon. I can hardly wait. I'm so excited. I guess I'm as ready as I'll ever be . . . thanks to more than a little help from my friends. I am wearing a beautiful, new blue dress. My hair has been professionally styled. My face has been professionally made up. David even polished my gold crucifix to a brilliant luster.

Speaking of David . . . He brought his video cam over, earlier. He said it was to "capture the moment for posterity". I made him promise me not to turn it on until the Webers' arrival. I really wasn't thrilled about being filmed. Hey, let's be honest. Even with professional help, it doesn't take a genius to figure out that I ain't feeling none too healthy! Anyway, you should be the one worrying. I might just prefer talking to a camera . . . then where would you be? Huh?

"Please God. Don't let the Webers . . . see me suffer." I pray.

An image of old Bill flashes through my mind. It is quickly replaced by a memory of Gus, my friend Kari. This is marvelous . . . like a video game . . . sort of. Suddenly the horrible faces of Mr Handy and his son fill my brain. As swiftly as they appeared, they fade . . . only to be replaced by Derek's sneer. Now, Cliff . . . Oh, they're changing faster. Lots of doctors: Doctor Holladay, Dr. Lacey, Dr. Davidson . . . Dr. Dixon, Dr. Long, even Dr. Jerrell's here now. Mr Landis, Slim, Fr. O'Hara . . . The Warners, Virginia, The Webers. When did Amy and Sylvia get here? How did everybody know where to come?

"Ding-dong!"

"Oh, my Lord! It's them. They're here . . . "

Now I can see the blackness approaching. I can vaguely hear a muffled conversation . . . far away. I can feel the blackness . . . making its way stealthily . . . towards me . . . from across the room. I can't fight it . . . this time. I can't . . . fight it . . . anymore . . .

"Jesus . . . forgive me . . . I'm so sorry . . . "

The blackness . . . is all around . . . me . . . all . . . around . . .

Wait! I see Kevin . . . waving . . . No, beckoning me . . . to follow. Oh! Erica, my beautiful little girl . . . running . . . running . . . towards me. They're waiting . . . waiting for . . . me . . .

THE EPILOGUE

When I was first approached about doing this . . . er . . . I must admit, I wasn't thrilled with the idea. I'm still not convinced that I should even attempt it. Please understand that I am doing it for Tarah. In case you haven't figured it out yet, I'm David . . . Tarah's ever-faithful brother.

This project hasn't been easy for me. I still miss my sister very much, but I know how much of herself she put into these recordings. Maybe too much. Sometimes I get to think . . . Maybe if she had saved her strength . . . No! This is what she would have wanted me to do. It was so important to her. Since she didn't live long enough to finish it, I will. At least, I'll try. Here's what happened that night as I entered the room with the Webers hurrying behind me. As I passed the machine I noticed it was running so very discreetly I reached over and turned it off. For some unknown reason I was glad that the Webers had not noticed my action.

I escorted Gerta and Frank Weber into the room where she lay so quietly. Just looking at her face . . . I knew. She was at peace.

From out of the silence, I heard Gerta Cry softly, "My little Libchen. Look how tiny she is. Poor little thing!" She knew, too.

Frank did nothing to hide his sorrow. His tears slid down his weathered cheeks unchecked. He knew, too.

The remainder of the night was agony to us all. We did our best to console each other. The Webers helped me get through that night. There were phone calls and arrangements that had to be made, quickly. The Webers said that they'd take care of all the funeral expenses. Out of pride, I politely refused their generous offer. Frank, however, was not about to be so easily dissuaded.

We continued to discuss the matter until Frank became adamant. He offered the following explanation for his insistence.

For the entire time that Tarah had worked for them, the Webers had garnered fifty dollars per week from her paycheck, supposedly for room and board. They had, however, saved every penny of those monies and had eagerly anticipated its timely return to Tarah during this visit. They felt that they had been twice cheated out of the chance to surprise her with this small windfall. The first time she had run away for some unknown reason. This time, death stole her away.

I recognized the determination in Frank's very attitude. Before long I acquiesced. In all honesty, his timing was impeccable . . . at least where the money was concerned.

Being barely 26 years old, Tarah had not considered the need for life insurance. Any policies from her time with Kevin had been terminated at his death. Of course, I was ready and willing to accept the financial responsibility for my baby sister's funeral. This would, however, surely have imposed some unfair penalty on my growing family. Hey, don't get me wrong. I make a good living . . . but funerals are extremely expensive. I mean, I would never be able to "say goodbye" to her the way I felt my beautiful sister deserved. Obviously, the Webers felt the same way. They insisted on making these difficult arrangements. I will always be grateful for their love and support.

Everything was perfect at the private viewing. The room was full of flowers. Some were from people I, personally, did not even know. Condolences came from every "corner" of the globe. Mother was a big help in keeping the flow of correspondence moving. I'll spare you a descriptive narrative of the mourners who attended suffice it to say that our earthly grief was only slightly anesthetized by our Christian joy.

I was also selected to deliver the eulogy. I feel that my words were not only a fitting tribute to my baby sister, but also an appropriate closure for this recording. With encouragement from Mother and tears flowing freely, I began.

"Today we say goodbye to a daughter, a sister and a friend. Somewhere, this wife and mother is being greeted at Heaven's gate by her devoted husband and beautiful baby daughter. Amen, I could say!

Consider, then, my human and mortal nature. My heart aches with the loss I suffer. Tarah was my very own baby sister and I loved her from the very first day. We shared the joys and sorrows of childhood. We teased each other. We hurt each other. We forgave each other.

My human tears belie the joy of my Christian soul. I rejoice that my Tarah is finally at peace. She now shares the universe with us . . . in the presence of God. Again, I say Amen.

Now, we must remember Tarah . . . her laughter, her energy, and her love. Lest she died in vain, remember that AIDS was the minacious cloud of 'gloom and doom' that cast its deadly pall over her fragile body . . . and over our spirits.

We must not allow the brouhaha involving the fear, the prejudice and the hatred that surrounds this disease to overshadow the importance of education and self-protection, for which Tarah was such a courageous advocate.

Remember her as one of the sacrificial lambs that had been led to slaughter by life. Remember also the lovely, loving and much-loved woman she became in spite of it all.

As she remained strong during her illness, we must remain strong through our grief. This would be our final tribute to Tarah. I know my sister would have wanted it that way.

Amen I say . . . and thank you."

*   *   *

Warrior

A Warrior for God...

Seeks the Lord's glory, not his own

Is uncommonly devoted in his walk with God

Enjoys and embraces challenge

Lives adventurously

Has a warrior spirit

Does not complain in the face of difficulty or hardship

Does whatever it takes to accomplish God's will

Seeks to excel

Expects more of himself than others expect of him

Does the unexpected, does more than expected

Is eager to learn from others

Embraces accountability

Helps the weak and needy

Rejoices with and assists others in their
accomplishments and efforts

Is devoted to the church

Keeps his word

Goes and makes disciples

Sam Laing

Warrior

A Call to Every Man Everywhere

ILLUMINATION
PUBLISHERS

Warrior—*A Call to Every Man Everywhere*
© 2015 by Sam Laing

ISBN: 978-1-941988-13-8.

Printed in the United States of America.

Unless otherwise noted, all Scripture quotations are taken from the *Holy Bible,* New International Version, copyright ©1973, 1978, 1984, 2011 by Biblica, Inc. Used by permission. All rights reserved worldwide.

Scripture quotations marked HCSB are taken from the *Holman Christian Standard Bible®*, Copyright © 1999, 2000, 2002, 2003 by Holman Bible Publishers. Used by permission.

Scripture quotations marked NRSV are from the *New Revised Standard Version Bible,* copyright © 1989 National Council of the Churches of Christ in the United States of America. Used by permission.

Scripture quotations marked NKJV are from *The Holy Bible, New King James Version®.* Copyright © 1982 by Thomas Nelson, Inc. All rights reserved.

Scripture quotations designated as NET are taken from the NET Bible® copyright ©1996-2006 by Biblical Studies Press, L.L.C. All rights reserved.

Cover design by Roy Appalsamy of AMDesign, Inc.

Interior book design: Toney Mulhollan

Illumination Publishers cares deeply about the environment and uses recycled paper whenever possible.

About the author: Sam Laing serves as an elder and evangelist in the South Florida Church of Christ. He and his wife, Geri, have four adult children and nine grandchildren. The Laings have coauthored five books on family, the most recently being *The Essential 8 Principles of a Strong Family.* They maintain a busy schedule traveling in the U.S. and abroad, ministering to churches and conducting seminars on marriage, family and spiritual life. For more information about Sam's ministry visit his website at **www.WarriorfortheLord.com.**

Dedication

To my sons,
Samuel David Laing III and Jonathan Mark Laing;

to my sons-in-law,
Kevin Thompson and Jesse Ghoman;

to my grandsons,
Blake Thompson, Samuel David Laing IV, and Isaac Laing:

At the turning of the new year in 2015, these members of my family (with the exception of two-year-old Isaac!) gathered after sunset on a beach beside the Atlantic Ocean. We prayed and pledged to God to be his warriors. We all placed chains on our necks bearing this inscription:

They were brave warriors, ready for battle.
1 Chronicles 12:8

May we all be warriors for our God
for all the days of our lives!

Contents

Contents

Acknowledgments

Writing this book has been a long battle. It has required perhaps the greatest effort and hardest work I have ever put into a book. As I finish, my hand, like that of the Mighty Man Eleazar, is "frozen to the sword"—in my case, a computer keyboard and mouse (2 Samuel 23:9–10)!

I thank my daughter Elizabeth Laing Thompson for her invaluable contribution to the creation of this book. She has been my editor. Her spirit of faith, excellence, and devotion are nothing short of amazing. Her skill with words and language, her creative mind, her perceptive heart, her gift for sensing what is important, her ability to organize material has been crucial—*no, essential*—in the completion of this volume. It is ironic, but also a verification of what I write in this book: the role of godly women in the lives of warriors is one of God's most important means of making us the men he wants us to become.

Our first child, the daughter my wife and I brought into the world and raised up through her childhood and teen years, has grown up to bless the life of her father, more than I can ever express.

> *Our daughters will be like pillars*
> *carved to adorn a palace.* (Psalm 144:12)

She is truly a *warrior princess*!

I certainly hope this volume accomplishes what I have hoped, dreamed, and prayed: to inspire the men who read it to become mighty warriors for our God.

Introduction

This is a book for men, based upon the life of David.

In it I hope to present a picture of manhood that will inspire, inform, and revive the spirit of every man who reads it. I am hopeful that groups of men will study it and band together to help each other become the mighty men that God wants us to be.

In this volume I have included short fictional vignettes to bring to life some of the key parts of David's story. They are written for that simple purpose—to help the story live. I do not assert that this is the precise way these events happened—only the biblical record can do that. These vignettes are just for fun, to add some color and drama.

The vignettes (with the exception of "The Lion") are told from the perspective of Eleazar, one of David's Mighty Men (2 Samuel 23:9–10). Eleazar was one of this storied group of warriors, and I enjoyed exploring what Eleazar and his friends might have witnessed, felt, and experienced in David's service. In these vignettes, Eleazar and his friends Shammah and Jashobeam all start out as young armor bearers in Saul's army, and later become the Three, some of David's most renowned Mighty Men (2 Samuel 23:8–12; 1 Chronicles 11:10–14). Together they witness David's life—first as a young warrior, and then as a warrior king—unfold. I hope these vignettes breathe life into the biblical record, and light the fire of your imagination as you read God's word.

Some of the chapters open with a Battle Cry (a call to action) to introduce the material, and conclude with a Battle Plan (an action plan) to help you apply the material to your daily life.

If you want to apply the principles in *Warrior* in more specific ways to your daily life, *The Warrior Workbook* provides more in-depth study, questions for reflection, and practical ideas to implement. *The Warrior Workbook* also supplies guidance in how you can create your own Warrior Group within your home church—a fellowship of men who commit to help one another along the path to godly and glorious manhood. As with the Mighty Men of David, I think we will discover that in order for men to become mighty for God and *stay* mighty for God, we need to surround ourselves with a group of warriors who inspire us, encourage us, advise us, admonish us, and keep us on the right track. I encourage you to build a Warrior Group among your friends. Only in the company of other Mighty Men can we fully experience life as men in our Lord's service.

May we all become Mighty Men. And may we, like our brother David, rise to become warriors after the heart of God!

—Sam Laing
Palm Beach County, Florida

Vignette: The Lion

But David said to Saul, "Your servant has been keeping his father's sheep. When a lion or a bear came and carried off a sheep from the flock, I went after it, struck it and rescued the sheep from its mouth. When it turned on me, I seized it by its hair, struck it and killed it."

1 Samuel 17:34–35

The amber eyes peered through the brush at the sheep grazing in the valley below. The stream flowed beside them in cool, sparkling laughter over smooth stones. The soft noise would soon serve as a muffling cover for the attack.

The lion was hungry. Young and powerful, but still inexperienced, he had been recently driven from the pride by his own sire, whose dominance he had challenged. He had wandered aimlessly for days, nursing his wounds and finding little to hunt, until his cravings drew him to the flock.

Accustomed to stalking wild game in the hills, he viewed this opportunity with alert, wary instincts. The sights, sounds, and smells were unfamiliar. Though his hunger pressed him hard, something raised his caution. The creature with the long stick hovered near the sheep, guarding them—this must be a human. Unlike any being the lion had ever encountered, this young human's presence slowed his approach, made him wary. For several days the lion waited, watched, and learned.

The lion was patient, but though he waited long, the human shepherd never left the flock. He was always watching, walking in front of the sheep, or in their midst. He stayed nearby, usually perched on the rocks above. Then he would go down to them, call, and they would follow him away from the stream in a tight grouping as he led them back up the narrow trail to the grassy plateau to graze.

The shepherd spoke. He called out to the sheep, sometimes in staccato sounds, at other times in unbroken, sonorous tones that went on for long periods during the day and deep into the night. As he listened, the lion would sometimes, like the sheep, drift into peaceful sleep.

At dusk each day the shepherd guided the sheep into an enclave in the rocks, where they crowded together and slept through the night. One evening the lion waited until all was quiet, and crept closer. Reaching the entrance of the canyon, he froze. The shepherd was blocking the narrow opening, his sleeping body stretched across the gap. With the pathway to his prey blocked, the lion turned back and melted into the brush.

The next day, his opportunity came. The flock went down to the stream to drink, and when they finished they followed the shepherd as usual back up the path to the grassy plateau. But this time, one lamb strayed. Unseen by the shepherd, the little one, hidden by boulders, lingered too long. She looked up from her drinking, and not seeing the others, began to trot up and down the stream. She could not find the path. Fearful and anxious, she made a soft crying sound, but the rush of the stream on the rocks drowned her out. She was alone, lost and vulnerable.

The lion moved quickly. Gliding in a half crouch, he moved intermittently through the tall grass toward the stream. The lamb ran in smaller and smaller circles, faster and faster, bleating louder. Still the cascading stream muffled her cries.

He was closing upon her now, blending into the brush and sand on the opposite bank. With easy grace he leapt across the stream, turned, rose to his full height and ran along the bank, his gaze intent, his left paws splashing in the water. The lamb saw him and froze in terror. He sprang.

She bolted, her hooves clambering desperately for a hold on the slick, rounded rocks. He almost missed with his extended left paw, but caught enough of her wool to send her tumbling, bleating and crying, into the sand and rocks by the water's edge. He flew over her, and turning in midair tried to catch himself before he slammed into the creek bed wall. He pushed down with his front feet, sinking his claws into the sand, slowing himself enough to spin his rear legs around behind him. She struggled to rise, but he lunged. Fully extending his body, he managed to hook the talons of one paw into the woolen coat of her rear quarters, pinning her to the ground. She fought to free herself, but the talons held firm. The lion, holding her down with his extended left paw, tried to stand quickly. His rear legs spun and thrashed, slipping on slick rocks and loose sand.

He finally regained his footing, stood above her and clamped his jaw down onto the wool above her neck. Getting a mouthful of wool but no flesh, he began to trot across the stream, back into the haven of brush, with the flailing, bleating sheep dangling from his mouth.

He sensed movement. He stopped. Turned his head. Froze in place. He heard a hissing sound.

The stone caught him square in left eye. With a thud it lodged inside the socket. Dropping the lamb and pawing desperately at his eye, the lion roared in agony. He sensed more movement. With his good eye he saw the shepherd running toward him, staff in hand.

Pain forgotten, the lion crouched, then bolted forward. The boy kept coming. The lion attempted to stop, but slipped on the rocks. The shepherd swung his staff and caught the lion in the side of the head, driving the stone deeper into the eye socket. Again and again the boy swung the staff. The lion stumbled, swatting wildly, slipping on rocks in the streambed. With an angry roar, the lion swiped at the boy with one paw. The blow drew blood—he could smell the tang in the air—but it was not enough. The boy was on top of him now, on his back, gripping his thick mane with his right hand. The lion spun and rolled, but could not shake him.

The boy tightened his grip, shouted, and dug his heels into the lion's sides. Something sharp sliced across the lion's neck, a searing pain. Spurting blood, he roared and ran wildly down the streambed, the boy still clinging to his mane. The lion rolled, smashing the boy against the rocks. The boy held on. With another desperate twist of his head, he threw the boy off.

The lion turned and gathered himself to charge, but his legs were strangely weak. He stood in the reddening water, unable to do more than stagger forward. One front knee buckled under him, then the other. He slowly sank into the water, felt it wash over him, and closed his amber eyes.

The boy turned and sprinted back down the stream, looking for the lamb, calling her by name. He found her hiding between two rocks, shivering and soaked with water.

A quick examination yielded no broken bones, and only a few flesh wounds. He took off his tunic and wrapped it around the matted wool. Retrieving his staff and his sling, he went back to the carcass. Taking his bloodied knife, he clipped off three of the lion's talons, placing them in the leather bag tied around his waist. He limped back downstream to the lamb. He draped her small trembling body across his shoulders and carried her up the trail, back to the rest of the flock.

As he ascended the pathway, the shepherd began to sing. The lamb on his back shut her eyes and dozed, safe at last. The flock waiting around the bend, hearing the voice they knew so well, bleated in quiet, gentle reply.

Part One

The Call of the Warrior

Chapter One

The Call to War

Praise be to the LORD my Rock,
who trains my hands for war,
my fingers for battle.

Psalm 144:1

And what more should I say? For time would fail me to tell of Gideon,
Barak, Samson, Jephthah, of David and Samuel and the prophets—who
through faith conquered kingdoms, administered justice, obtained prom-
ises, shut the mouths of lions, quenched raging fire, escaped the edge of
the sword, won strength out of weakness, became mighty in war, put for-
eign armies to flight.

Hebrews 11:32-34 NRSV

Men, we are called to be warriors.

Deep in our souls, God has placed the heart of a warrior. It beats within every man. It is the part of us that longs for battle, for struggle, for conquest, for victory. We sense it: *I have a battle to fight. A struggle to face. A war to win. I need to rise up. I need to fight.*

The men of the Bible were all engaged in battle. They fought different battles—in different situations, times, and ways, with their own distinct personalities—but fight they did. Consider our Old Testament heroes, men like Abraham, Joseph, Moses, Joshua, Elijah, David: they were all warriors in the cause of faith. And the same is true of men in the New Testament, men like Peter, John, Paul, Barnabas, Timothy: they all fought in a mighty spiritual conflict. And last, but not least, consider Jesus himself. He experienced more conflict and endured more opposition and resistance than any man before or since. He faced it every day of his life, culminating in the great victory he won on the cross and in his resurrection from the dead.

And now brothers, it is our turn. Today God is still calling each man, every one of us reading this book, to be his warriors in the same conflict that even now rages on around us. Just as the heroes of the faith went to war for their God, so must we. Fighting and winning the battles God has placed before you—whatever they may be—is *the* defining struggle of your life and your manhood.

And what are our battles today? They are many. They are around us and within us.

- The struggle to overcome our selfishness and sin, our personal temptations and weaknesses.

- The fight to conquer our fears, doubts and pride.

- The battle to uphold God's name and honor; to defend and proclaim his word, to stand up for his truth and justice.

- The calling to be the husbands and fathers we need to be.

- The summons to meet the needs of the poor and the suffering.

- Above all, it is the great mission to help build and advance God's church, to share the gospel, to win souls for Jesus.

This is our great purpose; the great calling from our Father, our Lord and our God. There is no more worthy thing we can do with our lives; there is no greater cause.

Brothers, we cannot be fulfilled as men unless we are warriors for God. *That is what he has created and called us to be.*

God calls a mighty warrior

In the dark days of the book of Judges, we find the man Gideon threshing wheat in a wine press. An angel comes to him and says, "The Lord is with you, mighty warrior" (Judges 6:12). *What? Gideon, a mighty warrior?* He's hiding from the enemy in a winepress! But nonetheless that is how God views Gideon. God sees him as his warrior, and he tells him so.

Gideon is a lot like you and me. He immediately starts making excuses, asking questions, and expressing his doubts: "If the Lord is with us, why has all this happened to us? Where are all the wonders that our fathers told us about? Now the Lord has abandoned us!" (Judges 6:13). But the angel of God does not buy into Gideon's fear and doubt. He tells him, "Go in the strength you have and save Israel." Then he asks Gideon a crucial question: "Am I not sending you?" (Judges 6:14).

Brothers, isn't that enough, to know that God himself has summoned us, that Jesus has called us to battle? Our Lord will give us the strength! We can answer whatever challenge God calls us to face; we can fight—and win—whatever battle he summons us to fight. The issue is not our personality. The issue is not our temperament. It's not even our talent. All that matters is this: God has called you. As men, we can—we must—rise to answer.

Finally, Gideon steps up and answers the call. And from that day forth, his life, his family, and his nation will never be the same.

My brother, please hear me: God sees you as a mighty warrior. No matter where you may be right now, no matter how you may have failed, or how afraid or lacking in confidence you may be, God sees you for the warrior you *can* be and not just for who you are.

The calling of David

Young David is just a shepherd boy. He is minding his own business, taking care of his dad's sheep. One day, his father asks him to carry food to his brothers who are serving as soldiers in Israel's army. David packs up and heads out.

When he arrives, he finds the army of Israel cowering in fear. The soldiers of the army of the living God are discouraged, dismayed, and disrespected. There is a huge giant standing in front of them, mocking them. Goliath is calling for one of their number to come and meet him in battle, man to man.

No one steps up. No one has stepped up for forty days. That's a long time to refuse to be a mighty warrior, my brothers!

David gets upset. The army of God has been disgraced. He wants to do something about it.

King Saul is so desperate that when he hears that a young shepherd boy is talking about taking on the giant Goliath, he sends for him. At first Saul doubts David can do the job, but when David tells him of his past exploits, he changes his mind. Saul tries to suit David up in his tunic, armor, and weapons. David tries them on for size, but they don't fit. And so he heads out to face a nine-foot foe armed with a shepherd's staff, five smooth stones, and a slingshot.

We know the rest of the story. God gives David the victory. The giant falls. The Philistines break and run. The army of Israel surges forward, transformed from cowards to heroes in a matter of seconds. The whole world knows about the greatness of God because of what happened that day! In all of human history, there is no story of combat and courage that is better known or more inspiring than this one.

My brothers, take careful note: God did not speak directly to David that day. There was no angel like the one Gideon met. There was no vision. No prophet. No burning bush. No fire and smoke. No miracle. There was only a sad, cowering army and a mocking, cursing giant. And that was all David needed. He saw and heard enough to know that God was calling him to battle.

My brother, what do you see around you that calls you forth to war? Are you hearing the voice of your God?

God is calling you

> For the eyes of the LORD range throughout the earth to strengthen those whose hearts are fully committed to him. (2 Chronicles 16:9)

Do you know that God is summoning you? Do you realize that he sees you as a mighty warrior? Yes, my brother, you too are a mighty warrior in the eyes of your God. He is offering you a life of greatness, conquest and victory. He is beckoning you to an inspiring but challenging life that will require the best you have to give. He is calling you to the highest standards of morality, purity, nobility, and courage.

I know you feel it. You read it in your Bible. You hear the voice of the Spirit speaking to your heart. You see it in the faces of the people around you who desperately need you to rise up. You see men around you who are dull, dead, asleep, empty, and frustrated because they have lost their warrior spirit and their manhood. They are waiting for someone like you to inspire them. Yes, you.

The victory has already been won

My brothers, there is good news. *Great* news!

"I have told you these things, so that in me you may have peace. In this world you will have trouble. But take heart! I have overcome the world." (John 16:33)

Jesus, through his cross and resurrection, has already fought and defeated our Enemy. If we join Jesus's army, faithfully obey his word, and persevere to the end, the outcome is assured. We will win, because Jesus has already won.

For everyone born of God overcomes the world. This is the victory that has overcome the world, even our faith. Who is it that overcomes the world? Only he who believes that Jesus is the Son of God. (1 John 5:4–5)

You may be wondering, *But what if I get off track, mess up and lose a battle?* When that happens, all we have to do is come back to our Commander, admit our failure, gain forgiveness, and reengage. He will not hold defeats over our heads. He is more interested in helping us get back into the fight than in punishing us for our failures and sins.

So, men, let us engage—or reengage—with confidence. Let's think and live like victors. Let's stride forward to face our own Goliath with the knowledge that although he may be bigger, stronger, and more powerful than we are, our God will guide our small, smooth stone straight, and that our giant will fall.

With God we will gain the victory,
and he will trample down our enemies. (Psalm. 60:12)

Men, let's answer the call and go to war. If we have stepped back, let's step back in—back into the fight. Let's strap on our armor and wield the sword of the Spirit once again. Only as we do this will we find our deepest selves, fulfill our destiny, and discover our true manhood. Only in going to war for God will we find lasting joy and peace within.

My brother, are you beginning to hear the call? As you read this book and study the story of the warrior David, I pray it will inspire you. May it call you forth to battle. May it renew and revive the heart of the warrior within.

Even today, even now, God is summoning his army. I pray that you and I, and all whom God calls, will rise up to be his mighty warriors!

Vignette: Off to War

All the days of Saul there was bitter war with the Philistines, and whenever Saul saw a mighty or brave man, he took him into his service.

1 Samuel 14:52

Next to him was Eleazar son of Dodai the Ahohite. As one of the three mighty men, [Eleazar] was with David when they taunted the Philistines gathered at Pas Dammim for battle. Then the men of Israel retreated, but he stood his ground and struck down the Philistines till his hand grew tired and froze to the sword. The LORD brought about a great victory that day. The troops returned to Eleazar, but only to strip the dead.

2 Samuel 23:9-10

Here we meet young Eleazar on the day he sets out to join Saul's army as an amor bearer.

It was a time of darkness. The voice of the prophets was a faint and distant memory. The priests had become mere officiants, doing their duty with heartless repetition. Our nation's first-ever king, Saul, had begun his reign with promise and fire, but now, pagan enemies were threatening, and borders that were once secure were falling to their increasingly bold advances. Israel was gripped in despair, dismay and fear. Even the once-proud army was losing its nerve, its numbers shrinking with desertion.

I was but a boy in the dark times, the times of King Saul. We were at war, our king was going mad, and God had left us. How long could our nation survive? But I was young, with the fire and faith of the unseasoned and untested—faith more in myself than in my God. Eager, willing, full of zeal and dreams of glory, I begged my father to let me join the armies of Saul.

"No, Eleazar. You are too young. An army needs grown men to do its fighting. Not boys like you. Or even cripples like me."

Years earlier, a neighbor's rogue ox had gored my father's leg, and ever since he had walked with a limp. He was still the strongest man in our village, but no longer the fastest.

"Father, I am old enough to fight. Somebody needs to go and teach the Philistines a lesson; somebody needs to stand up to them," I said.

"That somebody is not going to be you," he shot back. "I have said it a hundred times—you are too young."

"But I hear they're taking younger boys as armor bearers. That's how Zal got in."

"Well, I happen to know that Zalmon's father feels the same way I do. I still don't know why he let him go."

But I was stubborn, just like Father. I persisted. I wore him down. When I told him I would feel less than a man if I could not be in the army, he heard me. In spite of the tears of my mother and the wails of my sisters, he gave me permission. Finally, the day came for me to leave.

"Go son, and may God be with you," Father said, grasping my shoulders with his strong hands, hands that had worked the soil for a lifetime. I felt small and weak in his grip. I had seen him pick up and toss aside boulders half his weight with those hands.

Mother clung to his arm, shuddering through her tears. Her long henna hair shone in the morning sun. She was strikingly beautiful, even when she cried. She looked at me, then turned to Father, searching our eyes for a shred of doubt, an opening that might dissuade me from what she believed would be my journey to certain death.

Her green eyes flashed, hurt and maybe a little angry through her tears. "But he's too young, and we need him here," she said to Father, for the thousandth time.

He stared silently at the ground. She turned to me.

"But you don't know anything about fighting. There are soldiers who are trained for that. Let them do it. Stay here with me and Father and your family where you belong. Do you want your sisters to grow up without you? Do you think your father and I can manage the work alone?"

She was making sense, but I'd made my decision a long time ago. My throat tightened. I tried to speak, but neither my mind nor my mouth seemed to work.

Father would not meet her eyes, or mine. He peered at the ground and then over my shoulder, as if he saw something the rest of us could not. He spoke to me as if I were already far away, already leaving him, and Mother, and the life I had known in the hills and valleys of the Jordan.

"Pray every day, Eleazar. Remember the words we taught you, the words of God. Remember Joseph. Remember Moses. Remember Joshua. Remember that your God is always with you. Remember . . ." He sucked in a long breath through clenched teeth. He shook his head, as if willing himself not to weep, not to show weakness. He lost his resolve and threw his arms around Mother and me, crushing the breath out of us with his embrace. My feet came off the ground and my face was pressed between his chest and Mother's shoulder. I could smell the delicate fragrance she always wore.

"Son, I . . ." He searched for words, but they would not or could not come.

"Son, Eleazar, my son . . . I want you to know . . . I wanted to say—I have always wanted you to know . . ." His voice broke. His strong body shook. His huge hand pressed between my shoulder blades, and he kept gathering my robe up with his fingers, wadding it up into his fist. I hung there, limp and helpless, like one of my sisters' dolls. I had only seen him cry one other time, at the funeral of his mother, years ago when I was a child. His tears came unashamed and in a torrent now, just as they did then. I wanted to hear him say the words I had never heard him say, but he stopped short.

At last he loosened his grip, cleared his throat, and lowered us back to the ground. He put two strong hands on my shoulders. "Son, take care of yourself. Come back to us—to your mother and me, and to your sisters. We will be right here. We will pray for you. May God watch over you, my son, my only son."

I nodded and took a deep breath. "I will come back to you. God will bring me back. When we have defeated our enemies, I will come back."

My mother smoothed out my robe, running her hands from my neck to my shoulders, and around to the front of my robe. She tried to smooth it out, and patted me on the chest with the palms of her hands. She forced a smile.

"Father has wrinkled your new robe. There now, we don't want you going to see the king looking like a beggar. You are so handsome, they need to see you at your best."

She reached up and tousled my hair with her fingers, doing whatever secret thing it is that mothers think they need to do to make their sons look presentable.

"Red curls, just like your father when I met him," she said, smiling through her tears. "So handsome."

"Good-bye, Mother. Good-bye, Father. I . . . I will come back to you. I will come back to you all," I said, gesturing toward the house where my three young sisters had come to stand in the doorway. They clung to each other, cheeks wet and flushed with tears.

Eyes burning, I turned, and grabbed the leash of my little donkey, which Mother and the girls had loaded with more provisions than I could ever hope to use in my journey. Giving the leash a tug, I set out down the road.

At the great rock at the crest of the hill I turned back to wave to my family and gaze one last time at my home, the only home I had ever known. Already the distance had made the house, and my family, look small. Still standing in the doorway, Father put his arm around Mother and she laid her head on his chest, as I had seen her do countless times. I looked long and hard, to engrave the scene in my memory forever. I waved one last good-bye. When I crested the hill, hidden from their view, I fell to my knees and wept.

Chapter Two

The Warrior Who Might Have Been

"Your glory, O Israel, lies slain on your heights.
How the mighty have fallen!"

2 Samuel 1:19

"You acted foolishly," Samuel said. "You have not kept the command the
LORD your God gave you; if you had, he would have established your king-
dom over Israel for all time. But now your kingdom will not endure."

1 Samuel 13:13

The Bible tells the story of a man who might have been.

Had that man—Saul, the first-ever king of Israel—listened to, obeyed, and humbly served God, his name could have gone down among the great heroes of the faith. Jerusalem might today be known as the City of Saul. The flag flying over Israel could have upon it a symbol called the Star of Saul.

After the time of the leadership of Moses and Joshua ended and the Israelites settled into the Promised Land, they were guided by leaders called judges. They did not have kings, as did the pagan nations around them. God was Israel's true king; the judges were servants and stewards, charged with keeping the people loyal and faithful to their true Leader—God himself.

But the time comes when the people approach Samuel the judge and ask him to appoint a king for them: "So all the elders of Israel gathered together and came to Samuel at Ramah. They said to him, 'You are old, and your sons do not walk in your ways; now appoint a king to lead us, such as all the other nations have' " (1 Samuel 8:4–5). Samuel's sons are not godly men; the nation is under military threat and the people simply want to be like the other nations around them. God accedes to their request, but only after warning what their human kings will do to harm them, and explaining in no uncertain terms that the real issue is that they have rejected him as their king (1 Samuel 8:10–18).

God graciously sets up the whole situation to go as well as it possibly can. He reveals to Samuel that Saul son of Kish is to be the new king. He arranges for the two of them to meet, and Samuel privately anoints him as king. God gives Saul some amazing signs to confirm that he has indeed selected him. Saul receives the Holy Spirit, and he prophesies. Some "coincidences" occur that could have only been orchestrated by the divine hand of God (1 Samuel 10:1–12). Later, in a great public assembly, Samuel announces Saul as the new king, and he receives an overwhelmingly positive response from the people (1 Samuel 10:20–24).

Saul starts out well enough. Getting started well is good. Good beginnings can lead to good endings—if we stay faithful to the end.

Here are some of the early positives about Saul:

- He is *physically impressive.* He is a head taller than any other man in the whole nation (1 Samuel 9:2).

- He is *humble.* When Samuel alludes to him being the next king, Saul responds by saying that he is the least in his clan, and that his clan is the least in the nation of Israel (1 Samuel 9:21).

- He is *decisive and bold by the power of the Spirit.* When he learns of a threat to the nation from Nahash the Ammonite, he calls on the people to follow him to battle, and they do. The result is a great victory (1 Samuel 11:1–11).

But along with Saul's strengths, some of his flaws soon begin to surface. What this tells us, warriors, is that our talents and strengths do not cancel out our character weaknesses. Our weaknesses must be recognized and dealt with, or they will undermine us.

Here are some of his flaws that begin to assert themselves:

- *Insecurity.* When the people have all assembled and Samuel is ready to appoint him king, Saul can't be found—he is hiding among the baggage (1 Samuel 10:22)! This at first seems to be humility, but it is more likely a portent of deep insecurity, self-focus, and self-absorption.

- *His righteous anger crosses the line into human anger.* When he learns that the nation is in danger of attack, the Spirit of God moves in Saul's heart to stir up righteous indignation, and he calls the people to follow him into battle. But he overdoes it, resorting to threats and intimidation as a source of motivation (1 Samuel 11:6,7).

- *Fear, faithlessness, and desire for success lead him to usurp God's authority.* Later, the Philistines once again gather in huge numbers to attack Israel, and they appear to have the upper hand. Samuel the prophet has agreed to come before the army and offer the sacrifices and ask God's blessing on the coming battle. Saul knows that when the men see this, morale will improve and his army will be stronger and better prepared to fight. Samuel is set to come in seven days:

    > When the men of Israel saw that their situation was critical and that their army was hard pressed, they hid in caves and thickets, among the rocks, and in pits and cisterns. Some Hebrews even crossed the Jordan to the land of Gad and Gilead. Saul remained at Gilgal, and all the troops with him were quaking with fear. He waited seven days, the time set by Samuel; but Samuel did not come to Gilgal, and Saul's men began to scatter. (1 Samuel 13:6–8)

Saul sees more and more of his men deserting, and he makes a terrible decision. In his pride and fear he preempts the priestly role of Samuel, and offers the sacrifice himself: "So he said, 'Bring me the burnt offering and the fellowship offerings.' And Saul offered up the burnt offering" (1 Samuel 13:9).

Samuel arrives on the seventh day, just as he said he would, but it is at the very end of the day and Saul has already made his fatal error. Rather than trusting God and Samuel, Saul has opted to go through the motions of seeking God's blessings so as to improve morale. His actions reveal that he is more about putting on a religious show than genuinely calling upon God in the manner he has prescribed. This is an attitude and an error that will cost him the throne. God wants things done in the right way and for the right reasons. Only then will he bless our efforts.

The Bible tells of another leader who lost men from his army at a time of crisis. Gideon was facing terrible odds and was already outnumbered when God told him he had too many men. God took his army down from thirty thousand to only three hundred, and then gave them a mighty victory (Judges 7). Could Saul not have remembered this story?

We also see Saul's first occasion of excuse-making and rationalization:

> Just as he finished making the offering, Samuel arrived, and Saul went out to greet him.
>
> "What have you done?" asked Samuel.
>
> Saul replied, "When I saw that the men were scattering, and that you did not come at the set time, and that the Philistines were assembling at Micmash, I thought, 'Now the Philistines will come down against me at Gilgal, and I have not sought the LORD's favor.' So I felt compelled to offer the burnt offering." (1 Samuel 13:10–12)

He spins what he has done to make himself look better. He probably buys his own excuse and believes his own rationalization. And that is a fatal error: The first lie we tell is the one we tell to ourselves.

• *Unreasonable personal demands.*

It has been said, "Pride makes you stupid." We are about to see one of those moments for Saul.

At a time when the armies of Israel are without weapons and at a very low point of stalemate and discouragement, God uses the daring initiative of Saul's son Jonathan to bring about a huge victory (see 1 Samuel 14:1–23). After Jonathan's bold two-man attack, the enemies of Israel are suddenly panicked and on the run. In the midst of this great moment, Saul makes a selfish, foolish, and unreasonable demand of the army: "Now the men of Israel were in distress that day, because Saul had bound the people under an oath, saying, 'Cursed be any man who eats food before evening comes, before I have avenged myself on my enemies!' So none of the troops tasted food" (1 Samuel 14:24). Saul won't let the men eat anything all day until they have won a complete victory. What is he thinking? Soldiers need to eat to have the strength to keep fighting!

Jonathan, not knowing of the oath Saul has imposed on the army, comes across a beehive during the midst of the battle, dips the tip of his spear into the honey, and has a taste. Later, when this becomes known, Saul is ready to take Jonathan's life to honor his imprudent vow. Only the intervention of his soldiers prevents him from enforcing this harsh and unreasonable oath.

When we make unwise decisions like this, there is usually much more at work than meets the eye. Saul is making the battle about himself and his personal vengeance. His life and leadership have become twisted to be about *him* instead of about God and God's glory. Saul's pride and hunger for achievement are becoming more and more evident. His pride and selfishness will eventually cause God to determine that Saul is unfit to lead.

But Saul still has victories

Even after his failure with the offering and with the foolish oath, Saul still has some victories:

> After Saul had assumed rule over Israel, he fought against their enemies on every side: Moab, the Ammonites, Edom, the kings of Zobah, and the Philistines. Wherever he turned, he inflicted punishment on them. He fought valiantly and defeated the Amalekites, delivering Israel from the hands of those who had plundered them. (1 Samuel 14:47–48)

We might ask: *If God is unhappy with Saul, how can Saul still lead Israel to victory? How can he still do great things? If he is such a sinner, why doesn't God immediately remove him from being king?*

These are great questions. If you have been in the church very long, you have probably seen a version of this very thing happen. You may have seen leaders rise to influence, position, and power, and have it go their heads. You have seen trusted, well-known, and respected men (and women) turn from their good beginnings and go down a path of selfishness, pride, and folly. And perhaps you saw these people stay in a leadership position, and even have great success, only to have their hidden sin or prideful spirit exposed later on.

When something like this happens, does this mean that the whole kingdom of God is a sham and a pretense, and that the church is really no different than the world? The message from the way God deals with the disobedience of King Saul is: No, it does not!

Here are some important lessons to learn from the example of Saul:

Early success does not mean permanent success.

We can begin with God's blessing and with a good heart, but we also have an Enemy who will stop at nothing to corrupt us. One of the ways he does so is by deceiving us with pride when we are successful. Success should humble us, not make us arrogant. Experiencing success should convince us that success comes from God, not from us. If we let success make us prideful, we are headed for disaster.

Character weaknesses may take time to reveal themselves.

Saul starts out his journey in a great way. He rallies the people. He has some impressive victories. But over time, his flaws begin to assert themselves. Under the pressure of leadership, his weaknesses become more and more evident. Pressure has not created his weaknesses; it has revealed them.

Insecurity and pride often go together.

Saul's early reluctance to lead appears to be motivated by humility. But later, his insecurity shows itself to be based in pride. Even when we lack confidence, that does not mean that pride is not lurking inside our hearts. It has been my sad observation that a man can be profoundly unsure of himself, yet at the same time have an arrogant spirit. Exactly how that works, I am not sure. But as it happened with Saul, it can happen to any of us.

Power, popularity, and position can become more important than the glory of God.

When Samuel approached him to become king, Saul was not ambitious or expecting to be selected as the next leader. But what happens when we get a taste of glory and power? We didn't know it could become addictive until we experienced it! And so we find Saul, who had hidden himself in the baggage on the day of his appointment to the kingship, building a monument in his own honor only a short time later (1 Samuel 10:22; 15:12).

When we fight against the will of God, we ultimately lose.

> *When Saul realized that the LORD was with David... Saul became still more afraid of him, and he remained his enemy the rest of his days.* (1 Samuel 18:28–29)

Saul has already been told that God is going to replace him as king (1 Samuel 13:14; 15:26–29), but still he fights to retain his position. Determination is one thing; foolish stubbornness is quite another. When we set ourselves against the clear will of God in our lives, we are headed for disaster.

God will deal with sin in our lives, and in the lives of leaders.

Sometimes leaders remain in power, even when they have seemingly disqualified themselves. Why would a just and righteous God allow this? Perhaps he is giving them a chance to repent—he is, after all, a God of mercy and redemption. It also may be that God is using the situation to teach all of us deeper lessons—that *he* is the ultimate head of his kingdom, no matter what anyone may do or how they may fail. He may also be waiting to see how his people will respond when a leader falls. Will we stand up for God and his word even when the one in charge goes astray? Will we lose our faith in God because of what that person does or does not do? Will we give in and go along with his sin? Will we deal with the situation righteously when it is exposed? Is our faith in God and his word, or is it in a human leader?

Later we find Saul in another terrible moment. God sends him on a mission—to bring judgment on the Amalekites, the people who had refused to help Moses and the Israelites in a time of distress years before. He is told to "devote to the Lord" all the people and their possessions. That means that all were to be destroyed and that no plunder was to be taken. Saul does obey these instructions. Here is what he does:

> *Then Saul attacked the Amalekites all the way from Havilah to Shur, to the east*

of Egypt. He took Agag king of the Amalekites alive, and all his people he totally destroyed with the sword. But Saul and the army spared Agag and the best of the sheep and cattle, the fat calves and lambs—everything that was good. These they were unwilling to destroy completely, but everything that was despised and weak they totally destroyed. (1 Samuel 15:7–9)

Once again Saul shows his penchant for excuse-making and blame-shifting as he tells Samuel that *he* destroyed the Amalekites and their possessions, but that *the army* saved the good stuff. And then he adds another deception by saying that he planned to sacrifice it all to God at a later time anyway! Does Saul really believe his own rationalizations? Has he convinced himself that this is the truth, or is he just plain lying? My own opinion is that he has convinced himself of his rationalizations. And that is what makes his character so flawed—he can no longer tell truth from falsehood; he is self-deceived.

God is so upset at Saul's disobedience that he tells Samuel he is grieved that he ever made Saul the king (1 Samuel 15:10–11). My fellow warriors, when we grieve God, we really have fallen! God presents us and others with opportunities, hoping we will use them well. We assume God always knows exactly how everything will turn out, but perhaps he may choose *not* to know. He waits and sees. He gives us talents, a position of leadership in the church, a good job, material blessings, a great wife, children...what are we going to do with those blessings? Will we be good stewards, or will we, in faithlessness, pride and fear, turn away from the Giver and become abusive of, consumed with, or unappreciative of the gifts he has given us?

Speaking of grief, God has gotten past his—but Samuel has not:

The LORD said to Samuel, "How long will you mourn for Saul, since I have rejected him as king over Israel? Fill your horn with oil and be on your way; I am sending you to Jesse of Bethlehem. I have chosen one of his sons to be king." (1 Samuel 16:1)

God did mourn for Saul, but he has moved on past his grief. He has chosen a new leader for his people—a young shepherd boy whom he will anoint and raise up to serve as king in Saul's stead. God comes to Samuel and tells him it is time to move ahead. It is time to stop mourning for Saul and look to the future. A new leader is coming—a man after the heart of God.

Fellow warrior, do you need to hear what God said to the prophet Samuel? Are you grieving over a fallen leader? Are you suffering in pain, disappointment, or anger over someone who once led God's people to victory—someone who inspired, encouraged, and helped you? Has this grief persisted too long? Is it affecting your faith, your confidence, and your motivation? Has it caused you to question God, or to diminish or damage your commitment to his church?

Brother warriors, remember this: We signed up to follow Jesus. He is our Lord; he is our commander. Human leaders will rise and fall. They may lose their faith, get off track doctrinally, or fall into sin. They may even pass on and go to be with God. But Jesus never changes.

I have seen strong and trusted men fall. When they do, I remind myself of this: *I signed up to serve as God's warrior because of Jesus. I am loyal to him and to his body, the church. I will not allow my faith to be shaken, nor will I desert the bride of Christ because human leaders fail. I will do what I can to help. I will stand for righteousness. But I will not leave God or his people because a leader stumbles or gets off track. There is a time to grieve, just as God did over Saul. But then there comes a time to move on and rebuild the kingdom.*

> *A thousand may fall at your side,*
> *ten thousand at your right hand,*
> *but it will not come near you.*
> *You will only observe with your eyes*
> *and see the punishment of the wicked.* (Psalm 91:7–8)

Brother warrior, keep serving Jesus and his church no matter who or how many may fall at your side!

What Saul thinks and what he says are not the same.

Later on we see Saul engaging in some more interesting, but deadly behavior.

After David slays Goliath, the women are singing songs of celebration, saying how David has slain *tens of thousands* and Saul only *thousands*. Saul reacts with jealousy and fear. He starts thinking some dangerous things he does not say out loud, but says only to himself.

> When the men were returning home after David had killed the Philistine, the women came out from all the towns of Israel to meet King Saul with singing and dancing, with joyful songs and with tambourines and lutes. As they danced, they sang:
>
> > "Saul has slain his thousands,
> > and David his tens of thousands."
>
> Saul was very angry; this refrain galled him. "They have credited David with tens of thousands," **he thought,** "but me with only thousands. What more can he get but the kingdom?" And from that time on Saul kept a jealous eye on David.
>
> (1 Samuel 18:6–9, emphasis added)

Later, he does this again. He says things to himself that are different than what he says to others:

> **Saul said to David,** "Here is my older daughter Merab. I will give her to you in marriage; only serve me bravely and fight the battles of the LORD." **For Saul said to himself**, "I will not raise a hand against him. Let the Philistines do that!" (1 Samuel 18:17, emphasis added)

The tendency to hide what is really going on in his mind and heart finally hardens into a pattern in Saul's life. He says one thing, but thinks another.

We just can't conceal who we really are forever. The truth of our inner self will finally come out of us one way or another. Saul begins to act more and more angrily. For no apparent reason, he starts throwing spears at David, who is serving him by playing his harp to help soothe Saul's jangled emotions. To others, this may have seemed irrational. But really, it was not. It was the product of Saul's anger, ambition, pride, and jealousy. He has tried to put on a good face, but he can no longer conceal the truth of what has been happening in his mind and heart. He is jealous, threatened, and afraid. He had been given the kingship by the grace of God, but he has lost it through his own pride and disobedience. Instead of humbly accepting God's verdict, he fights against it and destroys himself.

Brother warriors, when we have evil thoughts like these in our hearts, who knows about them? Do we tell anyone our real thoughts? To whom are we confessing? What righteous, godly men do we have in our lives to whom we are opening our hearts? If we don't want to end up like Saul, we need to get honest, humble, and open—and fast!

Brothers, I know this is not the most encouraging story in the Bible. Yet it is here for a reason. We need to hear the lessons loud and clear.

There is one more lesson we need to learn, and it may be the most important one we can learn from Saul; indeed, it may be one of the most important ones we will ever learn in our life.

What is that lesson?

Know yourself.

We have an enemy who knows us. He studies us. He contemplates, schemes, and dreams of the best way to bring us down. He is looking for the chink in our armor, the weak place in our character, the blind spot—and that is where he will strike. If we aren't men who are honest with ourselves—who see ourselves clearly—our adversary will know us better than we know ourselves, and we are headed for certain defeat.

Don't we remember? At the heart of the call of Jesus is the call to deny ourselves: "If anyone would come after me, he must deny himself and take up his cross daily and follow me" (Luke 9:23).

Let me ask what may seem to be some obvious questions:

If we don't know ourselves, how can we deny ourselves? If we are blind to who we are apart from Christ, how can we make the changes we need to make?

Read carefully these profound words from James, the earthly brother of Jesus:

> *Do not merely listen to the word, and so deceive yourselves. Do what it says. Anyone who listens to the word but does not do what it says is like a man who looks at his face in a mirror and, after looking at himself, goes away and immediately forgets what he looks like. But the man who looks intently into the perfect law that gives freedom, and continues to do this, not forgetting what he has heard, but doing it—he will be blessed in what he does.* (James 1:22–25)

Brother warrior, do you see yourself as God sees you?

Do you know who you really are?

Do you know well your own character?

Do you know your strengths, but also clearly see your weaknesses?

Do you have blind spots?

You have an enemy who knows you. He is scheming *right now* to bring you down by exploiting your vulnerabilities. The more clearly you see them, the more prepared you are to win the fight. But if you are unaware and blind, or if you just don't take your weaknesses seriously, you are set up for defeat after defeat after defeat. You are headed for a hard fall—perhaps a fall beyond recovery.

A message to the "seasoned warriors"

As a veteran of many battles myself, I have a special message for my fellow seasoned warriors: *As older men, we must know ourselves better than anyone else in the fellowship of warriors.* We must be the men above all others who are the most easily convicted, most readily humbled, and most quickly perceptive of our sins and weaknesses. Nothing is worse than to witness an older man who is unaware of himself; a man who, after years of life and service to God, still has blind spots that he does not see or admit. Let us as seasoned warriors lead the way in humility, in self-knowledge, and in openness. Let us not imitate the tragic example of Saul, whose blindness to himself increased as he aged, ultimately causing him to fall from the faith.

I have now lived as a disciple for more than four decades. I have seen how Satan attacks me. I have seen how he has overthrown great men who have done mighty things for God. Most of the time, it was because these men had a weakness (or weaknesses) they would not recognize or deal with. These men were either completely blind to their own flaws, or they convinced themselves that the weaknesses were not that serious. These men fell defeated, not even sure how or why they had fallen. Some of them even convinced themselves they were doing just fine, even as their souls slipped away.

Brother warrior, may this never happen to you and me! *Know yourself.* Never forget your sins. Never forget that those very sins put Jesus on the cross. Know who you are and who you will become apart from Christ. Know with clarity your "old self" that you decided to put to death so that your "new self"—your *true* self—could live (Luke 9:23, Ephesians 4:20–24). Then you will know what part of your nature must be crucified all the days of your life (Galatians 5:19–25, Colossians 3:5–11).

These clear-eyed, self-aware men are the, honest, humble servants and warriors whom Satan cannot deceive, the brothers who will stand victorious at the end, who will one day hear the glorious words, "Well done, good and faithful servant.... Come and share your master's happiness" (Matthew 25:23).

My brothers, these are the warriors whom God is seeking: men like David, men after God's own heart.

Chapter Three

The Warrior After God's Own Heart

But now your kingdom will not endure; the LORD has sought out a man after his own heart and appointed him leader of his people, because you have not kept the LORD's command.

1 Samuel 13:14

But the LORD said to Samuel, "Do not consider his appearance or his height, for I have rejected him. The LORD does not look at the things man looks at. Man looks at the outward appearance, but the LORD looks at the heart."

1 Samuel 16:7

Saul, the first king of Israel, has fallen. The warrior who might have been has failed. God is looking for a replacement, someone to lead his people in his ways. What kind of man will he seek?

The Bible tells us what God was looking for in this man, and this description tells us what he still looks for in every man who would be his warrior: God was looking for *heart*. Yes, heart. Above all else—above talent, above skill, above appearance, it was *heart* that God longed to see in his new king.

It was heart that set David apart above all the other men in Israel.

It was heart that got David anointed as a shepherd king.

It was heart that kept David going as a warrior king.

It was heart that earned David the title of Israel's greatest king.

And heart, my brother, is what God wants from you and me.

Heart is not just a part of what God wants—it is the *most important thing* that he wants. Heart is the summation and essence of everything God is looking for in his warriors. And why is that? What makes it so important? Heart matters because God knows that if he has our hearts, he has us. If we try to give God a part of ourselves without giving him our whole heart, we are doomed to defeat—we cannot be his warriors.

God does not just want your service—he wants *you.*

God does not just want you to fight for him and for his cause—he wants a relationship with you, Father to son.

God wants your heart.

He has given you *his* heart, and his greatest gift—his Son—and he wants your heart and your self. That is the only way it works!

Heart is the most important thing in your life

Many a man has vainly tried to serve God by giving only a part of himself. Perhaps he gave God some time. Perhaps he gave some effort, some money. Perhaps he intellectually believed in God—even respected God. Maybe he kept a few rules, got some bad stuff out of his life, even got involved in church. But down inside, his heart did not belong to God. God was not his greatest love. God was something or someone he made a donation to, but not the greatest love of his life. There is only one way to be a warrior for God, and that is by becoming a man, like David, who is after the heart of God (1 Samuel 13:14).

Superficiality is one of the greatest reasons men have lost their warrior spirit, or have become warriors in the wrong cause. We simply cannot be warriors for God unless he has our whole heart, unless he is our first and greatest love. More than our career, our wife, our children, and yes, even our own selves, God must be the greatest passion in life.

And why is that? Why does God need to be the greatest love in our hearts? The answer is as simple as it is profound: *Because he alone is worthy.* God is our Creator, he is our Life-giver, he is the Source of everything. If we put him first, the other loves and priorities in our lives sort out just fine. We still love our wives, our friends, our families, our lives... but we understand where they all came from, and we love the Giver more than we love the gifts. When we love the Giver first of all, then we are free to love his gifts with a fervent love that is ordered in its proper place.

What exactly is *heart*? How do we define it?

Heart is the real you. It is the deepest part of your soul, your core, the essence of who you are. It encompasses the entirety of your being—not just what you do but who you *are*. It includes, but is more than, your emotions and your intellect. It includes, but is more than, your physical body. Heart is the inner part of you that directs the way you use and employ the other parts of your Self. Let's not make it too complicated—I think you probably get it by now!

Heart is different than talent. Talent is wired into us at birth. Yes, we can and should develop our talents, and we can, later in life, discover talents we didn't realize we had. But even though you may long to sing rock and roll or dunk a basketball (these are a couple of my fantasies— what are *you*rs, brother warrior?), those kinds of things are, by and large, inborn capacities that you either have or don't have from the get-go.

If we are a man after the heart of God, we care about what God cares about. We think like he thinks, we value what he values. We work for what he wants to accomplish. We avoid what he does not like. We embrace what he loves. An as warriors, we fight against what God opposes and fight for what he promotes. It's that simple.

This tells us that if we are to be God's warriors, we first must be his sons. We must love him if we are to fight for him. We must give God our first allegiance, making Jesus our Savior and Lord. We must be born again of water and the Spirit, baptized into Christ.

Relationship precedes duty. We must be close to God if we are to conquer for him. Duty to God without love for God produces men who harsh and self-righteous, or who are half-hearted and weak. Such men cannot be the godly warriors who will carry God's cause, word, and work forward with compelling force. Men motivated by duty alone and not by closeness to God will, by their harshness and pride, alienate those they seek to reach for Christ, or they will simply give up when hard times come. To avoid these traps, become a man who is a warrior for God because he has your heart. Let God's love, shown through the life and death of his Son, capture and compel your heart to its highest love and greatest destiny.

The heart of David

What shows a warrior heart? Let's look at the heart of the man who God said was a man after his own heart—let's look at David.

David poured out his heart to God

> *I cry aloud to the LORD;*
>   *I lift up my voice to the LORD for mercy.*
> *I pour out my complaint before him;*
>   *before him I tell my trouble.* (Psalm142:1–2)

Nothing reveals our relationship with God more than our prayer lives. Prayer is the heartbeat of our relationship with God.

It is essential that we cultivate a deep level of heart-communication with God in prayer. Pouring out our hearts in prayer means that all of our hearts' inmost contents are laid out, poured out before our Father. It means that we are not merely superficial or dutiful in our prayers, but that we are heartfelt. We hold nothing back. We tell him what we really feel, what we really think.

As we noted earlier, superficiality and lack of depth may be the single greatest problem that men have in their lives, and in their walk with God. As a matter of fact, if we are superficial, we cannot have a walk with God—he won't walk with us unless we are committed to him heart and soul. Perfunctory obedience and shallow religion just don't cut it with God. He wants us to be real and genuine, or he cannot and will not be close to us—and we certainly cannot be his warriors.

This is what David wanted with God: genuineness, honesty, and depth—nothing fake or phony. David was a great warrior for God because he knew God so well. He went to battle for God because he was close to God and down inside, he knew God heart to heart. How about you and me? If you have lost your warrior heart, maybe the first place to look is at your closeness to your heavenly Father.

David spent time with God

How do we know this? Well, look at the psalms he wrote. David sings of God being his shepherd. We know that a shepherd spent night and day with his sheep for months, and knew them each by name (John 10:3). Reading David's psalms, we can sense that David spent hours and days out in nature, singing, playing his harp, writing his music, and being with God. He could face Goliath, deal with relentless pursuit by Saul, and face warfare with the pagan tribes around him because he was intimately acquainted with the God who called him into battle.

David cared about what God cared about

In Acts 13:22 God says, "I have found David son of Jesse a man after my own heart; *he will do everything I want him to do*" (emphasis added). David longed to please God; he cared about the same things God cared about. All alone as a young shepherd, with neither his brothers nor his father beside him, David cared for the defenseless flock. When the lion and the bear came, he courageously protected his sheep. This is the heart that God wanted in the man who would look after his people. "And the LORD said . . . 'You will shepherd my people Israel, and you will become their ruler' "(2 Samuel 5:2).

David's heart was full of praise and thanksgiving to God

His psalms are songs full of praise and thanksgiving. With all of the trials he endured, with all the pressure he experienced, he never stopped being grateful. The theme running through the psalms is one of overwhelming and heartfelt gratitude. This tells us so much about David's heart, and about the nature of his relationship with God. He was full of appreciation. He was a warrior, but not a warrior of grim and angry determination or begrudging and resentful dutifulness. No, he was happy warrior, serving his Commander with joy and thanksgiving, even when his heart was torn with anxiety, confusion, and heartache. This is the kind of warrior God wants all of us to be.

David was a warrior who deeply trusted in God

The basis of his confidence as a soldier was that he knew his cause was just, and that God was with him in whatever God called him to do. When he says in Psalm 23:4–5 that he does not fear when going through the valley of the shadow of death, and that God prepares him a table of plenty in the face of his enemies, David is telling us that as God's warrior he has absolute confidence in God's ultimate provision of victory.

Getting our hearts right

The great news is that anyone can have a great heart, and anyone who has lost his heart can get it back.

You're not sure about that? If God commands us in his word to have a good heart, then that means *it is possible!* What God expects, he enables. His commands are not burdensome; they are not beyond us

(1 John 5:3). We can *decide* to have a good heart. We can *choose* to open our closed heart and soften our hard heart—and when we do so, God responds; he comes to our aid.

Consider this prayer of David:

> *Create in me a pure heart, O God,*
> *and renew a steadfast spirit within me.*
> *Do not cast me from your presence*
> *or take your Holy Spirit from me.*
> *Restore to me the joy of your salvation*
> *and grant me a willing spirit, to sustain me.*
> (Psalm 51:10–12)

David offers this prayer when has fallen deeply, horribly into sin—committing adultery and murdering a friend to cover it up. He has deceived himself; he has hardened his heart so severely that we wonder how he could ever recover. He is praying, trying to make his way back to God. As he prays, he realizes that his heart, turned to stone by his sin, is not where it needs to be.

What can David do? How can he get his heart back? He asks God to create within him a pure heart. He asks for the Spirit of God to renew, revive, and restore his heart.

Brothers, we can get in such a state that we need can't even get our attitude right. We can sink so low and grow so hard that without divine assistance, we can't get our hearts tender and sensitive. But the good news is that God loves us enough to help us get there. Thankfully, our Father "knows that we are dust" (Psalm 103:14) and stoops down to help us in our worst, most desperate moments.

My wife has taught me an invaluable life lesson about this. She says that when she is not doing well spiritually, she has to have "Gethsemane Prayers," where she gets on her face and re-surrenders her life to God, giving up her will in order to do God's will. And she says that when she has done all she can to get her heart tender, penitent, broken, and sorrowful, but is still left wondering—still doubting if her heart is where it needs to be—she then asks God to take her heart the rest of the way home. She does her very best, and then she calls upon God to finish the work, to complete what she cannot do. When she first told me that, I was so very encouraged. I don't know about you, but sometimes I get to stuck in a place where I have fought hard to get my heart to a better place, but it is still hard, angry, dull, damaged, or hurting. God is aware of our struggle, and when we are in that difficult place, he will help us get our heart where it needs to be. Amazing grace!

So what does it mean to have a "good heart"?

Here is where I have come out on this (and I hope it doesn't sound like heresy!):

A good heart means knowing that I don't always have one, and that I need God's help to get there.

When our heart is not where it needs to be, may this be our prayer: "Father, I don't have a great heart right now, but I want one. God, I am coming to you, asking for a tender and renewed heart. Please help me. Please move in my heart."

Consider this great promise from the Old Testament, when God brought his sinful, fallen people back from captivity:

> For I will take you out of the nations; I will gather you from all the countries and bring you back into your own land. I will sprinkle clean water on you, and you will be clean; I will cleanse you from all your impurities and from all your idols. I will give you a new heart and put a new spirit in you; I will remove from you your heart of stone and give you a heart of flesh. And I will put my Spirit in you and move you to follow my decrees and be careful to keep my laws. (Ezekiel 36:24–27)

This was an awesome promise for the returning Israelites, but how much more is it fulfilled in the New Covenant, when we can be born again and receive the indwelling Spirit! Brother warriors, baptized into Christ—dead, buried, and raised with him—you who long to have good hearts before God, let us rejoice, and so come to God, knowing he will help us to be men with good, tender, noble, and honest hearts. If we want it, God will enable it!

What about emotion?

Heart is more about *will* than about *emotion*. It is more about the direction you have decided to go—the ultimate loyalty of your life—than about how you feel from day to day. Heart, although connected to emotion, is not the same thing as emotion.

Some of you, when you hear the term "heart" and expressions like "love God with all your heart," immediately become discouraged. You are concerned because you do not feel a continuous sensation of connection to God. You lack the "warm fuzzies" and tears that others seem to have. And that can make you wonder about your relationship with God: *Am I for real? Do I truly love God? Am I missing something?*

Certainly, we want to grow in our feelings of closeness to God. God made us with emotions, and he wants us to enjoy and experience them. But there is a big difference between experiencing emotion in our walk with God and *being based upon* emotion in our walk with God. Some men are readily emotive, and feelings come easy to them. They cry, they rejoice, and they often "feel" God's presence as they worship and pray. I think David was one of those men. It is certainly a good thing to have those feelings—as long as they are based upon a genuine walk with God. But we need to be careful to seek *God himself*, and not a *feeling about God* as we build our relationship to him.

Emotions are ephemeral. Depending on our mood and our experiences in a particular day, they can go up, down, and all around. Let me say it again: let's seek God himself—a genuine relationship of honesty, commitment, and integrity. Let's not seek emotion as an end in itself. To do so is to open ourselves to being deceived or dictated to by our own changing feelings rather than the truth of God.

I love my wife dearly. Sometimes I am swept away with feelings of love just by looking at her. Suddenly, all that she means to my life will rush over me like a surging, pleasant waterfall. In those moments, I go to her with tears in my eyes, hug her, and tell her how much I love her. I remind her that she is the greatest blessing God has given me in this world. Those are great moments . . . but I don't experience them every day. I love it when I do (and so does she!), but when I don't happen to be emotionally swept off my feet on a particular day, that does not mean that Geri is in any way lacking my full love, heart, and commitment. She has my heart *all the time* —whether or not I am feeling an ecstatic connection to her in one particular moment.

That being said, if you rarely have deep feelings of connection with the Father, I would encourage you to grow emotionally, both as a man and in your walk with God. If you are completely devoid of those kinds of feelings toward God, I would urge you to do some soul-searching and be sure your heart is still fully given to the Father. The feelings of emotional closeness will come back when you give your heart to him again.

A man after the heart of God

To summarize all of this, what does a man the heart of God look like? How does he act? How does he feel? A man after the heart of God:

- is in love with God and wants to know God.
- wants to spend time with God.
- wants to spend eternity with God.
- wants to please and honor God.
- wants to serve God's people.

Heart. That is what being a true warrior for God is all about. And so I ask you, brother warrior:

- Who are you in your core being?
- Who are you when the exterior is stripped away?
- How are you doing today? How is your heart?
- Are you at peace with God?
- Are you growing?
- Do you still long to know the Lord and follow him?
- Do you still have dreams of faith?
- Are you in love with God?

Being God's warrior is not about position. It is not about glory for yourself. It is all about knowing, loving, serving, and being near to God.

Who was David, after all? Is it really so complicated? He remained throughout his life the man he was when we first met him out working in his father's fields: A simple shepherd. A man who sang and wrote songs. A man who played his harp, prayed, and practiced slingshot. That's really who David was.

He was the man who:

- sought to know God.
- sang songs about God.
- saw and celebrated the beauty of God's world.
- shepherded the sheep.
- stepped up with a slingshot.
- simply and sincerely trusted God.

Brothers, let us be the same man on the outside as we are on the inside. And may that man be, like David, a man after the heart of God.

Chapter Four

The Warrior's Walk with God

One thing I ask of the L̲ORD̲,
*   this is what I seek:*
that I may dwell in the house of the L̲ORD̲
*   all the days of my life,*
to gaze upon the beauty of the L̲ORD̲
*   and to seek him in his temple. . . .*

Hear my voice when I call, O L̲ORD̲;
*   be merciful to me and answer me.*
My heart says of you, "Seek his face!"
*   Your face, L̲ORD̲, I will seek.*

Psalm 27:4, 7-8

Warrior, what is the greatest need in your life?

Is it to be saved? To go to heaven? To be righteous? To fight and win battles for your Lord? All of these are worthy, even essential, things in your life. But they are not your greatest need. You wouldn't be reading this book if you were not motivated to be a better man—and that is admirable. But behind the desire to improve, behind the good deeds, there must be a greater purpose, a greater need, a greater destiny. That purpose, that need, that destiny, is to know God himself.

Your greatest need is to know God.

The greatest thing in life is knowing God. The rest is just details.

Think about it:

Why are we saved? *That we might know God and his Son, Jesus.*

Why do we go to heaven? *To be with God and with his Son, Jesus, in eternal fellowship.*

Why are we righteous? *Since God is righteous, we must also be righteous, that we might know him.*

Why do we fight battles? *Because in doing so, we come to know the Lord, and we help others to know him.*

"Now this is eternal life: that they may know you, the only true God, and Jesus Christ, whom you have sent." (John 17:3)

Brother warrior, *knowing God* is the heartbeat behind all that you are, all that you do, and all that you need to become. It is your life.

As we talked about in the previous chapter, God wants a Father-son relationship of intimate fellowship with each one of us. Perhaps David's heart has already inspired you to draw closer to God. But you may be wondering what closeness to God really means, and how you can develop it.

What is intimacy with God like, and how do we get it?

Let us turn now from the profound to the practical. Shift gears with me, brother, while keeping the same heart.

Let us examine some of the real-world examples we find in David's life, realizing that behind these very down-to-earth practices is a profound reward—the reward of knowing God. Let us discipline ourselves to imitate these practices, because these tools will help us to seek—and find—connection with our Father. I pray these practical suggestions provide the means you need to become closer to God than you have ever been before.

Here are some ways we can draw close to God as David did:

Seek God's face

Reread the verse at the beginning of the chapter. As we've already seen, David was the man after the heart of God (1 Samuel 13:14). What did David's heart tell him? *It told him to seek the face of God.*

David wanted to know God—to genuinely, deeply know God. He longed to gaze upon the beauty of God. He longed to spend time with

God. He longed to listen to God. He longed to speak with God. He longed to think about and meditate upon God. He longed to please and serve God, and to be his warrior. And that is what David did, all of his life. And that, brother warrior, is just what you and I must long—and learn—to do.

Speak aloud to God; cry out to him

Here is what David has to say:

> To the LORD I cry aloud,
> and he answers me from his holy hill. (Psalm 3:4)

Prayer is speaking to God. We don't always have to speak verbally to communicate with God; he has the ability to "hear" what we say and think even when we do not speak aloud. We can certainly speak to God with our minds alone. But if you are in the habit of silent prayer, I would encourage you to speak aloud in prayer more often. Speaking aloud in prayer may provide a way for you to get more real with God than you have ever been before. I don't know about you, but sometimes in my silent prayers I can begin to feel as if I am just talking to myself! When I change and begin to speak aloud, I connect with God in a deeper and more profound way. Praying audibly may be a key way for you to communicate more closely with God, to tell him more clearly and deeply what is on your heart.

And here is how Jesus prayed to his Father: "During the days of Jesus' life on earth, he offered up prayers and petitions with loud cries and tears to the one who could save him from death, and he was heard because of his reverent submission" (Hebrews 5:7).

Jesus' example shows us that we can take it even further—when we feel the need, let's cry out loudly to God, just like Jesus did!

Spend time alone

Modern warriors are constantly surrounded by people. And even when we are alone, we are not really alone...we have our phones and computers with us, constantly beeping greetings and messages and requests from people demanding our attention. We have to fight to find true solitude with God—away from people and from the demands and distractions of technology.

Warriors, let's find ways to get alone with God, in a place where we can open our mouths and speak aloud. Let's take Jesus' advice when he tells us to go into our room, close the door and pray (Matthew 6:6). Who we are when we are alone with God is who we really are. Being alone with the Father allows us to speak honestly, knowing we will not be overheard or interrupted.

On our knees, bow down

> But I, by your great mercy,
>   will come into your house;
> in reverence will I bow down
>   toward your holy temple. (Psalm 5:7)

> I will bow down toward your holy temple
>   and will praise your name
>   for your love and your faithfulness,
> for you have exalted above all things
>   your name and your word. (Psalm 138:2)

> Come, let us bow down in worship,
>   let us kneel before the LORD our Maker. (Psalm 95:6)

We are physical beings. Our bodies are created in the image of God. We cannot artificially separate our relationship with God from our physical bodies. Our body language communicates as much to God as do our words and our expressions.

Perhaps no postures are more associated with prayer than those of kneeling or bowing down. Such positions show humility, reverence, respect, and submission. I have found in my own prayer life that when I am on my knees before God, my heart becomes more humble. I sense that I am in the physical position I *ought* to be in heart—the position of need and humility. I find that my heart will more readily go to the *place* of humility when I assume the *posture* of humility.

There are times when we are so moved that we need to fall prostrate before God. Such a time occurred when David charged the people and his son Solomon to build the temple:

> *Then David said to the whole assembly, "Praise the LORD your God." So they all praised the LORD, the God of their fathers; they bowed low and fell prostrate before the LORD and the king.* (1 Chronicles 29:20)

Jesus himself fell prostrate on his face in the Garden of Gethsemane (Matthew 26:39). During the earthly ministry of Jesus, people often came to him and fell on their knees, asking for help. Our fellow warrior Paul knelt before the Father (Ephesians 3:14).

When is the last time you fell on your knees to pray? When is the last time you lay prostrate before God, praising and honoring him, or pleading for his help and seeking his presence? Brothers, if our walk with God has become stale, rote, and routine, let's get on our knees and fall on our face in prayer.

Lift up and spread out our hands

> *Hear my cry for mercy*
> *as I call to you for help,*
> *as I lift up my hands*
> *toward your Most Holy Place.* (Psalm 28:2)

Next to our face and voice, our hands may just be the most expressive part of our bodies. As we speak with others we use our hands to express and emphasize what we are saying. If someone speaks to you and maintains a motionless posture with little or no hand movement, the conversation can easily become boring, unexpressive, and passionless. Rigidity and lack of movement can betray a lack of concern.

True, some of us (and some cultures!) are naturally more active and energetic in conversation than others. We don't all communicate in the same way, nor should we. And there is a time for stillness and repose in our interactions with people and with God. But we all use our hands to some degree when we speak. Why would we leave them out of our prayers to God? If we are not using our hands, we are overlooking a powerful, valuable, and I would say necessary, part of our communication with the Father.

Warriors, let's imitate David and the other great heroes of the faith. Let's become more physically expressive in our communication with God. Let's stop being so uptight and self-conscious. Let's open our hands in prayer as we ask God for his forgiveness, mercy, and blessing. Start in your devotional times—let the physical expression become real and genuine there, just between you and God.

Then take it out there in front of others. Let us raise our hands as we thank and praise God for his greatness and goodness. Let's obey what Paul told us men to do: "I want men everywhere to lift up holy hands in prayer, without anger or disputing" (1 Timothy 2:8). Let's raise our hands in our prayer groups with other warriors and in our family devotionals. As we sing at church, let's give it a try: If raising your hands during a song means "Praise God!" to you, then go ahead and raise your hands, even if you are the only one in the room doing so! It may take a while to feel comfortable with a different expression, but isn't that always the way it is when we learn something new?

Put variety in your prayer life

Taking a prayer walk outdoors is a great way to draw near to God. I do this many a morning as I walk the quiet streets of my own neighborhood. I often use this as an opportunity to pray my way through a psalm, using the inspired words of Scripture (and of David) to take my heart to wonderful places of praise and petition that I would not have gone on my own. For some of us who need new life and freshness in our prayers, a walk outside may be just the answer we have been looking for.

Emotions in the Psalms

We are emotional beings. God made us that way, and God himself has powerful emotions.

Some men consider emotion to be the exclusive realm of women and children. Some even view it as a weakness, or at best as territory outside the bounds of real manhood. A cursory look at the great men of the Bible shows this to be mistaken thinking. Go through the list: Moses, Joshua, Joseph, David, Jonathan, Elijah, Jeremiah, Peter, Paul, John—all were men of deep passion and powerful emotions. And no man who ever lived felt and expressed emotion more powerfully and righteously than did Jesus. Yes, emotion—godly emotion—is meant to be a vital part of the life of every true warrior, and of his walk with God.

Here are some of the emotions of pain and anguish that David experienced and expressed in his walk with God:

Anxiety:

> *Search me, O God, and know my heart;*
> > *test me and know my anxious thoughts.* (Psalm 139:23)

Distress and sorrow:

> *Be merciful to me, O LORD, for I am in distress;*
> > *my eyes grow weak with sorrow,*
> > *my soul and my body with grief.* (Psalm 31:9)

Sighing:

> *All my longings lie open before you, O LORD;*
> > *my sighing is not hidden from you.* (Psalm 38:9)

Groaning:

> *I am worn out from groaning;*
> > *all night long I flood my bed with weeping*
> > *and drench my couch with tears.* (Psalm 6:6)

Tears and weeping:

> *Record my lament;*
> > *list my tears on your scroll—*
> > *are they not in your record?* (Psalm 56:8)

Faintness of heart and weariness:

> *From the ends of the earth I call to you,*
> *I call as my heart grows faint;*
> *lead me to the rock that is higher than I.* (Psalm 61:2)

David, we thought you were a courageous warrior! What's up with all this emotional stuff?

Brothers, it is time for us to understand something: *Being a courageous warrior does not mean we are immune to feelings of fear and discouragement.* As men we all feel these kinds of emotions from time to time. When we do, it does not mean we are failing to be real men, it just means we need to turn to God!

I have often seen men, in a mistaken attempt to be strong, decide not to acknowledge or share their feelings. Or perhaps they do acknowledge their emotions, but they do so only with other people, and not with God himself. Brother warriors, let us learn to share our deepest feelings with our Father. As we do so, our relationship with God will go to new depths of honesty and sincerity, and ascend to new heights of closeness and intimacy.

Sometimes we may feel such a sense of emotion or pain that we may not even be able to put into words what we feel. What do we do then? God, as always, has a solution:

> *In the same way, the Spirit helps us in our weakness. We do not know what we ought to pray for, but the Spirit himself intercedes for us with groans that words cannot express. And he who searches our hearts knows the mind of the Spirit, because the Spirit intercedes for the saints in accordance with God's will.* (Romans 8:26–27)

Brothers, when we come to a place where we feel so deeply we cannot put it into words, let us know that the Holy Spirit within us is expressing to God on our behalf those feelings that are beyond human words or language. And when that happens, may we praise God for his grace in meeting our every need.

But there is more to emotion than anxiety, stress, pain, and grief. Our Father wants to share joy and exhilaration with us as well. Let us once again learn from our brother and fellow warrior David:

Joy and gladness:

> *But let all who take refuge in you be glad;*
> > *let them ever sing for joy.*
> *Spread your protection over them,*
> > *that those who love your name may rejoice in you.* (Psalm 5:11)

> *I will be glad and rejoice in your love,*
> > *for you saw my affliction*
> > *and knew the anguish of my soul.* (Psalm 31:7)

We have just seen some amazing expressions of David's joy and gladness. Joy is wonderful. Gladness is glorious. I always think of joy and gladness as two different levels of feeling. Joy is an amazing, awesome, wonderful feeling. But gladness—well, that's joy on steroids! If joy is laughter, then gladness is falling on the floor and cracking up until you embarrass yourself. Probably not the most scholarly way to look at it, but it works for me!

Brothers, let's learn to be joyful and glad in our relationship with our Father. Let's share with him the moments of celebration, ecstasy, delight, and just plain old fun. Your father wants you to be happy. Your joy makes him happy. Go ahead and party!

So how might we express our joy and gladness? How would they show up? We will use two of David's psalms. Here goes . . .

Shouting:

> *Then my head will be exalted*
> *above the enemies who surround me;*
> *at his tabernacle will I sacrifice with shouts of joy;*
> *I will sing and make music to the LORD.* (Psalm 27:6)

Let's have some moments where we shout out our praises to God. Let's cry out with joy, victory, and celebration! Why do we confine loud celebration to sporting events or rock concerts? Why not shout for God and his glory? For victories over sin and Satan? To thank God for answered prayers? To celebrate the blessings of God? You say shouting is irreverent? Take a look at the word of God—his people shouted for joy, time after time. Let's yell it out. Let's roar it out, privately and publicly.

Why not have some moments in church services where God's people cheer and shout? Do we have less to celebrate than our brothers in the Old Covenant? I think not! Jesus had people criticize him for letting the children shout aloud in the temple. They told him to tell them to be quiet. What did he do? He said this:

> *But when the chief priests and the teachers of the law saw the wonderful things he did and the children shouting in the temple area, "Hosanna to the Son of David," they were indignant.*
> *"Do you hear what these children are saying?" they asked him.*
> *"Yes," replied Jesus, "have you never read,*

> *" 'From the lips of children and infants*
> *you have ordained praise'?"*

> (Matthew 21:15–16)

Jesus wasn't going to allow some stuffy people to quell the joyful, exuberant spirit of the kids who were there that day. Let it be so with us: let's not quench the spirit of joy when it breaks out in the church or in our own heart!

> *When he came near the place where the road goes down the Mount of Olives, the whole crowd of disciples began joyfully to praise God in loud voices for all the miracles they had seen:*
> *"Blessed is the king who comes in the name of the Lord!"*
> *"Peace in heaven and glory in the highest!"*
> *Some of the Pharisees in the crowd said to Jesus, "Teacher, rebuke your disciples!"*
> *"I tell you," he replied, "if they keep quiet, the stones will cry out.*

> (Luke 19:37–40)

This time it's the Pharisees trying to shut down the joy of the kingdom. Jesus once again says, "No way!" It is not irreverent, disrespectful, or inappropriate to shout and rejoice at church. Let me ask us, brothers, do we want to be like Jesus, or like the cranky, sour Pharisees? Let's start some shouting in our own lives and at church!

Oh, but there is even one more level. Here we go again! Check out one last way David expressed his joy before God:

Dancing:

> *When the men were returning home after David had killed the Philistine, the women came out from all the towns of Israel to meet King Saul with singing and dancing, with joyful songs and with tambourines and lutes.* (1 Samuel 18:6)

> *As the ark of the LORD was entering the City of David, Michal daughter of Saul watched from a window. And when she saw King David leaping and dancing before the LORD, she despised him in her heart.* (2 Samuel 6:16)

Dancing may be the ultimate form of joyful physical expression. It is held forth in the Scriptures as a holy, happy, and entirely acceptable manner to praise God. Jesus used it to describe the joy of celebration when the prodigal son returned home (Luke 15:25). As in the case of David's dancing before the Lord, there were some folks around who had words of criticism. I say, brothers, that if David could dance for joy, and Jesus could teach dancing as a godly response to repentance, then we are clear to bust some pure and righteous moves for God!

Why does all of this matter?

How do expressive acts like dancing, rejoicing, raising our hands, bowing down, and speaking aloud help us walk with God? How does physical expression tie in to emotional connection?

- It helps us to express our true feelings—our true selves—to God.

- It makes our relationship with God just that: *a relationship*, filled with all the modes of expression we would use with a human father or friend.

- It helps us to relate to God in a more honest and open way.

- It brings our walk with God out of the ethereal, theological sphere, and into the real world. The world of the heart.

Emotion and your walk with God

Emotion is integral

As you seek to draw closer to God, brother warrior, let David's example remind you that emotion is an integral part of your relationship with your Father. David shows us that emotion and deep expression are entirely appropriate in our walk with God. Not only are they appropriate, they are natural. They are meant to be a part of who and what we are as warriors for God. From the despair of defeat and discouragement to the exuberance of victory and blessing, we need to be real and honest with God, and share with our Father all that we feel.

Emotion helps God heal us

We need to open our hearts to the Father so he may repair our broken and damaged places. We need to express to God any negative emotions so that he can help us overcome and get past them. As we learn to share those feelings more openly, we do so with the prayer that God will give us deliverance, healing, forgiveness, and the strength to endure.

Emotion makes our Christian life a joy, and makes it last

Brother warriors, let your walk with God be filled with joy! Let it not be a stale, depressing, or boring relationship. God wants to share your greatest joys and triumphs with you.

I pray we all learn to rejoice exuberantly in the Lord. May our greatest joys be shared with God and with a clear conscience. Men who seek celebration, happiness, ecstasy, gladness, and joy apart from God may have their moments of fun, but they will not have a life of real and lasting joy. They may mistakenly come to believe that joy and happiness can only be found apart from God, That, fellow warriors, is a lie from Satan. A life of true pleasure is found only in our Father's house.

David's heart can become our heart, too

Perhaps when you began reading this chapter, you expected instructions on how to study your Bible or pattern your prayers—both valuable skills to learn as we seek to walk with God. But David's example gives us something even more memorable: a real-world example of intimacy with God. A heart and a lifestyle we all can imitate.

When we study the life of David, we find a multicolored tapestry of a beautiful, lifelong, intimate walk with God. A walk that began in the fields, among flocks of sheep; spent years in the desert, hiding among caves, valleys, and mountains; and ended in a palace, resting in peace. In all these places and stages David walked (and ran, and hid, and fought, and—finally—rested) with God. His honest and emotional prayer life was the sustaining force that kept him going through every trial. David sought the face of God, and God graciously turned, looked, and smiled upon him. My brothers, God longs to do the same for you and me.

Let us seek the face of our Father. May we know him, and may he know us. May his smiling face shine down upon us, filling our hearts and lives with love, joy, and gladness!

Vignette: Eleazar Meets Shammah

Next to him was Shammah son of Agee the Hararite. When the Philistines banded together at a place where there was a field full of lentils, Israel's troops fled from them. But Shammah took his stand in the middle of the field. He defended it and struck the Philistines down, and the LORD brought about a great victory.

2 Samuel 23:11-12

Only a few hours have passed since Eleazar said good-bye to his family. Here he meets Shammah, who is also on his way to serve Saul.

The road from my village was as narrow as it was deserted. Several times I had to unpack my donkey, Jezebel, and lead her through the tight passages between the rock walls. Each time I had to tie her down while I went back and hauled the baggage through on foot.

"Why do mothers pack so much?" I asked Jez, sweating and scrambling through another passageway. "You don't know? It's because they think we can't do anything for ourselves. They want us to be babies all our lives, to stay in the house and help them in the kitchen, that's why." Jez turned and looked at me. I don't think she had ever before been given instruction in the ways of mothers and sons.

Removing her load for what must have been the fifth time, I saw something sticking out of the bundle, something that had worked loose. I reached in and pulled it out. It was a piece of leather, wrapped up and bound tightly with twine. I untied the twine and unrolled the leather. A sword glittered up at me. I gasped, and looked around as if someone seeing me might assume I was a thief.

"But there are no swords in Israel, only those of Saul and Jonathan," I said to Jez. "Where did this come from?" A flick of the tail, a batting of an eye, a stamp of the foot. No help from Jez. I looked up into the sky, as if I might see the angel who had given me such a priceless gift. No one there. My mind raced, my throat constricted, my breathing became shallow. Who? Father? But I had never seen this sword before. Where had he kept it? Where did he get it? Then I remembered, from years ago, a conversation I had overheard between Mother and Father. One night he woke the house with his shouts, and I could hear Mother calming him, telling him it was just a dream, that he was home, that those days of battle and blood were past. I had not understood it then, but now it came to me: Father had once been a soldier! Why hadn't he told me? Why did he wait until now to let me see this magnificent weapon?

I held it gently in my hands, turning it over again and again. It was beautiful. It shone in the sunlight. The handle was carved out of a piece of some sort of wood, so dark it was almost black. The blade was shiny and bright. I felt the edge. Razor sharp. "This has just been sharpened," I said to the donkey, noticing the brighter hue along the edge. I stood up, held it in my hand. I extended it forward in mock combat. I swept it from side to side. I turned and faced my imaginary foes, attacking me from behind. A few deft thrusts and they were done for. Easily dispatching them, I turned and dared the next group to do battle. They cut and ran at the sight of such a fearsome warrior.

"That's right, run, you Philistine dogs! And if you come back, there will be more of the same for you!" Jezebel turned, looked at me, snorted and shook her head. I bowed to an invisible crowd. "Why, thank you ladies. It was nothing, really. There were only twenty of them. Brave? Me? Well, I have experience, you see, and when our other men turned and ran, well, somebody had to make a stand. Somebody had to save the village. Well, if you insist, I will lead the victory procession. No, no, please, no songs for me. All glory to God."

I wrapped up the sword and carefully placed it back in the bundle on Jez's back. "Let's get through this next pass. I think there's water on the other side, and we can camp there for the night," I said to her.

In spite of my pulling, Jez and the bundle once again got stuck in the narrow opening. "I'm not taking that thing off you again," I said. "I'll push it through."

I went round to her backside, braced myself against her hindquarters, and shoved. No movement. She brayed and stamped her feet. Another push. I lowered my head further, and braced my feet against the ledge so I could push harder.

Jez decided, right in the middle of one of the hardest shoves, with my hands on her hindquarters and my head angled low under her tail, to relieve herself. All over my head, all over my new robe. Shouting and cursing, I drew back to kick her in the backside. She moved faster than I had ever seen her move, out of the way of my rising foot. My leg swung up wildly, my other foot followed, and then my whole body was extended in the air, parallel to the ground. I landed with a crushing thud, flat on my back, gasping for air, sputtering and soaking wet.

A voice echoed loudly in the narrow passage: "Well, Master Swordsman, if the Philistines attack with their donkeys, you're done for. Especially if they turn them around and come at you backwards!"

I scrambled to my feet, fumbled to pull my sword out of the pack, and looked around. I saw no one. Right. Left. Still no one.

Laughter echoed through the passageway.

"Up here, Swordsman. No, look higher. Up here. That's right. A little higher. To your left. Got some of that stuff in your eyes? In your ears? Ah, now you see me, brave warrior."

He was sitting cross-legged on a ledge about fifteen cubits above me, with his hands clasped in front of his knees, like he was ready to sit with his family and have the evening meal. My age or younger. Blonde hair. Short red tunic. Leather leggings from the thighs down. Small dagger in his leather belt. His long, curved bow was propped up on the ledge next to him, along with a quiver of arrows. He looked so relaxed, it made me even more embarrassed and angry than I already was.

"Come down here and we'll see how you do, pretty boy," I shouted, my voice cracking. I sounded like my little sister Hannah when she didn't get her way. I didn't know which was hotter: my flushing face, or the stream of donkey urine oozing down my neck.

"Alright, alright, I'm coming down, but you have to promise not to swing that thing at me. You'll hurt both of us. And maybe while I'm heading down, you can get yourself a little cleaned up!"

"So, Master Swordsman, do you have a name?"

He moved down the rocky slope, softly stepping from one boulder to the next. He kept his eyes on me, and his feet seemed to find their own way from stone to stone. I looked back, still shaking and fuming with embarrassment and anger. I didn't know what infuriated me more, the donkey anointing me or the huge smile on this arrogant stranger's face.

"Yes, I have a name. And I have a father and a mother, and I have something you don't have—respect and manners."

"Oooh, look out now, Swordsman, or your anger and stubbornness might get you in trouble again."

"You want trouble, pretty boy? I'll give you all the trouble you need, right here, right now." He paused on top of a huge boulder almost twice my height. His bow was strapped at an angle across his back, reaching across his body on both sides. His quiver of arrows reached straight up over his right shoulder. There were so many fletched arrows in it that it looked like a bird may have been perched on his shoulder. The sun glinted off his small dagger on the right side of his waist, and off his straight blonde hair that reached down to his shoulders.

"Are you going to let me come down there or not? I don't really mind fighting you, that wouldn't last too long. But it's the donkey stench that really scares me."

"Just what I thought," I said, "easy for you to shoot off your mouth and your arrows from up there where you don't have to face me man to man."

The stranger laughed. "Look, boy, you're starting to take this a little too seriously. Maybe you take yourself too seriously. I'm coming down there. Let me help you get your stubborn beast through the pass. I'm coming down, all right? I'm on way to join King Saul and fight the Philistines, and I don't want to waste any more of my efforts on a stupid argument. Here I come."

He jumped off the boulder, almost as if he thought he could sprout wings and fly. It seemed for a moment that he did. It seemed to take him longer to cover the eight cubits or so to the ground than it should have. His hair flowed behind him. He held out his upraised arms out to either side. He landed almost soundlessly on both feet, went into a crouch, and sprang up, turning to face me. He never stopped smiling.

Now that he was on my level, I realized he was taller and bigger than I had thought.

He gave another easy grin. "Here, climb up on the ledge, go around in front of her, take her bridle and coax her forward. I'll help you get her through." He sprung up onto a narrow ledge just above the donkey, and as she passed beneath him, he pressed sideways on her backpack with one foot. Jez walked through with room to spare. "See, not so hard after all. Maybe you need to keep things a little simpler, donkey herder."

I sniffed. "I was doing just fine before you came along. If I need your help or your advice, I'll ask. Otherwise, just keep your mouth shut."

"Look, I meant no disrespect," he replied, "It's just—well, look at you!"

His eyes we so full of life and sparkle, his smile so warm, that I began to mellow, if only a little. At last I said, "Well, thanks for helping, anyway. Did I hear you say you were going to join Saul and fight the Philistines?"

"You got that right," he said, smiling broadly. "I hear the army is gathering at Gilgal. Saul's son Jonathan attacked the Philistines at Geba a few weeks ago. He routed them! It's about time somebody stood up to those dogs!" He talked so fast and with such force I could barely keep up with the torrent of words. "Saul's messengers came to my town to enlist men in the army. You should have seen them! All clad in blue, with their silver trumpets. Their horses"—he whistled—"you should have seen them! Those trumpets, I think you could have heard them for miles! Men came from everywhere."

"They came to my town too," I said, "and all of the young men were begging to go. I left as soon as—well, as soon as . . ." I didn't want to say as soon as my mother let me.

"You mean as soon as you got the courage? Or as soon as your mother gave you permission?" he said with a knowing grin.

That did it. He had pushed too far, and something inside erupted. I was on him before he could react. I slammed into him headlong, and we rolled off the side of the trail in a cloud of dust, rocks, sand, and donkey dung. I had both my arms around him and hung on as we crashed down the hill. We rolled down until I smashed my back into a huge boulder. As my grip momentarily relaxed, he pulled out my grasp and jumped to his feet.

"Just what is wrong with you?" he said, brushing the sand off his tunic, arms and hands. "God knows you are one pompous, touchy fool!"

"And God knows you should not us his name so lightly, and that you should show some respect." I said back, spitting the sand out of my mouth.

"All right, all right, I'm sorry," he said, both palms in the air. "You could have killed us both. Or worse, you could have broken my bow." He pulled it off his back and checked it over, stroking it with his finger tips, caressing it as he would a lover, wiping it clean of sand. "I meant no disrespect, for God's sake."

"Well, you could have fooled me," I said, swiping a streak of blood from one cheek. "I tell you again, stop using God's name so carelessly, you come close to blasphemy."

"Look, can we call a truce?" he said, regaining his smile. "Let's call it even. I insulted you, and you pushed me down the hill. Fair enough?"

"Fair enough," I said as I slowly got to my feet, checking for broken bones, "Fair enough."

"I'm Shammah son of Agee," he said, sticking out his hand.

I looked down at my hand, wiped my palm off on my tunic, and held it out to him. "And I'm Eleazar son of Dodai."

Chapter Five

Friendship and the Warrior

After David had finished talking with Saul, Jonathan became one in spirit with David, and he loved him as himself. From that day Saul kept David with him and did not let him return to his father's house. And Jonathan made a covenant with David because he loved him as himself. Jonathan took off the robe he was wearing and gave it to David, along with his tunic, and even his sword, his bow and his belt.

1 Samuel 18:1–4

Jonathan said to David, "Go in peace, for we have sworn friendship with each other in the name of the LORD, saying, 'The LORD is witness between you and me, and between your descendants and my descendants forever.' "

1 Samuel 20:42

Warriors need friends. And we need to be friends to others.

Warriors are not called to be independent mercenaries, waging solitary war; they are called to be part of an army, fighting—perhaps dying—alongside their friends.

One of the great stories of friendship in the Bible is that of David and Jonathan.

Sometimes, warriors, the friends we need to make could just as easily be our rivals, or even our enemies.

Jonathan was the son of Saul, the king of Israel. He was next in line to inherit the throne. As a young man he was already a hero in the land, the one who inspired the army to victory with his bold attack on the Philistines at Micmash (1 Samuel 14:1–23). But when Goliath comes on the scene, brave Jonathan, along with all the other mighty men of Israel, is afraid. Day after day the giant taunts and defies the army, daring them to send out a warrior to face him in single combat. The obvious choice to meet this challenge is Saul himself, or his son Jonathan, who has already proven himself the brave warrior in spectacular fashion. When Goliath shouts out his challenge, we can imagine the eyes of the warriors turning to first to Saul, then to his dashing and daring son, Jonathan. But instead of stepping up, Jonathan shrinks back. He hangs his head in fear. Where are his faith and courage now? Surely this is a humiliating moment for this brave young prince, Saul's son, the next in line to be king.

But then, out of nowhere comes the young shepherd boy David. He volunteers to face Goliath. Turning down Saul's offer of armor and weapons, he strides out to meet the giant armed only with a slingshot and five stones. And almost miraculously, he brings Goliath down with one shot! In a matter of seconds the army turns from being cowards to heroes—they surge forward and rout their enemies. It is one of the most amazing, memorable victories not only in the Bible, but also in all the long and storied history of warfare.

When David returns from defeating Goliath, Saul honors him with a commission in the army.

If you were Jonathan, how would you be feeling at this moment? Ashamed? Embarrassed? Insecure? How about envious? This kid David has in one fell swoop supplanted you as the most celebrated warrior in the nation. The eyes that used to look to you for leadership are now on him. The praise and the adulation once lavished upon you are now his. The respect of the strongest, bravest men in the army has been transferred elsewhere. David is the hero now.

Brothers, let's face it: We all want to be respected by other men— especially brave, strong men. When we have respect, life is good. When the respect we long for is given to someone else, if we are not careful to guard our hearts, we can lose our confidence, grow angry, or become resentful and jealous.

But there is more to come. Take a look at this next scenario:

When the men were returning home after David had killed the Philistine, the women came out from all the towns of Israel to meet King Saul with singing and dancing, with joyful songs and with tambourines and lutes. As they danced, they sang:

> *"Saul has slain his thousands,*
> *and David his tens of thousands."* (1 Samuel 18:6–7)

My, oh my! The women of Israel are lining the streets, dancing and singing about Saul and David. Okay, brothers, let's keep it real. These are soldiers, mighty warriors. They are strong, tough men. They have risked their lives to fight for God and country. The song the women sing only names Saul and David. Some of the soldiers probably feel a bit unappreciated when they hear this song, but *what about Jonathan?* How does it make him feel? Just a short while ago he was the superstar, the hero, the darling. He is not even mentioned in the song. He is ignored, left out, marginalized. If his heart were in it for himself, he would have been eaten alive by jealousy and rivalry (which, by the way, is exactly what happens to his father, Saul).

But that is not how Jonathan responds. He does just the opposite. Instead of being jealous and threatened by David, he is overwhelmed with admiration. He gives this young hero his heart. With a solemn vow to God, in a decision that will endure through terrible trial and grave personal risk, he pledges David his respect and friendship.

Brothers, some of your greatest friendships can be forged with people who might become your rivals—unless you decide to make them your friends. Know this: whatever you may accomplish, however great you are (or think you are), someone will one day come along who is greater, does things better, and who gets more applause, more attention, and more adulation than you. *What will you do then?*

Isn't it ironic that jealousy is a sin that destroys our chance to have a relationship with the people we admire the most? Who among us is jealous of someone unless they have something we wish we had? Yes, jealousy and envy can block us from friendship with those men who, deep down, we actually esteem the most, and most long to be like.

When David bursts onto the scene, Jonathan does not give in to this satanic temptation. Instead, he gives David his heart, and in so doing, he helps to create one of the greatest stories of friendship we find in all of Scripture. He could have taken the route his father Saul took—the pathway of jealousy and envy. Had he done so he would not only have lost the opportunity of enjoying David's friendship, but he also would have ruined his own life, just as his father did. Instead, Jonathan chooses the path of friendship, and he is now considered one of the great men in the Bible.

Sometimes you're David; sometimes you're Jonathan

How about our friendships, brothers? Sometimes we may be the "David" in a relationship. We step in at the right moment and God uses us to do a great deed to inspire and encourage others. We will be loved, appreciated, and lifted up. Other times, we may need to be like Jonathan. We will have to be the man who steps aside so that another might rise. This may sound bad at first, but in the eyes of God, it is a great and valued role. The Lord may assign us to help someone else succeed in his task, knowing that without us, the victory will not be won. You will be the wind beneath another man's wings, the unsung hero, the one in the background whom God uses mightily but that others do not see or appreciate.

Brother warriors, let us deal with our competition and pride. Let us be a friend of other soldiers who fight the battles of God beside us. Let us not allow our selfishness to cheat us out of friendship with the men we respect and need the most. Let us be like Jonathan.

Let's get a bit more practical. How did Jonathan and David form their friendship?

Jonathan gave his heart

To have a friendship, sometimes you have to make the first move. And that move may be to simply open up your heart. Paul tells the church in Corinth to "open wide your hearts" (2 Corinthians 6:13), but he only made that request *after* he had first opened his heart to them (2 Corinthians 6:11). Some of us are frustrated that we don't have more friends or very deep friendships. But our problem may be that we are too cautious—that we are holding back, waiting for the other guy to come our way first. Let's remember who went first in our relationship with God: "We love because he first loved us" (1 John 4:19). If God were waiting for us to love him first, he would still be waiting! We have the love of the Father—it is already ours. Let's imitate him in our love for others. Let's extend our hearts first.

You may be thinking, "I tried that, but it didn't work. I got little or no response." Men, when we give our hearts we cannot determine what we are going to get back, only what we are going to give. Yes, friendship is a two-way street. Jesus offered his friendship to the whole world, and yet how many have responded? Love is given freely, but a relationship requires a response. So don't be discouraged if you have reached out, but not received a reciprocal response. That is not your decision to make. Your decision can only be that, like Jesus and our fellow warrior Jonathan, you will give your heart in the offer of friendship, and let God work it out from there.

Some relationships are almost magical in the way we connect with another brother in the faith. It is as if we are "brothers from another mother," and we just "get" each other. We bond rapidly and easily. Those relationships are as wonderful as they are rare. When God gives you one of those, thank him and enjoy that friendship all the days of your life.

Most relationships take much more effort than that. We have to initiate. We have to spend time together, sometimes over a long period of time. We have to go through things together. We have to hurt each other's feelings and let each other down; we have to forgive and be forgiven. We may even have to go after the other guy when he seems to be disinterested. But over time, and with God working in our hearts, the bond and the understanding will begin to form. We look back one day and say with gratitude, "We have become close friends!" And we have a treasure we can enjoy for a lifetime.

Jonathan and David committed to each other

And Jonathan made a covenant with David because he loved him as himself.
(1 Samuel 18:3)

It is one thing to care about and admire someone. It is quite another thing to make a promise that you will be their friend. Many of us have good feelings toward other brothers, but we have never spoken them aloud, and we have never promised them our love and loyalty.

We see this all the time in men who will not make a commitment to a woman. We want to be her friend, to go out on dates, but we will not commit. Yes, that has to do with marriage, a unique commitment exceeded only by our commitment to God himself. But the principle works in friendship as well. If we are going to be the kind of man who is there for our friend day in and day out, year in and year out, we need to make a decision, and we need to make it known to them. You may ask, "Why say anything? Aren't actions louder than words?" True, words without actions are no good. But we also need to put our commitment of friendship into words because *words have power.*

Think about it: God makes promises to us, and he puts them in writing. He gives his heart, and then he also gives his word. He showed us his love through Christ, and then he wrote it down in the Bible. Both are necessary. We men are sometimes reluctant to do things like this, especially in relationships with other guys. But warriors, when we do so, we are imitating the actions and methods of our Father, who teaches us how to love.

Jonathan and David's relationship was spiritually based

We just read about the commitment that these two warriors made to each other. But let's take a closer look and see what it was based upon. We see it in the nature of the oath they made to each other:

> Jonathan said to David, "Go in peace, for we have **sworn friendship with each other in the name of the LORD,** saying, 'The LORD is witness between you and me, and between your descendants and my descendants forever.' " (1 Samuel 20:42, emphasis added)

Their promise to each other was based upon the Lord—it was "in the name of the Lord." It was about God, not just about the fact that they happened to like each other or were close friends. Brothers, our relationships must be built upon *our common love for God and our shared commitment to Jesus as Lord.* Only then can we build a permanent bond.

Too many men want buddies to hang out with—we want a golfing buddy, or a workout partner, or a guy who will come over to watch the game with us while we both inhale bucketfuls of hot wings—but we don't want spiritual friendships that draw us closer to Jesus. And by the way, fun things like that are actually essential to a great friendship! But none of them are the *substance* of a great friendship. They are needed, but they are not the heartbeat or the foundation of what God intends us to have in our brotherly friendships. Our common love and commitment to Jesus is the *root* of great friendship, and those other things are the *fruit.*

Even in the church, we see the worldly pattern of superficial friendships all too present among our men. Brothers, evaluate your relationships. Ask yourself: *Does this relationship draw me closer to Jesus, to his church, and to his mission? Or is it superficial? Is it helping me to mature in the Lord, or is it neutral—maybe even detrimental to my growth in Christ?* My advice is this: Don't let unspiritual relationships hold you back. If any relationship—even with a brother in the faith—is not helping you become a stronger warrior for Christ, then either change its direction and emphasis, or move on to different relationships with men who will help draw you closer to God.

Jonathan gave David his valued possessions

Jonathan took off the robe he was wearing and gave it to David, along with his tunic, and even his sword, his bow and his belt. (1 Samuel 18:4)

Look at the gifts Jonathan gives David. He gives his own robe and tunic. He gives him his bow and his sword. In the warrior culture of their day, the sword was the warrior's most prized possession. When Jonathan gives his sword to David, he is showing immense love and respect. He is treating him like a brother. Actually, he is treating him better than David's own brother did—David's older brother Eliab had belittled him earlier that day for even showing up on the battlefield!

What gifts do we give to show other men our love and friendship? We men are notorious for failing to remember birthdays, anniversaries, and special occasions. We think, "Giving presents is just being materialistic and superficial. Friendship is more than that." Certainly gift-giving can be superficial, and some people even try to buy friendships with gifts, or dutifully give gifts to people they don't really care about. And we need to keep in mind that not every friendship is on the level of depth and commitment that David and Jonathan had. Those kinds of friendships are unique. So be assured that we don't need to break the bank anytime we claim friendship with another man. That would discourage us from making too many friends—we just couldn't afford it!

What we are saying is that to show deeper friendship for special people in our lives, there will need to be gift-giving along the way. Somewhere, sometime, we need to give something that is so valuable or treasured in heart that our brother just cannot miss what we are saying: "You are my friend. This gift represents the value you have in my life.

This present shows what I feel about you. You have my heart, and this is how I am letting you know."

Jonathan and David expressed emotion and affection

After the boy had gone, David got up from the south side of the stone and bowed down before Jonathan three times, with his face to the ground. Then they kissed each other and wept together—but David wept the most. (1 Samuel 20:41)

Showing emotion and affection in friendship can be a difficult and awkward thing for men. Some warriors reading this may be thinking: *Warriors are supposed to be tough! Aren't tears a sign of weakness and fear? Isn't weeping the domain of women and children? Didn't we leave tears behind when we grew up and became men? Shouldn't we be strong? Wouldn't our crying make people who depend on us feel we have no faith and confidence in God?*

Let's rethink this by looking at David and Jonathan:

David and Jonathan are warriors. They are brave men. They have defeated giants, fought the enemies of God, and endured hardship and suffering. So here we see them weeping together. They are still the same guys they were before this moment, and they will be the same men after they finish.

They are sharing one of the most difficult moments in David's life. This is the moment when David realizes that from this time forth he will be an outcast, an outlaw. He is being driven from his wife and his home, and his reputation is going to be torn to shreds. It grieves and saddens them—and they, in manly friendship, embrace each other and weep. Picture these two great warriors at this moment. This is not effeminate, sexual, weak, or faithless. It is just two strong men showing raw, honest grief.

What attitudes would hold us men back from shedding tears at a moment like this?

- How about our pride?
- How about fear that we might be looked down upon or laughed at for being weak?
- How about just not wanting another man to know, deep down inside, that our heart is breaking?

There was another time when David wept, and when all his Mighty Men wept with him and with one other:

When David and his men came to Ziklag, they found it destroyed by fire and their wives and sons and daughters taken captive. So David and his men wept aloud until they had no strength left to weep. (1 Samuel 30:3–4)

Their wives and children have been captured. For all they know, they have been killed, raped, or taken away as slaves forever. What do the Mighty Men do? *They weep.* They weep until they have no more strength left.

We may be thinking: *Wait, aren't these warriors? They are being wimpy! They are wasting valuable time! Come on guys, strap on your swords, mount your horses and go save your families! Stop being cowards!*

Well, that is just what they do—*after* David turns to God, and God tells him to lead his warriors to save their captured wives and children. The men get up, dry their tears, and set out to rescue their families. They find the other army in a drunken celebration, and to put it mildly, David and his warriors take care of business! Not one woman or child is lost.

Brothers, let's learn something here: *Strong men will sometimes need to grieve and cry.* It is hurtful to our souls, our manhood, and our friendships to hide, stifle, or ignore our emotions. It is a serious mistake to pretend we do not feel pain, or to fail to grieve or shed tears when we are sad. It is also hurtful to shut down our feelings and act as if we don't need them. It limits us and prevents us from being close to other men. Stifling our emotions will make us *hard* men, but it will not make us *strong* men.

Warriors, I have some questions for us—we'll call this the warrior's emotional gut-check:

- Have you ever told another male friend, even your own son or father, how much he means to you in the deepest part of your heart?
- Do we just assume that our brothers know how we feel about them?
- Do we even *want* them to know?

- Are we willing to risk looking a bit foolish to say it or write it?
- Isn't it odd that we would even think we could look foolish for speaking to another man in this way?

My friend JP Tynes and I have a relationship that has lasted decades, all the way back to our college days. He was—and still is—the crazy, laughing, fun guy. I am the intense, introspective, focused guy. Together we make a better picture of Jesus than either of us does by ourselves. JP makes me happy—and I tell him so all the time. His laughter, faith, and trust in God help me to face life with joy and optimism. I, on the other hand, help to keep us thinking, praying, and talking deeply. I do most of the crying, and show most of the emotion. And when I do, JP never makes me feel weird about it. He knows he needs it. He values me and I value him. As I often say, "JP keeps me sane; I keep him spiritual." Ours is a great lifelong friendship, and I thank God for my dear brother.

Jonathan and David sacrificed for their friendship

A friend loves at all times,
and a brother is born for adversity. (Proverbs 17:17)

David finally has to flee for his life to escape Saul's jealousy. Saul attempts to kill him, and David has to leave behind his wife, his home, and his position in the army to save himself. Jonathan now has a decision to make. He can just let it go, or he can be loyal to his friend. He can quietly go on his way, or he can try to help David in spite of the danger that such a choice will bring upon him.

A man of many companions may come to ruin,
but there is a friend who sticks closer than a brother. (Proverbs 18:24)

Jonathan proves himself a true friend. He goes to see David, the fugitive. He even agrees to risk his life to speak to his father Saul on David's behalf. When he does, he is rewarded with venomous insults and a spear slamming into the wall near his head, hurled by his father. Such is Jonathan's love and friendship. As for his part, David never asks Jonathan to take revenge upon or abandon his father. David never asks his friend to fight back against Saul or to forsake his own family for the sake of their relationship.

The last recorded meeting of David and Jonathan is deeply moving. (See 1 Samuel 23:15–19.) Saul and his army are in hot pursuit of David. Jonathan seeks David out, knowing that if he is found out, it could mean death. He finds his friend, and here is what he says and does:

> *And Saul's son Jonathan went to David at Horesh and helped him find strength in God. "Don't be afraid," he said. "My father Saul will not lay a hand on you. You will be king over Israel, and I will be second to you. Even my father Saul knows this." The two of them made a covenant before the Lord. Then Jonathan went home, but David remained at Horesh.* (1 Samuel 23:16–18)

At one of the lowest moments in David's life, his friend Jonathan comes to him. And what does he do? *He helps him find strength in God.* That is what a real friend does:

- He comes after you.

- He finds you.

- He helps you turn to God, to put your trust in him.

- When all around you seems to be crashing down, when your faith is failing, your loyal and loving friend finds you and helps you to believe once again.

Jonathan reminds David of the promise God made to him through the prophet Samuel when he was just a teenager, when he was anointed king so many years ago. He reminds him that although it may seem dark, and that although the promise spoken through Samuel may seem but a distant, hopeless dream, God himself is behind that promise and will keep it without fail. What an amazing moment, and what a huge source of joy and encouragement this must have been for David!

The two friends renew their covenant before God, and Jonathan returns home. It is the last time they will see each other. Jonathan, the most loyal friend David ever had, is soon to die. His example and name will be recorded in God's book as one of the most giving, unselfish, and courageous friends a man could ever have.

The many facets of friendship

We have described in this chapter a uniquely close friendship. It is a wonderful story that can inspire us, as men and as warriors for God, to strive to take our friendships to another level.

That being said, let us realize that not every friendship can be, or needs to be, just like that of Jonathan and David. That would be an unrealistic and unattainable expectation. No, we will have many different kinds of friendships at different levels of closeness.

- Every friendship will meet different needs in distinctive ways and at special times in our lives.

- Some brothers will be more like mentors and teachers to us.

- Others will be encouragers and visionaries.

- Others will be younger men whom we mentor and help to mature in the faith.

- Others will be our advisors and counselors.

- Some relationships will change over time as we both mature in years and experience.

- Some relationships will literally come into and out of our lives as they or we move from place to place.

Relationships are marvelously dynamic, and over the course of our lives we will need the good influence of many different men to help us become mighty warriors for God. Let us welcome into our lives the men God sends our way, and let us reach out to other men and be the friends they need.

Seek to gather around yourself a group of men who share your desire to fight God's battles:

- Get with them regularly.

- Share your dreams and goals.

- Be open about the battles you are fighting.

- Be open about your victories and defeats, your strengths and weaknesses.

- Challenge each other to be the best you can be.

- Encourage each other to keep going and never give up.

- Hold each other accountable.

- Call upon each man to be spiritual, to live by the word, to follow Jesus, and to be a fisher of men.

- Help each other be better men.

May these verses be your watchword together:

As iron sharpens iron,
    so one man sharpens another. (Proverbs 27:17)

Two are better than one,
    because they have a good return for their work:
If one falls down,
    his friend can help him up.
But pity the man who falls
    and has no one to help him up! (Ecclesiastes 4:9–10)

Let a righteous man strike me—it is a kindness;
    let him rebuke me—it is oil on my head.
    My head will not refuse it. (Psalm 141:5)

Fight for friendships

Brothers, we just can't make it alone. We need God above all, and no one can replace him and what he gives. But it is his plan that we also rely on each other. Where would David have been without Jonathan in his early years? We know that David descended into terrible sin after his friend's death. Could Jonathan have made the difference in helping David to remain strong during his middle season of life? We will never know. We do know that Jonathan's love, devotion, and friendship were a crucial part of David's life during some of his greatest trials as a young warrior. We know that David wrote a song to honor his friend after his death. We know that more than any other relationship in his life, David could count on Jonathan to care, to love, and to help him be near to God.

May God give us friends like Jonathan as we fight the battles of life, and may God help us to *be* a friend like Jonathan to our fellow warriors!

Author's note: In this chapter we introduce the *Battle Cry* (a call to action at the beginning of a chapter) and the *Battle Plan* (an action plan at the end), to help you apply the material to your daily life. Each chapter in Part Two will have a *Battle Cry* and *Battle Plan*.

BATTLE CRY

Brother warriors, God included Benaiah's story in the Bible, along with the exploits of David's Mighty Men, for a reason…he put them there for *us*.

As boys, we drove the women in our lives crazy and scared them to death. We pretended we were superheroes, firefighters, and warriors. We ran, raced, and rode. We crawled, climbed, and clambered. We smashed, bashed, and crashed. We heaved it, hurled it, and hit it. We jumped it, jarred it, and jammed it.

> We craved adventure.
> We took risks.
> We had fun.
> We laughed a lot.

And you know what? God made us this way, and he likes us this way.

So what happened? When did we become dull, boring, and predictable? Somewhere along the way, many of us lose the zany, courageous, daredevil spirit we had as boys and young men. The Bible invites us to get it back. The stories of Benaiah and the Mighty Men are God's invitation:

> Come on.
> Jump down into that pit.
> Take on that lion.
> I DARE YOU.

Chapter Six

Adventures and Exploits

They were brave warriors, ready for battle and able to handle the shield and spear. Their faces were the faces of lions, and they were as swift as gazelles in the mountains.

1 Chronicles 12:8

Benaiah son of Jehoiada was a valiant fighter from Kabzeel, who performed great exploits. He struck down two of Moab's best men. He also went down into a pit on a snowy day and killed a lion.

2 Samuel 23:20

Men need adventure. We need to test our limits. We need to have fun. We need to do some out-of-the-box things—and sometimes, we need to tear the box to shreds.

I was raised from the age of twelve by a widowed single mom. I also had three older sisters who had a great influence upon me as a young man. All of these women taught me invaluable life lessons. I am the husband and father I am today partly because they taught me how to treat women, how to be a gentleman, and how to care for children. I will be forever grateful. But the good influence of women in my life did not stop there; I also married an amazing woman. She is the most wonderful person I know, and I get to live with her every day of my life! She is my greatest earthly blessing, and there is no one I have ever known whom I respect more. But my wife, my mom, and my sisters are very different people than I am. "Male and female he created them" (Genesis

1:27). They are women; I am a *man.*

It shows up in our idea of a good movie. I always say that my wife likes to watch movies where everybody is sick and in the hospital. And me? I like to watch movies that *put people in the hospital!* It shows up in our idea of fun. Women like to shop and have girl talk; men want to go outside and throw things, kick things, and hit things. It shows up in our feelings about motorcycles. My wife sees a motorcycle and thinks "death trap"; I see a motorcycle and think, "FREEDOM! WHEN CAN I GET ONE OF THOSE?"

I like—actually, I *love*—being a man. A man cannot be fully happy until he learns to enjoy his manhood and his masculinity. Brothers, we need to be glad that women are women and that we are men! Let's stop apologizing for our uniqueness as males, and while we're at it, let's start acting like strong, Mighty Men.

I remember reading the Mighty Man stories while on my twenty-fifth wedding anniversary cruise in the western Caribbean. I got all fired up, reading about these great warriors for God. I got so excited I could hardly sit still. I later decided to write a book about them, *Mighty Man of God.* I realized, I need to push myself. *I need to take things to another plane. I need more adventure in my life.*

ADVENTURE

Adventures are things that don't absolutely *have* to be done from a practical point of view, but that we would *like* to do, just for the fun of it. "Adventure" is of Latin origin and has at its root the idea of "about to happen." So, fellow warrior, I ask you:

- What is *about to happen* in your life?
- What are you looking forward to?
- Do you have true excitement in your life?
- Are you pushing yourself out of your comfort zone?
- Is anything a little dangerous in your life or somewhat risky?

Nothing, you say? Then I say it's time for some adventure.

When we were little boys, life was all about adventure. Our moms used to worry about us getting so adventurous that we would get hurt. They were always trying to hold us in check, keep us out of trouble. Keep us safe. Well, now that we are adults, we don't want to do unsafe, foolish things, but we still need to do *exciting* things! Why are little boys so fired up, and adult men (all too often) so boring? It is because little boys are adventurous, and adult men—well, many of us stopped living exciting lives a long, long time ago.

Benaiah didn't have to kill that lion. He just wanted to. I bet he was thinking something like this: "If l let this opportunity go by, I'll regret it later. I'll always wonder if I could have done it. But if I kill this lion, I'll remember it the rest of my life. This is just too exciting to pass up!" And so down he went, into the pit; down went the lion, at the end of a dagger; and down went Benaiah's name, memorialized in biblical history. And afterwards, David put Benaiah in charge of his bodyguard (2 Samuel 23:23). Sounds like a good exploit to me!

Come on men, let's get out there with God, live adventurously, take some risks, and create some stories worth telling.

Aren't you tired of living a boring Christian life?

Do you really think Jesus called you to follow him just so you could plod your way through a safe, dull, lackluster existence?

Adventures take us to new places, often outside

Men, we need adventure to stay vibrant and alive. We need real adventure, where there is some risk and uncertainty involved. Out there in nature, out where things are not fully under our control. Out there where we are going to be challenged to *think differently*. Out there where we are going to be challenged to *act boldly*. Out there where we have to learn something new or *master a skill we don't yet have*.

Going down the rapids in a kayak? That's adventure. Climbing a mountain? Hiking a trail? Going on a camping trip? Those are real challenges. Sailing? Boating? Surfing? My son tells me surfing is "just plain awesome." Men need waves. Sand. Dirt. Mud. Rain. Snow. Cold. Heat. Fire. Sun. Moon. Wind. Rocks. Streams. Rivers. Lions. Bears.

Video games just don't cut it here. Tell me, where's the manly adventure in sitting in front of a screen *pretending* to be at war? Where's the risk? Where's the danger? If you lose, so what? If you win, so what? We don't need virtual adventure—we need *real* adventure! Television? That's just watching *someone else* be adventurous. No wonder we fall asleep in front of it.

David was a shepherd. He lived outside with the flock. He lived under the stars and the sun. He had to take on a lion and a bear just to do his job—and he was probably just a teenager when he did it. He also wrote songs and practiced slingshot. Both of those skills changed *his* life, and through both skills *he* changed the world. (Oh, by the way, have you ever heard of Goliath, and have you read the book of Psalms?)

But David was not the exception; he was the norm of godly masculinity. Do you realize that most of our Bible heroes were outdoorsmen? That most of them lived their lives in tents?

- Abraham lived in tents for most of his life, not knowing exactly where God was leading him.

- Moses, Joshua, Caleb and the people of Israel camped out in the desert for more than forty years.

- Paul walked the roads or sailed on the open water to most of the places he journeyed.

- John the Baptist was raised in the wilderness. He preached outdoors, in the desert, near the Jordan River, where he baptized multitudes and ate grasshoppers and wild honey. He wore clothing of camel hair, bound up with a leather belt.

- Jesus was outdoors most of his ministry. He preached on the shores and the hillsides, sailed on boats, and walked everywhere he went.

Don't get me wrong here. I am not saying that we have to be farmers or country boys to be warriors. In Scripture we can see that many of God's great men lived in homes and in the city. I am saying, though, that nature has a special place in God's scheme of things—especially for men. And I *am* saying that too many of us aren't out there in it nearly enough. We live every day under a roof and in artificial light, and we stay that way most of the time. We are missing the consciousness of God that can be found only when we are outside, under the glory of the heavens, beneath the splendid sun and starlit sky. No wonder we lack the awareness of God's presence and a sense of awe!

Many of us, unlike David and most of our Bible heroes, don't spend much time outside. If you live in an urban or suburban setting, try getting out to a park. Walk out onto a bridge and watch the river flow beneath you. Get up on the top of a building and look up at the sky and the stars. Schedule a day out in God's world, out of the city, out of the suburbs, away from traffic and buildings—away from an environment altered by man. Try it, and see if it doesn't refresh you and draw you closer to God the mighty Creator!

Never stop seeking adventure

I started studying about the Mighty Men on my twenty-fifth wedding anniversary, and I became convinced that I needed more adventure in my life. Not too long afterwards, my oldest child got married. I was happy and sad at the same time. I was happy that she was marrying an amazing young man who has powerfully proven his love for God and for her, over and over again. But I was also sad—sad that I would no longer have my daughter with me in my home, sad that a wonderful season in my life was drawing to a close. To make matters worse, I was also scheduled to have my second knee surgery soon, and I had the feeling that my joyful days of long-distance running were coming to an end.

For years, I had wanted a motorcycle, and for years, I had not been able to afford one. And—more importantly—my wife had never gotten fired up about the idea. Finally, in the midst of my sadness about my daughter leaving, my wife changed her mind. She said, "Maybe a motorcycle is what you need right now. Just promise me you'll wear a helmet, stay off the Interstate, and take riding lessons." It took me about four seconds to agree! That very week, I bought my first bike, a Harley Davidson Sportster (God got me an amazing deal, by the way). Before my daughter was even back from her honeymoon, I was out on country roads, helmet on my head, riding lessons learned.

It was the beginning of a great new adventure, a new passion in my life. My bike gave me a sense of freedom and fun like nothing else ever had. It set me free from the mundane grind of daily life. While I was riding, I couldn't talk on the phone—I could only talk to God. I rode up into the Appalachian Mountains on the Blue Ridge Parkway. I rode the Tail of the Dragon in Deals Gap, Tennessee, the biker's legendary ride: 318 curves in 11 miles.

The beauty of the mountains awed me. The majesty of God in the cascading rivers and sparkling streams moved me to tears. The glory and grandeur of mountain cliffs and the spectacular beauty of golden leaves in autumn left me breathless. All this I experienced because I wanted, sought, and *found* adventure.

But that is my story. What could it be for you, my brother? What adventure is calling you? The mountains? The sea? The desert? The forest?

The plains? The rivers? All of the above? I say get up, get out, and have the time of your life! If not now, when? Go ahead and plan it, even if it is out in the future. Just knowing an adventure is on your calendar will make you a happier man!

EXPLOITS

But Mighty Men for God need more than adventure; they also need to accomplish great exploits. What are exploits, you ask? And why do I need to seek opportunities to achieve them? What difference will exploits make in my life? Let's take a look at the exploits of David and his Mighty Men.

On one occasion, David was in a stronghold. Nearby, the Philistines had taken control of his hometown of Bethlehem. Here is what unfolds:

> *During the harvest time, three of the thirty chief men cam down to David at the cave of Adullam, while a band of Philistines was encamped in the Valley of Rephaim. At that time David was in the stronghold, and the Philistine garrison was at Bethlehem. David longed for water and said, "Oh, that someone would get me a drink of water from the well near the gate of Bethlehem!" So the three mighty men broke through the Philistine lines, drew water from the well near the gate of Bethlehem and carried it back to David.* (2 Samuel 23:13–16)

These Mighty Men just happen to hear David expressing a wistful thought—he wants a drink of water from his hometown well. We can only imagine how this transpires: These men look at each other, seeing that warrior gleam shining in their brothers' eyes. They nod and smile. They know what they are going to do. They head out of the safety of their camp, strong-arm their way through the Philistine lines, and while two of them hold off the enemy soldiers, the third lowers the bucket down into the well and gets the water. They fight their way back, and present their hard-won gift to David.

My fellow warriors, *that's an exploit!* It does not *have* to be done; it is not an order from their commander . . . which is just what makes it awesome. It is something these three warriors decide to do on their own. By doing so, they show courage, loyalty, and initiative—just the kind of qualities it takes to be a real warrior.

You may be thinking this is a foolish, wasted effort, a needless risk that accomplishes nothing of value, and does nothing to advance the position of David's army. *But think again.*

Exploits define us, and inspire others

What impact did these three men's exploit have on the other soldiers? You know the answer—the whole army must have been inspired! I'll bet that some other soldiers were so moved by this tale that they started thinking, "This is the kind of soldier I need to be. What can I do to show my bravery, to encourage my king and my brother warriors?" And what about David? How do you imagine he felt when they brought him that jar of water? David was so moved by their devotion, risk, and courage that he would not drink the water, but instead poured it out as an offering to God (2 Samuel 23:16–17).

Exploits intimidate the enemy

What message did the three Mighty Men send to the enemy that day? The Philistines were probably left shaking in their boots! *Look out guys; we've got some real warriors coming against us. These men are tough, committed, skilled, and fearless. They risked their lives and fought through our lines just to get a drink of water for their king! What will they be like when we meet them on the field of battle?*

In the same way, when we accomplish spiritual exploits for God, we intimidate *our* enemy, Satan. We show him that God's people mean business. We set him back in his plans. We make him think twice about attacking God's people.

That is what exploits do:

- They inspire.
- They raise the bar.
- They make us better.
- They redefine our lives.
- They tell us something about ourselves.
- They say something to our loved ones, to our friends, to our fellow warriors.

We are better for doing, and witnessing, exploits.

Exploits are things we decide on our own to do.

An exploit is something burning inside of us. The Spirit of God moves, and we feel it in our heart and conscience:

No, we don't *have* to do this thing.
No one may have even asked us to do it.
But *we decide* to do it.
We pray about it, seeking God's will and wisdom.
Then we step up and step out.
And we are never the same.

Exploits of generosity

Exploits are not limited to acts of bravado or physical courage. They take many forms. Consider the example of the Macedonian disciples, who surprised their spiritual leaders:

> *And now, brothers, we want you to know about the grace that God has given the Macedonia churches. Out of the most severe trial, their overflowing joy and their extreme poverty welled up in rich generosity. For I testify that they gave as much as they were able, and even beyond their ability. Entirely on their own, they urgently pleaded with us for the privilege of sharing in this service to the saints. And they did not do as we expected, but they gave themselves first to the Lord and then to us in keeping with God's will.* (2 Corinthians 8:1–5)

Giving to people in need is a great kind of exploit. Note that the Macedonians gave out of their poverty, not out of their wealth. When they learned of the need of their brothers in Judea (people they didn't personally know), they volunteered to give—they were *begging* to help!

My friend Kevin Broyles is a physician, a disciple I have known since his days in medical school. He spent years building a good medical practice, but felt he was a bit stuck where he was, and that there was more he could do with his life. He sensed God calling him higher. He had entered the medical field in order to help people, and he was a strong and committed disciple of Christ. Yet he felt the urging within to do more, to make more of an impact for God. And this, mind you, is a physician who was already successful in the eyes of the world. When Kevin was a member of my Mighty Man group, he decided to go back to school and get his Master's degree in leadership from Duke University. It was a challenging decision for a physician and family man to make, but make it he did. Upon graduation, he was given the opportunity to begin and build Duke Urgent Care, a network of clinics to serve community health needs. His efforts were so successful that he was able to retire early. But Kevin and his wife Noelle were not done yet! They started dreaming, praying, and looking to see what else might be out there for them to do in their (young) retirement years. They now reside in La Paz, Bolivia, where they minister to medical and spiritual needs in one of the poorest countries in the western world. Here is a man and his wife who have done amazing exploits for God. Their lives are an upward call.

An exploit does not have to be something quite like this. You may never get a Master's degree, begin a business, or move to another country. *So what?* Exploits can be on a grand or small scale. They may take a long time, or they may be achieved in one day. They simply need to be out-of-the-ordinary feats, performed for the glory of God, the good of others, and our own growth.

My mid-life exploit

I had no intention of becoming an author. When I went to college, I thought I was going to be a dentist! Decades deep into my life, I had never written anything longer than twenty pages—a term paper for a high school history class.

But when I was in my forties, a publisher asked me to contribute a chapter to a parenting book. It was to be an anthology, composed of a collection of essays from various authors. I thought to myself, "I would like to write the whole book myself!" I took my idea to a friend who knew the publisher. He liked it. He called the publisher and they offered me the opportunity to write the whole book.

After I got off the phone with them, reality hit. Fear struck. I said to myself, "Sam, what were you *thinking?* You must have been out of your mind!" But I had made a commitment, and I set out to accomplish it. I recruited my wife to coauthor with me, and after many months and countless moments of doubt and frustration, we turned in our manuscript. The book went on to become a real source of help to many parents, and also launched our writing career—something we have done "on the side" of our ministry life ever since. Writing is one of the most fulfilling and helpful things I have ever accomplished. It began, however, as a crazy exploit, a terrifying leap of faith. I am so glad I jumped into the pit and wrote that book. (And that is usually how we feel after we complete an exploit!)

Exploits transform us in a moment

Some exploits, in a single decisive moment, will launch us further in our faith and personal growth than we could ever go in years spent in our normal routine. Think about David stepping out to face Goliath. He has worked behind the scenes for months—probably years—practicing slingshot, shepherding sheep, and dealing with lions and bears. So when Goliath comes along, David is ready. But still, he has to step out. *He has to seize the moment.* This exploit is his first big step on the road to fulfilling his God-ordained destiny.

Much of the growth and change God gives us comes incrementally, throughout long seasons of steady, persistent effort. And we need to be the warriors who persist for the long haul, never giving up, letting God do his mighty work in us over the months and years. But sometimes, a moment comes—or we *make* a moment come—when we step out and do something amazing. Something out of the ordinary. We ride to victory in a powerful, rapid rush. Such is the power of an exploit!

If you feel frustrated where you are, and have been stuck for a long time, maybe the thing you need to do is have a breakout moment. Step out like a mighty man: Do the deed, make the stand, do the exploit that forever changes your life! Training and consistency are essential, but there is a time to make the big step, to take on the huge challenge. Read the stories of the exploits of the Mighty Men in 2 Samuel 23:8–23. They were warriors. But when the right moment came, they took all their years of training, faith, and heart, and put them into decisive action. In one day, they changed their lives forever. They became Mighty Men.

What exploits should a Mighty Man of God seek?

For our purposes, we will define an exploit as something that is a bit more substantial and *necessary* than an adventure. By necessary we mean that an exploit has more to do with advancing the gospel of Christ, helping someone, completing a needed project, building a ministry, conquering bad habits, overcoming a weakness, or the like.

An exploit is something:

- Inspiring to your family—your parents, siblings, wife, children
- Inspiring to other men
- Unique that sets you apart
- Exhilarating, adventurous, risky
- Rarely done in your fellowship or social circle
- Urgently needing to be done in your family or community
- That will alter your life, your marriage, your family
- That will alter someone else's life: that will save a soul or souls
- That will help others in need

- That will alter your future, and take you to a new level: learning a new skill, gaining education, etc.
- That will take your church or God's kingdom to a higher level
- That has been on your heart or conscience for a while

Here are seven areas where you can challenge yourself to accomplish some exploits:

- Spirituality
- Evangelism
- Service or benevolence
- Family
- Fitness
- Finances
- Profession or education

Look through the list of seven areas. In what area can you step up and do something to challenge yourself? Where do you most need to have a breakthrough? What out-of-the-ordinary act can you take to help yourself grow and change? What exploit can you do to inspire your church? To help others? What would be a life-changing feat for you? What would be something that would be exhilarating and just plain fun? Let your walk as a warrior become one of challenge, accomplishment, and growth. That's when life gets exciting!

Let's go, brothers!

If there is any need in churches today, it is for our men to step up and inspire the fellowship with some mighty deeds. As the armies of David were energized by the exploits of his Mighty Men, so will the modern-day army of God, the church, be stirred and taken to new levels by men just like you, men who do the extraordinary. Pray, fast, study the word, and seek godly counsel, but come to a decision. And when you do, step out, and step out boldly!

My fellow warrior, are you ready to live an exciting life again? The life you wanted to grow up to live when you were just a crazy kid running around, wreaking havoc? God made you to live life on the edge, my friend. He made you to crave adventure, to yearn for the next big thing. He designed us as men to push ourselves to experience great things, and to do great things. So, warrior, what are you waiting for? Adventure awaits, and exploits beckon! Let's go!

BATTLE PLAN

1. Plan an adventure.

What would be something you could do either alone, with a group of warriors, or with your spouse or family that would be fun, exciting, enjoyable, and refreshing?

When can you do it?

Put it on your calendar, and begin to plan for it now!

2. Plan two exploits.

We don't have to be one of David's Mighty Men to attempt and achieve great exploits. Brother warrior, I encourage you to seek out exploits of your own. Get out there and try something great. Something that challenges you. Something that inspires you. Something that inspires others. Watch what happens in your heart, your relationships, your influence, and your walk with God.

3. Read 2 Samuel 23:8–23.

As you read, think about these things:

- What inspires you about these exploits?
- What made them unique?
- What are some exploits that God has given or is giving you the opportunity to pursue right now?

In this chapter we mentioned seven areas where we can achieve exploits:

- Spirituality
- Evangelism
- Fitness
- Family
- Service or Benevolence
- Profession or Education
- Finances

Battle Plan

4. Consider these seven areas, and select two areas to focus on for your personal exploits:

> 1) Which area would address your greatest spiritual need?
>
> 2) Which area would most motivate and excite you?

Decide upon an exploit you can accomplish in both areas!

As you make this decision, keep these things in mind:

- The exploit does not need to be complicated or complex. It should be challenging, but doable.
- The exploit should have a definite beginning and end, and a specific plan of action.

Some practical guidelines in choosing your exploits:

- Seek inspiration and direction from Bible study. (Suggestion: Study the exploits of the Mighty Men in 2 Samuel 23:8–23, or read through the book of Acts.)
- Seek God's guidance in prayer and fasting. (See Mark 9:14–29, James 1:2–6.)
- Seek godly counsel from fellow warriors. (See Proverbs 21:31; 24:6.)
- Take no more than one week to make your decision. Share it with key warriors in your life who can encourage you, pray for you, hold you accountable, and possibly participate with you.

Part Two

The Battles of the Warrior

BATTLE CRY

Fear may be the greatest battle a warrior ever has to fight. It is the enemy we face before we can even step into the battle.

Even the bravest warriors of God feel fear. The issue is not *if* we will experience fear; the question is, how will we respond when we do?

Some of us are disturbed and discouraged because we experience fear. We think, "If I am supposed to be a mighty warrior for God, why am I afraid? I must not be much of a man."

Brother warrior, feeling fear does not make you a coward. Being afraid does not mean you can't be a warrior for God. It means you are human, just like the rest of us. The man who would be a warrior for God learns to face his fears and overcome them by the power of God. Yes, my fellow warrior, you too can become brave by the power of God!

Chapter Seven

The Battle of Fear

Goliath, the Philistine champion from Gath, stepped out from his lines and shouted his usual defiance, and David heard it. When the Israelites saw the man, they all ran from him in great fear.

1 Samuel 17:23-24

Fear may be the greatest battle you ever have to fight. It is the enemy you have to face before you can even get into the battle! As Winston Churchill said, "Courage is rightly esteemed the first of all human qualities because it is the quality which guarantees all others."[1]

Everyone feels fear. There is no one who is not tempted to be afraid. The bravest warriors of God feel fear. I will go so far as to say there is no one who is fearless. If Jesus was tempted in every way that we are (Hebrews 4:15), then even he was tempted by fear. The issue is not whether we will experience fear; the question is, *How will we respond when we do?*

Some of us are disturbed and discouraged because we feel fear. The very fact of fear's presence in our hearts and minds brings shame, and causes us to lose confidence. We think, "If I am supposed to be a mighty warrior for God, why am I afraid? I must not be much of a man."

No, my brother, feeling fear does not make you a coward. Feeling fear does not mean you can't be a warrior for God. Feeling fear means you are human, just like the rest of us. The man who would be a warrior for God has to face his fears and overcome them with God's help. Yes, my

---

1. James C. Humes, *The Wit and Wisdom of Winston Churchill* (New York, New York: HarperCollins, 1994), 23.

fellow warrior, you too can become brave by the power of God!

When the young shepherd David arrives on the scene in the Valley of Elah, the armies of Israel are in a terrible state. For forty days they have been facing the Philistine army across the valley. Each morning and evening they draw up the battle lines, preparing to go into battle. They shout the battle cry and line up, ready to go to war. And each morning and evening, a huge giant named Goliath steps out of the Philistine ranks to challenge them. He calls on them to send one man to fight him in single combat, and the winner of that fight will be the winner of the entire conflict. Sounds fair enough: saves lives, avoids a lot of bloodshed, and conserves energy.

You can imagine the men looking up and down the battle lines, wondering who among them would rise to meet the challenge. But not a single soldier from Israel's army steps up.

What about Jonathan, the brave son of King Saul? Not long ago, he had sallied forth against the Philistines, accompanied only by his armor bearer—together they climbed a cliff, took on an entire Philistine outpost, and routed them, winning a huge victory for Israel (1 Samuel 14). *Where is Jonathan?* He holds back, he does not step forward. *He is afraid.*

What about Saul? He is a head taller than anyone in the army (1 Samuel 9:2), so he's the biggest guy on the field—that is, besides the nine-foot-plus Goliath. *Where is Saul?* He also stands back, afraid of meeting his end before the huge warrior taunting them. *He is afraid.*

What about David's brothers, Eliab, Abinadab, and Shammah? Aren't they experienced warriors? Don't they believe in God? The famed prophet Samuel had visited them not long ago. Didn't that build their faith? And what about all the guys who will one day become David's Mighty Men? (It's likely they were already soldiers by this point.) Where are they? *They are afraid.*

All of these mighty men—these tough, brave, skilled, battle-proven soldiers—are full of fear: "On hearing the Philistine's words, Saul and all the Israelites were dismayed and terrified" (1 Samuel 17:11).

But they are more than fearful; they literally run away (1 Samuel 17:24)! Do you realize how demoralizing it is for soldiers in an army to see their brother warriors running away from a fight? This was the era of individual combat, where men wielded a sword or a spear and engaged the enemy face to face. If you were scared, you could not conceal it—everyone around you was close enough to see your fear.

Cowardice is the worst thing a soldier can be guilty of. It leaves him empty, friendless, and discouraged, with no respect from others or for himself. His self-worth is gone.

Well, that is now how the *whole Israelite army* feels—and has felt for forty days! Think about it: six weeks of disgrace. Six weeks of humiliation. *Six weeks!* Time enough, you would think, for someone to work up the courage to say, "Okay, guys, I'll go out there and fight Goliath." But nobody steps up. Depression and discouragement grip the army like a sickening disease. When men lose their courage, life becomes a terribly depressing thing.

Besides that, where is their faith? Hasn't God proven to them over and over again that there is no foe, no army, no king, no challenge so great that he will not get them through—no enemy too powerful for God to defeat? From Pharaoh to the Amalekites to the Philistines to the Red Sea—whatever, wherever, or whoever the foe has been—God has always been with his people. Why not now?

The Bible uses some provocative words to describe the situation.

They were *defied*. Goliath taunted them. He humiliated them. He not only challenged them; he attacked their sense of manhood. That is what fear does to us.

"This day I defy the ranks of Israel! Give me a man and let us fight each other."
(1 Samuel 17:10)

They were *dismayed*. All of them were dismayed, including their once confident and brave King Saul, who had led them to so many victories in the past.

On hearing the Philistine's words, Saul and all the Israelites were dismayed and terrified. (1 Samuel 17:11)

They were *disgraced* by their intimidating foe:

David asked the men standing near him, "What will be done for the man who kills this Philistine and removes this disgrace from Israel? Who is this uncircumcised Philistine that he should defy the armies of the living God?" (1 Samuel 17:26)

They, along with David, were *despised* by Goliath:

Meanwhile, the Philistine, with his shield bearer in front of him, kept coming closer to David. He looked David over and saw that he was only a boy, ruddy and handsome, and he despised him. He said to David, "Am I a dog, that you come at me with sticks?" And the Philistine cursed David by his gods. (1 Samuel 17:42)

When someone despises you, they have no respect for you They hold you in utter contempt. They sneer at you. You are nothing to them. To be opposed by your enemy is one thing; to be scorned and dismissed as worthless by him is quite another. And so Goliath disdained the armies of the living God!

Defied. Dismayed. Disgraced. Despised. Isn't that what fear says to us, and about us? Isn't that what it makes us feel about ourselves? Fear not only beats us down, it also causes us to beat ourselves down. Fear destroys our manhood because it strips us of confidence. It diminishes our self-worth. And yes, it causes others to wonder about us, too.

But thankfully, there is another "D-word" in the story: *David.*

When this young man arrives on the scene, he brings a completely different perspective. He brings God into the picture.

Look through the story as it unfolds in 1 Samuel 17. You hear a lot of talk from the men. You hear a lot from Goliath. You hear criticism from David's brother and words of doubt from Saul. *But not one soul mentions God.* No one, that is, until the young shepherd arrives. David immediately brings up the honor of God. He asks the cogent and crucial question: "Who is this uncircumcised Philistine that he should defy the armies of the living God?" (1 Samuel 17:26)

Brother warriors, the heartbeat of this story really isn't David's courage, or even his faith. The heartbeat of the story is discovered when we realize what moved David to do what he did. And what was that? David was moved to act courageously because of one thing: He was concerned for the honor of God.

David's words to Goliath say it ever so clearly—he fought the giant, not to win a victory for himself or for the army; David fought for the glory of God:

*David said to the Philistine, "You come against me with sword and spear and javelin, but I come against you in the **name of the Lord Almighty, the God of the armies of Israel, whom you have defied.** This day the Lord will hand you over to me, and I'll strike you down and cut off your head. Today I will give the carcasses of the Philistine* army to the birds of the air and the beasts of the earth, and the whole world will know that there is a God in Israel. All those gathered here will know that it is not by sword or spear that the Lᴏʀᴅ saves; for the battle is the Lᴏʀᴅ's, and he will give all of you into our hands." (1 Samuel 17:45–47, emphasis added)

Many centuries later, this story is known the world over. And we know this: God gave the victory and it was God who won the battle.

Honor God

Do you want to be a man of courage, a man who overcomes his fear? Then forget about proving yourself. Forget about proving your manhood. Forget about trying to be brave, or be braver than someone else. Forget all of that—instead, become consumed with the glory of God. Become concerned about what God is concerned about. Become passionate about the honor of God and of his people. And when you see that honor being trampled, when you see God's people around you fearful and intimidated, you will go out and do something about it. Courage will fill your soul and drive out your fear. You will act bravely, because you are no longer concerned about yourself. And in that moment, you will become a Mighty Man—*of God*.

In his conversation with Saul before the battle, David described God with an interesting word. He said, "Your servant has killed both the lion and the bear; this uncircumcised Philistine will be like one of them because he has defied the armies of the living God" (1 Samuel 17:36).

The living God! Do you want courage? Then know that the God you serve is *living*. He is not dead. He is not asleep. He is not disengaged. He is in heaven, to be sure, but he reaches down and gives you what you need, whenever you need it. There is no foe he can't handle. No problem too big, no enemy too powerful, no obstacle too difficult, no task too great, no...nothing...that the living God, Lᴏʀᴅ Almighty cannot handle. What is a nine-foot-tall guy to the God who made the universe? Compared to you and me, Goliath is huge; to God, he is a pushover. A harp-playing teenager with a slingshot is quite enough to deal with him.

Becoming a courageous warrior is really a matter of who you fear the most. You heard me right: Who do you fear the most?

Fear God

Read through the Psalms, and look for phrases that mention people fearing God. They will jump out at you like you've just put on 3-D glasses in the movies. My quick count finds at least 41 times in the 150 Psalms that mention the fear of God. Fear of God is a positive character-istic. It is a *necessary* characteristic. You may be thinking, *But I thought we were talking about overcoming fear—now you are telling me to fear God?* Well, yes I am, because the Bible tells us that fearing God is the pathway to true courage.

Take a look at this small sampling from David's psalms:

> The fear of the LORD is pure,
> > enduring forever. (Psalm 19:9)

> Fear the LORD, you his saints,
> > for those who fear him lack nothing. (Psalm 34:9)

> Teach me your way, O LORD,
> > and I will walk in your truth;
> give me an undivided heart,
> > that I may fear your name. (Psalm 86:11)

These are only a few of the Psalms we could cite. The man after God's heart (1 Samuel 13:14) tells us we actually do need to have fear—fear of God. And isn't it amazing that when we fear God, it cuts the rest of our fears down to size? The problems and people that used to loom so large and intimidate and discourage us shrink down to nothing, when they fall beneath God's all-encompassing shadow.

You might be thinking, "But that is the Old Testament—we aren't supposed to live in fear anymore, right?" No, my brother, this great concept is not limited to the Psalms or to the Old Testament; it is found throughout the Bible. Stay with me on this, and it will become clear.

Jesus said the same thing:

> "**Do not be afraid** of those who kill the body but cannot kill the soul. **Rather, be afraid of the One who can destroy both soul and body in hell.** Are not two sparrows sold for a penny? Yet not one of them will fall to the ground apart from the will of your Father. And even the very hairs of your head are all numbered. **So don't be afraid;** you are worth more than many sparrows." (Matthew 10:28–31, emphasis added)

So basically, Jesus says:

Don't be afraid of people.

Instead, be afraid of God.

Be afraid of God, but not afraid of life—God will take care of you.

So is your head spinning a little?

Looks to me like the Bible is saying we *do* need to be afraid of God—to revere him, stand in awe of him, know that he is our righteous Judge...and when we get that fear on straight, we can still know that God loves us, delights in us, and will take care of us.

We can fear God and at the same time know that he loves us:

> *For as high as the heavens are above the earth,*
> *   so great is his love for those who fear him....*
> *As a father has compassion on his children,*
> *   so the LORD has compassion on those who fear him....*
> *But from everlasting to everlasting*
> *   the LORD's love is with those who fear him,*
> *and his righteousness with their children's children* (Psalm 103:11, 13, 17)

Loving God is not the same as loving other humans. People are our equals. God is far, far above us, and that changes everything. The element of respect, awe, and fear must be deeply and essentially present in our relationship with the Lord.

Fear God, but do not fear man. That is the message of the Bible. We need to care much more about what God thinks of us, and far less of what people think. Many of our fears exist because we are too attached to what people believe about us, even to the point of sacrificing God-given principles in order to please them. If you want to be a warrior for God, you will need to decide that God's word and will come above what any human thinks. That is not to say that we do not give respect to others, or that we dismiss their convictions or feelings. But it does mean that when the two come into conflict, we go with God, not with people. And we don't let fear of people's disapproval or of losing a relationship keep us from standing up for, and fighting for, the will and truth of God.

Trust God

Trusting in God's faithfulness and promises is one of the primary ways to get fear out of our lives. When David went out to face Goliath, he was in one sense staking his life on the character of God and some promises that God had made (and kept) a long time ago. He was harkening back to Abraham, to Moses, to Joshua, to Gideon—to all the men and women that God had sustained when they stood up for him. David did not quote a single Bible verse that day, but he stood upon the rock of God's word and faithfulness nonetheless. And so he was able to say without a shadow of doubt:

> "You come against me with sword and spear and javelin, but I come against you in the name of the LORD Almighty, the God of the armies of Israel, whom you have defied. This day the LORD will hand you over to me, and I'll strike you down and cut off your head. Today I will give the carcasses of the Philistine army to the birds of the air and the beasts of the earth, and the whole world will know that there is a God in Israel. All those gathered here will know that it is not by sword or spear that the LORD saves; for the battle is the LORD's, and he will give all of you into our hands." (1 Samuel 17: 45–47)

Brother warriors, when we stand up for God, and his glory, he will be with us! If we are doing what God wants to be done, we have nothing to fear. We may feel fear, but we can put it aside and let it go, knowing that the God of heaven is by our side all the way.

So what do you do when stand up for God but you feel fear gripping you so tightly that it seems to be choking the life out of you? Does that mean you have failed, that you have no faith, and that you are a disappointment to God? No, far from it!

Consider this passage:

> When I am afraid, I will trust in you.
> In God, whose word I praise,
>> in God I trust; I will not be afraid.
> What can mortal man do to me?. . .
>
> Then my enemies will turn back
>> when I call for help.
> By this I will know that God is for me. (Psalm 56:3-4, 9)

First, notice that the passage begins with the words, "When I am afraid." Okay, so we know that David the giant slayer felt fear! But what is his response to his fear? He says that when he feels afraid, he has a solution—and what is it? *When I am afraid, I will trust in you.*

When we feel fear, we must trust God. It's that simple.

The next line says that David praises God's word. So, brother, when you are afraid, get into your Bible. Find a promise or a story that relates to what you are dealing with, and live there. Think about that story. Memorize that passage. Claim it. Trust it. Trust God.

David asks the question: What can mortal man do to me? Well, they can slander you and hurt your reputation, just as they did David. They can attack you and try to take your possessions and your life, just like they did David. "They" can do lots of things—but God is bigger and stronger than they are. And although they may inflict some damage, God is keeping accounts, and he will pay them back—and he will pay you back, too!

So look carefully again at the psalm. In essence it says, "When I am afraid...I will not be afraid." How about that? I was afraid, but I decided to trust God, and now I am no longer afraid. This is how a warrior needs to live!

Here then is the cure for fear:
>Honor God.
>Fear God.
>Trust God.

Honoring God means . . .
>Remember who God is
>Remember what he can do, and has done.
>Respect and seek to please him above all others.

Fearing God means . . .
>Fear God, not man.
>Fear God, not circumstances.

And while you are fearing God, know that he loves you, delights in you, has compassion on you, and will never leave you.

Trusting God means . . .
>Trust God; he his bigger than man.
>Trust God; he is bigger than circumstances.

When fear comes, deal with it before God the way David did. Honor God. Fear God. Trust God. Step out, pick up your five smooth stones and your slingshot, and take on your Goliath!

BATTLE PLAN

Honor God. Fear God. Trust God.

1. Think of one of the greatest righteous victories you have experienced in your life that involved fighting a battle against fear.

2. How did you feel at the conclusion of that battle? What were the keys to the victory you experienced?

3. List three battles you are facing right now that trigger feelings of fear.

    Now consider:

    - How can you honor God in these battles?

    - How do you need to fear God in these battles?

    - How do you need to trust God in these battles?

4. Find a story in the life of David or in the life of another Bible character that most resembles what you are facing in your current battles. Read that story over and over again in your personal devotionals, asking God to help its message to fill you with courage.

5. Share your three battles of fear with a fellow warrior who can be your friend, encourager, and companion as you take on these challenges.

Vignette: Jonathan and David
Based on 1 Samuel 17 and 18

The stone sank into [Goliath's] forehead, and he fell facedown on the ground....

David ran and stood over him. He took hold of the Philistine's sword and drew it from the scabbard. After he killed him, he cut off his head with the sword.

When the Philistines saw that their hero was dead, they turned and ran. Then the men of Israel and Judah surged forward with a shout and pursued the Philistines to the entrance of Gath and to the gates of Ekron. Their dead were strewn along the Shaaraim road to Gath and Ekron. When the Israelites returned from chasing the Philistines, they plundered their camp.

1 Samuel 17:49, 51–53

Eleazar is now an armor bearer in Saul's service. He has befriended two other young men, Jashobeam and Shammah. Together they have just witnessed one of the greatest moments in Israel's history, as David—another young man around their age—killed Goliath and inspired the Israelite army to rout their enemy.

After pursuing the fleeing Philistines along the Shaaraim Road all the way to Gath and Ekron on the day David slew Goliath, my friends Jashobeam, Shammah and I loaded up our horses with plunder and headed back to our base camp in the Valley of Elah. As we drew near to the camp, we saw a group of men, growing larger by the moment as warriors streamed back triumphantly from the battlefield. In the middle stood King Saul. His height made him impossible to miss.

"I wonder what's going on?" I asked Jashobeam. But I was too late; Jash was already galloping off toward the gathering crowd.

Shammah and I looked briefly at each other, laughed and spurred our mounts forward. When we caught up with him, Shammah shook his fist and shouted as we flew past, "Jash, your new Philistine horse may be faster than ours, but not with you riding him, big boy!"

As the three of us neared the group of warriors, we slowed to a trot and rode up side by side. We quietly dismounted, tied our horses to a nearby sapling, and walked up to the group.

Saul was standing on the elevated flat rock he always spoke from when he addressed the army. Jonathan stood just below him, to his right. I noticed Abner, the commander of the army, approaching with the young shepherd boy David at his side. The men parted widely to let them pass. Some ducked their heads or thumped fists against their hearts in a gesture of respect. And no wonder—this young man was the hero of the hour—maybe of our lifetime.

Abner paused at the base of the rock, clasped David by the shoulders, embraced him, and led him up to stand beside Saul. Jonathan climbed up and stood beside them. It was obvious that Abner was introducing David to the king. I thought they had already met, but maybe this was the formal introduction. What do you know anyway, Eleazar? You're only an armor bearer, I thought to myself.

Saul's officers stood on the ground below, intently looking up. Men were still pouring in from all around, creating a growing circle. We all sensed something important was about to happen.

Saul turned to address us. He held both his hands in the air and raised his voice. "Men of Israel, we have been given a great victory today! God has answered our prayers! He has given us a mighty deliverance!" Our shouts merged into one and echoed like thunder. "Young David, son of Jesse, has defeated the giant Goliath! The Philistines lie slain all the way to the gates of Gath and Ekron!"

"Yes!" "Amen!" "Praise God!" Our shouts resounded in a cacophony of joy. All around me, men punched each other on the shoulder and slapped each other on the back.

David stood beside Saul, dwarfed by the king's height, passing his slingshot from hand to hand, looking uncomfortable with the attention. He looked down at the ground, then up into the heavens as if he saw something or someone that the rest of us did not see. I wondered why he was not cheering along with us or holding Goliath's severed head and captured sword aloft.

"I as your king hereby appoint David a captain in my army and give him command of a thousand men!" Saul shouted as he grabbed David's right hand, raising it high. David smiled, but his eyes were wide with surprise.

Jashobeam cheered for a moment, then he looked over at me, lean-ing in to mutter, "I'm grateful for his courage, but how does one lucky shot and watching a flock of sheep prepare you to lead a thousand warriors?" I shrugged at him and kept on clapping, but what he said made sense.

I looked up at Jonathan, standing a step behind David, and won-dered what he must be feeling. Was he not the son of Saul, Israel's prince and heir to the throne? Was he not the hero of the stunning victory at Geba? Hadn't we all just a few weeks ago been cheering for him? Had he not been, until today, the bravest and most admired warrior in our army? Now all eyes were on David, and Jonathan was standing off to the side, not the star he once was. Had the men already forgotten what he had done?

I had watched Jonathan when Goliath came out day after day to challenge one of us to fight him. The men would look up and down the battle lines to see who among us would step out. All eyes had turned to Jonathan—over and over again, day after day. Surely if anyone was going to fight Goliath, it would be Jonathan. But although his eyes had glit-tered with anger and fire every time Goliath insulted us, he never made a move. Nor did Saul. None of us did, day after shameful day, for forty days. But then this redheaded shepherd boy armed with nothing but a sling-shot had come from nowhere and killed the giant, and now the whole army was cheering for him.

Watching Jonathan stand there, watching his army cheer for David, I couldn't help thinking, We could be cheering Jonathan's victory today. He's no longer our greatest hero. What does his future hold? If I were Jon-athan, I would be seething with jealousy or shame—or both.

But Jonathan was not seething or scowling; instead he had begun to laugh and shout and smile—more than anyone else. He jumped down off the rock and ran around the inside the circle of warriors, slapping their upraised hands. Then he leapt back up onto the rock beside his father and David, and started leading the cheers. He mimicked the motions of a slinger throwing a stone, then shaded his eyes with his hand as if watch-ing the rock soar. Then he crouched down with his fists clenched by his knees and sprung straight up in the air, arms extended full length over his head, shouting wildly in mock victory. The men went crazy. The whole army erupted in pure, joyous bedlam.

Jonathan ran around to David's side, grabbed his hand and raised it up in the air. Saul grabbed David's other hand and did the same. David stood there between them, the king and the prince each holding an arm aloft.

The shouts and cheers shook the ground beneath us. David was so much shorter than Saul and Jonathan that he had to stand on his toes. They finally actually lifted him off the ground between them. He looked small, boyish, dangling there between those two tall noble men.

Finally they lowered David to the ground. Jonathan embraced him, clasping and shaking him by the shoulders and banging his forehead against his.

Jonathan grabbed his father and began saying something in his ear. It looked like he was shouting to be heard above all the noise. I wondered how Saul was taking being shouted at—even in a moment like this. Saul looked at Jonathan, eyes narrowed for a moment, then smiled and nodded.

Saul raised his hands to the men, palms out, motioning down toward the ground. The men gradually quieted down. Saul's regal baritone boomed, "Yes men, this day is a glorious victory from God! Jonathan has asked to lead us in a prayer of thanks to him. Here is my son!"

Jonathan stepped forward. As one we knelt on the dusty ground. Many raised up hands in thanksgiving. Jonathan prayed, "Thank you O God, for you are the Giver of victory!"

Voices sounded all around me: "Amen!", "God be praised!", "Glory to God!"

"Our God, we thank you for your mercy. We were facing a foe mightier than we had ever seen. We were afraid. We lacked faith. But you, O God, are strong when we are weak, and faithful even when our faith in you falters.

"You chose a young man to fight this battle. He showed a heart of humility and reverence, of faith and courage. You, O God, directed his steps. His stone flew true. Our mighty foe and his army were defeated.

"We give you glory and praise! Amen and amen, forever and ever!" As one man, we all added our "amen."

"I have one more thing to say, brother warriors!" Jonathan shouted, rising from his knees. Jash and I stood, wiping dirt from our knees.

We all grew quiet.

"David, son of Jesse, please step forward and stand between my father and me."

David stepped up, looking uncertain.

Saul shot Jonathan a puzzled look.

"I have some gifts for you, David my friend." Jonathan's gaze swept over his men, his hand resting on David's shoulder. "My father has just given you a commission in the army. Your shepherd's garments have served you well, but you now need a soldier's attire. I hereby give you my own officer's robe and tunic. They may be a little large for you right now, but you'll grow into them."

Jonathan slipped out of his beautiful royal blue robe and tunic and draped them over David's shoulders. Beside me, Shammah gave a small gasp of surprise. All around us, the men clapped and cheered.

Jonathan wasn't done yet. "Your slingshot has served you, your Lord, and all of us well today. But every warrior should have a sword." The crowd roared its assent. "Most of us now have returned today with new swords, taken from our enemies." Even louder cheers. "You have won in battle the great sword of Goliath, the largest sword any of us have ever seen." At this Jonathan reached down, picked up the huge blade of Goliath, placed it in David's hands, and motioned for David to raise it up into the air. When David did so, the warriors erupted once more.

Jonathan slashed a hand out to quiet everyone. "But I have one more sword for you, David. It is not as mighty as that of Goliath, but is the sword of my own heart, given to me by my father."

Beside me, Jash whispered, "I don't believe it."

Chills crept down my back.

Jonathan drew his sword and held it high. "David, today I present you this, my sword, along with my bow and my belt, to show you my respect and honor. I give you these, my most valuable possessions, as a sign of the covenant and vow I make with you this day. I pledge to you before God and these men that I will be your friend and brother in love and loyalty all the days of my life."

The prince knelt in front of David, offering the young shepherd his gifts. David stood stunned for a moment, and then dropped down on his knees in front of Jonathan with his head bowed and his hands open. Jonathan laid the weapons in his hands and clasped his own hands together as if in prayer.

The soldiers all stood silent. Never had any of us seen a warrior give away his sword and bow to anyone other than his own son or brother.

My throat tightened with emotion. I gripped Shammah's forearm, who used his other hand to wipe tears from his eyes. Jashobeam stood silent, his mouth agape in wonder. Soldier after soldier bowed his head, while others just stood there, weeping silent tears. Finally, the men began to join arms until every warrior was connected in line after line of a soldier's embrace.

Jonathan stood up and said, "Men, let us prepare to return home. All glory to God! May his peace be with you all. Remember this day of victory all the days of your lives!"

Jashobeam, Shammah and I turned looked at each other. I swallowed hard, cleared my throat and said to them, "I can't believe Jonathan did that—and in front of his whole army! What a man of God. He may not have slain Goliath, but he is a true Mighty Man." I paused, gathering my courage to imitate my prince and put my own heart on the line. "My brothers, may we have this same friendship with each other. God being my helper, I pledge to both of you my loyalty and love for life."

With shining eyes, Shammah said, "Yes my friends. By the living God, that is my promise and pledge to you both, for all the days of my life."

Jashobeam's voice quivered, "And I too, before the living God, this day, make the same oath to you, my brothers, friends, and fellow warriors."

We bowed our heads and clasped our hands together for a moment. Then we turned and silently walked back to our mounts and readied to return to camp, not knowing what way lay ahead of us, but knowing our lives would never be the same.

BATTLE CRY

Every warrior gets discouraged.

Maybe you feel discouraged now: Maybe life isn't going the way you had planned. Maybe you've faced a series of disappointments, heartbreaks, and failures.

When discouragement seeps into our bones, it saps our strength and destroys our spirit. It puts us right where the Enemy wants us: Listless. Uninspired. Unable to fight.

Fellow warrior, God does not want us to live in perpetual discouragement. And we have every reason not to.

Feeling discouraged, brother warrior? Let David's story, and the way he overcame discouragement, help to restore your faith, revive your hope, and reinvigorate your spirit.

Let's go to battle! Let's rise up and defeat discouragement!

The Battle of Discouragement

But David thought to himself, "One of these days I will be destroyed by the hand of Saul. The best thing I can do is to escape to the land of the Philistines. Then Saul will give up searching for me anywhere in Israel, and I will slip out of his hand."

1 Samuel 27:1

*The enemy pursues me,
    he crushes me to the ground;
he makes me dwell in darkness
    like those long dead.
So my spirit grows faint within me,
    my heart within me is dismayed.*

Psalm 143:3—4

Fear is a hard battle to fight, but the battle of discouragement may be even harder.

Just what is the difference between fear and discouragement?

Fear can come upon us in a moment. It can be shocking, terrifying, and sudden. Fear is often connected to a specific situation or person. Kind of like when a Goliath shows up in your life. But after a while, the situation resolves, our fear subsides, and we get past it.

Discouragement is different.

Discouragement is fear stretched out over time. It is fear that settles in. It is apprehension that does not go away.

Discouragement comes when we face long-term, difficult situations that seem to have no end. We get worn down and lose our motivation. We aren't necessarily living in terror, but we have lost the hope, the expectation, and the confidence that we, or the situations around us, could ever change for the better. Instead of living with the joy and hope of better things to come, we plod along with a sense of defeat, dullness, and resignation.

As I often say, discouragement comes when our courage has been "dissed" for a long period of time.

It was discouragement, not fear, that almost took David down at one point. We know the story: Samuel privately appoints young David as king; David slays Goliath and is selected by Saul to be an officer in the army. David grows successful and popular. Saul, consumed by jealousy and fear, seeks to kill David to prevent him from displacing him as king. David has to flee for his life. He runs from Saul for months, perhaps years.

Situations like this are some of the most difficult to deal with in our spiritual lives. They wear us down over a long period of time. Let's step back and look at some of the challenges David endured during this time, sufferings that could bring discouragement to the heart and mind of any man who would be a warrior for God. Perhaps, brother warrior, you have also experienced some of these struggles.

David's discouragements

Irrational, unnecessary suffering

David has been privately anointed by Samuel to be the next king. Shortly afterward, at the moment of Israel's great need, he steps up and does the courageous thing: he faces and defeats Goliath. And then, in spite of being the hero of the moment, he does not push himself forward to be recognized as the rightful king; instead, he does the humble, noble thing: he submits himself to Saul and serves as a captain in his army. He seems almost naïve in his trusting obedience to this twisted, disturbed ruler.

The next thing David knows, Saul has turned against him, and he is running for his life.

Sometimes, we just can't figure out what God is up to. We look at his promises of deliverance and victory, and wonder why certain things happen to us. Here is what David could be thinking: *If God is with me, if God wants me to be the next king, why is this happening? Why would God put me in a position like this? I did not ask to be king. I stood up for God and killed Goliath. I did the right thing. Why doesn't God come to my rescue and free me from this suffering and pressure? This makes no sense whatsoever.*

When things happen to us that we don't understand, difficulties that make no sense and we can't figure out, discouragement can set in and darken our days, robbing us of the joy we once knew.

We might wonder, "Why didn't David just leave the country and go far away? Why stay right there in Judah, where Saul would be provoked to pursue him?" We don't know the full answer, but we can formulate a reasonable guess from the information we have.

When David first fled Saul, he at first was completely alone. But eventually his family and others came to join him:

> *David left Gath and escaped to the cave of Adullam. When his brothers and his father's household heard about it, they went down to him there. All those who were in distress or in debt or discontented gathered around him, and he became their leader. About four hundred men were with him.* (1 Samuel 22:1–2)

David realizes that it will be difficult to hide from Saul with such a large company of people around him. He is concerned for his family. He goes to the pagan king of Moab and asks him to allow his mother and father to stay there until he can learn God's will:

> *From there David went to Mizpah in Moab and said to the king of Moab, "Would you let my father and mother come and stay with you until I learn what God will do for me?" So he left them with the king of Moab, and they stayed with him as long as David was in the stronghold.* (1 Samuel 22:3–4)

David then looks to discover God's will by seeking the counsel of the prophet Gad. God has some very challenging direction for David:

> *But the prophet Gad said to David, "Do not stay in the stronghold. Go into the land of Judah." So David left and went to the forest of Hereth.* (1 Samuel 22:5)

From a human point of view, this advice just doesn't make sense.

Judah was very close to where Saul lived. It is as if God is saying to David, "Don't flee Israel and live in pagan territory, where Saul will leave you alone. Instead, remain in Judah, right under his nose. I know that means he will hunt you relentlessly, and that you, your family and your men will be continually in danger, on the run, and under pressure. But that is the way I want it."

Have you ever sought God's guidance and gotten back a message that was difficult to hear? Have you wondered why God would allow a trying, unfair or unjust situation to go on and on, with seemingly no end in sight? Have you gone through a tough circumstance in your life that you asked God to take away and that he seemed unwilling to remove? That is what happens to David here. God actually directs him to move his family and his warriors into a difficult, dangerous place.

I wonder how David took that news. I wonder if he wrestled with it and struggled to accept and understand it. Here is my guess on some of the thoughts that may have gone through his mind—it certainly is what I might have thought if I were in his situation:

> *God knows that King Saul is an evil, selfish, angry man. He has already told him that he is unworthy to be king, and that I am going to replace him. Why doesn't God go ahead and take him out of power? That is hard enough for me to understand, but now God has told me to stay in Judah where my family and my men will face danger every day. Why can't we just move cross the border away from Saul and live our lives in peace until he dies? I will stay faithful to God even though I reside in pagan territory. Every day that I stay here in Judah I provoke Saul to greater anger. Why would God want me to do this?*

Unjust treatment

What is happening to David is just not fair. He has done nothing to deserve it. He has faithfully, humbly, and loyally served Saul as one of his commanders. Although God has appointed him to be king, David does not try to usurp, undermine, or overthrow Saul.

David knows that Saul has brought judgment upon himself. God has declared his intention to do take him out because of his pride and disobedience. But it is *David* who is unjustly suffering at Saul's hands.

But as if becoming a fugitive is not bad enough, there is even more pain and injustice for David to endure: Saul takes David's wife, Michal, away from him and gives her to be the wife of someone else. Michal (who is the daughter of Saul) had faithfully helped her new husband escape from her father, but she had to remain behind when David fled. So now David has to bear up under the knowledge that Saul has stolen his young wife, given her away, and that she is now having intimate relations with another man (1 Samuel 25:44).

But in spite of this injustice, David maintains a good attitude. While on the run from Saul, he learns that the Israelite city of Keilah is under Philistine attack. At great risk and against the wishes of his own men, he goes to Keilah's aid. David and his men drive off the Philistines and save the city (1 Samuel 23:1–6). When Saul learns that David is in Keilah, he comes with his army to capture him. As Saul approaches Keilah, David prays to God, asking him if the citizens of the city he just saved will turn him over to Saul. And what is God's answer? *They will* (v. 12). Talk about injustice! He just saved their lives!

Have you ever experienced unfair treatment in your life? How discouraging has it been? Mistreatment can come from evil, greedy people who seek to take what is ours. Or it can come from angry people who think we have done them wrong. But sadly, it can also come at the hands of people whom we have helped, loved, and served—people who ought to be our biggest fans. When that happens, deep discouragement can set in. We did the good and noble thing, and here is what we get in return! And as we have seen with David and Saul, we may suffer abuse at the hands of people who are who are supposed to be our spiritual leaders and protectors. Sometimes unfair situations like these can go on and on, with no end in sight.

Unfair criticism, loss of reputation

Saul does not just seek to capture David, he does more: he and his cronies slander David's name. Saul sets out to undermine the popularity and heroic reputation David has earned by his victory over Goliath and his amazing success as a commander in his army. (See 1 Samuel 22:6–8 and Psalm 54.)

Fair, just criticism can be hard enough to take—how much more when we are falsely accused? Nothing can make us feel more discouraged than knowing our reputation is being assailed and that our good name has been unfairly damaged or destroyed.

David is helpless, completely unable to defend himself. He cannot tell his side of the story or explain what really happened. He who was once praised throughout the land in joyful songs of victory is now mocked in drunken revelry. In a matter of days he goes from being the rising young star of Israel to being an object of contempt, ridicule, and hatred. He goes viral on the ancient Internet—all as a result of being selected by God to do something he never asked to do! Right about now, David may be thinking, "No good deed goes unpunished!"

Alienation from friends and family

Saul's attacks begin to take a fearsome toll. Now some of David's closest friends turn against him. How would we feel if a fellow warrior who once worshipped God at our side turned and became our enemy? That is what happens to David. And the damage does not stop with his friends. Some members of David's own family believe Saul's slander. Psalm 69 says that David's brothers also joined in mocking him. It is painful to lose our reputation among people who used to admire and trust us; it is heartrending to be stripped of the love of closest friends; it is devastating to be estranged from our own family.

Upheaval and instability in our living situation

David has to flee for his life. He has no money, no food, no home, no nothing. He ends up living in the wild. No house. No job. No way to make money. Soon we find him and a few companions begging bread from Ahimelech the priest (1 Samuel 21:1-3). He later tries to earn income by providing free, unsolicited protection to rich guys like Nabal and then later going to ask for a donation (1 Samuel 25:4-11). In return for his deeds of service, he receives contempt and humiliating insult from Nabal. How discouraging must this have been!

Have you ever had to take a cut in pay? Ever lost a job? Did it put you in financial distress? Did you have to sell or forfeit your home and move to a smaller, cheaper place? How did that affect your confidence and your sense of manhood? Deep discouragement can set in when we as men feel as if we have failed to succeed in our careers or to properly provide for our wife and children.

I wonder if God has placed these stories in Scripture to help those of us who face struggles in similar areas. Perhaps you have faced unfair criticism. Perhaps you have been falsely accused. Perhaps you have lost respect and a good reputation. Perhaps you have lost your job, your savings, your home, your family, or the place you had fought to carve for yourself in the world. If the man after the heart of God endured such sufferings, then we can learn from his mistakes, defeats, and victories.

We can make it through. We can learn. We can turn things around.

Intensity of pressure

Pressure can bring upon us profound discouragement, especially when we must endure pressure for a long period of time.

> *David stayed in the desert strongholds and in the hills of the Desert of Ziph.* **Day after day** *Saul searched for him, but God did not give David into his hands.* (1 Samuel 23:14, emphasis added)

> *Saul was going along one side of the mountain, and David and his men were on the other side, hurrying to get away from Saul. As Saul and his forces were **closing in** on David and his men to capture them . . .* (1 Samuel 23:26, emphasis added)

Here we find David and his men under intense pressure, and we see that the pressure kept up for days on end. The Scripture says it went on "day after day." It also says that Saul was "closing in." Ever felt that way? *Day after day*, the pressure *closes in*? If you are under this kind of stress, it can slowly, surely wear you down. It can rob you of your strength. It can rob you of your faith and confidence. Discouragement can set in.

Sometimes, fellow warriors, God lets things like this happen to us. We may wonder why. We may weaken. We may get down. But, if we remain faithful, God comes through. And when he finally does, we can know without a doubt that it was God himself who delivered us! Just when it seemed David and his men were finally going to be captured, God providentially intervenes:

> *Saul was going along one side of the mountain, and David and his men were on the other side, hurrying to get away from Saul. As Saul and his forces were closing in on David and his men to capture them, a messenger came to Saul, saying, "Come quickly! The Philistines are raiding the land." Then Saul broke off his pursuit of David and went to meet the Philistines. That is why they call this place Sela Hammahlekoth.* (1 Samuel 23:26–28)

At the last minute, just when Saul was about to capture David, God yanks the evil king out of the picture. Isn't that the way it works sometimes? We are on the verge of losing, and God turns it around! David was so inspired that he changed the name of the place so that he would never forget what happened. He renames it "Rock of Parting"—the place where God turned Saul away. Brothers, we all have victories like this. Let's remember our own Rocks of Parting, the times and places in our lives when God stopped Satan in his tracks. And may those memories inspire us when we are once again under pressure, and it seems defeat is imminent. God is a mighty God, and he is our deliverer!

Long-term pressure

Two times, David fled to Philistine territory.

The first time was fairly soon after he was exiled. It happened when he sought refuge with Achish, the Philistine King, who lived in Gath. In this case, his actions are somewhat understandable, since he at this point had no definite word from God on where he wants him to be. But it was still a mistake:

> *That day David fled from Saul and went to Achish king of Gath. But the servants of Achish said to him, "Isn't this David, the king of the land? Isn't he the one they sing about in their dances:*
>
> > *" 'Saul has slain his thousands,*
> > *and David his tens of thousands'?"*
>
> *David took these words to heart and was very much afraid of Achish king of Gath. So he pretended to be insane in their presence; and while he was in their hands he acted like a madman, making marks on the doors of the gate and letting saliva run down his beard.*
>
> *Achish said to his servants, "Look at the man! He is insane! Why bring him to me? Am I so short of madmen that you have to bring this fellow here to carry on like this in front of me? Must this man come into my house?"* (1 Samuel 21:10–14)

The next time David flees Israel, his decision is much more grave. He has received definite instruction from God telling him not to leave Judah, but David does so anyway. Discouraged from months and possibly years of living on the run, David allows his weariness to get the better of him. He tells himself that he will perish at Saul's hand—in spite of God's promise that he would be king, in spite of God protecting him from Saul time and time again (see 1 Samuel 19:18–24; 23:14).

That is what discouragement does. It wears us down; it drains us over time. The long days, weeks, months, and years of not seeing definitive deliverance or relief can do things to us that a moment's shock will never do.

We get tired.

We wonder why God does not act.

We don't understand why God's timetable is different than ours.

We don't see things ever working out.

We begin to overlook God's promises.

Our faith weakens.

We doubt God, we doubt ourselves, and we doubt our destiny.

When we forget that God is good and that he is working out everything for our good (Romans 8:28), we become weary, vulnerable to spiritual compromise. Maybe we don't leave God in a single, dramatic moment, but we leave him nonetheless.

David ends up back with the pagan king Achish (1 Samuel 27). He ends up lying to Achish to protect himself. He goes raiding against pagan peoples, but to cover it over, David tells Achish he was raiding against his own people. Achish believes David, and starts trusting him. We see here that when we allow ourselves to be "unequally yoked" with unbelievers (2 Corinthians 6:14), we usually end up compromising our convictions. We start twisting the truth, and eventually we end up outright lying. We bend the rules a little at first, but once we cross the line, we end up in serious sin.

Here is how bad it gets for David: King Achish and the Philistines once again go to war against the Israelites (see 1 Samuel 29). And when they do, Achish insists that David and his men attack the Israelites—their own people!—with them. What does David do? Does he make a stand? Does he say, "No way, Achish. I will not fight God's people, they are my people, too"? No, he does not. He wants to go to war with Achish against Israel!

What has happened to the pure-hearted, brave young man who stood up to Goliath? Where is the noble man who refused to take the life of Saul on two different occasions? Where is the man who wrote the psalms, who trusted God so amazingly? That man has become discouraged, and because of that, he has compromised. And now he is on the verge of treason, ready to go to war against his God and his people, ready to throw away his own life and destiny...all because he has grown discouraged.

God graciously uses the suspicion of other Philistine leaders to block David from his folly. The Philistine warlords decide that David can't go to war alongside them because they fear he might turn against them in the midst of battle. Achish protests their decision, and so does David! David is actually offended that he can't go out and go to war against his own people—this is how severely his heart, attitude, and judgment have deteriorated. But God is merciful. Just as he did when he sent Abigail to stop David from killing Nabal, so now God intervenes to save him from a horrible mistake. Banned by the Philistine commanders, David turns around and goes back to his "home" in Ziklag.

When David and his men return, they find a terrible scene. The city is burned to the ground (see 1 Samuel 30), Amalekite raiders have come and taken their wives, their children, and all their possessions. The very people David has compromised himself to protect—his family—he has lost. What a lesson! It is better to suffer daily difficulty and pressure, still following the will of God, than to seek a false peace by compromising God's plan. How many of us have seen people leave God and his church looking for an easier life, only to end up in utter misery: divorce, the loss of children to the world, and other problems too many to mention? Brother warriors, stay in the will of God, no matter how difficult or wearying it may be. Compromise produces far more pain and regret than we can imagine.

Look what happens now: David's own Mighty Men blame him for the disaster. They are ready to stone him: "David was greatly distressed because the men were talking of stoning him; each one was bitter in spirit because of his sons and daughters" (1 Samuel 30:6).

Isn't it amazing, brothers? If we lead our family astray, away from God, at first it may seems like all is well. We, and they, may even feel some initial relief. But in time, we start to reap what we have sown. And you know what? The people who cheered when you first led them astray will turn against you when it all comes crashing down.

I have seen this terrible pattern hold true over and over again: a man leads his family out of the church and into spiritual compromise.

It may take months or years, but eventually the horrible repercussions begin to reveal themselves. Then the man's friends, and perhaps his own family, turn against him in bitterness. "What have you done?" they ask. And just like David, that brother weeps until he can weep no more (1 Samuel 30:4).

The solution

What do we do in the face of discouragement? What do we do when we are weary? What if we have given in and compromised our faith?

It's really pretty simple. We need to do just what David does: he turns back to God.

David was greatly distressed because the men were talking of stoning him; each one was bitter in spirit because of his sons and daughters. But David found strength in the LORD his God.

*Then David said to Abiathar the priest, the son of Ahimelech, "Bring me the ephod." Abiathar brought it to him, **and David inquired of the LORD**.* (1 Samuel 30:6–8, emphasis added)

David humbles himself. He turns back to God. He does what he failed to do when he abandoned Judah—he inquires of the Lord. And God is merciful. He hears David's prayer and gives him the guidance he needs. David and his Mighty Men recover their families, all safe and sound (1 Samuel 30:7–20).

Fellow warrior, are you discouraged?

Does it seem like you have some problems that just won't go away?

Is your zeal waning?

Are you just plain tired?

Are you beginning to doubt God?

Are you thinking it is just not worth it to serve God, to keep putting him first, to keep serving in the church?

Does it feel like a long time since you have seen God move in your life, answer a prayer, or give you a victory?

Let me encourage you not to give up. God still loves you. God is still with you. You may not understand what is happening, or why. You may no longer be a young man, or young in the faith. My brother, *stay faithful* over the years, and over the decades. Some of the greatest and sweetest moments of your life will come only after years of difficulty and trial.

Here is how this part of David's story ends:

Saul goes into battle against Achish and the Philistines. His army is defeated. Rather than be killed by his enemies, Saul takes his own life by falling on his sword. It is not long after this that the promise God made to David years ago finally comes to pass. The long, discouraging ordeal with Saul is finally over, and David is crowned the new king!

David pulls through this long season of discouragement to become a great king. He lives to write these words of praise, looking back over his trials to his ultimate victory and vindication:

> For the director of music. Of David the servant of the LORD. He sang to the LORD the words of this song when the LORD delivered him from the hand of all his enemies and from the hand of Saul. He said:
>
> I love you, O LORD, my strength.
>
> The LORD is my rock, my fortress and my deliverer;
> my God is my rock, in whom I take refuge.
> He is my shield and the horn of my
>   salvation, my stronghold.
> I call to the LORD, who is worthy of praise,
> and I am saved from my enemies.
>
> The cords of death entangled me;
> the torrents of destruction overwhelmed me.
> The cords of the grave coiled around me;
> the snares of death confronted me.
> In my distress I called to the LORD;
> I cried to my God for help.
> From his temple he heard my voice;
> my cry came before him, into his ears. . . .
>
> He reached down from on high and took hold of me;
> he drew me out of deep waters.
> He rescued me from my powerful enemy,
> from my foes, who were too strong for me. (Psalm 18:1–6,16–17)

Thoughts for discouraged warriors

Brother warrior, if you are dealing with discouragement, keep these truths in mind:

- Realize that God has a longer-term plan in view than your immediate situation.

- Realize that God's purpose is greater than your personal needs.

- Realize that God is using the situation for your good and that God's definition of "good" is often different than ours.

- God wants a closer relationship with you, and if this situation draws you closer to him, that is of greater value than your personal comfort.

- God wants to help you be more like Jesus. If this situation makes you more like Jesus, then that growth is of greater value than your personal comfort.

- God wants you to understand and respect Jesus better than you ever have, and to love and appreciate Jesus more than you ever have. God uses hardships to accomplish those purposes.

- God can use difficulty to help you more deeply understand the needs and feelings of other people, and to make you more compassionate.

- God may be using this situation to help other people. His greater plan is to help people to come to faith in Jesus, and then become more like Christ over time. He may be using your challenging situation to help accomplish those purposes.

- In the end, God will bring justice and righteousness about in whatever unjust or painful situation you have faced. God may not do so on your timetable, but he will set things right in his own good time.

Brother warriors, let us not allow discouragement to take us away from faithful, zealous, joyous, service to our Lord. Let's be the warriors who refuse to surrender to discouragement. Let's stand strong with God. He will never fail us or forsake us!

Battle Plan

1. List three of the most discouraging situations you have faced in the past that have turned out well.

2. What was the key that turned each of those situations around?

3. What was crucial in your attitude that enabled you to not give up or give in?

4. List the good that came about in (1) your life, and (2) the lives of others as a result of these victories.

5. What would have happened had you given up or given in?

6. What are the three most discouraging long-term battles you are facing right now?

7. Read Romans 5:1–5 and James 1:2–8.

8. List a character issue that God could be helping you to grow in through each of these battles.

9. List the good that could be coming into the lives of other people as a result of these battles.

10. Share these situations with a fellow warrior who can be your companion and fellow soldier as you "fight the good fight" in each one.

BATTLE CRY

God's warriors are not angry men.

We might think that being a warrior for God means that we are to be flammable, volatile, and full of indignation. And in one sense, we are right. Passion is a good thing, when we are on fire for the glory and honor of God. But anger —our personal anger—can be dangerous, destructive, and deceptive.

God wants his warriors to be gentlemen. He wants us fueled by faith, hope, and love, not rage, bitterness, and frustration.

Fellow warriors, let us look deeply into our hearts. Let us guard our thoughts, rein in our tempers, and watch our mouths.

Let us distinguish between godly anger and personal affront.

And let us fight to uphold our Commander's honor, filled with conviction, compassion, and courage.

Chapter Nine

The Battle of Anger

"It's been useless—all my watching over this fellow's property in the desert so that nothing of his was missing. He has paid me back evil for good. May God deal with David, be it ever so severely, if by morning I leave alive one male of all who belong to him!"

1 Samuel 25:21–22

God's warriors are not angry men.

On one occasion, David was almost ruined by his anger. (Read the full story in 1 Samuel 25.) This incident from David's life teaches us profound lessons about how anger can defeat us, even as warriors in God's service.

Anger can come unexpectedly, and after we have done well

Just before this incident occurs, we find David and his men desperately seeking to escape Saul and his advancing army (1 Samuel 24). They take refuge in a cave, and Saul unknowingly enters the same cave to relieve himself. He is defenseless and vulnerable. David's men urge him to take the (supposedly) God-given opportunity to kill his enemy, but David, ever the righteous warrior, refuses to place himself in the role of judge and executioner. Instead, he quietly cuts off a corner of Saul's robe. When Saul exits the cave, David follows, calls out, and shows Saul the cloth. The cloth is proof that David could have taken Saul's life, but that he showed mercy instead. It is proof that David does not consider Saul his enemy. On hearing this, Saul is moved to tears, and declares openly that David is not his foe. Saul admits that he has unjustly accused and pursued him, and that God is indeed with David.

What a victory for David! What a demonstration of his humility, faith, forgiveness, respect, and self-control. This is one of the noblest moments in David's life, an occasion in which he rises high above the injustice and mistreatment he has suffered, and is rewarded by God with open (albeit temporary) vindication.

But anger is no respecter of our past victories. Anger shows no honor to our previous humility, faith, or patience. Anger can blindside us. It can strike from unexpected places and in unexpected moments. And it can flare up even when an offense is not a big deal... we may have handled other, greater offenses with grace and wisdom, but a small offense can still make us lose it.

Anger can come from angry, difficult people

While they were camped in the region of Carmel, David's six hundred men provided protection for the shepherds and farmers who grazed their flocks and herds there. David's men could have been bullies and thieves, but instead they became an informal vigilante police force protecting people from the lawless bandits who roamed the countryside. They had an invaluable and honorable role. They were loved, trusted, and respected by everyone they served.

Well, *almost* everyone.

> *A certain man in Maon, who had property there at Carmel, was very wealthy. He had a thousand goats and three thousand sheep, which he was shearing in Carmel. His name was Nabal and his wife's name was Abigail. She was an intelligent and beautiful woman, but her husband, a Calebite, was surly and mean in his dealings.* (1 Samuel 25:2–3)

Do you realize that some people are just flat-out arrogant and mean? Ever figured that one out? Yes, there are people who are angry, cocky, and superior in their attitudes. When you deal with them, you are going to be insulted, put down, and disdained. Don't take it personally; that's the way they treat just about everyone they encounter. If you are not careful, they will provoke you into acting just like they do.

We are about to learn about a man whose name in Hebrew, *Nabhal*, sounds remarkably similar to the Hebrew word for "fool," *nebhalah*. There you have it: *Nabhal* (Nabal) and *nebhalah* (fool). Just what were his mom and dad thinking when they stuck that moniker on him?

Nabal was so mean and angry that his servants said that no one could reason with him (1 Samuel 25:17); even his own wife said he was a wicked fool (1 Samuel 25:25).

Let's see how Nabal's arrogance and folly come perilously close to defeating David.

David sends some of his younger soldiers to Nabal to tactfully ask if he might be so gracious as to give some sort of reward for their service. David's envoys do not demand or threaten; they are respectful and courteous in their approach, delivering the message David had given them:

> " 'Long life to you! Good health to you and your household! And good health to all that is yours!
>
> " 'Now I hear that it is sheep-shearing time. When your shepherds were with us, we did not mistreat them, and the whole time they were at Carmel nothing of theirs was missing. Ask your own servants and they will tell you. Therefore be favorable toward my young men, since we come at a festive time. Please give your servants and your son David whatever you can find for them.' "
>
> When David's men arrived, they gave Nabal this message in David's name. Then they waited. (1 Samuel 25:6–8)

You would think Nabal would bend over backwards to reward these men who, free of charge, have protected his herdsmen and his flocks. Not so!

> Nabal answered David's servants, "Who is this David? Who is this son of Jesse? Many servants are breaking away from their masters these days. Why should I take my bread and water, and the meat I have slaughtered for my shearers, and give it to men coming from who knows where?" (1 Samuel 25:10–11)

Anger can come from injustice and insult

The men return and report Nabal's insulting words to David. He is outraged. He immediately tells his men to follow his example and strap on their swords, and they head out to take vengeance. David is so angry that he vows to kill not only Nabal, but also every male in his household: children, kinsmen, and servants.

Yes, there has been injustice. And what is more, the perpetrator has added insult to injury. It is one thing to be done wrong. But it is quite another thing to have your dignity and manhood denigrated as well. If you are a man, and especially if you are a strong man who tries to do the right thing, it may be that anger and rage come even easier to you than to most other people. That doesn't make your anger right, but it is true nonetheless.

I don't know about you, fellow warrior, but when I treat someone courteously and respectfully, but receive insults in return, the anger-demon rises within me in full, raging force. "I did him right, now look at how he is treating me! This is unfair and outrageous! It is time for payback. Justice must be served!"

Know this: Oftentimes, these kinds of insults come from people who do this to pretty much *everybody*. In the first verse of the first psalm we read that some people "sit in the seat of mockers." They have a sneer, a jeer, and a leer for anyone they don't like, and that includes the whole world. They play by their own rules. I remember a difficult conversation I once had with a particularly insulting guy. When he treated me with contempt, I responded, "I am playing a gentleman's game of flag football; you are playing tackle! To play with your style, I would have to break rules that neither God nor my conscience will allow me to break." In soccer parlance, I was playing a friendly match, while he was getting red card after red card, but staying on the field!

In one sense, anger is a righteous emotion. It is a natural response to injustice and maltreatment. We think, *As a warrior for God, how can I back down when I am right?* Yes, we need to stand up for God, for his principles, and for the weak and downtrodden. But standing up for God does not mean we need to become angry. We need to be especially careful when our own personal pride and feelings are involved. Yes, we may need to stand strong in such a situation, but we need to be sure our thinking is clear, our heart is pure, and our actions are righteous.

There are some people you may have to stand up to, but with whom you will never win an argument. They want to have the last word. They are not interested in *what* is right but *who* is right. They are not seeking God's will; their goal is personal victory. You simply cannot win in a conversation or debate with someone like that.

Insults and provocation may come from people who are in power, like a boss, a supervisor, a coach, a teacher, or a leader. Some people in these positions think that their status gives them the right to treat those "under" them with contempt and disdain. Disrespect may come from people who are wealthy, successful or popular. (True, Nabal wasn't popular, but he was successful and wealthy!) It is as if they think, "My money and my success mean I am better and smarter than you. You need to cater to me and show me deference. I have a free pass to be rude."

As warriors for God, we might think it is our personal duty and mission to straighten such people out—to humble them, to humiliate them, to put them in their place. And you know what? They do need to come to their senses. But can you help them do that when you yourself are out of control with anger? The problem is, when we feel personally insulted, we are easily swept into sinful anger. Our indignation is no longer about God; it is about us. *Our* pride has been wounded; *our* dignity has been (supposedly) sullied. We have been humiliated and embarrassed. And we are determined to fix it by fighting back!

Which voices will you value?

Let me ask you, brother warrior, where does your dignity come from, really? Is it derived from how this person thinks about you? Is it from how *anyone* thinks about you? Or does your sense of who you are depend upon how *God* thinks about you? If you are going to allow yourself to care about someone else's opinion of you, choose those people wisely. Decide to value the perspective of people who are seeking to place God and his word first in their lives. Don't let the opinions of worldly, arrogant, selfish people get under your skin. We should be willing to hear the truth, even from a flawed source, but we must be careful not to count on worldly people to build up our confidence. We need to draw our confidence from God, and then select godly friends to influence, encourage, and shape us. Let us choose friends who will tell us the truth of God even when it is hard for us to hear—but make sure those friends are spiritual people who form their judgments based upon God's word, and not upon their high view of themselves (Proverbs 25:12, Ephesians 4:15). I will say it again: *Choose wisely!*

Consider these verses:

> *Do not make friends with a hot-tempered man,*
>> *do not associate with one easily angered,*
> *or you may learn his ways*
>> *and get yourself ensnared.* (Proverbs 22:24–25)

Stone is heavy and sand a burden,
but provocation by a fool is heavier than both. (Proverbs 27:3)

Yes, the Bible says there are fools in this world. One way we recognize fools is by their pride and anger. The problem is, if we are not careful, they can draw out our own sinful nature, and we end up acting just as foolish as they do. We live to regret our words and our actions.

It is hard to know how to deal with people like this. If we are nice to them, it inflates their pride and increases their sense of superiority. If we come back at them, we get into foolish arguments and lose our temper. The Bible says as much:

Do not answer a fool according to his folly,
or you will be like him yourself.

Answer a fool according to his folly,
or he will be wise in his own eyes. (Proverbs 26:4–5)

A summation of these contrasting verses: *Fools are hard to deal with!*

If at all possible, avoid engaging petty people like this. If you must do so, don't let them pull you into anger and wars of insult. Leave them to God to straighten out.

Anger causes overreaction

When you find yourself becoming angry, watch out! Anger is dangerous. Anger can lead to temporary loss of judgment and to words and actions that you may regret for the rest of your life. And yet the problem is, at the moment, you feel entirely justified in what you feel, say, and do.

After hearing Nabal's insulting response, David saddles up four hundred of his guys and heads out, intending to kill Nabal and all the men in his household. Not only is the vengeance he plans wrong before God, it is also completely out of proportion to the level of provocation he received. He has been insulted, but Nabal has not killed any of his men, or even harmed them. He has only humiliated and embarrassed them. Isn't murdering Nabal and his innocent male servants and family members a complete overreaction?

When our pride is hurt, we want payback. When our dignity as a man is torn down or sullied, we want to humble the guy who did it. When you are angry and enraged, guard against the demon of pride welling up in your heart. Pride responds to pride. Yes, we want to be strong men, but we don't want to be proud men who are controlled by the pride of others. We don't want to sink to the level of the arrogant bearer of insults. If we do, we are, oddly enough, allowing the controller to control us:

> *A fool shows his annoyance at once,*
> > *but a prudent man overlooks an insult.* (Proverbs 12:16)

Be careful not to equate your own wounded pride with righteous indignation:

> *The end of a matter is better than its beginning,*
> > *and patience is better than pride.*
> *Do not be quickly provoked in your spirit,*
> > *for anger resides in the lap of fools.* (Ecclesiastes 7:8–9)

When we are angry, we lose perspective. We blow things out of proportion. That is why James warns us:

> *My dear brothers, take note of this: Everyone should be quick to listen, slow to speak and slow to become angry, for man's anger does not bring about the righteous life that God desires.* (James 1:19–20)

Anger can cause us to fight the wrong battles

Nabal is the last guy David needs to be worrying about. Saul is hunting him. The Philistines, Amalekites, and other enemies of Israel surround him. But how easily the wrong fight sidetracks him! Brother warrior, pick your battles carefully. Be sure they are the ones God wants you to fight, and not just the ones where you have gotten angry. Avoid any battle that has nothing to do with God's great purposes. Fight the "good fight of the faith" (1 Timothy 6:12), not the battle to defend your own anger and pride.

Listen to voices of reason

When we are angry, we need to listen to voices of reason. Nabal's servants warn his wife Abigail that David is probably not going to take Nabal's insults sitting down (1 Samuel 25:14-17). Abigail takes quick action. She prepares a generous gift of food for David and his men (the gift her foolish husband should have given) and sends it out ahead with the servants while she comes following after. Listen to her words of wisdom, words that prevent David from destroying his own destiny:

She fell at his feet and said: "My lord, let the blame be on me alone. Please let your servant speak to you; hear what your servant has to say. May my lord pay no attention to that wicked man Nabal. He is just like his name—his name is Fool, and folly goes with him. But as for me, your servant, I did not see the men my master sent.

"Now since the LORD has kept you, my master, from bloodshed and from avenging yourself with your own hands, as surely as the LORD lives and as you live, may your enemies and all who intend to harm my master be like Nabal. And let this gift, which your servant has brought to my master, be given to the men who follow you. Please forgive your servant's offense, for the LORD will certainly make a lasting dynasty for my master, because he fights the LORD's battles. Let no wrongdoing be found in you as long as you live. Even though someone is pursuing you to take your life, the life of my master will be bound securely in the bundle of the living by the LORD your God. But the lives of your enemies he will hurl away as from the pocket of a sling. When the LORD has done for my master every good thing he promised concerning him and has appointed him leader over Israel, my master will not have on his conscience the staggering burden of needless bloodshed or of having avenged himself. And when the LORD has brought my master success, remember your servant." (1 Samuel 25:24–32)

Abigail is the heaven-sent voice of reason, faith, and humility:

- She acknowledges the wrong that has been done.
- She reminds David of who he is before God.
- She reminds David of God's plan for his life.
- She assures David that whatever insults Nabal may have hurled at him, they in no way change God's destiny for him, or define who he is as a man and warrior for God.

To David's credit, he listens, comes to his senses, and backs off.

Men, when you are insulted, when you are out of patience and full of anger, listen to the voices of reason around you. It may be the voice of a friend. It may be the voice of your wife. It could even be a young child, or people who serve under our leadership, like the servants who reasoned with Naaman (see 2 Kings 5). It may be the voice of the Spirit, or of your own better judgment. *Listen!* Put on the brakes. Hold off saying or doing anything while you are in a state of anger. Only when your feelings have abated should you speak or act, and even then, use the greatest of caution. Yes, be a warrior—but do not be an angry fool.

David ends the encounter by recognizing that God has sent Abigail to save him from his folly. He realizes his recklessness, praises God for his deliverance, and turns around and heads home, wiser and richer.

Is it not wonderful, brothers, that God will work to save us even when we are out of control and careening down a dangerous course? Is it not a testimony to God's amazing grace and mercy that even when we are tempted by anger, he will work to prevent us, his warriors, from fighting the wrong battle, a battle based on our pride and emotion, and not upon his greater purposes?

We can do our part by remembering these things:

- Being a warrior means guarding against anger, especially anger over personal insult or jury.

- Being a warrior means heeding the voice of reason, in whatever form God sends it.

- Being a warrior for God does not mean that you are always right, no matter how strongly you *feel* you are right. If you are angry, you need to stop and *think* before you act. Even if everything in you feels that you are right, wait until your anger dies down before making what could be a rash decision that you will later regret.

- Being wronged does not mean you have permission to return evil for evil or insult for insult.

- Being a strong man of God means being strong enough to resist the temptation to assert your own sinful will when you have been wounded or insulted.

Rise above anger

I once attended a class about birds of prey at a national park in the mountains of North Carolina. These majestic birds—hawks and eagles—soar above the mountains and are beautiful creatures.

We learned that crows pursue these great birds and surround them, seeking to drive them down out of the air to the ground, where they will literally peck out their eyes. Sounds awful, doesn't it—a cawing crow taking down a majestic eagle?

The solution for the eagle or the hawk is a simple one: *Fly higher! Don't fight with the crows. Don't get down there among them. Sail up over them. They can't fly as high as an eagle. They don't have the wings for it.* Crows have to pump their wings ferociously to catch up with the eagle. The mighty eagle needs only spread its wings, catch an updraft, and he will soar high above the world of the crow.

Brothers, like the eagle, let us rise above petty people and petty conflicts. Warriors for God are meant to soar with eagles, not quarrel with crows.

Let God work it out

But we have not finished our David story! The end is amazing: When Abigail returns home, she finds Nabal in a drunken stupor. The next morning, she informs her husband of how she went out and stopped David and his warriors who were on their way to slaughter Nabal and all his men. When Nabal hears this, his heart fails him. Ten days later, God ends his life (1 Samuel 25:36–39).

David learns the news and asks Abigail to marry him, an invitation she readily accepts. David now not only has the gifts Abigail gave him, but a beautiful and intelligent new bride as well! And most of all, he has preserved his righteousness and integrity and his relationship with God. When David honored God, God blessed David in return.

So, my fellow warrior, is there something or someone arousing your anger right now?

Are you filled with anger and resentment?

Is there an injustice or insult simmering inside?

Do you have a Nabal in your life, someone whose arrogance and rudeness is getting under your skin, and into your heart and mind?

Are you tempted to treat them as they have treated you, or even worse?

If so, let David's story inspire you. Let it instruct you. Let it save you. Let it bring joy and confidence back into your life. Let it free you from surrendering to angry passion. Let it reassure you that you are not a coward if you do not retaliate when you are wronged. Let it comfort you with the realization that sometimes, as a warrior for God, the best thing you can do is put away your sword, and let God draw his.

BATTLE PLAN

1. Think of a situation where you lost your temper and acted in anger. (This can be a recent event or a significant incident from earlier in your life.)

2. What was the result or results?

3. What was it about the person(s) or situation that provoked your anger?

4. If you had it to do over again, what would you do differently?

5. Have you ever faced a situation like that of David and Nabal, where you were about to lose your temper but God sent someone to help you come to your senses? Briefly describe it in one or two sentences.

6. What would have happened had God not intervened through that person?

7. Are any situations or people in your life tempting you to anger right now? Write them down.

8. What is it about these situations that upsets you the most?

9. Find scriptures or a story in the Bible that will help you to handle these situations in a righteous way that honors God.

10. Share these situations with a spiritual person—someone who, like Abigail, can help you to respond wisely and righteously. (Be sure to select someone who has the maturity and strength to advise you without also becoming angry!)

BATTLE CRY

Like all sin, bitterness deceives us. It promises a reward, but gives only misery.

Satan is a wily adversary. If he cannot destroy you one way, he will try another. If he cannot defeat you with lust or adultery or greed or deceit, perhaps he can bring you down with bitterness. Bitterness has felled many a man who has stood strong for God against other foes. It has taken down men of courage, integrity, talent, and faith.

Let us see how David faced and conquered this great enemy. Time and again, it tried to wrap its icy tentacles around his heart; time and again, David resisted its snare. Brother warriors, let us resist the inviting, deceptive lure of bitterness, keeping our hearts unfettered and our minds uncluttered to fight the battles of the Lord.

Chapter Ten

The Battle of Bitterness

Be still before the LORD and wait patiently for him;
do not fret when men succeed in their ways,
when they carry out their wicked schemes.

Refrain from anger and turn from wrath;
do not fret—it leads only to evil.
For evil men will be cut off,
but those who hope in the LORD will inherit the land.
Psalm 37:7-9

Bitterness is anger gone to seed. It is anger planted in our hearts. As discouragement is long-term fear, bitterness is long-term anger.

David and bitterness

Bitterness could have easily destroyed this great warrior from within. His unjust and unfair treatment at the hands of Saul would have filled most men with hatred. But David never allows himself to take vengeance. On two different occasions, while Saul is pursuing him to take his life, God delivers Saul into David's hands (1 Samuel 24:10; 26:23). The king is defenseless and vulnerable. David has the opportunity to take his life. The enemy who has made David's life a misery, who has stolen his wife and his reputation, who has tried to murder David on many occasions, is now at his mercy. David's warriors urge him to take Saul's life, believing that this is a God-given opportunity to fulfill God's promise to David—that he will be king (1 Samuel 24:4).

What will David do?

These moments are perhaps David's finest hours. Both times, he turns away from revenge and retribution. He appeals to Saul to listen to reason, assuring him that they need not be enemies. Saul is (temporarily) humbled and repentant, David returns to the desert and his life of exile, and Saul returns to his palace.

Brother warriors, one of the greatest and most insidious enemies we will ever face is bitterness. Bitterness has felled many a man who has stood strong for God against other foes. It has taken down men of courage, integrity, talent, and faith.

Satan is a wily adversary. If he cannot destroy you one way, he will try another. If he cannot get you with lust or adultery or greed or deceit, perhaps he can bring you down with bitterness. Bitterness is one of his worst weapons. Be on your guard against it throughout your life.

Had David given in to vengeance and bitterness, he could never have become king. All of the promises God had made to him would have fallen to the ground, useless and dead. David would have disqualified himself. Bitterness is a sin that will take you down and out. How heartbreaking it would be to overcome our own "King Sauls"—our enemies from without—only to be conquered by bitterness, our enemy within. If you let it, bitterness will destroy you, ruining your heart and life.

Dangers and deceptions of bitterness

As someone once said, "Bitterness is the poison we drink, hoping it kills the other person." Bitterness grows when we indulge in resentment and anger. And instead of hurting the person who has harmed us, we find ourselves destroyed.

Like all sin, bitterness deceives us. It promises a reward, but gives only misery, heartache, and pain. Oddly enough, it gives even more power to the people who have hurt us by their unfair, disrespectful treatment. Now that we are indulging in bitterness, we relive the pain they inflicted over and over again.

Harboring bitterness against people we do not love can destroy our feelings for the people we *do* love. How does that happen? It happens the same way infection or cancer takes over our bodies. These foreign bodies get a foothold, and if they are not removed or defeated, they reproduce and spread. What started in one place ends up moving into another. If you find yourself becoming angry with people you hardly know, or with people you love dearly—and you can't figure out why—check your heart and mind for bitterness. Bitterness can sour your attitude towards everyone. Scary, right? That's why we need to guard against bitterness with our best spiritual weapons.

Causes of bitterness

What are the causes of this terrible malady? When are we most tempted by bitterness?

The causes of bitterness are not hard to figure out. The difficulty is not in identifying the sources of bitterness, but in *uprooting* bitterness once it has been sown in our hearts.

When we feel disappointed by God, life, or people.

When we feel let down by God, by life, or by people, bitter thoughts may begin to fester. "Why did God let that happen?" we ask. We think if God is sovereign and runs everything, then why did we suffer that loss, get that disease, have that accident, or lose that job? I would not minimize for a moment the pain we feel when such things happen, or even try to explain it all. But when hardship comes (as it will come to all of us in various ways), we have to confront it with the truths and promises of God. (We will come back to this topic at the end of the chapter.)

When we experience unjust treatment.

When people do us wrong or treat us unfairly, it opens us up to bitterness. Think about Jesus. He never committed a single sin, and we crucified him. If anyone had the right to be bitter, it was Jesus. But instead, he died for our sins, with love in his heart.

When we feel that others are more blessed than we are.

We can look at the material, social, and even spiritual blessings of others, and feel shortchanged. This is especially difficult when we think those people are less devoted to God than we are. How come they have a better job, more money, and better health than we do? Maybe we should call this by another name: envy.

> Surely God is good to Israel,
>   to those who are pure in heart.

But as for me, my feet had almost slipped;
*   I had nearly lost my foothold.*
For I envied the arrogant
*   when I saw the prosperity of the wicked.*

They have no struggles;
*   their bodies are healthy and strong.*
They are free from the burdens common to man;
*   they are not plagued by human ills.* (Psalm 73:1–5)

While David did not write this psalm, the Holy Spirit certainly did, through Asaph. Here Asaph speaks to an issue deep in our hearts. There are some things that are just plain hard to understand. (And oh, by the way, he gives the answer to his problem at the end of the Psalm!)

When we are insulted or disrespected.

Need we say more?

When we, or our efforts, are unappreciated.

Uh, need we say more, again?

When people we have trusted and loved let us down.

This is a big one. And do you know why? Because it is the people we love and trust the most who have the most opportunity to hurt us. We have given them our hearts. We have let them inside. And then they let us down. They disappoint us. Maybe they fail to do something we needed them to do. Maybe they fail to encourage us when we need it.

Yes, the people around us, the ones we love—try though they may to do right by us—will still fail us at times. Just like we fail them. The only person who will never let us down is Jesus. We will have to forgive our friends and loved ones just as he taught us to do, or we will end up having a shrinking—or disappearing—intimate circle.

But what about a person we have trusted in the past, who later proves to be so flawed that we cannot count on them at all, ever again? Here I would cite the example of David and Saul. King Saul proved he was unstable and untrustworthy. David (and God) gave Saul many opportunities to prove himself a man of integrity, but he failed the tests. So, brother warrior, remember this: forgiving someone does not mean you have to entrust your life to them. *Forgiveness is given, and trust is earned.* Even Jesus would not entrust himself to some people (John 2:23–25) and he told us to be as innocent as doves and as wise as serpents (Matthew 10:16). But in being as wise as a snake, let us not *turn into* one! Let's keep our hearts open to others, and not become negative, angry, cynical men.

Characteristics of bitterness

Let me share some simple, straightforward thoughts:

The more you have given your heart, the greater the chance for bitterness.

The more you have trusted, the greater the chance for bitterness.

Bitterness is the weapon Satan uses against the trusting, against the good, against the righteous.

Sure, he uses it against everyone, but it is especially powerful against humble, spiritual people. Why? Because Satan cannot usually get people like this to go out on a binge of self-indulgent, wild living, he uses another tactic: Exploit their trust and goodness. Use their best traits as weapons that hurt them. Test them and see how deep their faith is, how pure their heart is, and how much they will trust when it seems that someone they love, or even God himself, has let them down.

Bitterness is the weapon Satan uses against the submissive and the humble.

Yep, here he goes again! Let's say you trust your parents, your boss, or your church leaders. But they fail you somehow. They sin. They even deceive you. What is the temptation that will come your way? *Bitterness.* "I trusted them, and look where it got me. I'll never trust them, or anyone, again. I'm on my own now. I'll hold back my heart now. Fool me once, blame you; fool me twice, blame me."

Can we see why bitterness is such a destructive sin? It tears apart that which is most precious inside us: our trust, innocence, and love. And it does so by making us feel completely justified in our attitude. Warriors, let's fight off bitterness with everything we've got!

Bitterness is the weapon Satan uses against the sensitive.

If we weren't so sensitive, if we just didn't care, we would not be as vulnerable. The more we love, the more we care, the more we feel for people, the more we are susceptible to being hurt by them. So what do we do—stop feeling? Stop caring? That is what some sensitive people have chosen to do after being hurt. The result? *Bitterness. Loneliness. Isolation.* We seek to protect ourselves, and in so doing, we harden our hearts. All of this is a dead-end street. We end up with nothing but emptiness, pain, and misery.

Bitterness is a weapon the Enemy uses against thinkers.

Bitterness can ruin a thinker's life. It is a product of the wrong kind of rumination. And oftentimes, the people who hurt us are not very deep thinkers—if they were, they may have never hurt us in the first place! They go on their merry, unthinking way, and the wounded thinker can't stop thinking about what happened! Those angry and bitter thoughts can intrude upon some of the most beautiful times of our lives to bring darkness, anger, and sadness. That is why Jesus told us to forgive, and Paul told us to fill our minds with pure, noble, and good thoughts (Philippians 4:8). We can't win the battle by just fighting off the bitter stuff; we have to *replace* it with good stuff from God—happy, grateful thoughts.

Bitterness is a weapon Satan will use against older warriors.

Bitterness may be the final deadly weapon the Enemy will use to seek your defeat. Older warriors have endured many painful situations over the years; after a while, it can all become too much. Satan will seek to use bad memories to hurt us, paralyze us, and change us. As I have matured, the temptation to bitterness has come at me harder. I have had to remind myself that I am saved only by the blood of Christ (the same blood that also saves any brother or sister in Christ who hurts me). There is no other way for me to forgive "them" (and for "them" to forgive me!) but by the cross of Christ.

Conquering bitterness
Decide whether or not a conversation is in order.

Sometimes, our love and understanding can cover an offense without a word having to be spoken. We realize that someone made a mistake, and we let it go. We overlook it. We give grace.

At other times, we are going to have to go and have a talk with another person, or even a fellow warrior. We need to let the other person know what happened and how we felt. Be careful to approach such conversations with humility, even as you speak the truth in love. If all goes well, your conversation will resolve the conflict. If not, get help from a friend or friends that you both trust. That is God's plan. To be sure, this is not a full explanation of righteous conflict resolution, but it gives you the basics.

Resolve conflict as quickly as you can.

Staying in a wounded, angry state can lead to bitterness. Either decide to forgive on your own before God, or go and talk it out as soon as you can. (See what Jesus says about this in Matt. 5:23-24)

Keep your eyes on Jesus, and on the cross.

Knowing what Jesus suffered at the hands of sinful people (including you and me) gives us the means to forgive anything that anyone does to harm us.

When the bitter thoughts come back, dismiss them quickly. Forgiveness is granted to someone by decision, but that decision will have to be reaffirmed every time the painful memory comes back, and you once again find yourself tempted with bitterness. Bitterness is similar to lust—both are sins of passion and desire. Just as you run from lust, run from bitterness. Lust is not conquered by simply saying, "I will not think about it." That is only the first step; then you also have to quickly put your mind on something else. Bitterness works the same way. Once you have forgiven a person, you have to redirect your thoughts. Angry, vengeful thoughts may try to return. Don't just stand there in a defensive position: Refocus your thoughts. Turn your attention elsewhere. Remind yourself, "I have forgiven this person, just as I have been forgiven by God. Time to think about something else now!"

David was a great warrior. He had every opportunity and excuse to become a bitter man. As a teen he had been appointed to be the next king, but before he knew what was happening, he was dodging spears from King Saul! David never asked to be king. He did not know what God was getting him into. And yet he accepted the life God assigned to him, and the drama that came with the promise.

Think about this:

Had there been no Saul, there would not be so many great psalms.

If David had not suffered injustice at the hands of an evil man, many of the psalms that we warriors love—the psalms that have saved our souls—would never have been written. Think about that for a while!

God brings good out of evil.

God may have allowed you to experience some difficult and dirty situations. Some of them you may have walked into deliberately, all on your own. Others may have come to you, seemingly out of nowhere. Whatever the case, God is bigger than you, bigger than me, bigger than the devil. He is smarter than all of us. He loves us more than we can ever understand. If we turn to him, he can and will forgive us, and will carry us through even "impossible" situations. He can bring us out as better men and stronger warriors than we were before.

And who knows what greater purpose God has in mind for all your sufferings? Perhaps your pain, like David's, will be used to help others one day.

The best psalm I can recommend on this subject is Psalm 37. Read it over and over and over again when you are tempted to be bitter. The promises it contains, the wisdom it provides, and the hope it brings to a wounded heart, are unsurpassed. Let the Spirit-inspired words of the warrior David comfort you, instruct you, inspire you, and set you free.

Do not fret because of evil men
or be envious of those who do wrong;
for like the grass they will soon wither,
like green plants they will soon die away.

Trust in the LORD and do good;
dwell in the land and enjoy safe pasture.
Delight yourself in the LORD
and he will give you the desires of your heart.

Commit your way to the LORD;
    trust in him and he will do this:
He will make your righteousness shine like the dawn,
    the justice of your cause like the noonday sun.

Be still before the LORD and wait patiently for him;
    do not fret when men succeed in their ways,
    when they carry out their wicked schemes.

Refrain from anger and turn from wrath;
    do not fret—It leads only to evil.
For evil men will be cut off,
    but those who hope in the LORD will inherit the land. (Psalm 37:1–9)

Battle Plan

1. List the top three situations or circumstances in your life that most tempt you to bitterness.

2. Did David face any situations like these? How did he handle them?

3. Read Hebrew 4:14–5:3. This passage says that Jesus was tempted in every way we are. In reflecting on the situations you have identified, how and when was Jesus tempted in the same way as you? How did he handle it?

4. Is getting past your bitterness simply a matter of dealing with your own attitude before God? Or do you need to have reconciling conversations with someone?

5. Making these kinds of decisions requires insight and perception of the highest order. Ask God for wisdom on how you should respond. (See James 1:2–8.)

6. Seek wise counsel. Share these situations with a fellow warrior who can pray for you and with you. (See Proverbs 13:10; 13:20; 15:12; 15:14; 24:5–6.)

7. Decide whether or not you need help in resolving a conflict. (See Philippians 4:2–3.)

Vignette: Sparing Saul's Life

Based on 1 Samuel 24

David left Gath and escaped to the cave of Adullam. When his brothers and his father's household heard about it, they went down to him there. All those who were in distress or in debt or discontented gathered around him, and he became their leader.

1 Samuel 22:1–2

David's ragtag army has grown to a band of six hundred, including Eleazar and his friends Shammah and Jashobeam. For months they have been running from the vengeful King Saul and his army. After several narrow escapes, Saul and his soldiers are now closing in. David and his men are vastly outnumbered.

There were about thirty of us, running up the pathway to the Crags of the Wild Goats. Saul and his handpicked warriors— three thousand elite fighters—were looking for us. We had barely escaped being seen earlier in the day. They had come so close we could hear their shouts and feel the pounding of their horses' hooves, making the ground tremble beneath us. Now we had divided our six hundred men into small units so we could hide more easily.

Asahel, our scout and fastest runner, came racing up the trail behind us, breathless. "They have split up into search parties of about a hundred each! One of them is right on our trail! They are almost upon us! We have to find a place to hide or get ready to fight—right now!"

"Quick, men—into this cave. Go in, go deep, and whatever you do, keep quiet when you get inside." David's hushed, urgent voice came from up ahead, farther up the mountain. He crouched beside a barely visible cave, half-hidden behind a thicket of scraggly bushes.

"Eleazar, Shammah, Jashobeam," David summoned us, speaking low and fast, his voice half-whisper, half-shout. "After we go in, get on your hands and knees out here and cover over our tracks! Asa, hide at the entrance and tell us what you see. Go, go, go!"

When the men had all disappeared into the cave's black mouth, we smoothed out the sand from the trail to the cave, scattering rocks on top of it as best we could. I peered down the mountainside. A cloud of dust was drawing near—Saul's troops were close, so close.

"We'd better get inside," I said, "or it'll be three versus one hundred."

"That could be fun," said Shammah, a smirk on his face. "We can take 'em, just us."

Jashobeam stood and pulled out his sword. "Thirty to one odds—I say let's do it! They don't stand a chance."

"Uh, I was kidding, Jash," said Shammah. "We may be mighty, but we're not that mighty."

Shammah and I turned to walk into the cave, motioning Jash to join us.

"You never know how mighty you are until you face the biggest, the best and the bravest," Jash said, sheathing his sword with a grunt of frustration. "Sooner or later we're going to have to stand up and fight."

We crept into the cave. Asahel remained just inside the entrance to serve as lookout, while the rest of us picked our way slowly through the inky blackness until we met the amber glow of a few torches. As our vision adjusted, we saw the men huddled in small groups all along the dripping cave walls. We jostled to find a place to sit among the tightly packed bodies. Jashobeam pushed a few guys out of our way, forcing them to move farther down the line so we could claim a place along the cave wall near David. David had stationed himself at the front of the men. If Saul's soldiers found us, ours would be the first swords to fight . . . just the way we liked it.

The damp cave was thick with the smell of sweat and metal, mildew and goat dung. Whispers filled the hollow space with anxious sound. "Calm yourselves, men," David said, quietly. "God will protect us. We are under the shadow of his wings."

I raised an eyebrow at Jashobeam and Shammah. "God's wings better be pretty thick, or we're all dead men," I muttered.

We sat in strained silence for a long while. David began walking among the men, offering quiet words of encouragement.

The stench in the cave began to get to me. "The wild goats must use this place as their private toilet," I said, to no one in particular.

Soon, Asahel came pelting back, slipping on the rocks in his haste. "My lord David!"

David rushed over to him. "What is it?" David's taut voice was pitched low. He leaned in to Asahel, as if he did not want the men to hear.

"Sire, you are not going to believe this! King Saul has entered the cave."

"What?"

Asa spoke a little louder, "King Saul is in this cave! Our cave!"

My heart clenched. An excited whisper rose among the men near enough to overhear. They crowded in closer to listen. David waved an arm to silence them.

Asa spoke fast. "He has removed his helmet, his breastplate and his greaves. He's just sitting there!"

David gave Asa a skeptical look. "Are you sure it's him? Why would he come in the cave? Is he searching for us here?"

"Yes sire, no doubt it's him. And sire, he's alone. He, uh—well, he came in by himself, squatted down, and relieved himself! He must be ill, from the awful sound and smell of it," Asa said, with a crooked smile. The men snickered.

David started pacing, as he always did when thinking. The cave grew quiet but for the pad of his footsteps and the dripping of water down the walls. I could almost hear all thirty of our heartbeats pounding, waiting for our commander to give us the order to rush forward and attack. I heard the metallic ring of a sword sliding out of its scabbard.

"Sire, if you want me to—," said Jash, stepping forward.

Shammah silenced him with a shake of his head.

David turned and walked a few paces toward the entrance of the cave and dropped to his knees, opening his hands out in front of him.

When David did not arise for long minutes, Jash nudged me forward. "He's prayed long enough now," he whispered in my ear. "Saul won't sit in this cave forever. And the men are getting restless. Speak to him."

I gripped the handle of my sword and stepped toward David, speaking quietly. "Sire, your prayers have been answered. God has delivered your enemy into your hands! Let us take off his head and end this now!" Behind us, the men nodded agreement, getting to their feet. More swords glinted in the torchlight.

David looked up at me, then stood and turned to face the men. His voice was low but firm. Confident. "Everyone stay here. Don't move. I'll be right back!" He turned and strode toward the cave entrance, melting into shadow.

"Men, get ready," Jashobeam said, holding his sword high with a grin. "God is with us. Remember Goliath? Our day of victory has come!" Eager voices murmured assent.

"Shhh," someone said. "I want to hear Saul scream."

We all strained to listen. Our restless breaths filled the cave. I wondered if the others could hear the hammer of my heartbeat.

In a moment, David's silhouette reappeared, taking nimble, cat-like steps across the rocks.

Jash stepped forward, a hungry gleam in his eye. "So, sire, do you need help dragging his large corpse out the door? And can we see his head?"

David stood framed by the torchlight, a funny expression on his face. He waved a hand to silence us. "Men, it is not for any of us to kill the Lord's anointed!" he said in a loud whisper.

"Wait, what are you saying, my lord?" said Jash. "You—you didn't kill him?"

I could tell that what he wanted to say was, "You let him get away?" Shammah jabbed Jashobeam in the side with an elbow.

David shook his head. "I did not kill him."

No one spoke. Water dripped down the walls, filling the silence.

David waved a piece of cloth in the air—it shimmered golden in the amber light. "I cut off a corner of Saul's royal robe! I hope God does not judge me for what I am about to do, but I am going to show Saul in front of his men that he is in the wrong for pursuing me. As soon as he leaves the cave, I'm going to follow him out, show this cloth to him in front of them all, and let them know that they have no reason to hunt us down. Although the Lord delivered him into my hands, I had mercy on him. I leave him in the hands of God!"

While we all gaped at him, too stunned to speak, he turned and sprinted toward the front of the cave. Shammah reached an arm out as if to grab him, to stop him, but he was already gone.

We all traded shocked looks. A low babble began to spread among the men as the news was passed down the line.

"He just threw away the chance to end all of this!" Jash said, clenching his teeth and jamming his sword back into its sheath.

"What was he thinking?" Shammah said. "Isn't this the opportunity he has been praying for?"

And suddenly, my feet were moving toward the mouth of the cave. "Saul and his men will kill David as soon as they see him," I said. "He's going to need us. Let's get out there. At least we'll die with swords in our hands!"

Jash and Shammah followed me, and together we ran through the cave, sliding on rocks, barely keeping our footing, until the darkness broke. Dim light streamed in through the cave entrance, ahead. Jash pushed me forward, and as one we rushed out into the sunlight—eyes squinting, swords drawn, ready for a fight.

And there outside the entrance, we froze.

Just a few feet away, David was kneeling before Saul, holding up the jagged piece of Saul's golden robe.

Saul's warriors stood behind their king, weapons drawn.

My stomach twisted.

This was it.

David had been caught.

Saul was going to behead him right here in front of us.

I was about to lunge forward when Jash grabbed my arm and stopped me. Wait," he said, "David is about to speak."

Loud enough for all to hear, David said, "Listen, my lord!"

Saul locked his eyes on David and held up his hand, keeping his men at bay behind him.

Jash released my arm.

What was going on?

"See, my father, look at this piece of your robe in my hand! The Lord delivered you into my hands in the cave. I cut off the corner of your robe but did not kill you. Now understand that I am not guilty of wrongdoing or rebellion." David kept speaking, pouring out his heart. Saul and all his men stood frozen in place, listening. I peered more closely at Saul. His expression first grew shocked, then stricken, as David continued to speak. "Against whom has the king of Israel come out? A dead dog? A flea?"

Jash winced.

"May the Lord be our judge and decide between us. May he consider my cause and uphold it; may he vindicate me by delivering me from your hand."

Saul wept aloud now, his huge body heaving with sobs. David bowed his head. Saul spoke up. "May the Lord reward you for the way you have treated me today!"

I cannot remember all Saul said that day, but he admitted in front of all his men that he was wrong, that David was right, and that David would be the next king.

Saul walked forward and helped David to his feet. They embraced, and Saul spoke loudly, so all the men could hear. "Swear to me an oath, my son, that when you become king, you will not wipe out my family line."

David stood up, raised his hands to heaven, and swore it before God.

Saul gave a single regal wave, and his men all knelt before David, laying their weapons on the ground.

Jash, Shammah, Asahel and I all blinked at each other in disbelief. Uncertain, we sheathed our own swords and took a few steps back. We all knew we had seen David do something that we would never forget for the rest of our lives.

Saul turned to his men. "Warriors, mount your horses. Return home. God has spared my life, and all of our lives, this day." His soldiers moved slowly. Not a man spoke. They mounted their horses, cast a few nervous glances back over their shoulders at us, and made their way down the mountain.

Later, as our entire company walked back down the trail to find the rest of our brother warriors, the men were strangely silent, with none of the usual banter.

I finally spoke to Shammah, Jash and Asa. "I don't know whether that was the wisest, most courageous thing I have ever witnessed, or the most foolish. Saul has never been one to keep his word. We'll soon find out. But . . . no matter what Saul does, you have to admire a man for not taking vengeance on his mortal enemy when he has the chance."

Asa groaned, "Yes, it was noble, but at what cost to our families and to us? When will this misery ever end?"

"True, it's not over," Shammah said. "It won't be over until Saul is rotting in his grave, food for worms. But at least we know one thing." He stopped walking, and we all stopped, too. "We know without a doubt that our next king is worthy to wear the crown. I have never known a man braver, nobler, or more honorable than David son of Jesse. Perhaps this is why God chose David to shepherd us," he said, looking up at the sun sinking behind the mountains. "He has a good heart—far better than mine. And God is certainly with him."

Jashobeam looked at us all, his eyes gleaming with tears. I had never seen him so moved. "None of us knows when it will be over, but one thing I do know: I have never beheld anything like what I saw today. We have just witnessed David do a deed even greater than his defeat of Goliath." I looked at my brother warriors, feeling the warmth of conviction heat my chest. "The Lord giving me strength, I will follow this man of God all my days, to whatever end."

All of them bowed their heads in silent agreement. We stood quietly for a long moment, looking together at the magnificent sunset beyond the towering mountains. Then we turned and walked together down the road, to whatever end God might bring our way.

BATTLE CRY

Sexuality is one of the greatest gifts God has given us. The greater the gift, the greater is its potential for joy and fulfillment in our lives. And conversely, the greater the gift, the greater is its power for abuse and pain.

Many a warrior has been brought down by sexual sin. Let that never happen to you and to me, brother warrior.

Remaining sexually pure is one of the greatest victories a warrior can ever win. To refrain from sexual relations while single, and to remain faithful to your wife throughout your life, is one of the warrior's most sacred commitments.

Let us appreciate the great gift of sexuality given us by the Creator, and respect the boundaries he has placed upon it.

Let us be warriors who esteem women, honor our wives, and direct our passions in godly ways. Let us always bring God glory with our hearts, our thoughts, and our bodies. Let us show the world how beautiful true purity, and real romance, can be.

Chapter Eleven

The Battle of Purity

Keep yourself pure.

1 Timothy 5:22

One evening David got up from his bed and walked around on the roof of the palace. From the roof he saw a woman bathing. The woman was very beautiful, and David sent someone to find out about her.

2 Samuel 11:2–3

David is now reigning in Jerusalem as the king of Israel. This man—who once lived a simple, innocent life tending sheep and playing the harp—was chosen by God, anointed by the prophet, and finally, crowned king. The promise of God, made to David years ago through the prophet Samuel, has at last come to pass. The man after the heart of God is no longer in exile, no longer under stress, no longer an outlaw fleeing from the evil King Saul. He has fought the battles of fear, discouragement, anger, and bitterness, and has come out victorious. Here is what God says to him through the prophet Nathan:

"Now then, tell my servant David, 'This is what the Lord Almighty says: I took you from the pasture and from following the flock to be ruler over my people Israel. I have been with you wherever you have gone, and I have cut off all your enemies from before you. Now I will make your name great, like the names of the greatest

men of the earth.... I will also give you rest from all your enemies.

" 'The LORD declares to you that the LORD himself will establish a house for you: When your days are over and you rest with your fathers, I will raise up your offspring to succeed you, who will come from your own body, and I will establish his kingdom. He is the one who will build a house for my Name, and I will establish the throne of his kingdom forever.' " (2 Samuel 7:8–9,11–13)

What an amazing series of promises, and what a wonderful, loving God whom David serves! God reached down and lifted up this young man from a life of obscurity to make him the leader of his people. God has been with David through the battle with Goliath and the terrible loneliness and heartbreak of his rejection and pursuit by Saul. He has delivered him from his enemies, and protected him from his own weariness and weakness. Now he promises him ultimate rest from his enemies. Now he assures David that he will build a lasting dynasty through his family, and through his son that will follow him. He pledges that he will make David's name great, like that of the greatest men who ever lived. David goes forth from this moment and experiences victory after victory over his enemies.

How overwhelmingly wonderful was the grace of God in David's life! Brother warriors, how wonderful is God's grace to us all! God has reached down to wash us clean from sin, to give us a new life, to bestow on us new purpose and power, and to help us build our lives on a foundation that will bless us, our children, and the generations that follow in ways beyond our imagination.

Why would anyone ever stray from such a good God, and from his word and ways? Who, after being loved, blessed, and cared for so well, would ever turn aside or away from a Father like this one?

But brothers, our Enemy is evil, vicious, wily, and unrelenting. He never stops seeking to harm, defeat, and destroy us. And so he devises a plot and a plan to bring David down. When all else fails, he resorts to sexual temptation. David loses the battle, and darkness descends—upon him and his family.

In the spring, at the time when kings go off to war, David sent Joab out with the king's men and the whole Israelite army. They destroyed the Ammonites and besieged Rabbah. But David remained in Jerusalem.

> *One evening David got up from his bed and walked around on the roof of the palace. From the roof he saw a woman bathing. The woman was very beautiful, and David sent someone to find out about her. The man said, "Isn't this Bathsheba, the daughter of Eliam and the wife of Uriah the Hittite?" Then David sent messengers to get her. She came to him, and he slept with her. (She had purified herself from her uncleanness.) Then she went back home. The woman conceived and sent word to David, saying, "I am pregnant."* (2 Samuel 11:1–5)

David, David, David! How could you do such a thing? You are the man after the heart of God. You have been through battle after battle. God has protected you, blessed you, loved you, comforted you, and instructed you. He is your Shepherd. He is your Rock. He is your Song and your Salvation. He is your Provider. He has never let you down. He is the source of everything good in your life. How could you do such a thing?

How did this happen to David? How could he fall like this?

First, notice where David is.

He is at home in Jerusalem. The army has gone out to war. In the past, David had always gone out with them. He had led them into battle himself. Why not now? The Bible does not say, but it appears as if David is now laying back, letting other people do the work he used to do. David is not too old to fight. In the previous chapter, he has just gone out and led a campaign (2 Samuel 10:15–19). And even if David has now aged past the time of being able to fight on the front lines himself, he can still go out with his troops as their king and commander.

Second, notice what he is doing.

He is wandering around on the roof of his house during the night. He notices a woman bathing. Okay, what are you doing up there, David? He set himself up for a fall by putting himself in the wrong place at a bad time. How many of us have also "wandered" into lust, into inappropriate late-night television, into late-night Internet porn?

Third, notice what he doesn't do.

The minute David saw Bathsheba, he could have averted his eyes and walked away, but he stopped and took a second look, which led to a full gaze, which led to lust, which led to inquiry, which led to... At any point along the way, David could have turned this thing around. The

Bible charges us to "flee sexual immorality" (1 Corinthians 6:18). And, that, by the way, is just what young Joseph did when a lustful woman aggressively pursued him—he took off running (Genesis 39:11–12).

Brother warriors, sometimes the way to win is to retreat! Hit the road. Get out. Beat it. Leave! Lust is a sin of momentum. One step leads to another, to another, to another, and before you know it you've run full-tilt into a trap, and you're hip-deep in quicksand. Don't let lust get started. Don't let it get going. Don't dip a single toe into Satan's trap. Stop looking before Satan pins you down and sinks his talons into you.

Fourth, notice that David takes action to get involved with her.

David sends word to find out who she is. *Oh yeah, I'm just getting her number, just looking her up on Facebook, just connecting in a chat room.* Hey, David, you are a married man! You have no business reaching out in this way to any woman other than your wife—unless she is your mother, sister, or grandmother!

Single warriors, if you find yourself inappropriately initiating with or getting involved with a woman who is married, stop now. Keep a righteous, respectful distance. And brother, before you start drawing close to any single woman, find out how she is doing spiritually. If she is not a godly disciple, wake up! You are setting yourself—and her—up for a huge fall.

Fifth, notice that what he does in secret comes out in the open.

Somehow, we think we can get away with impurity. We tell ourselves, "This is just between the two of us." We act as if God is not watching. My brother, God is always watching, and if you, like David, get into sexual sin, God will bring it out into the open. "Be sure . . . your sin will find you out" (Numbers 32:23).

Satan himself will betray you. He led you into sin, but now he will use it to destroy you. He is a traitor. He will embarrass and humiliate you with what you have done. You may be thinking that your private lust on the Internet or with videos or other kinds of pornography will never come out. Oh yes it will, my brother. It will come out one way or another. It will probably come out in this life, and it will most certainly be exposed on the day of judgment:

For God will bring every deed into judgment,

including every hidden thing,
whether it is good or evil. (Ecclesiastes 12:14)

But whether or not you are publicly exposed and even disgraced, the signs of your sin will show up in your life now. They will show up in your lack of joy. They will show up as you lose your manliness and confidence. They will show up as you become spiritually lukewarm. They will show up as you become defensive and ashamed. They will show up as you stop being effective in reaching others for Christ. They will show up in your closeness and your sexual relationship with your wife—they will put a cloud between you and her, taking away the joy and thrill of your marital intimacy. They will show up in your children—you have allowed the devil to slink through the door of your home, and your children will be hurt. One day, your children may even find out what you have done.

Brothers, sexual sin is a terrible enemy. The greater the gift, the greater the potential for evil. The greater the blessing, the greater the potential for abuse when we strip it away from God's purposes and use it selfishly, outside of his plan. Sexuality is meant to be one of the most precious gifts God ever gave to men. Let us not take it and use it for our own destruction.

Nothing can harm a man's entire life more than sexual sin. Paul puts sexual impurity in a special category: "Flee from sexual immorality. All other sins a man commits are outside his body, but he who sins sexually sins against his own body" (1 Corinthians 6:18). All sin is abhorrent to God; all sin crucified Christ. But Scripture here says that sexual sin carries greater consequences, because it is a sin against our own bodies. I do not pretend to understand all that that means, but I tremble before these words. *Brother warriors, stay away from sexual impurity!*

This sin in David's life releases a torrent of pain and misery. From this one sin, the floodgates of evil are set loose. To cover it up, David will kill a close friend, and will use another friend to carry out the murder. He will lie. He will undermine his own leadership within his family. He will sow seeds of rebellion and disrespect into his sons' hearts. He will plant the seeds of sexual sin and murder into his sons' lives. He will live to see incest, murder, and open rebellion disgrace his home and his nation. All because he took a careless evening stroll on the roof of his house.

God's plan

Exactly what are God's standards in this area? The laws of society and governments change from place to place and from age to age. Depending on where and when we live, cultural standards will vary. As Christians we must look to God and his word for the truth—the unchanging truth—that will set us free and guide our lives to fulfillment and victory.

One man, one woman, for life

This plan is set forth in the first book of the Bible. God intended marriage to be between one man and one woman, until death separated them:

> So the LORD God caused the man to fall into a deep sleep; and while he was sleeping, he took one of the man's ribs and closed up the place with flesh. Then the LORD God made a woman from the rib he had taken out of the man, and he brought her to the man.
>
> The man said,
>
> "This is now bone of my bones
>   and flesh of my flesh;
> she shall be called 'woman,'
>   for she was taken out of man."
>
> For this reason a man will leave his father and mother and be united to his wife, and they will become one flesh. (Genesis 2:21–24)

Jesus affirmed this standard in his teaching:

> "Haven't you read," he replied, "that at the beginning the Creator 'made them male and female,' and said, 'For this reason a man will leave his father and mother and be united to his wife, and the two will become one flesh'? So they are no longer two, but one. Therefore what God has joined together, let man not separate." (Matthew 19:4–6)

While this book is not the place to do a detailed or lengthy study on marriage, we can summarize biblical teaching as follows: God's plan is for one man and one woman to marry, and to stay married until death. The only things that can break a marriage before God are death or un-faithfulness.

The only person with whom we can be sexually intimate is our spouse. In marriage, our bodies belong to each other, and to no one else. That means that any sex before or outside of marriage is forbidden and sinful before God—always. It matters not if we love each other, or if we intend to be married one day. Until we are married in the eyes of God and before the laws of the land, sex is off-limits. Her body does not belong to you until you get a marriage license and the preacher or Justice of the Peace says, "I now pronounce you husband and wife." It's that simple. If you touch each other in a sexually inappropriate manner before marriage, you are touching a body that belongs to God, not to you. And that is a huge mistake.

Once we are married, we are free to enjoy the intimacies of sexual love. Sex is not inherently evil—far from it—*it is inherently wonderful!* We are the ones who, in our folly and pride, have taken sex out of its proper context and made it a tool for harm and destruction.

Jesus raises the bar

Some may object, "But isn't that just Old Testament rules? Sounds a little legalistic to me." Well, take a good look at the New Testament, where Jesus takes the standard even higher. He teaches that sexual sin is not just what happens with our bodies; it is what happens in our minds and in our imaginations as well. Remember, God is all about heart, not just what we *do*. So when Jesus spoke about sexual purity, here is what he said:

> *"You have heard that it was said, 'Do not commit adultery.' But I tell you that anyone who looks at a woman lustfully has already committed adultery with her in his heart. If your right eye causes you to sin, gouge it out and throw it away. It is better for you to lose one part of your body than for your whole body to be thrown into hell. And if your right hand causes you to sin, cut it off and throw it away. It is better for you to lose one part of your body than for your whole body to go into hell."*
> (Matthew 5:27–30)

Do you get the idea that Jesus means business here? I would say so. He mentions eternal punishment. This means, warriors, that we need to fight the battle for purity not only at the action level, but at the thought level. We need to value God and our minds so much that we will not allow our thoughts to go past noticing an attractive woman to the point of desiring her.

Some of us might be overly sensitive here. Merely noticing that a woman is beautiful is not a sin. That is quite normal. But going beyond that and allowing our desires to be awakened and aroused is where we need to draw the line. When we start becoming attracted to a woman, or feeling aroused in any way, we need to quickly avert our eyes and *get our minds on something else*. It is the lustful *intent* with which we look—and keep looking, thinking, and imagining—that is wrong before God.

Careless behavior and talk can also cross the line and become sin. We shouldn't engage in flirtatious, inappropriate conversation with women. The moment we sense a conversation moving in a questionable direction, we need to change the subject or remove ourselves from the situation. Never should we bring up sexual discussions with women. If a conversation begins to provoke lust or sexual interest within us, we should immediately remove ourselves.

Guard your steps

God warns us to stay far away from situations that could bring us into sin:

> Now then, my sons, listen to me;
>> do not turn aside from what I say.
> Keep to a path far from her,
>> do not go near the door of her house." (Proverbs 5:7–8)

What kinds of places do you go, brother warrior? There are some places you should avoid: certain parties, certain kinds of restaurants and social gathering places. The warrior of God does not need to set himself up to be ambushed by Satan. Stay out of his traps!

Guard your eyes

Okay, men, we need to talk about pornography.

I know of nothing that is undermining the righteousness, confidence, and integrity of more men today than Internet pornography. Far too often, I speak to men who are "struggling" with porn over the airwaves. Brothers, it is time to stop "struggling" and start *winning*! What do I mean by that? I mean that we should stop Internet porn before it ever gets into, or out of, our computer. You may be tempted to look, but you need to set up roadblocks *that make it impossible* for you to look.

You can block sensual websites on your home Wi-Fi. You can set up your server so that it will cut off that garbage at the source, never letting it get to your computer or to your phone. You can put blocks on your PC and cell phone. You can build a team of fellow warriors around you with whom you communicate daily, or as often as need be, to hold one another accountable. Each one of us as God's warriors needs to put on our armor, pick up our shield, wield our sword, and go into battle. You do not have to be defeated by Satan in this area. You can be free! *Yes you can!*

Keys to sexual purity

What attitudes and beliefs will help us win the battle for purity?

- Deep conviction that God has spoken clearly and strongly on the matter
- Deep conviction that God knows what is going on in your life
- Deep conviction that sexual impurity will destroy your life and soul
- Openness with other men who can help you
- Openness at the *temptation* level, not just after you fall
- Openness when you have sinned—*immediately*
- Knowing that lust promises *much* and gives *nothing*
- A simple decision to stay away from sensual movies and videos
- When you do watch movies or TV, have your wife or other strong disciples with you

Do not become discouraged if, early on in the battle, you have to fight every day, and even throughout the day. But know this: the farther you get away from lust and the longer you stay away, the easier the battle will get! You will see it for all its emptiness, and your determination and confidence will grow.

What about masturbation?

The Bible is silent on the subject, but some principles clearly apply.

- *Masturbation goes counter to God's purpose.* Sexual pleasure was created by God to be enjoyed and experienced in the marriage relationship with our wives, not for solitary gratification. Masturbation is a solitary and selfish experience. It turns sex into a selfish, private act, and it will ultimately hurt your ability to experience loving sexual union in marriage.

- *Masturbation leads to impurity, and is often directly associated with lust.* Most men who masturbate do so while fantasizing. Even if that was not our original intent, it can easily lead to impure thinking.

- *Masturbation becomes addictive.* Once we start, we become enslaved to the practice.

- *Masturbation leads to guilt and shame, and robs men of confidence.* Down inside, we feel weak and defeated, knowing we are controlled by this selfish habit. We feel bad about ourselves.

- *Masturbation in marriage deprives our wives of our partnership and love.* We have replaced our wife's love and pleasure with our own. God's plan is for the two of you to be partners in pleasing one another sexually in lovemaking, not for you to please yourself, by yourself.

What about homosexuality?

We have seen what God says about sex between men and women: it is confined to married couples. What does God have to say about same-sex or homosexual involvement? Here are some key verses:

Because of this, God gave them over to shameful lusts. Even their women exchanged natural relations for unnatural ones. In the same way the men also abandoned natural relations with women and were inflamed with lust for one another. Men committed indecent acts with other men, and received in themselves the due penalty for their perversion. (Romans 1:26–27)

Do you not know that the wicked will not inherit the kingdom of God? Do not be deceived: Neither the sexually immoral nor idolaters nor adulterers nor male prostitutes nor homosexual offenders nor thieves nor the greedy nor drunkards nor slanderers nor swindlers will inherit the kingdom of God. (1 Corinthians 6:9–10)

"Do not lie with a man as one lies with a woman; that is detestable." (Leviticus 18:22)

The Bible is clear: sexual involvement is designed for, and limited to, men with women, to males joined with females in lifelong, exclusive marital union. Every other kind of sexual involvement is forbidden, including same-sex unions or same-sex contact. The passage in Romans makes it clear that homosexuality is not a natural, God-given desire, but a learned one. It is not a part of the order of creation. The Bible plainly says this is not the way God created us. Yes, some men are tempted in this way. If so, we need to resist this temptation just as we would any other. Experiencing homosexual temptation does not exclude us from being a mighty warrior for God! Whether we are tempted by the opposite sex, the same sex or both sexes, we as warriors of God need to fight and resist any sin that tempts us, and live righteous, pure lives.

We live in a day when society around us is changing rapidly. Same-sex attraction and homosexuality are now being advocated as acceptable lifestyles. While society may change, God's word is the unchanging standard for his people. We must remember that our standards about sexuality or any moral issue come from Scripture and not from society. The temptation has always been for God's people to conform to the standards of the world around them. May we as God's warriors hold unflinchingly to what God has said.

The amazing blessing of sexuality

So how should we as men look at the whole idea of our sexuality? Most of us would probably agree that sex and our sex drive are a major shaping force in the male makeup. I would guess that sexuality is, or has been, a huge issue in the life of just about every man who reads this book. And in this chapter we have rightly identified sexual purity as a battle. But brothers, is that what that the sexual element of our masculine nature was intended to be—a battle? A source of struggle, stress, and shame?

Marriage and sexuality were a vital part of God's creative order:

The LORD God said, "It is not good for the man to be alone. I will make a helper suitable for him...."

For this reason a man will leave his father and mother and be united to his wife, and they will become one flesh.

The man and his wife were both naked, and they felt no shame.

(Genesis 2:18, 24-25)

God made us sexual beings. Sex was not the forbidden fruit of the Garden of Eden. Sex was presented to Adam and Eve—and to all of humanity—as a gift from God. That's right, a *gift*. A good thing. A blessing to be appreciated and celebrated, not hidden and feared.

Read the creation story in Genesis. Everything God made was, and is, good. This means that our bodies are *good*. The sexual side of our nature is good. Sexual attraction is inherently good. Sexual love between husbands and wives was designed by God to be good. Sexual pleasure in marriage is good.

But I'll take it even further than that, because the Bible takes it further. Read *Song of Songs*. The message of this neglected little jewel of a book in the Old Testament is this: Married sexual union between husbands and wives was designed and planned by God as a thrilling, adventurous, and fiery experience to be celebrated and enjoyed.

Yes, you heard me right!

God designed sexual union not only for procreation, but also as a way for married men and woman to express their love to each other. It is the unique way God provided for husbands and wives to be close, to unite, and to bond in body and spirit. Explain this to me: If God didn't want sexual lovemaking to be enjoyed, why did he design it to feel so good? And since he is the creator of sexuality and sexual desire, God knows how and where it is best carried out: in the relationship of marriage. Therefore, brothers, of this we can be sure: *married sexual love is the hottest and best sex on the planet*. God just flat-out knows how to do things right!

Single men who plan to marry one day: Know that God has a great woman out there for you, one who will love Jesus first and you second. Be thankful for what is coming your way. Save yourself for *her*, and for *marriage*. Be patient and pure until you meet her and marry her.

Single men who plan to stay single: God will honor your commitment to serve him as a single man. Remain pure all the days of your life. Go and be God's warrior!

Married men: Enjoy life with your wife!

Let's listen as the Bible says it:

> *You have stolen my heart, my sister, my bride;*
> > *you have stolen my heart*
> *with one glance of your eyes,*
> > *with one jewel of your necklace.*
> *How delightful is your love, my sister, my bride!*
> > *How much more pleasing is your love than wine,*
> *and the fragrance of your perfume than any spice!*
> > > > (Song of Songs 4:9–10)

> *May your fountain be blessed,*
> > *and may you rejoice in the wife of your youth.*
> *A loving doe, a graceful deer—*
> > *may her breasts satisfy you always,*
> > *may you ever be captivated by her love.* (Proverbs 5:18–19)

Warriors, let's not allow our definition of sexual manhood to be twisted by the Enemy. He would like to deceive us into thinking that a "real man" is someone who can draw women—lots of them—into sexual impurity; that this kind of "success" proves how masculine you really are. In God's view, the opposite is true. A "real man"—a godly man—is someone who has *self-control*.

So, my brothers, who is the *real man*? It is the single brother who stays sexually pure. It is the married man who wins the trust, love, and respect of one woman—his wife—and keeps it all the days of her life!

Sex is a gift from God. Let us respect and appreciate it, and enjoy it in its proper context. Let us never abuse it. Let us trust that God's plan for our lives—including our sexual lives—is one of the most amazing and wonderful gifts he wants to give us. Let us be pure warriors, trustworthy men of integrity and honesty. Let us be noble knights who honor our bodies, honor women, honor our wives, and honor our God.

May we ever be warriors of purity!

BATTLE PLAN

1. How would you say the battle for purity is going in your life? Are you feeling encouraged or discouraged in this area?

2. Is purity an occasional struggle or a continual one? How would you rate the level of intensity of your battle on a day-to-day basis?

3. Are you being consistently open with godly, spiritual men around you about this area? Who are they? Write down their names.

4. How often do you see and speak to these brothers?

5. Is purity a topic that you are readily and easily open about? Are you completely forthcoming? Is there anything you are hiding or holding back?

6. Is there a person (or persons) who is a source of temptation for you? If so, who? Have you become involved emotionally, physically, or conversationally (through spoken or written conversations) with this person? Are you being open about this?

7. Are you facing battles in the area of pornography (Internet, movies, television, smart phone, magazines, etc.)?

8. Are there any other activities, relationships, or situations you are involved in or tempted by that you need to talk about with spiritual brothers (for example, people at work, places you go, social situations, etc.)?

9. If you haven't already done so, establish a relationship with a fellow warrior or group of warriors who will help you to fight the battle for purity. Who do you plan to contact? Talk to them this week.

BATTLE CRY

Selfishness is a killer.

It is the skulking, underlying flaw that takes us down, the secret passage that the Enemy uses to infiltrate our hearts and undermine our defenses.

It seems simple enough: put Jesus above Self, and you will be fulfilled and victorious; place Self above Jesus, and you will be empty and defeated.

It's harder than it sounds.

Building a godly life, a close family, and fulfilling friendships takes a warrior who is willing to give of himself:

His energy.
His time.
His resources.
His emotions.
His heart.

As God's warriors, let us break the mold. Let us put Jesus first, then choose to be noble, sacrificial men who place the needs of others above our own.

Chapter Twelve

The Battle of Selfishness

Then Nathan said to David, "You are the man! This is what the LORD, the God of Israel, says: 'I anointed you king over Israel, and I delivered you from the hand of Saul. I gave your master's house to you, and your master's wives into your arms. I gave you the house of Israel and Judah. And if all this had been too little, I would have given you even more. Why did you despise the word of the LORD by doing what is evil in his eyes? You struck down Uriah the Hittite with the sword and took his wife to be your own. You killed him with the sword of the Ammonites. Now, therefore, the sword will never depart from your house, because you despised me and took the wife of Uriah the Hittite to be your own.'"

2 Samuel 12:7-10

What was the real issue behind David's sin with Bathsheba? What caused him to use his kingly power to take advantage of her, to attempt to hide it, and then, finally, to have his friend and loyal warrior Uriah killed? What could possibly cause the man after the heart of God to descend so deeply into sin? Did lust take hold of him? Did his newly acquired power go to his head? Was he empty and bored? While all of these motives are possible, none of them seem an adequate answer for such a despicable series of events.

I have a theory. It may seem overly simplistic, but I encourage you to take a hard look. Consider what God said to David through Nathan the prophet. Look at the world around you. Scrutinize your own heart. I think the answer becomes clear.

In one word, David's problem was *selfishness*.

Yes, just plain old selfishness. He wanted what he wanted. He had the means to get it, and he took it. He took what he wanted from someone else. Not only that, he took it from people who were weaker than him in power and influence. He used the power of his position in an attempt to cover up his wrongdoing. His selfishness blinded him to what he was doing. It hardened his tender heart and allowed him to sin against God. His selfishness created the empty place inside of him that he sought to fill with an illicit union. He took advantage of another man's wife—a man who was a loyal, noble soldier, and one of his trusted, renowned Mighty Men (1 Chronicles 11:41). David's selfishness enabled him to rationalize his actions.

Fellow warriors, selfishness is a battle that *every one of us* has to fight. Selfishness (coupled with its cousin, pride) is the most basic and profound battle we will ever fight in life. It is the problem behind and at the root of every other struggle we have. Whatever other sins and weaknesses we are battling, selfishness is somehow intertwined with them. One way or another, the placement of Self above God is behind every sin we face.

Exactly what is Self? It is the "I," our core, the center of our being. It is our essence, the person we really are.

The problem is not that Self is inherently evil—we are made in the image of God. The problem is our priorities. If we place God, our Creator, at our lives' center and as our first priority, then our attitudes will be rightly aligned. But if we place Self above God and his will, we have made the most fundamental error we can make in life, and the rest of our decisions will miss the mark. (That is, by the way, a good definition of sin: "to miss the mark.") We want to have a good life, but when we are self-focused, we misfire and go the wrong direction, with horrible results.

God before Self

If you reread the passage we cited at the beginning of this chapter, when Nathan confronts David with his sin, you'll see how Nathan spotlights the real issue behind David's evil actions: David has put himself above God; he has exalted himself and despised his Lord. God has blessed David richly. God has given David everything he could possibly ever need and would gladly give him even more. But in his selfishness, David wanted what he wanted, even if God forbade it. And he has gone against the will of God to get it. When Self displaces God on the throne of our hearts, we never have enough.

Let's take a deeper look.

Self-will

The primary way selfishness reveals its presence is in our desire to have our own way. Like David with Bathsheba, we want *what* we want, *when* we want it. And we want it without reference to the will and plan of God. Putting God above our own selves takes a great deal of faith, but also a deep attitude of loving surrender.

Jesus is the ultimate example of this kind of faithful surrender. His deepest attitude is reflected by these words, "I seek not to please myself but him who sent me" (John 5:30). And brothers, what he expected of himself, he expects of you and me. Let us lay aside *our* will for the will of the One who loves us and knows what is best for us.

Self-centeredness

What is David thinking when he takes Bathsheba and has Uriah killed? He is thinking about *himself*. He has grown so blinded that he has not only shut down his conscience, but his common sense. Does he really think he can get away with it? The young man after the heart of God is no longer who he used to be. The young man who once stood up to Goliath because of his concern for the glory of God, no matter the personal cost, has now grown selfish. He sees a woman he wants, and he takes her. She belongs to one of his trusted warriors, one of his Mighty Men. No matter. He takes her, and then takes the life of his friend to protect his own reputation. Such is the path of Self.

Self is forever preoccupied with itself. The two most used words in Self's vocabulary are the pronouns *I* and *me*. When we are selfish, we are not first concerned about God, or about our wives, our families, our neighbors, or our church—no, it is all about us.

Our words tell us a lot about ourselves. Self loves to hear itself talk, to keep the conversation focused on its greatest love—itself. It always has a better story, a greater accomplishment, a worse illness, a better cure. Others may seek to turn the conversation in a different direction, but Self can find a way to point the needle back to its own North Star— itself. And all the while, Self is oblivious to the effect this is having on others. When we are selfish, we don't realize that others are frustrated by our self-focus and insensitivity. We don't see that they would like to share some things with us, to tell us about their day, their life, their feelings, their needs. And we wonder why we aren't close to people and why we are lonely and without friends; we wonder why our wives and children don't enjoy our company or want to be around us. It is because we always talk about ourselves.

Is it any wonder that at the very core of following Jesus, of being his disciple, is the concept of self-denial? If we are to be warriors for God, if we are to be like Jesus, then we will need to decide, *at our deepest core*, to put God's will above our own selfish desires, plans, ambitions, and dreams:

> *Then he said to them all: "If anyone would come after me, he must deny himself and take up his cross daily and follow me."* (Luke 9:23)

We are not warriors for our own selves, fighting for our own ambitions and wishes. No. We are warriors for *Jesus*. We are warriors for *the good news*. We are warriors for *others*. Let's give up Self and give him to Jesus. Paradoxically, only then will we be deeply fulfilled and soul-satisfied. And only then will we be victorious warriors.

Self-seeking

Self longs for admiration, appreciation, and praise. It wants power. It wants prominence and attention. It loves to be noticed. It is essentially competitive. It wants to be better, more liked, more influential, more popular. Jealousy and envy are always lurking nearby. When another person is lifted up or given recognition, Self has a hard time.

It was a self-seeking attitude that ultimately destroyed Saul, the first king of Israel. The kingship was not Saul's by right or familial inheritance; it was a gift from God. God gave it, and God took it away when Saul sinned. Samuel had clearly informed Saul of this punishment; he knew it was coming. You would think that he would accede to God's plan and graciously step aside when the new king was revealed.

But no, that is not what Self does. Self seeks to hang on to what it has, even if God says to give it up. So when young David shows up, slays Goliath, and is praised by the singing women, given greater credit than Saul, Saul is distressed.

"They have credited David with tens of thousands," he thought, "but me with only thousands. What more can he get but the kingdom?" And from that time on Saul kept a jealous eye on David. (1 Samuel 18:8-9, emphasis added)

Saul began to fight the wrong battle—and so do we all when we grow selfish. We start fighting for our own glory and ambitions rather than for God. And we always lose that fight in the end.

Saul started out as a seemingly humble, self-effacing man (1 Samuel 9–10). Brothers, we can be insecure and lacking in confidence, *but still* be selfish and prideful in our inner heart. Selfishness is so slippery and deceiving that it can appear to be humble. But if, deep down inside, the center of our being is not focused on God and surrendered to him, our insecurities are only a mask for selfishness.

When I was a college sophomore I served as president of my Christian student group on campus. I completed my term, took a year off, and ran again at the beginning of my senior year. The other candidate was a year younger than me. Surely the students would select me, now that I had another year of maturity under my belt! But much to my shock and dismay, I was defeated. I then decided to run for vice president, thinking that with my great wisdom I could help my younger friend as he served as president. This time, my opponent was only a sophomore, and new to the faith. Surely I would be elected! The vote was tallied, and again, I lost. I was devastated. As we sang during the church service later that night, my campus minister walked up beside me and whispered in my ear some words I have never forgotten: "Now we'll see whether you are in it for yourself or for God." Those words struck deep into my heart. My selfish motives had been exposed. I went home, read my Bible, prayed, and got my attitude right. I decided to fully accept the result, and to serve God and my student group with all my heart. I went on to have a great year, and learned a life lesson that I have been reminded of many times since then.

Selfishness can be loud or it can be quiet; it can be swaggering or it can be subtle; but it is a battle that we *all* have to fight regardless of our personality or temperament.

Self-indulgence

When we live by our own feelings and desires, we descend into selfishness. Ask yourself: "Am I controlled by my emotions, or by God's will?" The answer to that question will tell you by what principle you live your life—whether by God's will or by the rule of Self. When our own desires triumph over principle, and they win out over what is right and just, we are living by the rule of Self.

This was obviously the case when David takes Bathsheba. He looks at her and sees that she is "very beautiful" (2 Samuel 11:2). She is attractive. He wants her. *Why not take her?* David's actions are motivated by his own lustful desires, to be sure, but lurking behind his lust is another, more sinister motive: *selfishness*.

Brothers, God knows how to fulfill us. He knows what is good for us, and what is not. The way to find our Self is to give it away to God and his purposes, not to seek to fulfill our desires in our way.

Sexual sin, drug abuse, alcohol abuse, greed, popularity, the desire for an easy, comfortable life…all these sins are rooted in the same thing: selfishness. God wants us to be happy and fulfilled—he made us with those kinds of desires woven into our being. But we have to trust that when God gives us a priority or a rule, it is for our benefit. It is for our own well-being. If we follow his way, we will be fulfilled and satisfied in the long run.

Again our perfect example is Jesus, who said, "I always do what pleases him" (John 8:29). He lived a life of pleasing God, and not himself. Why do you trust Jesus and follow him? Why do you let him guide and lead you? Why are you his warrior today? Because he put God's will and your well being above his own comfort, happiness, and desires.

Self-justification

We might ask, "How could David have rationalized his behavior in this situation? How could he have convinced himself to take another man's wife? How could he try to cover it over by having a loyal soldier and friend murdered? How did the man who started with a great heart get himself here?"

The answer is self-justification. Someone once said, "For many people, their minds exist only for the purpose of giving them an excuse to do what they already want to do."

The human mind, when driven by selfishness, is capable of rationalizing any behavior, no matter how terrible, no matter how egregiously wrong. Sin is always accompanied by deceit in some form or other. Satan first deceives us, then we deceive ourselves, and finally we deceive others as well. The first and greatest lie is the one we believe ourselves. Satan is a liar and the father of lies (John 8:44). He is the one actually behind our self-deception—he is the one who is causing us to rationalize our sins.

So, fellow warrior, where is Satan lying to you today? Have you begun to believe any of his lies? Is there any sin in your life that you are rationalizing? Anything you are minimizing? Do any of these justifications sound familiar?

- "Oh, that's just the way I am."

- "There are worse things I could be doing. This is not so bad."

- "Look at what that guy is doing. At least I'm not that bad off."

- "Doesn't everybody sin? What's the big deal?"

- "Can we know what the Bible really means? Everybody interprets it differently."

- "I know what I am doing is wrong, and I plan to deal with it one day."

- "No we are not legally married, and yes, we are sleeping together, but we are already married in our hearts."

- "If my wife was more sexually responsive, I wouldn't be having this affair or be involved in pornography."

Where else does selfishness manifest itself in our lives?

The warrior's selfishness often appears at home with his wife and children

Men, who we are at home is who we really are.

How we treat our wives and children, or how we treat our siblings and parents, tells us more about ourselves than just about anything else.

How are we treating our wives?

God tells us that our two jobs are to *love* and *lead* our wives (see Ephesians 5:22–6:4).

First, we are explicitly told to love our wives "just as Christ loved the church and gave himself up for her" (Ephesians 5:25). Your wife's greatest need from you, aside from needing you to love God first, is for you to *love her* as Jesus loves the church: passionately, sacrificially, practically, and with deep emotional connection, just as Jesus repeatedly showed compassion for people during his ministry.

Second, we are meant to be the leader, the head of our households. Our wives are told to follow (submit to) us as they also follow Jesus himself (Ephesians 5:22–24). If they are supposed to follow us, then we are supposed to lead them! This means we need to set the spiritual example in our own walk with God and in our commitment to Jesus and to his church. It means we are to be concerned for the spiritual well-being of our wife and children.

How are we treating our children?

Fathers are told, "Do not exasperate your children; instead, bring them up in the training and instruction of the Lord" (Ephesians 6:4). Our children need our loving attention. They need our nurturing. They need our diligent teaching, correction, and discipline. They need us to be deeply, consistently involved in their lives.

We need to be able to say with Joshua, "But as for me and my household, we will serve the Lord" (Joshua 24:15). Leading a household takes effort, commitment, sacrifice, affection, and love.

Tell me, brothers, what kind of man do you have to be to be this kind of husband, this kind of father? I will tell you in one word: *unselfish*.

The young warrior still at home

And how about our younger warriors? You may be still be living at home, under the roof of your father and mother, and with your siblings. What kind of son are you? What kind of brother are you? You need to be selfless and humble enough to honor your parents. They are not perfect, but God does not say they have to be perfect before you start respecting them. Respect for our parents is mandated simply because it is God's order of things.

Nothing tests our "selfishness index" quite like living in a household with parents and siblings. Even if your parents are committed disciples of Jesus, they will make mistakes—yes, they will even make mistakes in dealing with you! You can't always have your way. You have to adjust to other people. You will get hurt. Your siblings will provoke you, offend you, and be selfish at times. And guess what? You will do the same things to them! We have to learn to submit to and respect our parents, to be patient, to be honest without losing our temper . . . on and on we could go. We all, of course, fail and fall short, but the question is, *Are we trying to be respectful and loving at home, or are we just thinking about and looking out for ourselves?*

The reason so many marriages and households are failing is simply this: men are not fighting the good fight of the faith at home. They are not engaged. They are not giving their best effort. Maybe they try for a while and find it difficult, and so they just back off. They just slide into the pit of selfishness.

Brothers, it takes faith, perseverance and humility to be unselfish at home. Let's make a decision. Let's get down on our knees and ask for help. Let's go to other men for help. Let's go to war against our own selfishness so that we can be the men we need to be under our own roof.

Getting practical: How do we fight the battle against selfishness?

Selfishness is a battle we lose when we are not aware—when we are blinded and insensitive. There are some classic ways that we as a gender tend to be selfish. Here are a few examples:

Married men and fathers face:

The battle of distraction and connection

Sometimes when my children were younger and we would sit around the dinner table, my wife would lean over and gently whisper in my ear, "You aren't *here!*" She was letting me know that although my body was seated in my chair at the table, my mind was elsewhere. Here in front of me were my children and my wife, here was a chance to shed my worries and engage with my family, and I was letting it pass me by. I was not yelling or being mean—I was just being quietly, nicely selfish. To this day, even now that my children are grown and married and have families of their own, I still have to consciously decide to disengage from my own world and get into theirs. Yes, even grandfathers can be selfish! I must choose to fight and win the small battles of engaging in each moment. These "little victories" add up to define what kind of husband, father, and grandfather I am, and what kind of family I have. The reward of selflessness is beyond my ability to describe.

Brother warriors, let us not lose the battle of selfishness at home. Let us win the "small" battles of distraction. Let us stop what we are doing, free our minds from whatever preoccupies us, look at our family members, and really *be with them*. Let us be present. Let us win the victory over Self at home.

The battle of interruption and inconvenience

Jesus was constantly interrupted by human need. In Mark 5 he sails across the Sea of Galilee with his disciples, disembarks from his boat, and is immediately confronted by a disturbed, demon-possessed man. (Kind of like coming home to a kid or family in high drama!) He heals the man, and is then begged to go and save the life of a dying child. While on his way, struggling to make his way through the pressing crowds of people, an ill woman manages to touch his garment and receive a cure. He stops, pronounces her healed and forgiven, and moves on. Before he reaches his destination he is informed that he is too late—the sick little girl has died. Undeterred, he presses on to her home, where he is met with scorn and laughter from those who doubt his ability to heal her now. He ignores his critics, enters the home, and brings her back to life.

Aside from the miracles, does all this chaos sound a bit like a day in your life? Some days, the problems seem to fly at us in every moment and from every angle. One reason I know Jesus is the Son of God is because of the way he handled pressure, interruption, and inconvenience. I appreciate his miracles. I stand in awe of his wisdom. But let me tell you, a man who handles the stresses and pressures of life with the unselfish poise that Jesus demonstrated just *has* to be divine!

How about you and me? Do we always have to get our way? How do we take it when our plans are interrupted? Can we graciously let go of our own desires and even our schedules to make someone else happy? As fathers and husbands we certainly need to lead our families, but our model in how to do this is Jesus, who gave up his own will to serve and to save his bride, the church.

Rising to the challenge

Then he said to them all: "If anyone would come after me, he must deny himself and take up his cross daily and follow me. For whoever wants to save his life will lose it, but whoever loses his life for me will save it." (Luke 9:23–24)

The battle against selfishness is fundamental to our following Christ. The call is still the same: Give up your life to save it. Lose it to keep it. Give it away to get it back.

Give your Self to Jesus and he will give you life.

Accept that God knows best.

Trust him.

Let go.

Brothers, the greatest battle of all is the one in which we surrender to God. We do this at first when we initially decide to repent, give our lives to Jesus, and be baptized. Then daily, step by step, we must continue to take up our cross, give up Self, and follow Jesus.

Let's go to war against selfishness!

BATTLE PLAN

1. Examine your priorities:

   - Are you resisting God's priorities in your life in any way?
   - Is there anything you want so much that it is causing you to compromise your commitment to Christ and his church?

2. Assess your behavior at home:

   If you are a young warrior:
   - How are you treating your family?
   - Are you obeying your parents, or are you ignoring, fighting, and arguing with them?
   - Are you showing consideration, humility, and love to your siblings?

   If you are a married warrior:
   - Do you greet and embrace your wives and kids when you come home?
   - Do you smile at them, look them in the eyes, and find out how they are doing and how their day went?
   - Do you connect emotionally?

3. What is one simple change you can make at home to help you be more present and engaged with your family?

BATTLE CRY

Every warrior longs to be victorious, to be respected, to prove himself. And in seeking those things, every warrior is tempted with pride.

No warrior is exempt from pride:

It is the one sin we all have in common.
It is our primary sin—the reason we commit all other sins.

Pride may strut about in the open: gloating and boasting, sneering and jeering. Or it may lurk in the shadows: disguised as something else, the secret, unseen driving power behind our anger, insecurity, jealousy, and envy.

Scripture warns of the dangers of pride:

God hates pride.
God opposes pride.
God humbles pride.

Jesus calls his warriors to a life of humility, sacrifice, and service: "For everyone who exalts himself will be humbled, and he who humbles himself will be exalted" (Luke 18:14).

Brother warriors, let us not be ambushed by pride. Let's take up the sword with a mantle of humility, and let God do the exalting.

Chapter Thirteen

The Battle of Pride

My heart is not proud, O LORD,
my eyes are not haughty;
I do not concern myself with great matters
or things too wonderful for me.
Psalm 131:1

Behind every battle you fight, you are also fighting the battle of pride. Pride is the primordial sin: the sin that lost Satan his place in heaven, the sin that lost Adam and Eve their place in the garden, the sin behind all other sins that crucified Christ.

No one is exempt from pride. It is our fundamental sin. It is the one sin we all have in common. It is the reason we commit all other sins. Every time we sin, we sin twice. Behind our every wrong, somehow, some way, pride is present. We may lie, lust, steal, cheat, get angry, give in to fear… but pride is connected to them all, its pervasive and pernicious presence invisible and unrecognized, but hiding in the background nonetheless.

Pride may strut about in the open—arrogant, boasting, contemptuous, sneering, leering and jeering. Or it may lurk in the shadows—disguised as something else, the secret, unseen driving power behind our anger, insecurity, jealousy, and envy.

God gives pride a unique place of condemnation and correction. No other sin elicits such a strong and powerful response from him. Throughout Scripture, no other sin merits the same level of outright rebuke from the Lord that pride receives.

What is it about pride that brings on such strong response from God? Why would he reserve for this sin such a place of denunciation and warning?

A major part of the reason is that pride is the underlying fundamental attitude that breaks our fellowship with God. Nothing else obstructs our relationship with the Father and his Son Jesus like pride does.

Look at these powerful statements from God and you will see how he feels:

. . . whoever has haughty eyes and a proud heart, him will I not endure. (Psalm 101:5)

Though the LORD is on high, he looks upon the lowly,
but the proud he knows from afar. (Psalm 138:6)

"You save the humble,
but your eyes are on the haughty to bring them low." (2 Samuel 22:28)

To fear the LORD is to hate evil;
I hate pride and arrogance,
evil behavior and perverse speech. (Proverb 8: 13)

The LORD detests all the proud of heart.
Be sure of this: They will not go unpunished. (Proverb 16:5)

Pride goes before destruction, a haughty spirit before a fall. (Proverb 16:18)

What is pride?

First, pride involves *exaltation of Self*. When we are proud, we place ourselves above God. Pride says that we, the created, are superior to or equal to God, our Creator. At its essence, pride overestimates itself and underestimates God.

Next, pride declares our *independence from God*. When we are prideful we think we do not need God. We are sufficient on our own. We are righteous on our own. We can handle life on our own.

Then, pride causes us to show *contempt for others*. We think we are better than them. We look down on them. We are critical of others.

And last, pride is essentially competitive. To paraphrase what C.S. Lewis observed in *Mere Christianity*, we are not proud because we are smart, good-looking, or successful—we are proud because we are smarter, better-looking, or more successful than someone else.[2]

Pride and Satan

Pride is what caused Satan to rebel against God. It got him thrown out of heaven. He asserted his will against God's. This is in essence what Satan tries to get us to do—to assert *our* will, *our* plan, *our* way against God's plan and purpose for our lives.

Listen to what Satan said to Eve in the Garden of Eden, and see if you do not sense the underlying pride within him, and the pride within Eve that the snake seeks to engender:

> Now the serpent was more crafty than any of the wild animals the LORD God had made. He said to the woman, "Did God really say, 'You must not eat from any tree in the garden'?"
>
> The woman said to the serpent, "We may eat fruit from the trees in the garden, but God did say, 'You must not eat fruit from the tree that is in the middle of the garden, and you must not touch it, or you will die.'"
>
> "You will not surely die," the serpent said to the woman. "For God knows that when you eat of it your eyes will be opened, and you will be like God, knowing good and evil." (Genesis 3:1–5)

Has Satan ever whispered lies like this to you? *You can be like God! There is a better way than his way. He is holding out on you! You don't need to listen to him. Do what you want to do!*

In this next passage we see the story of Satan's rebellion against God, and of his desire to do what he wishes:

> And there was war in heaven. Michael and his angels fought against the dragon, and the dragon and his angels fought back. But he was not strong enough, and they lost their place in heaven. The great dragon was hurled down—that ancient serpent called the devil, or Satan, who leads the whole world astray. He was hurled to the earth, and his angels with him.
>
> Then I heard a loud voice in heaven say:

---

2. C.S. Lewis, *Mere Christianity* (New York, New York: Touchstone, 1996).

> *"Now have come the salvation and the power*
> *and the kingdom of our God,*
> *and the authority of his Christ....*
> *But woe to the earth and the sea,*
> *because the devil has gone down to you!*
> *He is filled with fury,*
> *because he knows that his time is short."*
>
> (Revelation 12:7–12)

All of this comes from a simple origin: *Pride*. Yes, pride. It was the driving force behind Satan's desire to be greater than who God made him to be— his desire to rise above God himself. His desire to go his own way, to have authority over his own life and future...these yearnings caused him to rebel and lose his place in glory. And even now, he still seeks to undermine God and the good that God would do in our lives.

David's pride attack

Did Pride ever assail and defeat David? Oh yes, it did! It led him to a terrible mistake. This is a story that presents some difficulties of understanding for the modern reader, and so it tends to be overlooked. But despite our inattention to it, this incident recounts one of the worst mistakes David ever made—in fact, in terms of the repercussions it brought upon the nation of Israel, it was the *greatest* mistake he ever made.

In 1 Chronicles 21 we find the story. We see that Satan has incited David to count the fighting men of Israel. In itself this seems harmless enough, but there is more to it than meets the eye. It seems that God views this census as arrogance, and as a sign that David, after all the amazing victories God has given him, is now forgetting where the successes came from. Perhaps David is now drawing confidence from the size of his army, rather than from the power of God. Calling the census is so egregious an error that Joab—yes, even worldly, scheming, unspiritual Joab—warns David not to number his men. David ignores him, and Joab reluctantly obeys the king's order.

God takes swift and strong disciplinary action. This may be hard for us to understand or accept, but we must recognize that our pride sometimes hurts others beside ourselves. Pride can easily spread from a leader to his followers. Was the whole nation now being led into pride and arrogance, boasting in its own power, and not its dependence on God?

God addresses the situation with decisive and firm action. He gives David three options to choose from: Three years of famine, three months of defeat by his enemies, or three days of plague. David chooses the latter discipline, and the destroying angel visits Israel with a deadly plague. David appeals to God for mercy, admitting his folly and sin. David's repentance and God's own grief causes the Lord to have mercy and stop the plague, but not before seventy thousand people have died. David's pride and self-assertion have caused more obvious suffering and pain than any other sin he ever committed. That is what pride does. The sin of the leader hurts everyone around him.

Guard your heart

We might find it more difficult to relate to this particular situation in David's life, with its high stakes and staggering consequences, because few of us carry the kind of weighty responsibilities that David bore. We don't rule a kingdom or lead an army, yet we still wrestle with pride, as David did. Consider this: Who knows how you and I would respond if given the kind of influence and authority David held? God gives us a "big" story to remind us that we need to watch out for pride as if our souls depended upon it—because they do.

Brother warriors, let us remember that pride kills. We must relentlessly defend our hearts against pride. This may be the most important internal battle we ever fight.

For you and me, pride will reveal itself in our own smaller world: in our families, among our friends, on the job, and at church.

We may be tempted to seek glory by being arrogant.

We may be tempted to compare ourselves to other warriors.

We may be tempted to think more highly of ourselves than we should.

We may be tempted to push ourselves forward.

We may be tempted to take all the credit for our victories, without honoring God.

We may be tempted to will and work our way to the top, without dedicating our work to God, depending upon God, or giving him credit for our success.

We could even temporarily succeed in our pride-motivated efforts.

We may achieve incredible results; we may do amazing things. But the crucial issue is, *for* whom and *from* whom did those results come?

Pride will always backfire in the end. Only *God* can permanently give success and raise us up. And when we display pride on our own small stage, it is just as offensive to God, and hurtful to others, as it was when David displayed it on a bigger stage. God is the ultimate judge, and he is sovereign. He has long known how to bring down proud people, *and he always will.*

Pride transforms blessings into curses

Pride defiles all it touches. It takes what should be a blessing and turns it into a curse.

- *Zeal* + pride = tyranny and cruelty

- *Strong will* + pride = stubbornness

- *Intelligence* + pride = intellectual smugness, arrogance, and disdain

- *Good looks* + pride = vanity

- *Speech* + pride = criticism

- *Wit* + pride = ridicule and sarcasm

- *Youth* + pride = folly, foolish decisions, disrespect

- *Age* + pride = stubbornness, rigidity, smugness, dullness

The greatness of humility

The opposite of pride is humility. Humility is a quality that some of us have a hard time regarding as a desirable characteristic for a warrior. We might even equate humility with weakness and lack of confidence. We have a difficult time understanding how a man can maintain a great sense of his own need for God and other people, and still be a Mighty Man of God.

My brothers, humility is not an add-on or an optional quality that some of us have, but not all of us need. No! It is essential to the character of every godly warrior. It is foundational. It is the food we eat and the air we breathe! Without humility, we cannot be admitted into the army, and if we lose it, we risk getting discharged.

Is it any wonder that Moses, the courageous deliverer of God's people and greatest leader of the Old Covenant was described in the following words: "Now Moses was a very humble man, more humble than anyone else on the face of the earth" (Numbers 12:3)?

Is it any surprise that in one of the few times when Jesus, the perfect Son of God, described himself, he said, "I am gentle and humble in heart" (Matthew 11:29)?

Brothers, what does this tell us? We should seek humility. We should ask God to humble us. We should study the subject and fervently seek to grow in our humility.

Many of us are afraid of humility. We think it will undercut us. We think it will make us weak. How wrong we are! Listen to what the Jesus says: "For everyone who exalts himself will be humbled, and he who humbles himself will be exalted" (Luke 14:11).

How opposite this is from the way that many men think about manhood and masculinity! We think that in order to be a real man, we need to push ourselves forward, to believe we are better than others. We think that a real man should never, *ever* admit that he has weaknesses.

What does Paul, one of the most courageous preachers who ever lived, have to say about pride and humility? "I will not boast about myself, except about my weaknesses" (2 Corinthians 12:5).

What does the Rock, the Apostle Peter, have to say about pride and humility? "All of you, clothe yourselves with humility toward one another, because, 'God opposes the proud but gives grace to the humble.' Humble yourselves, therefore, under God's mighty hand, that he may lift you up in due time" (1 Peter 5:5–6).

My brother, what do you have to say about your own humility? What would your friends say? What would your wife say? What about your kids? Your siblings? Your fellow warriors at church? Your church leaders?

Let us forsake our pride, and let us embrace humility. Let us fight the good fight against the Enemy, whose own pride took down and got him cast out of heaven. It destroyed his relationship with God. He wants us to join with him in his misery. Let us never give in! May we stand our ground and, clothed with humility, win the battle against pride!

BATTLE PLAN

1. Timely, consistent self-examination is a healthy practice for God's warriors. Read 1 Corinthians 11:23–32 and 2 Corinthians 13:5.

2. Take the Pride and Humility Test.
    Rate yourself one to ten, with one being poor, ten being great.

a. _____ I often ask for advice.

b. _____ I listen and carefully consider the advice I receive.

c. _____ I am continually in learner mode. I am eager to learn from anyone at any time, in any situation.

d. _____ I am approachable. People around me feel that they can tell me what I need to hear, even when I have hurt or offended them.

e. _____ On matters of opinion and judgment, I am persuadable. I will listen and give careful consideration when others present a different point of view. I am willing to change my mind.

f. _____ When others are praised and lifted up, I am happy for them.

g. _____ When I am overlooked or bypassed for promotion, or when my work or efforts go unnoticed, unrecognized or unappreciated, I am not easily offended.

h. _____ I am quick to examine myself, see my mistakes, and apologize when I have hurt or offended someone.

Add up your points. How did you do? (Hint: If you gave yourself a perfect score of 80, please fall on your knees and confess your pride!)

3. Read Proverbs 27:17. In the spirit of this scripture, seek out one or two mature, wise fellow warriors who know you well. Agree to take the test together, first for yourself and then grading each other. Share your test results with each other. Help each other fight and win the battle of pride!

Part Three

The Victories of the Warrior

Warrior for God's Church

Day after day men came to help David, until he had a great army, like the army of God . . . men . . . who understood the times and knew what Israel should do.

1 Chronicles 12:22,32

We have a battle to fight and an Enemy to face.

Warrior, you need a place to fight. You need fellow warriors to fight beside you. You need leaders to direct you, and you need to lead other warriors into battle. You need other warriors to keep you strong, and they need you to help them stay strong.

But where and how do we get into this battle? Where do we sign up and how do we serve? Where do we train and how do we fight? Where do we find our fellow warriors?

Jesus gives us the answer: "On this rock I will build my church, and the gates of Hades will not overcome it" (Matthew 16:18). *The church is the place where we go to war.* It is the group of people, saved and trained and united by Christ, whom he will use to assault the gates of hell.

Sometimes we hear people say things like, "Yes, I want to serve *God*. But the church? That's just *people*." How mistaken! How far we stray from the will of God when we think and act this way. And how it must grieve our Father when we say we want to serve him, but are not a part of the great assembly of people he wants to build to overcome the forces of evil! God's warrior does not go to war in a haphazard manner. He does not fight alone. He does not operate as a free agent—no—he is part of a body of people, a group that is divinely formed, commissioned, empowered, and entrusted to fight the battle against the Enemy and his forces.

The glory of God's church
A bride worth fighting for

The church, when properly built upon biblical truth and teaching, is not a mere human organization. It is a divinely designed, divinely empowered society of people that preaches, teaches, and lives out the word of God in this dark world. It is the dwelling-place of God himself through the Spirit, in which and from which we fight the battle. More than that, the church is the bride of Christ, whom he is sworn to protect against all evil, and rescue from the Evil One.

The body of our Lord, where every part fights together

The church is the body of Christ, and he is the head. Directed by our Lord (the "brains of the outfit"), we are the hands, feet, legs, eyes, ears, voice and heart of Christ himself in his war against Satan and the forces of darkness. It is the place where God intends his warriors to serve in the great conflict. If we do not serve there, we are not under his command. If we are not serving as warriors in a local church, we will be casualties, not victors, in the spiritual battle.

Do you remember what Jesus said to Peter on the night of his arrest? He predicted that Peter would turn coward and run. But he also told him that he would later come back to him again: "But I have prayed for you, Simon, that your faith may not fail. And when you have turned back, strengthen your brothers" (Luke 22:32). *Peter, strengthen your brothers!* Stand beside your fellow warriors! They will need you! And after his resurrection, when he graciously reinstated Peter to service, Jesus called Peter to take care of his flock (John 21:15–19). What message does that leave us? It says loud and clear that *the church* is the place where Jesus wants us to serve him in battle. The church is the warrior's place, alongside his fellow servants, to fight the Enemy.

Brothers, we need to be in the church—right in the middle of it. We are not meant to be marginal, back-row members. We need to be fully engaged with God's warriors, so that together we can assail the very gates of the Enemy!

There is no Plan B

But isn't the church full of fallible people? Haven't we all seen the church, and its leaders, make mistakes and misrepresent Jesus? Of course we have. But serving in the church is the only plan God has left us to follow. There is no plan B. Jesus calls us to go to war together with his church, in a local fellowship of disciples, where as a body we fight the good fight. No, the church is not perfect, but as someone once said, "If you find the perfect church, please don't join it, or you'll mess it up!" Churches can fall spiritually asleep and become lukewarm (Revelation 3:1–2,15–16). As warriors we are called to help our local church be on fire, and be fully alive. Let's be a part of the solution, not the problem. Let's set an example of zeal, commitment, and devotion, and help our churches rise to be a body that honors the name of Jesus.

Beware imposters

That being said, does this mean that any group or church that sets up shop in the name of Jesus is on the right track? No it does not! Let's not be naïve; Jesus himself said that false prophets would arise and in his name mislead and deceive many people (Matthew 7:15–23). Paul puts it this way:

> For the time will come when men will not put up with sound doctrine. Instead, to suit their own desires, they will gather around them a great number of teachers to say what their itching ears want to hear. They will turn their ears away from the truth and turn aside to myths. (2 Timothy 4:3–4)

Paul said that the time would come when there would be groups and leaders who had a form of godliness but who denied the real power of the gospel to change us into righteous people (2 Timothy 3:1–5). There are people bearing the name of Christ but not living the life—people who are not letting the power of God transform them into to the image of Jesus, but who are just going through the motions, talking the talk and not walking the walk of a true disciple of Christ.

If we want to be victorious warriors, we must be active members of a local church. But we must be sure that group is built on the solid rock of Jesus and his word—the Bible. We must check out a church's life and doctrine before we join with them to fight the battle, or we will find ourselves on the losing side.

The local church is where you are "discovered" and put to work

He went through Syria and Cilicia, strengthening the churches. He came to Derbe and then to Lystra, where a disciple named Timothy lived, whose mother was a Jewess and a believer, but whose father was a Greek. The brothers at Lystra and Iconium spoke well of him. Paul wanted to take him along on the journey, so he circumcised him because of the Jews who lived in that area, for they all knew that his father was a Greek. As they traveled from town to town, they delivered the decisions reached by the apostles and elders in Jerusalem for the people to obey. So the churches were strengthened in the faith and grew daily in numbers. (Acts 15:41–16:5)

Paul's former helper John Mark has stumbled along the way, and needs some time to recover. Paul and his partner Barnabas part ways, and Barnabas takes John Mark with him to get the rehab project going. When Paul and his new cohort Silas come to Lystra, Paul is looking for warriors to help in the ministry. He finds Timothy there, and when Paul invites him to join with him and Silas, Timothy becomes a key soldier in spreading the gospel and building the church.

How does Paul know Timothy is the right man for the job? *Because he has proven himself in his local church.* Young Timothy is a brother in the fellowship in Lystra, faithfully serving there. The church, which knows him so well, readily recommends him for this opportunity.

Do you want to be a warrior for Jesus? Do you want to make a difference for him? Then serve wholeheartedly in your local church. Get right in the middle of the ministry there. Give yourself fully. That is the place to begin. It is the only place you can really make a difference. We would have never known about Timothy had he not been a faithful servant in his home church. Are you fully engaged in the real work of your local fellowship? Would they commend you as Timothy's congregation did? Warriors, this is what Jesus wants all of us to do, and who he wants us to be!

Yes, we must decide and declare that we are warriors for God. But that is only the beginning; as warriors, we have to prove ourselves. And we prove our character, our heart, and our devotion in our local church.

*But you know that **Timothy has proved himself**, because as a son with his father he has served with me in the work of the gospel.* (Philippians 2:22, emphasis added)

*In addition, we are sending with them **our brother who has often proved to us in many ways that he is zealous**, and now even more so because of his great confidence in you.* (2 Corinthians 8:22, emphasis added)

The local church is where we are trained and equipped.

It was he who gave some as apostles, some as prophets, some as evangelists, and some as pastors and teachers, to equip the saints for the work of ministry, that is, to build up the body of Christ. (Ephesians 4:11–12 NET)

All of us need to be equipped, prepared, and trained to be warriors in service to God. When we become disciples, we are entering into service, but we do not yet know how to serve. God knows this, and he provides us the place and the means to get the training we need. And that place, fellow warriors, is in your local church family.

Most of us will not become evangelists or elders. But we all need to be warriors. We all need to serve Jesus in the local body of Christ. And we need to be taught how to do that. We need pastors (also known as shepherds or elders), evangelists, and teachers to train us to be effective. And that happens in the local church.

Whatever age we are—be we young warriors, mature warriors, or seasoned vets—we all need training and equipping. We need to learn how to serve in a way that brings glory to Jesus and joy to those around us. We can't just jump in with no spiritual coaching and mentoring. Without godly, experienced training, even our best intentions and efforts will fall short. And this isn't just for the young—we all need "refresher courses" to keep our skills sharp.

Warrior, place yourself under godly leadership in the church. Be the most teachable, hungry learner you know how to be. Don't be independent and difficult to work with. If you serve in any ministry, let experienced veterans teach and mold you into the best disciple you can be. If you are a member of a small group, allow the leader to help you to grow. If you serve your church in a specific ministry—children's ministry, youth ministry, campus ministry, or by serving the poor—whatever you do, learn from the people leading you. Make their work a joy. Let them help you become the best warrior you can be for Jesus.

As you grow, you may one day have your own opportunities to lead. Don't stop being equipped! Keep learning from others. Once we begin to lead, our hunger to learn and our humility of heart should *increase*, not decrease. Leaders must not become prideful men who think they know it all. Instead, leaders need to remain good followers all the days of our lives!

Some of us may be thinking, "Yes, but Timothy became an evangelist. I am not on the church staff. So, how do I fit in here?"

Consider this passage:

Deacons, likewise, are to be men worthy of respect, sincere, not indulging in much wine, and not pursuing dishonest gain. They must keep hold of the deep truths of the faith with a clear conscience. They must first be tested; and then if there is nothing against them, let them serve as deacons. . . . Those who have served well gain an excellent standing and great assurance in their faith in Christ Jesus.
(1 Timothy 3:8–10,13)

Most warriors will not be on the supported staff of the church. Nor should they be. *Brother, you should still be a mighty warrior in the church.* We all need to be servants (which is just what the word *deacon* means, by the way). As a matter of fact, without "laymen" serving in the body of Christ—"regular guys" going to school, working a job, raising a family, living out there in the workaday world—the church cannot win the battle. Warriors living the Christian life in the "real world" are the ones who will reach the world for Christ. The army doesn't just need generals; it also needs foot soldiers on the ground. It needs men on the front lines, fighting day in and day out against the forces of darkness; it needs soldiers advancing through smoke and fire in hand-to-hand combat. The church needs these warriors to effectively share the gospel in our communities, neighborhoods, and workplaces.

The local church is where our gifts are identified and developed

Just as each of us has one body with many members, and these members do not all have the same function, so in Christ we who are many form one body, and each member belongs to all the others. We have different gifts, according to the grace given us. If a man's gift is prophesying, let him use it in proportion to his faith. If it is serving, let him serve; if it is teaching, let him teach; if it is encouraging, let him encourage; if it is contributing to the needs of others, let him give generously;

if it is leadership, let him govern diligently; if it is showing mercy, let him do it cheerfully. (Romans 12:4–8)

Most of us think that being gifted is for the one-in-a-million person: the professional athlete, the mathematical genius, the rock star. Not so! God gifts every disciple with abilities and talents. And he gives us those gifts not just for our own benefit, but so that we might serve his church.

Many men in our world spend their lives feeling empty and useless. They are bored, selfish, and unproductive. They devote themselves to shallow, selfish pursuits limited to their own pleasure and entertainment. A warrior gifted by the Spirit of God and at work in his service is a powerful force for good. He sees the work of his hands and knows he is making a difference. He watches other people change and grow because of what he gives.

As warriors, the church is where our gifts come into focus and where we find ourselves being used to help others. The battle to win people to Christ, to help others grow, and to serve the needy both within and without the church is waged and won by gifted warriors—men out there on the battlefield serving, sacrificing, helping, and equipping others.

Brother, you have something to give. Let the leaders of your local church help you identify your gifts and put you to work ministering in your local family of believers. Your life will make a difference, and you will feel great satisfaction as God uses you to your highest and best potential.

The local church is where our weaknesses are exposed and our character is developed

We have already seen how character weaknesses in Saul kept him from fulfilling a destiny filled with incredible promise. We have also seen how David allowed his lust, pride, and selfishness to severely damage his nation, his family, and even—for a time—his own heart.

Satan studies us, discovers our weaknesses, and attacks us where we are vulnerable. He seeks to use our weaknesses to undermine and overthrow us. We all need other warriors in our lives to help protect us from Satan's attacks.

Consider these verses that tell us of God's plan for having people in our lives to help us resist and avoid evil:

Let a righteous man strike me—it is a kindness;
let him rebuke me—it is oil on my head.
My head will not refuse it. (Psalm 141:5)

Better is open rebuke
than hidden love. (Proverbs 27:5)

Wounds from a friend can be trusted,
but an enemy multiplies kisses. (Proverbs 27:6)

As iron sharpens iron,
so one man sharpens another. (Proverbs 27:17)

Welcome help from other warriors

Men, we need to surround ourselves with other strong men who love us enough to tell us the truth. And the stronger we are, the *more* we need strong men around us. Why is this so? For two reasons: First, when you are strong, you are a greater threat to the Enemy, which makes you his particular target. If he can take you down, he will do greater harm to God's cause. Second, if we are strong men, others around us are less likely to challenge us. Out of respect or fear, they may choose to leave us alone, even when they see something in us that is harmful and displeasing to God. Or they may just assume we are right, doubt their own opinion, and back off.

All of this leaves us vulnerable. We need, as warriors for God, to guard each other from Satan. And men, we need to invite other men into our lives, opening the door of our hearts and minds to their challenges, advice, and sharpening words. If we do not let other men help us, we will either never get going at all, or we will stall in our growth along the way. As warriors for God, we need to be the most humble, most teachable, most approachable men in the church. Otherwise, we are setting ourselves up for a huge defeat in our future.

What if Saul had actually listened to his son Jonathan? He would have gotten behind David and helped mentor him to become the next king. Instead, he did not listen, fought against David—and against

God—and destroyed himself.

What if David had a truth-telling Nathan in his life *before* he got involved with Bathsheba? What if someone had said, "David, you are a warrior! Why are you lounging around the palace while your men are out fighting? Now that God has given you the kingship, don't get lazy. Go out there and keep fighting the battles of God!."

Warriors, we need strong men like this in our lives to protect us from our own selves and from the devil. Let's go after these kinds of relationships in our local fellowship. Let's invite men into our lives, and call our fellow warriors higher in their service for God.

Real commitment brings out the real you—and that's a good thing

As you work together with others in your church family, your real self will emerge. Your strengths and weaknesses will be plainly seen. When my wife and I teach on family, we often say, "Who you are at home is who you really are." The same is true as you serve in your spiritual family. If you are just showing up at Sunday services and no one at church really knows you, no one will know the real you. When you work side by side with people—spreading the gospel together, helping people to reach spiritual maturity, serving in the church—the real you is right there. You aren't just putting up a front; you are being yourself. That means as you work together, people can see how you handle pressure, how you handle different or even difficult personalities.

Have you ever noticed the number of times that Jesus had to deal with pride, conflict, and disagreements among the Twelve? They argued about which one of them was the greatest (Luke 22:24). They were competitive and got indignant with each other (Matthew 20:24). They rarely, if ever, had open conflict with Jesus. It was with *each other* that their selfishness and weaknesses showed up. And so it will be with us. As we serve together, our sins and weaknesses will emerge. That does not mean we are not genuine disciples; it does mean we are disciples who have growing to do, and this will be our chance to do just that!

The letters Paul wrote addressed all kinds of issues between Christians in the local churches. They were followers of Jesus, yet their weaknesses and sins came out in the family setting of the church. Being disciples does not mean we never sin against each other; it means that when we do, we repent and make it right with God and the church. This is what we mean when we say that the local church is the best place to see and overcome our weaknesses.

I would highly suggest forming a Warrior Group in your local congregation—a group of men who get together frequently, and who hold each other accountable, inspire each other, challenge each other to be our best, encourage each other, and become godly friends. A group like this will change your life and change your church. And yes, the local fellowship of the church is where this ought to be happening. The trend in so many religious groups today is for people to attend worship, but not to have spiritually close, transformative relationships. One of the most wonderful things the church does is worship together, but the church is far more than a worshipping society—*it is a fellowship of warriors!*

The local church is where we learn to function as a team

David's Mighty Men were a team. Jesus built a team of twelve men. The Apostle Paul had a group of men around him who served together to preach the good news, win disciples to Christ, and build strong churches. He called them his fellow soldiers, fellow workers, fellow servants, fellow prisoners, yokefellows, and partners. A quick count of these words shows multiple times where this type of phraseology is used by Paul.[3] We may think of him as the consummate loner, the man who stood by himself with God and did not need anyone else. Far from it! Paul was a team player, a man who hated to be alone—he once left an open door of ministry opportunity just because his coworker Titus was not there:

> Now when I went to Troas to preach the gospel of Christ and found that the Lord had opened a door for me, I still had no peace of mind, because I did not find my brother Titus there. So I said good-by to them and went on to Macedonia. (2 Corinthians 2:12–13)

Whatever was on Paul's mind, we know this: he knew he needed partners, fellow servants and soldiers. Brothers, if a man as strong and faithful as Paul needed fellow warriors, how much more do we!

---

3 Rom 16:3, 9, 21; 1 Cor 3:9; 2 Cor 6:1; 8:23; Phil 2:25; 4:3; Col 1:7; 4:7, 10–11; 1 Th 3:2; Phm 1:1–2, 23–24

A call to engage in the local church

Be on your guard; stand firm in the faith; be men of courage; be strong. Do everything in love. (1 Corinthians 16:13–14)

I have said it before and I will say it again: the men are the ceiling of the church. A church can rise no higher than the faith, love, and spirituality of its *men*.

Brothers, we need to stop being mere observers at church. We need to get into the action. We need to dive into the lives of others, and invite others in our lives. Warriors need strong, iron-sharpening-iron friendships with other men (Proverbs 27:17).

Most women instinctively know they need friendships. They love to hang out together. They seek each other out. They talk on the phone. They share their hearts, their feelings, and their lives with their sisters. No wonder women are so often spiritually stronger than we are!

The sisters in the fellowship can serve, give, pray, beg, prod, push, and yes, even nag—but until we *as men* get together and get going, their most courageous and sacrificial efforts will be limited, at best. Until we get going, the sisters will not be able to move our local church forward the way God wants them to—not with us as a ball and chain around the legs of the body of Christ! No, I am *not* complaining about the sisters here—God bless them! They don't need to slow down—*we need to speed up.*

Brothers, when are we going to build strong, godly friendships? When are we going to become a band of brothers? When we do, the church will feel the power. Come on, brothers—let's stop being independent, foolish and isolated. Let's obey God and become a dynamic, powerful, loving spiritual fellowship of men that inspires the body of Christ and grows to the glory of God!

As I was writing this book, I met with a group of guys to plan a retreat for the men of our congregation. None of the men in the group are on the church staff. This group is a Mighty Man group that I had formed a year earlier to help each other and our church to grow.

We met together and began to plan the retreat. As we worked together, the brothers became more and more fired up. We selected the theme *Warrior*. We planned speeches, classes, and discussion groups. Those Mighty Men did most of the teaching, led the worship, made the introductions, and carried out the administration. They came up with the idea of giving every man who participated in the retreat a "dog tag" on a chain to wear around as a reminder and memento of what we learned and the commitments we made. On the tag we put this inscription and verse:

> ## WARRIOR
> *They were brave warriors, ready for battle.*
> 1 Chronicles 12:8

When the brothers who planned this event showed up that Friday night, they were already on fire! Their spirit began to spread through the room. More and more men began to catch the vision to be warriors for God. More and more men became convicted of their need to grow, to shake off lethargy, to step up, to lead their wives, their families, and our church. Lives were changed that weekend. We returned home on Saturday and took the spirit of the retreat into our church worship service the next morning. The whole church could feel the fire of the men who had gone to that retreat.

When men engage in the work of helping and leading their own brothers, great things happen! Mighty Men come forth. Men who were once floundering turn around and catch fire for God.

Look what happened with David's Mighty Men—they start out in bad shape, but become a mighty force for good: "All those who were in distress or in debt or discontented gathered around him, and he became their leader. About four hundred men were with him" (1 Samuel 22:2). Out of this fellowship of distressed, discontented and indebted men, the Mighty Men of Israel emerge. In short order, their numbers grow from four hundred to six hundred (1 Samuel 22:2, 23:13).

This same thing needs to happen in our churches and in our lives, and it can!

Try this, brother warrior: Get some men together who want to serve God and who are willing to bond to each other. Then watch as their faith builds, their love increases, and their number grows. Men long to be a part of a zealous fellowship of warriors. It is attractive. It is inspiring, fun, and exhilarating. It gets our blood boiling. It teaches us what real men and true manhood are all about. Can we say it? *It is just flat-out awesome!*

David's group of Mighty Men continues to grow after David becomes king. Look at this description, tallying David's warriors:

> Men of half the tribe of Manasseh, designated by name to come and make David king—18,000; men of Issachar, who understood the times and knew what Israel should do—200 chiefs, with all their relatives under their command; men of Zebulun, experienced soldiers prepared for battle with every type of weapon, to help David with undivided loyalty—50,000. (1 Chronicles 12:31–33)

David started out as an outcast with no one on his side. Then we see him with just a handful of men. Soon there are four hundred, then six hundred. Now there are thousands and thousands. The warrior spirit begins to sweep through the men of Israel, and before long, thousands join with David, because "they knew what Israel should do."

It reminds me of the prayer of Joel:

> Proclaim this among the nations:
>> Prepare for war!
> Rouse the warriors!
>> Let all the fighting men draw near and attack.
> Beat your plowshares into swords
>> and your pruning hooks into spears.
> Let the weakling say,
>> "I am strong!"
> Come quickly, all you nations from every side,
>> and assemble there.
> Bring down your warriors, O LORD! (Joel 3:9–11)

Brothers, I do not know how many Mighty Men will rally in your church or in mine, but I know this: When we get men together who love God and are dedicated to being his warriors, and dedicated to being a band of brothers, watch out—great things are going to happen! May the local church be the place where the warriors of God are roused. If we are to see revival now, the men of the church need to start the revolution.

Rouse your warriors in our day, O Lord! And, my brothers, may you and I be right there, ready for battle, in the midst of that mighty company.

Vignette: Benaiah and the Lion
Based on 2 Samuel 23:20–23

*Benaiah son of Jehoiada was a valiant fighter from Kabzeel, who per-
formed great exploits. He struck down two of Moab's best men. He also
went down into a pit on a snowy day and killed a lion.*

2 Samuel 23:20

Eleazar, Jashobeam, and Shammah have earned places in the company of David's
Mighty Men. David's growing army is still on the run, trying to escape Saul and his
murderous threats. But any time you get a group of daredevil young warriors together, anything can happen.

No one would ever forget the winter day Benaiah took on the lion.
A crew of David's Mighty Men were tramping our way through the
snow-covered woods. We weren't used to snow. We were slipping, sliding, falling—and freezing—all at once. We were supposed to be hunting
down dinner, but Jashobeam and Shammah were making so much racket
I was sure every bird and deer within earshot had already fled to safety.

"Hey!" Benaiah's booming voice stopped us all dead in our tracks.
"Come over here! You're not gonna believe this!" We found him staring
over the edge of a pit just off the trail ahead. "The villagers must have set
this up as a trap, and look what they caught—a lion!"

We ran over to see. Just as we got to the edge and looked down, the
lion sprang upwards with a vicious roar. We all jumped back, crashing
over each other in a heap.

"Some fearless Mighty Men you are!" Only Benaiah hadn't moved.
He stood laughing at us from the edge of the pit, tossing his dagger hand
to hand. "Aw, poor babies. Should I get your mama to take you home?"
When we all scowled at him, he grinned back at us. "That lion's not going
anywhere. Look! The pit's too steep and icy."

He bent over the side of the pit, waved and growled down at the
lion. It roared back at him.

Benaiah glanced back at us, a wild glint sparking in his eyes. We had
seen him get that look many times before. "Uh-oh," said Shammah. We
both took a step back, sensing what was coming next.

Benaiah said, "I think that cat needs some company down there. I heard the villagers talking about a lion prowling these parts. They've been scared to death. Well, I say it's time for this big bad kitty to go away—permanently!" He held up his dagger with his left hand, unsheathed his sword with his right, and whipped both blades around in mock combat.

"Don't even think about it, fool!" Jashobeam yelled, shaking his head.

That got everybody going:

"Are you out of your mind?"

"It's snowing, big guy—it'll be slippery down there! You've got only two feet; he has four—with claws!

"Feel like dying today, do you?"

"Nice knowing you!"

Benaiah looked at us and laughed his crazy laugh. "Nah, boys, this is gonna be fun. Be seeing you guys soon!" He grinned, turned, and leapt into the pit.

The lion roared.

Just once.

Chapter Fifteen

The Young Warrior

I was young and now I am old,
*   yet I have never seen the righteous forsaken*
*   or their children begging bread.*

Psalm 37:25

God calls us to be his warriors at every season of our lives: as young men, as maturing men, and as seasoned men. The challenges we face at these various stages are in some ways similar, yet significantly different. Whatever season we are in, we must, with God's wisdom guiding us, and his power strengthening us, live it victoriously.

Young warrior

Jesse had seven of his sons pass before Samuel, but Samuel said to him, "The LORD has not chosen these." So he asked Jesse, "Are these all the sons you have?"
*   "There is still the youngest," Jesse answered, "but he is tending the sheep."*
*   Samuel said, "Send for him; we will not sit down until he arrives."*
(1 Samuel 16:10–11)

"Now then, tell my servant David, 'This is what the LORD Almighty says: I took you from the pasture and from following the flock to be ruler over my people Israel.'"
(2 Samuel 7:8)

Saul, the first king of Israel, has failed in his leadership. God is looking for a new leader, one who will guide his people in the way he wants it done. He is looking for a special man, a person with the heart, the integrity, and the faith to do the job right. He is seeking "a man after his own heart" (1 Samuel 13:14). How will God determine who has such a heart? Where will he find such a man?

He finds a young boy, out tending his father's sheep.

The years of life from our teens to our mid-twenties are some of the most important of our lives. In them we lay the foundation for our future, and set the direction in which we will go. What are some of the key things that we as young warriors need to do?

Embrace what is in front of you and do it with all your heart

Meet young David, a warrior-in-training:

When we first meet David, he is a young shepherd. His older brothers are soldiers in the army, but David is away, alone, looking out after the sheep.

As a young man, David is chosen by God to be the next king of Israel. He is probably still a teen. But God sees something in him that causes him to select David above any other man in the whole nation as the man he trusts to lead his people.

Young warrior, do you want God to use your life? Do you want to make a difference?

Many of us want to do something great with our lives, and something spectacular for God. We imagine ourselves making a grand entrance with some epic victory. We want to start off the way David did, by being a giant slayer. But wait, brothers, defeating giants is not actually where David got his start. If you want to become a warrior like David, you can't skip the most important steps of all.

David got his start long before Goliath, back when no one knew him or noticed him. He began his ascent to being God's warrior in utter obscurity, all alone, looking after his father's sheep. He spent years alone in the wilderness, where no one else saw him or knew what he was doing. Many of us want to do the glorious thing and kill the giant. Who wants to tend the sheep and be an errand boy? But brothers, that is how we prove ourselves and our hearts before the Lord. There is no other way.

David's mindset

I wonder if David ever felt overlooked or insignificant. He is the youngest of eight brothers. His three oldest brothers are serving in Saul's army. They've got the glamor jobs. What is David doing? He's out in the desert, hanging out with a flock of sheep! He other job is to be the errand boy for his dad, taking his brothers their food. When he shows up at the battlefield, his oldest brother Eliab sarcastically says to him, "With whom did you leave those few sheep in the desert?" (1 Samuel 17:28)

We don't know exactly how this kind of treatment makes David feel, but we do know that he does not allow it to taint his heart or his walk with God. We also know that in spite of his brother's mocking, David makes great use of his time out in the wilderness, alone with the sheep and with God.

What are some of the things that David does while he is out with the sheep?

He draws close to God

First, David gets close to God out there in the desert. Read Psalm 23. My own best guess is that David wrote this immortal song while he was out herding sheep. Even if he wrote the psalm later in life, it tells you how David looked at God. He viewed God as his shepherd. He built a relationship with God that was so intimate, so trusting that God noticed, and David maintained that closeness for all the years of his life.

Young warrior, what do you do when you are all alone, when no one else is around? How do you use that time? How do you fill the empty hours, the quiet days? What is going on in your heart, your mind, and your life? If you want to be a young warrior for God, use those hours in a way that honors God—don't throw them away.

Young man, now is the time to get close to God. Now is the time to begin to walk with him. Now is the time to pour out your heart to him, to learn and embrace his love for you. Now is the time to walk with God as David did.

Look closely at Psalm 19. In it David describes the beauty of God he sees in nature— nature that he learns to love while he is out herding sheep:

The heavens declare the glory of God;
        the skies proclaim the work of his hands.
Day after day they pour forth speech;
        night after night they display knowledge.
There is no speech or language
        where their voice is not heard.
Their voice goes out into all the earth,
        their words to the ends of the world.

In the heavens he has pitched a tent for the sun,
        which is like a bridegroom coming forth from his pavilion,
        like a champion rejoicing to run his course.
It rises at one end of the heavens
        and makes its circuit to the other;
        nothing is hidden from its heat. (Psalm 19:1–6)

Pretty awesome, don't you think? David writes a song about the beauty of God that he sees in nature. I think that he wrote this as a young man, or about his life as a young man in the outdoors.

Notice the way David changes the subject in the middle of the psalm. He goes from the glory of God in nature to the glory of God in the word:

The law of the LORD is perfect,
        reviving the soul.
The statutes of the LORD are trustworthy,
        making wise the simple.
The precepts of the LORD are right,
        giving joy to the heart.
The commands of the LORD are radiant,
        giving light to the eyes.
The fear of the LORD is pure,
        enduring forever.
The ordinances of the LORD are sure
        and altogether righteous.
They are more precious than gold,
        than much pure gold;

they are sweeter than honey,
than honey from the comb.
By them is your servant warned;
in keeping them there is great reward. (Psalm 19:7–11)

Once again we see the heart of this man. He loves God as his Shepherd. He is in awe of God as the creator of all nature, with its beauty and might. And he loves God's word. He sings about it. He knows it. He memorizes it. He thinks about it. It is like honey to him (honey was pretty much the only sweet stuff available in David's day). God's word is worth more than money to him. He is warned and rewarded by it.

How about us, young warriors? How is our love of the Bible? Do we read it, devour it, memorize it? Or do we spend more time watching TV, playing video games, and just goofing off? Does God know you as a young man who passionately loves the word? Do you understand that the Bible is the voice of God, the voice of your heavenly Father, the voice you would rather hear than any other voice in all the world? How much time are you spending reading and studying?

Young warriors, let us love the word of God the way our brother and hero David did!

He appreciates opportunities to work hard and grow

David does not view his shepherd years as a waste of time before he gets to the "important stuff" like fighting and leading. He views shepherding as something honorable, something good, something wonderful. He does not get a bad attitude, thinking, "Why I am I out here away from other people, my family, my friends, just watching these stupid sheep?' No, he looks at the job his father has given him to do as a thing of honor, a privilege, and as a way that he himself could imitate the heart of his God. That is a young man who has a good heart! That is a young man whom God considered worthy to one day lead the whole nation with the integrity, courage and love that God himself would have. He is the young man after the heart of God.

So, young brother, what jobs have you been given at home or in your church? Do you feel they are menial and unworthy of your time and attention? Are you blowing them off as beneath you, as something for lesser men to do? Jesus says that the one who is least of all is the greatest (Matthew 20:25–28). God notices stuff like this. It speaks volumes about our heart.

When David is sent out to watch the sheep while his brothers go off to war, he does not sit there sulking, wishing he was in the army, wishing he was more respected and appreciated.

Young warrior, respect must be earned. You cannot expect it, you cannot demand it. You have to prove yourself worthy by who you are and what you do. Learn to love working hard at the little things now, so that God (and people) will entrust you with the big things later.

David practices courage

You might think that tending sheep is a boring job that requires minimal brains and talent, and no courage. You would think wrong. Tending sheep in the wilderness is a surprisingly dangerous job, one that tests David's courage, hones his fighting skills, and prepares him to slay giants and lead an army!

During his years as a shepherd, David faces off with lions and bears. Lions and bears! Most men I know, if given the choice between risking their life fighting a lion, and losing a few sheep to a predator, would probably let the sheep go. I imagine David could have thought, "Too bad, we lost a couple of sheep, but that's part of the risk in being a sheep, I guess." It's not like anyone was there watching—no one would have known if David had wimped out. And no one would have criticized him for saving his own life at the cost of a couple of sheep. But no, that is not the heart of this young warrior. Here is what he says:

> *"Your servant has been keeping his father's sheep. When a lion or a bear came and carried off a sheep from the flock, I went after it, struck it and rescued the sheep from its mouth. When it turned on me, I seized it by its hair, struck it and killed it."* (1 Samuel 17:34–35)

Did you catch that? *"I went after it."* Yes, the lion and the bear were trotting off with sheep dangling from their mouths when David went after them. He chased them down. He struck them, *and they turned on him*. He grabbed them by their hair and killed them in hand-to-paw combat. Dude, that took guts! And no one was watching! He could have just let the sheep go. Nobody told him to risk his life, no one challenged him to do it—he did it all by himself.

Young warrior, what job have you been given to do right now? Does it seem boring? Unexciting? Like there's no chance for you to prove yourself? Think again. Opportunities for you to stand the devil down are all around you in middle school, high school, college, in your family, on the job, in your neighborhood, with your friends, or all by yourself. The question is, when the lion and bear show up, do you go after them, or do you run away or hold back? Or are you sitting around sulking because your dad or mom have given you jobs to do around the house that you really don't want to do?

What else does David do out there?

He learns to be close to God

He prays. He seeks God. Instead of sitting around lusting, wasting time, just being bored, he prays. He sings. He writes songs. He learns to play musical instruments. Where does he learn to play the harp? My guess is that he practices and plays all the time out there with those sheep. It is probably how he got them settled down at night—a free concert under stars, starring David as the singer and harp player!

What else does David do?

He practices slingshot

David takes out Goliath with one shot. That is a long, long shot, under intense pressure: thousands of soldiers are watching, he's aiming for a moving target, and he has to hit a small spot just under the visor of the helmet. If he misses, he is down to four rocks, and Goliath will attack him with his spear the size of a weaver's beam. David better not miss. My guess? David has spent hours upon hours practicing out there in the desert. Instead of wasting his time goofing off, he has used the time to better himself. He has become lethal with a slingshot.

And so when Goliath shows up, David knows he can make that shot. Does he depend on God? Yes, of course. That is what he says: "The LORD who delivered me from the paw of the lion and the paw of the bear will deliver me from the hand of this Philistine" (1 Samuel 17:37). But he also takes the weapon of his choice—not Saul's sword, but the one David is familiar with, the one he has spent years mastering: the slingshot.

So, young man, what are you doing with your spare time? Playing video games? Watching TV? Chatting and texting on your cell phone? Or are you praying to God, singing to God, learning responsibility, embracing the jobs your parents have given you to do and learning some valuable skills? How about school? Are you doing your homework? Are you giving it your best, or just going through the motions? If we are supposed to do all things for the glory of God, how can we goof off in school and call ourselves warriors for God? Let's get the heart of David, and get it right now!

So let us summarize. To become a young warrior we must:

- Seek after God himself—to know, love, and be close to him.
- Seek to draw near to God in nature and in time spent alone with him.
- Seek God by learning, meditating on, and memorizing the word of God.
- Embrace whatever jobs, responsibilities, and tasks we have been given, even if they seem unimportant or unexciting, knowing that this is how we learn to love God, serve him, and serve others.
- Do whatever we do with honor and integrity, knowing that even if no one else is watching us, God is watching, and we do all we do for him and for the people who trust us.
- Learn helpful skills. Get good at some things—really good.
- Choose to have a good attitude when we are overlooked and it seems like other people are getting more attention and opportunities. Take what is in front of us and make the most of it. If we do that, God will give us more opportunities later. But it we give in to a bad attitude or a lazy attitude now, when our "Goliath" comes along we won't be ready to step up to the challenge.
- Even if other people make fun of you, go ahead and serve in the humble job. God exalts the humble young man. He will bring down the prideful man—of any age (Matthew 23:12).

My training days

When I began serving in the campus ministry I was twenty-one years old. I was single. I was in a fast-growing congregation with many student members and large crowds in attendance. This church was a training ground for young men going into campus ministry. Churches from all over the country came to us and hired our young graduates to come to work for them, to help their churches build campus ministries like we had in our home church. Many of my friends, and many of the students I had helped to train, were being called into the ministry. Guys were going out, and they were experiencing remarkable success. They, by the grace and power of God, were duplicating what they had seen in their home church. It was an exciting thing to be a part of.

Most of them were getting lots of opportunities to speak, teach, and preach. Me? I stayed in my church, continuing the work there. I was working in a strong church with a great preacher and two outstanding elders who were superb teachers. We had a Sunday school class with a couple of hundred college kids in attendance every week. One of the elders, a man whom we all loved and respected deeply, did the teaching. I sat in the audience. I enjoyed listening to him, but after a while, I got a bad attitude.

All my friends and trainees were calling me from their new campus ministry positions, telling me how they were teaching classes and getting to preach a lot. Here I was, leading small group discussions and some devotionals, but that was about it. Over time, I grew more and more frustrated. "I must be the only campus minister in the world not even teaching my students in Sunday School," I thought to myself. I got more and more sullen and upset.

Finally, the church leaders asked me to teach on Sunday , . . but it was not the huge college class I wanted to teach. No, they asked me to teach the Adult 4 class—the class for the oldest people in the church! I went reluctantly to class, and there they sat, about twenty-five elderly people using canes and walkers, who I thought could hardly hear me and stay focused on my lessons. At first I was so frustrated and insulted! In my youthful pride and ambition (and lack of compassion), I thought, *What a waste of my time and talent!*

But you know what? I repented. I decided to give my heart, make the best of the situation, and do the best I could do. I was unsure what to teach. I decided to just go through the books of 1 and 2 Samuel. Why not teach ancient history for an ancient Sunday School class?

Two wonderful things happened. First, I fell in love with those people, and they came to love me as well. I saw their love, their faith, and their hearts. I learned to respect people who had served God faithfully for years and who had courage and maturity I had never seen before.

In time they became so loyal to me that if the elders and preacher had ever decided to fire me (which never happened), the Adult 4 Class would have defended me to the death!

The second thing that happened was that I fell in love with the story of David in 1 and 2 Samuel. I had never taught David's story before, and would not have selected it had I been teaching the college class. But it was perfect for those folks in Adult 4. Teaching that material changed my life forever. I would not be writing this book some forty years later had I not come to love the David story when I was a young minister, teaching the oldest members of the church. I thank God for placing me with those wonderful people, and for using that opportunity to introduce me to David, the man who became, next to Jesus and his story, my greatest Bible hero.

God humbled me through all of this, but he also used it to lift me up. Eventually I got to teach the college class on Sundays, and I did so for many years. I also got to teach a special class on Monday afternoons as well. What did I teach on those Mondays? Among other things, I taught the David story. Today, many of my former students are now serving God as adults in churches all over the world. They still tell me that the teaching that I did on David (and other Old Testament stories as well) helped to shape the foundation of their faith, and to ignite in them a deeper love for God and his word. Truly, God moves in mysterious ways!

What else does the young warrior need to learn?

Develop a teachable spirit

For this principle, let's take a quick look at Jesus in his youth. The first glimpse we have of Jesus as a young man is enlightening:

When he was twelve years old, they went up to the Feast, according to the custom. After the Feast was over, while his parents were returning home, the boy Jesus stayed behind in Jerusalem, but they were unaware of it. Thinking he was in their company, they traveled on for a day. Then they began looking for him among their relatives and friends. When they did not find him, they went back to Jerusalem to look for him. After three days they found him in the temple courts, sitting among the teachers, listening to them and asking them questions. (Luke 2:42–46)

Jesus is twelve years old. What is he doing? What can we learn from him as younger men?

- He is in the temple courts.
- He is sitting among the teachers.
- He is listening.
- He is asking questions.

Young men, if you want to follow Jesus, imitate him by doing what he did when he was young. Go to church. Sit among the teachers. Listen to them. Ask questions. Take it all in. Be a sponge. Take every opportunity you can to learn from other men.

Look, Jesus was the Son of God—he could have just ignored these guys. He could have gone in there and straightened them all out. But instead, he shows respect. He sits. He listens. He asks. Those are three great ways for you to imitate him right now in your teens and early twenties.

- Sit.
- Listen.
- Ask.

Get a mentor

I don't know if David ever had a mentor, but many other young men in the Bible had them. Joshua had Moses. Elisha had Elijah. Timothy had Paul. Young brother, find an older man to learn from, and let him teach you.

Manhood is learned from other men. Manhood is transferred from man to man. If you had or have a father who has taught or is teaching you manhood, especially if your dad is a disciple of Jesus, be grateful! There is nothing more special than having a godly father to teach you the ways of the Lord as outlined in Deuteronomy 6 and Ephesians 6.

But many of us were not raised this way. We may have come from an unbelieving or unspiritual background. We may have had no male influence, or even a negative one. Whatever the case, make every effort to get and keep older men in your life now. Even if you have a godly father, I urge you to invite godly mentors to influence and shape your life.

Choose men who love God; men who have faith and deep spirituality and integrity. Humbly ask them if they can help you and spend time with you. If they agree, make it easy for them to get with you. You should be the initiator. Don't make them do all the work, or have to hunt you down and seek you out. Pursue them. Without being a pest, be persistent and eager to learn. Respect them and their time, and adjust your schedule to theirs. Seek their advice. In a good sense, pummel them with questions!

Let us not be the foolish young man of Proverbs:

> *The way of a fool seems right to him,*
> *but a wise man listens to advice.* (Proverbs 12:15)

Instead, let us be the wise young man:

> *Listen to advice and accept instruction,*
> *and in the end you will be wise.* (Proverbs 19:20)

Young men, God's church is full of mature and seasoned warriors who would love to train up a young warrior. I urge you: Don't let pride or awkwardness or insecurity come in the way of seeking the help you need to grow. Be eager to grow. Ask big. Do so not for yourself, but for God and his glory. And when you have learned, it will be your turn to pass your heart and skills on to others.

What do we learn from David's example as a young warrior?

Become warriors! But do so the way David did:

- Serve humbly where you are right now. Have a godly, giving spirit in serving behind the scenes.

- Serve faithfully.

- Serve with integrity.

- Do whatever you do with excellence.

- Do what you do for the glory of God.

- Demonstrate courage and integrity wherever you are and whatever you are doing at this stage in your life.

- Don't get upset if you don't get the glamor job. Don't be jealous when others get the glory and you don't.

- Work hard all the time, not just when people are watching.

Remember, *who you are when you are alone is who you really are.* Walk with God. Pray to God. Love his word. Learn his word. Memorize his word. Sing and worship. Claim God as your loving Shepherd. Know that he is with you always.

Then you will be able to say, as the author of Psalm 71:5 declares,

"For you have been my hope, O Sovereign LORD,
my confidence since my youth."

And when you are a seasoned warrior, you will be able to look back on your life and say along with David,

I was young and now I am old,
yet I have never seen the righteous forsaken
or their children begging bread. (Psalm 37:25)

Young warrior, let God shape and guide your life from the beginning, through the middle, and all the way to the end. Come what may, our God will bring you through every battle to the day of final victory!

Chapter Sixteen

The Mature Warrior

But David thought to himself, "One of these days I will be destroyed by the hand of Saul. The best thing I can do is to escape to the land of the Philistines. Then Saul will give up searching for me anywhere in Israel, and I will slip out of his hand." So David and the six hundred men with him left and went over to Achish son of Maoch king of Gath.

1 Samuel 27:1–2

When I was in my forties, I ran the Marine Corps Marathon in Washington, DC. Somewhere in the middle of the run that never seemed to end, I started asking myself, "Just what were you thinking, Sam, when you signed up to do this?" The finish line felt impossibly far away.

I imagine warriors fighting extended battles experience a similar slump: In the middle of the war, where is the glory? Where is the exhilaration and thrill we thought warriors should feel every day?

This is what happened to David in the situation that introduces this chapter. This event is not only right in the middle of 1 and 2 Samuel; it is square in the middle of David's life. (If you are unfamiliar with this stage of David's life, you will want to read 1 Samuel 27–31 as you go through this chapter.)

David's "mid-life crisis"

At this point, David is maybe a decade past Goliath. David's years as a young warrior were difficult, but they were also a succession of victory. After his legendary, life-defining defeat of the giant, King Saul makes young David a commander in the army. Overnight, David is lifted to fame and success. He defeats enemy after enemy. He marries a princess. But then, Saul becomes jealous and drives him away in disgrace. His reputation in tatters, David is forced to live as a fugitive and an outlaw in the desert.

In spite of terrible mistreatment by Saul, David does not become bitter and rebellious. He rises above. He builds around him an army of Mighty Men. He meets and marries Abigail. He has two opportunities to take Saul's life, but he graciously and faithfully refuses to do so. David's faith in God flourishes and grows even through hardship. And during these years, he walks closely with God and writes down his prayers—psalms that have moved the hearts of millions of people for thousands of years.

But right in the middle of the journey, even after so many amazing victories, David falters. In chapters 27–31 he flees to live among the Philistines, a tenuous and dangerous compromise that leads him to needlessly take lives and live dishonestly. God eventually brings David out of this situation and crowns him king of Israel. He finds peace and stability at last.

Some time later, he falls again. He commits adultery with Bathsheba and arranges the death of her husband. The Bathsheba affair does not happen during a moment of danger or defeat; it does not happen during a life-or-death battle against the forces of Saul or the Philistine enemy. It happens in the middle of the long journey. What has happened to David that he has fallen so hard? The answers are crucial for all of us who are fighting our way through this same mid-life stage.

For the men in the middle

This chapter is written for you men who are in the middle third of your lives. It is for those of you who are leaving, or have left, the years of your teens and twenties, and are now living out the next season: your thirties, forties, and early fifties. It is for those of you running the middle miles of the marathon.

I myself have lived through my young and middle years. Unless

I make an early exit, I am just now entering into the final third of my time on earth. I am excited about it. I look forward to it. But as I look back on my own middle season, and as I reflect on the many men that I have befriended and counseled, it is my observation that you "men in the middle" may be living out the most challenging segment of life you will ever experience.

I say this not to discourage you, but to validate what you may already be feeling. You may at times find yourself thinking, "Why is this so hard? Just when I solve one problem, three more come up. I can't seem to get traction. There is no end in sight. My life is just work, work, and more work. I have problems in my job, in my marriage, with my kids, in my friendships, and even at church. What is going on? Is this how it's supposed to be?"

Challenges of the middle years

1. A time of increasing responsibility
The middle years are a time when we are trying to construct a career. Competition for positions, influence, and promotions is intense. More is being expected of us at work. We have to continually prove ourselves to our employers. We can't play the rookie card anymore. By this time, we are supposed to know what we're doing on the job. Now we have to deliver results. And as the pressure grows, our financial commitments are also mounting; we may be accumulating debt.

2. A time spent building our family
On the home front, most married men are way past the honeymoon stage at this point. As busy as we are with work and children, it is difficult to keep the romantic fires burning, to maintain the closeness we once had with the bride of our youth. We are still committed to each other, but the old fires may be fading, perhaps even dying down to mere embers.

Or perhaps we have discovered some real issues in our relationship that just aren't going away. We have had some serious conflicts with our spouse, and they may be getting worse, with anger and bitterness only increasing over the days, months, and years. Situations like this are draining and demoralizing.

Where is the victory that God promised? Where is the exciting, life-long romance we expected when we said "I do"? Where is the triumph over sin and selfishness? It may seem that our marriage is either trapped and torn by anger, or mired in a lifeless state of dullness and boredom.

What about us fathers? Certainly we love our kids, but sometimes being a parent is just flat-out hard work! Feeding kids, changing diapers, wrestling kids into bed (only to have them wake us up in the middle of the night), getting kids dressed and off to school, helping with home-work, attending sports and school activities . . . it never ends! When do we get a break, much less a vacation? And besides all this, we need to shape our kids' characters, teach obedience and respect, nurture their love for God, help them come to faith and love the church . . . Wonder-ful as child-rearing is, the nonstop, day-after-day, year-after-year effort it requires can be draining.

3. A time when we are tempted with weariness and discourage-ment

Look what happens to David in the middle of his life. He doesn't go to battle with his men (2 Samuel 11:1)—why? My guess? David is weary. He has grown tired of fighting the battles every day. He feels like it is taking too long for God to come through for him. He just cannot see the end of his long ordeal. He loses heart, faith, and focus. He becomes selfish. We discussed this season in David's life in The Battle of Discour-agement. My fellow warriors, it is my observation that simple weariness and discouragement have taken down more men than fright and terror ever did.

4. A time when we can easily become independent in our thinking and actions

> But David thought to himself, "One of these days I will be destroyed by the hand of Saul. The best thing I can do is to escape to the land of the Philistines. Then Saul will give up searching for me anywhere in Israel, and I will slip out of his hand."
> (1 Samuel 27:1)

Because of this questionable decision, David begins living a life of deceit and murder. He nearly gets his family killed, along with the families of all his Mighty Men. He nearly loses his chance to become Israel's king.

At first, we develop a sincere desire to do something every man needs to do: to stand up and take responsibility, and to not be dependent on others for what we should be doing for ourselves. Those are noble ambitions. But they can easily turn in a selfish, prideful, and dangerously independent direction. Yes, we need to work hard and earn our own way. Yes, we need to take responsibility and make our own decisions. Yes, we need to leave our little-boy years behind, when we depended on our parents to take care of us.

All of this is absolutely true.

But just as true is the other side of the coin: In the midst of trying to prove ourselves by our hard work and strength we can become foolish, blind, and arrogant. That is what happens to David here. Notice what the Bible says: "David thought to himself" (1 Samuel 27:1). Yes, we need to think for ourselves. But no, we don't need to think by ourselves. We need to share our inner thoughts, decisions, feelings, and struggles with others, especially with other strong, spiritual men.

What if David had sought advice about his decision from the prophet Gad or the priest Abiathar? How much pain would he have spared himself, his family, and his friends?

We want to be warriors, right? Amen, my brother. But remember, *warriors need advice.*

> Make plans by seeking advice;
>> if you wage war, obtain guidance. (Proverbs 20:18)

> Listen to advice and accept instruction,
>> and in the end you will be wise. (Proverbs 19:20)

My observation is that seeking advice and being open to input is one of the greatest weaknesses in the male gender. *And this is especially true of men in the middle stages of life.*

Brothers in this stage are faced with a plethora of difficult decisions, one after the other, often all at the same time: career alternatives, financial questions (like buying cars and houses), educational choices, marriage problems, childrearing challenges…on and on the list can go. In our efforts to be confident, strong, and decisive men, we can end up being foolish and prideful. Many of us in the middle season of life struggle because we think that by now we should be stronger than we feel we are, and we become embarrassed and ashamed to ask for help. Brothers, let's clothe ourselves with humility (1 Peter 5:5) and remember that that not one of us ever outgrows the need for advice and help.

When the Bible speaks definitively, the choice is simple: *obey God*. But when we are facing a decision that is not spelled out explicitly in the Bible, but is a question of wisdom (wisdom being the application of biblical principle), we need to pray, study, and seek wise counsel. Advice is just that—advice. It is up to us to make the final decision. But let's obey the command to ask for advice, and let us sincerely consider that advice when we make our final decision. Brothers, let's be warriors who make plans and go to war after we have obtained advice and guidance!

5. A time when we are tempted to start compromising our spiritual principles and priorities

We have seen it happen time and again: A young warrior starts out zealous for God, and begins to build his life and his family with faithful passion for God guiding his steps. Over time, life beats him down. He gradually becomes weary, dull, and hard-hearted, and his zeal flattens into a lukewarm, uninspiring spiritual life. The once enthusiastic warrior becomes just another boring "church member." Just another nice, tame religious guy. The once radical Christian removes Jesus from his place at the head of his life and makes Jesus just a part of his life. We have all seen middle-aged warriors who have simply lost heart and faith, and taken themselves out of the battle. Out of meaningful, biblical, life-changing discipling relationships. Out of the mission of making disciples. Out of a spiritually healthy, doctrinally strong church.

My fellow warrior, don't let this happen to you!

David thinks he can save himself and his family by compromising. He decides to go over and live among the Philistines. He knows that if he does this, Saul will leave him alone. God had told him earlier to stay in Judah, in his own country (1 Samuel 22:3–6). It must have seemed so easy to concede, to cross the line and go and live among the Philistines. Even though he had tried it earlier and ended up in serious trouble (1 Samuel 21:10–14), now he does it again.

The Philistine king Achish readily gives David the town of Ziklag as a home for himself and his army. David tells the king that he and his men are surviving by attacking and plundering the neighboring Jewish settlements. This is a lie—David is actually attacking the pagan allies of

Achish. To cover up this ruse, he slaughters every man, woman, whenever he raids a nearby town. His compromise in leaving Judah was bad enough; now he descends into deceit and murder.

Brothers, compromise will always lead us and our families into disaster. In the hope of protecting our loved ones and relieving the pressures we feel, we may be tempted to weaken our commitment to God and his church. We may start putting work, school, and our busy schedules ahead of godly priorities. Have you been tempted with any of these compromises?

- We start missing church activities to go to sports events.
- We let the kids stay home from church to finish their schoolwork.
- We convince ourselves that our kids can't go to bed a little later one night a week so our family can attend midweek services.
- We feel overwhelmed at work, so we neglect our relationships with the body of believers.

It seems so innocent at the time. We think that this is just a phase. We tell ourselves that everything will work out, we'll get past this eventually, and one day we'll be back to our usual involvement in church. The problem is, once we start going down the road of compromise and half-heartedness, it gets easier and easier to make excuses. Over time, our hearts become dull. Our family becomes more and more worldly. What message do we think we are sending our kids when we make decisions like this? What will they do when they become adults and their job or other priorities pull them away from the body of Christ? They will compromise just like you have done. If they become Christians at all, they will become "Sunday Christians"—which actually means they are lukewarm and dull, and they have lost their first love for God.

Look what happens to David. One compromise leads to another. Soon he is marching alongside the Philistine army, ready to go to war against his own people! It is only the intervention of some of the suspicious Philistine kings that saves him from this fatal mistake. They spot David and his troops in their army, and they complain to King Achish that David and his men will turn against them in the middle of the battle. Achish disagrees, but gives in and sends David back to Ziklag. David is so far gone in his attitude that he actually gets angry. He argues to be left alone so he can go *fight against his own people*. That is what compromise does for us—we end up making decisions that at one time would have appalled us.

Thankfully, God is merciful and gracious to David. Through the intervention of the Philistine commanders, God saves David from his sinful folly, and in so doing prevents him from ruining his credibility and right to ever become the king of Israel. David is saved from a mistake that would have completely destroyed the plan of God for his life—the plan to be the next king of Israel.

Victory is coming, but things are going to get much, much worse. Here is the final chapter of the story.

> *David and his men reached Ziklag on the third day. Now the Amalekites had raided the Negev and Ziklag. They had attacked Ziklag and burned it, and had taken captive the women and all who were in it, both young and old. They killed none of them, but carried them off as they went on their way. When David and his men came to Ziklag, they found it destroyed by fire and their wives and sons and daughters taken captive. So David and his men wept aloud until they had no strength left to weep. David's two wives had been captured—Ahinoam of Jezreel and Abigail, the widow of Nabal of Carmel. David was greatly distressed because the men were talking of stoning him; each one was bitter in spirit because of his sons and daughters.* (1 Samuel 30:1–6a)

What David thought was going to relieve him and his family from difficulty and pressure has instead brought disaster. He returns home to find that the family he thought he was protecting may be dead, slaughtered by his enemies. Furthermore, he has alienated the men who trusted him. He has led them into him compromise, and now in their anger and grief they are ready to stone him to death. Let us learn from David the lesson of a lifetime: Compromise does not work.

Winning the victory

What do we need to do to avoid the mistakes of our middle years, or to recover when we have made them? What can David's story teach us?

Turn to God

In the midst of one of the darkest moments of his life, when it is all about to come crashing down around him, David makes a crucial decision. It is revealed in a simple phrase that breaks into this dark story like a sunbeam from heaven: "But David found strength in the LORD his God" (1 Samuel 30:6).

David turns to God. He gets his heart back. He returns to being who he really is. He now does what he should have done before making this terrible decision sixteen months before: *he seeks spiritual counsel*. He summons the high priest Abiathar and "inquires of the LORD" (1 Samuel 30:7–8). He pursues God's wisdom; he prays—and God answers.

God directs David and his men to track down the Amalekites. David and his men set out, find the enemy war party, defeat them in battle, and save their families. Not one woman or child is lost! And they recover a huge amount of plunder from their enemies.

Keep your heart, mind, effort, and soul fully engaged in serving God

Yes, things will get tough. You will see some defeats along the way. You will at times hit a wall in an area of growth and in your own character development. Your job may get tough. Your finances may be stressful. Your marriage may need help. Your children may challenge you. Don't let these kinds of midlife issues weaken your determination to fight the good fight.

Remember that you are a warrior

Remember that you have an enemy who wants to destroy you, your family, and your marriage. My brother, you are a warrior. *Go to war*. Fight the enemy with everything you have. Depend on God as you fight. Life is a battle, and sometimes we see quick victories. But more often than not, victory comes after a long season of fighting. In the midst of it all, we have to get up every day, put on our armor, and go to war. We take up our cross initially at baptism, but after that, we take it up *daily* (Luke 9:23). Stay in the fight. Be like the Mighty Man Eleazar. He fought so long and so hard that his hand "froze to the sword" (2 Samuel 23:10). Don't turn loose of your sword, and don't stop fighting. Victory will surely come if we do not give up!

Continue to grow in your prayer life and personal walk with God

Stay in the word. Stay in prayer. Paul admonishes us to be warriors who "pray in the spirit on all occasions, with all kinds of prayers and requests. With this in mind, be alert and always keep praying for all the saints" (Ephesians 6:18). Battles are won or lost, not on the battlefield, but on our knees before God. Never give up or go slack in your personal walk with God!

Build and maintain relationships with spiritual men

Where are David's friends when he makes this foolish decision? Jonathan is no longer there for David—he is ensnared under the power of his father, King Saul. Soon he will die in battle. What about David's Mighty Men? They go along with him in his compromise. And then, when it blows up their faces, they blame him and are ready to kill him!

Get the help and discipling you need. If for some reason the help is not available for you in your local situation, then reach out and find it elsewhere. Find an elder, an evangelist, an old friend—someone you can turn to help strengthen you in the Lord and give you the godly wisdom and encouragement you need to see you through to the end. Let me say it again: Get a mentor. Find an older man who is godly, wise, and spiritual, and let him advise you. You are no longer a young man, but you still need older men in your life.

Keys to victory

Here are some areas where we need to fight to keep ourselves strong during the middle years:

- **Our personal walk with God:** Spending time daily in prayer and the word. Not just going through the motions but pouring out our hearts to God and seeking his wisdom in the word.

- **Work-life balance:** Keeping God first; not letting work or kids' school or activities take over our schedules.

- **Wrestling with difficulty and disappointment:** Learning to keep our faith, our focus, and our connection to God during tough times.

- **Big decisions:** If we have important decisions to make about our careers or where we are going to live, let's make those choices by seeking God's kingdom first, and with the help of wise, godly advice.

- **Marriage growth:** Keeping our marriages strong over the years; nurturing the romance and connection while protecting ourselves from dullness and bitterness.

- **A thriving family atmosphere:** Building a spiritual family that worships God and honors him in all we do. Raising our children to love God.

- **Church life:** Maintaining our involvement in our local church as a first priority.

- **Keeping perspective:** Not allowing the lure of money and worldly success to take over our families.

Men, let us stay strong in the middle years. They need not be "middling" years defined by mediocrity and struggle. No! These years may have a generous share of difficulty, but even so, they can be some of the most victorious and fulfilling years of our lives:

- If we keep God first, we can—and we will—remain close to God all of our days.

- If we continue to stoke the fire of our faith, we can—and we will—grow in our trust in God, no matter what comes.

- If we love God's church, we can—and we will—experience the joy of helping it to grow and accomplish God's purpose in our city.

- If we nurture our maturing marriages, we can—and we will—find joy in the wife of our youth until our dying day.

- If we love God ourselves, and instill that love into our children, we can—and we will—raise Christian children who are a crown upon our graying heads.

Even great warriors struggle and fall during their middle years. If you have gotten off track like David did, then imitate him in turning back to God. If you have compromised, own up to it. Repent. Tell your wife and kids you are sorry and that you are from this day forth going to get your heart and priorities right once again.

Then, follow through. Get back in the fight. God will forgive you and restore you. Even if you have made terrible mistakes that have harmed you and your family, don't let shame keep you down. If God forgave David, he can forgive you. He will cleanse you of your sin and put you back in the army again. Brothers, let's get our fire back. Let's be warriors again. Let's get in the race and back in the fight. Let's take up our shield and sword once again.

Therefore, since we are surrounded by such a great cloud of witnesses, let us throw off everything that hinders and the sin that so easily entangles, and let us run with perseverance the race marked out for us. Let us fix our eyes on Jesus, the author and perfecter of our faith, who for the joy set before him endured the cross, scorning its shame, and sat down at the right hand of the throne of God. Consider him who endured such opposition from sinful men, so that you will not grow weary and lose heart. In your struggle against sin, you have not yet resisted to the point of shedding your blood.... Therefore, strengthen your feeble arms and weak knees. "Make level paths for your feet," so that the lame may not be disabled, but rather healed. (Hebrews 12:1–4, 12–13)

Chapter Seventeen

The Seasoned Warrior

Even when I am old and gray,
do not forsake me, O God,
till I declare your power to the next generation,
your might to all who are to come.

Psalm 71:18

The glory of young men is their strength,
gray hair the splendor of the old.

Proverbs 20:29

David is now securely enthroned as king. He is entering into the final stage of his life. What is God's plan for him now?

As we leave the middle stage of life we begin to think about the fact that our time here on earth is not indefinite—the end is coming. That end may be years away, but life as we have known it is slowly but surely drawing to a close. We are entering our final act. And so the questions begin to knock insistently at the door of our heart: How do we want to finish our battles? How can we bring honor to the One for whom we have fought for so many years?

Seek and see the plan of God

David has a great project on his heart. He wants to build a magnificent temple where the ark of the covenant can reside, and the people of Israel may worship the Lord. He speaks to the prophet Nathan about his idea, but finds out that God has something else in mind.

> *After David was settled in his palace, he said to Nathan the prophet, "Here I am, living in a palace of cedar, while the ark of the covenant of the LORD is under a tent."*
>
> *Nathan replied to David, "Whatever you have in mind, do it, for God is with you."*
>
> *That night the word of God came to Nathan, saying:*
>
> *"Go and tell my servant David, 'This is what the LORD says: You are not the one to build me a house to dwell in. . . . Now I will make your name like the names of the greatest men of the earth. And I will provide a place for my people Israel and will plant them so that they can have a home of their own and no longer be disturbed.'"* (1 Chronicles 17:1–4, 8–9)

As we get older, many of us have dreams like this. We have something we long to do, an accomplishment we may have dreamed about for most of our life. It is our great hope, our passionate aspiration. We may feel it is our particular calling and responsibility, something that God himself has laid upon our heart to do.

My fellow warriors, we must seek God's will throughout our lives, but it is particularly vital that we seek it at this critical juncture in our lives.

In the closing season of life, the stakes are higher. The clock is ticking; we have no time to waste. What job we take, where we move, which ministry we serve in the church, the home we rent or purchase . . . *we need to make the right choices.* We don't have as much luxury to experiment. When we were young, we figured, "Okay, I'll try this for a while. If it doesn't work out, I'll move somewhere else, get another job, try another career, date somebody else…I've got lots of time." Well, not anymore we don't!

David has a great dream in his heart—a noble aspiration, a glorious passion—to honor his God by building a temple to house the ark of the covenant, a place of worship in Israel that would stand for all time. What a wonderful way to complete his lifetime of devotion to God! What a great legacy to leave behind!

But God has another plan.

Because David has shed so much blood in his military campaigns, God wants someone else—a man of peace—to build his temple. He chooses David's son Solomon to carry out this great project. And so this magnificent edifice will be known not as the Temple of David, but as the Temple of Solomon.

Have you ever had a dream to which God said no? How did you take it? When David, the man after the heart of God, hears the news that his son Solomon will get to fulfill his dream of building the temple, he humbly, joyfully embraces it:

> Then King David went in and sat before the LORD, and he said:
> "Who am I, O LORD God, and what is my family, that you have brought me this far? And as if this were not enough in your sight, O God, you have spoken about the future of the house of your servant. You have looked on me as though I were the most exalted of men, O LORD God.
> "What more can David say to you for honoring your servant? For you know your servant, O LORD. For the sake of your servant and according to your will, you have done this great thing and made known all these great promises." (1 Chronicles 17:16–19)

Brother warriors, we need to remember that we are soldiers, not the commander in chief! As we live out this final season, we need to seek God's will with all our heart, and with faith and humility. Where and how does God want us to serve? Not where do *we* want to serve, not what is our plan, but what is God's will? It can be tempting to dig our heels in and insist that God give us a certain dream, a certain path. We can think, *This is the only way for my life to count. This is the only way I can feel fulfilled.* But what if God has different plans for our final season? We can rest assured that he wants this season to be our triumphant finale— but we must accept that sometimes God's idea of *triumphant* may look different than what we expected. After years of faithful service, let us not become self-willed and self-centered.

It is my observation and experience that this season of life brings change, and then…more change. It is rife with the unexpected and the unpredicted. As the changes unfold, we need to stay attuned to the voice of the Spirit. We want to live out these times in victory, knowing we are surrendered to the will of the Father. We don't want to be men who spiritually fade away or get off track in our autumn years.

As my wife and I approached sixty, the passion to seek God's will for a new period of life began to burn within us. *How* did he want to use us at this new stage? *Where* did he want to use us? We prayed. We fasted. We completely opened the door to God. We sought the counsel of our wisest, most spiritual friends. We cast our bread upon the waters (Ecclesiastes 11:1–2) and waited for God to speak. Then we prayed and fasted more. It took several years to find answers (longer than we thought it would!), but God made his plan clear to us.

At one point during the journey, we decided to put our house up for sale. We loved our home, but we wondered if, for practical and financial reasons, we should consider downsizing. The housing market had taken a severe downturn, so it was not a good time to try to sell a home. Far fewer homes than usual were selling, and most of the ones that did sell were going at way below the asking price.

But we put our house on the market, prayed, and asked God to make his will known. In less than two weeks we had an offer— and not just any offer: it was right at our asking price. We cried tears of joy and sorrow. We really didn't want to leave our home, but we had laid the question before God, and now we had a definitive answer.

In just a few short weeks, we were living in my daughter's basement. We went from just the two of us living in our own large home to a blended environment of four adults and three kids living together under one roof and did I mention their huge, rambunctious dog and our two finicky cats? This was not the scenario we had envisioned, and yet it turned out to be one of the most enjoyable and fulfilling seasons of our lives. We built memories with our daughter, son-in-law, and grandkids that will last a lifetime. And while we were at it, we saved lots of money, and helped them pay off some bills! In the next two years, we would make two more moves, finally landing in South Florida, the place we firmly believe God wanted us to live and to serve. Not only were we given the opportunity to help build a wonderful church, but we also got to live near my wife's aging parents—an opportunity we could scarcely have imagined when we first put our home on the market.

Today, as I sit on my back patio writing this book, looking out over a sparkling South Florida lake, I thank God that he guided us through a difficult time of seeking and uncertainty, and brought us to the place he wanted us to be. As David puts it in Psalm 16:6, "The boundary lines have fallen for me in pleasant places; surely I have a delightful inheritance."

Remain secure in the promises

How do we respond when God changes our plans? What do we do when he says "no" to one dream and points us in a new direction? Do we question God's grace, wondering if he is angry with us and is refusing to give us what we want? Do we question God's wisdom, doubting that he really knows what we need? Do we question God's kindness, wondering if he really wants us to be happy?

David's response to God's plans for his "seasoned years" is a model for us.

When the prophet Nathan delivers the news that David is not going to be the one to build the temple, David responds in this way:

"O Lord, you are God! You have promised these good things to your servant. Now you have been pleased to bless the house of your servant, that it may continue forever in your sight; for you, O Lord, have blessed it, and it will be blessed forever." (1 Chronicles 17:26–27)

David goes before the Lord and claims his promises. Once more, the great warrior surrenders his future to God. He realizes that when God takes away one dream, he replaces it with another: Not only will David's son Solomon build the temple, but one of his descendants will sit on the throne as long as the nation endures. What a great promise! What a great future!

Seasoned warriors, just like David, we also need to focus on God's promises and faithfulness as his plan unfolds. Will we continue to believe that God is looking out for us? Will we believe he has our best interests at heart? Will we continue to trust that God is working all things together for our good? And will we continue to believe, like David, that if God closes one door, he will open another that is even better?

It would be a sad thing if we seasoned warriors should lose our gratitude at this stage in our lives. Let us not become cynical. Let us not become complainers. Let us not begin to feel that we have been short-changed in life. Let us not focus on what we don't have; instead, let us focus on appreciating the blessings God has poured out upon us. Let us not spend our sunset years focused on ourselves; instead, let us celebrate the greatness of our God.

Brother warriors, as we enter and live out this final stage of life, let us remember that God is faithful and that he does not forget his promises!

"Let God be true, and every man a liar." (Romans 3:4)

God has said,
> *"Never will I leave you;*
> *never will I forsake you."*
So we say with confidence,
> *"The Lord is my helper; I will not be afraid.*
> *What can man do to me?"* (Hebrews 13:5–6)

Pass your convictions on to others

As David lives out his latter years, he sets his mind to give away all the wisdom and guidance that God has shown him through his lifetime. He wants to leave his children, his grandchildren, and the nation of Israel with the immense blessing of all that God has taught him.

Listen to the charge he gives to Solomon and all the leaders as he admonishes them to build the temple when he is gone:

> *"So now I charge you in the sight of all Israel and of the assembly of the LORD, and in the hearing of our God: Be careful to follow all the commands of the LORD your God, that you may possess this good land and pass it on as an inheritance to your descendants forever.*
>
> *And you, my son Solomon, acknowledge the God of your father, and serve him with wholehearted devotion and with a willing mind, for the LORD searches every heart and understands every motive behind the thoughts. If you seek him, he will be found by you; but if you forsake him, he will reject you forever."* (1 Chronicles 28:8–9)

David gives his son and the people an inspiring and sobering charge. In essence he says, "God will be with you, but you must remain faithful and obedient to him."

As older warriors in God's kingdom, we need to pass on our strong convictions to those who are younger than we are. We need to challenge them to trust and obey God. We need to urge them to obey the Scriptures. Let us help the younger men and women coming behind us to have a healthy fear of God, to go by the Bible, and to never compromise with the watered-down versions of Christianity that we see all around us. The religious world is promulgating massive doctrinal and lifestyle compromise. May we as seasoned warriors call upon everyone we know to never back away from the truth of the word and the commitment that God expects!

Share your wisdom. Teach others what you know. Tell them of the wonderful things God has done in your life. Tell of his grace. Tell of his judgments. Tell of his disciplines. Tell of how his plan for life so far surpasses what this world has to offer. Pass on your hard-earned lessons. Share the mistakes you made so that others can avoid them. Share what you did right. This is how you prepare yourself to leave this world, and prepare others to stay behind and live in victory.

Don't hold back, but do be humble

All too often, we seasoned warriors hold back. We fear sounding pompous and condescending. We don't want to come off like old guys reliving our glory days. We don't want to be looked upon as dull old men telling another boring story.

Well, brother, all I can do is refer you to Hebrews 11, where God recounts the stories of the men and women who lived before Jesus. He calls on us to learn from them. He provides their stories to inform us, warn us, inspire us, and build our faith.

Like those heroes before us, we need to pass on our own stories of faith. Certainly we should do so with great humility. And we shouldn't just talk all the time—we should listen, too. We need to hear the stories of the younger folks. Perhaps our experiences can help them deal with their own challenges. No, they don't need to mimic our every action or do everything just like we did. But they do need to imitate our faith, and learn from our victories and mistakes.

Share your war stories

There is nothing like sitting down and hearing the stories of a true, faithful disciple who has fought for God for many years. These warriors can teach us how to apply the Bible in the real world. They can share wisdom that we can never learn any other way. So, seasoned warrior, don't minimize the power of the life God has given you. Your past and your present have so much to offer—share them with the younger warriors coming behind you.

Be deliberate

We need to help others in a deliberate way. David prepared Solomon and other leaders to build the temple after his departure in a strategic and specific manner. Read 1 Chronicles 22–27, and note the amazing amount of work David put in to helping set up the nation to succeed after his death. He gave materials for the construction of the temple. He provided planning and organization for the worship and upkeep of the temple—the priests, the singers, the gatekeepers. He provided organization for the army.

We can imitate David's example in this. Our final season is not the time to back out of helping our churches and families. No, we need to spend these years setting others up to win battles after we leave. Too many of us think that just because we are no longer able to work as we once did, or because we are not as physically capable as we were as younger warriors, that we should just chill out and disengage. Far from it! Now is the time to re-engage and share what we know. You finally have some experience— you worked hard and suffered long to earn it; it is invaluable.

Someone once said, "It takes five years to get five years of experience." So true! Well, what about ten years of experience? Twenty? Thirty, forty, and more? No amount of money, no kind of schooling, no modern technology can replace the lessons God teaches us through the long years of our life. Don't let your "education" go to waste. Share it!

Stay passionate

Look back at David's charge to Solomon in 1 Chronicles 28:8–10. Do you sense that this is a man who has lost his fire over the years? Is this a man who has let his convictions weaken and wane? Is this a guy who no longer has a love in his heart for God, God's work, and God's people? Is he worn out, just wanting to go quietly away?

The answer is obvious—*absolutely not!* David remains a man full of fire and passion. He still has deep convictions. He is just as strong now as he ever was.

One of the worst things that can happen to us older warriors is if we weaken in our biblical convictions. Certainly we need to leave behind and of our past arrogance, when we may have thought that we were totally right in every judgment, and that everyone else was wrong. We need to have the humility to grow past our immature prejudices and overconfidence. But we must never leave behind biblical conviction. My fellow seasoned warriors, let us lead and inspire the warriors coming behind us to have firm convictions. On matters of opinion, we need to teach younger men to be flexible—rigidity there is a sign of immaturity. But when it comes to biblical doctrine, truth, and principle, we need to urge them to never compromise. We need to pass this on. If we do not, the church in the next generation is headed for lukewarmness, weakness, or even apostasy. It is always the temptation for God's people to blend in with the world. Don't let it happen to those who are coming behind you—pass on deep convictions!

Plead for purity of heart

*"And you, my son Solomon, acknowledge the God of your father, and serve him **with wholehearted devotion and with a willing mind**, for the LORD searches every heart and understands every motive behind the thoughts. If you seek him, he will be found by you; but if you forsake him, he will reject you forever."* (1 Chronicles 28:9, emphasis added)

As seasoned warriors we know that obedience and service to God can become rote and routine. This is especially true after the passage of time, and for young people raised in the church. We must keep our own hearts tender and alive, and encourage those around us to do the same.

David began his life as the man after the heart of God, and he stayed that way to the end of his life. Yes, he fell, and fell hard, but he repented and asked God to give him a right heart, and God answered his prayer. Here David calls upon Solomon and all the people to serve God "with wholehearted devotion and a willing mind." David has seen Saul go through the motions of obedience from selfish, shallow motivations. He wants no part of that, and he urges the people to serve God from the inside out.

Keeping our hearts tender, full of love and deep devotion will save us from becoming mere churchgoers—nice people who attend services but are no longer warriors for God. The great danger to the church today is to settle for the appearance of godliness without genuine commitment. Plenty of groups have cool worship services with exciting music and entertaining sermons. But there is no true call to, or expectation of, genuine discipleship. People come and go as they please. They don't really know each other. Who among them even knows what kind of life the other members are living outside the confines of the church service?

Too many are wearing the uniform, but are not in the battle. God forbid that should ever happen to you and me, or to our churches! Let us serve from the heart and call others to do the same.

Share generously

> Then King David said to the whole assembly: "My son Solomon, the one whom God has chosen, is young and inexperienced. The task is great, because this palatial structure is not for man but for the LORD God. With all my resources I have provided for the temple of my God—gold for the gold work, silver for the silver, bronze for the bronze, iron for the iron and wood for the wood, as well as onyx for the settings, turquoise, stones of various colors, and all kinds of fine stone and marble—all of these in large quantities. Besides, in my devotion to the temple of my God I now give my personal treasures of gold and silver for the temple of my God, over and above everything I have provided for this holy temple: three thousand talents of gold (gold of Ophir) and seven thousand talents of refined silver, for the overlaying of the walls of the buildings, for the gold work and the silver work, and for all the work to be done by the craftsmen." (1 Chronicles 29:1–5)

The temptation for us as we age is to become self-protective, cautious, and fearful—if we don't look out for ourselves, who will? This is why some men who were bold, giving, and caring warriors in their past fade away and disappear as they age. Instead of becoming more caring and giving like Jesus, they retreat into a shell.

I have spent enough time in this period of life, and observed enough seasoned men and women around me to have learned an important lesson: *Getting older doesn't automatically make you more like Jesus. You have to keep on carrying your cross to become more and more like him. If you don't stay in the battle, your old self will re-emerge, and you will grow increasingly selfish.*

How can we fight our natural tendency to selfishness and spiritual regression? David gives us the answer: *The older we get, the more giving and generous we need to become.* David liberally provides treasure for the building of the temple. As king, he gives funds from the public domain. But then he does more: He gives sacrificially from his personal treasures as well.

What is the result? His example inspires the other leaders around him! After his unselfish actions, David does not even have to urge, challenge, beg or command others to be generous. He just sets the example and asks a question: "Now, who is willing to consecrate himself today to the LORD?" (1 Chronicles 29:5).

And here is their response:

> Then the leaders of families, the officers of the tribes of Israel, the commanders of thousands and commanders of hundreds, and the officials in charge of the king's work gave willingly. They gave toward the work on the temple of God five thousand talents and ten thousand darics of gold, ten thousand talents of silver, eighteen thousand talents of bronze and a hundred thousand talents of iron. Any who had precious stones gave them to the treasury of the temple of the LORD in the custody of Jehiel the Gershonite. The people rejoiced at the willing response of their leaders, for they had given freely and wholeheartedly to the LORD. David the king also rejoiced greatly. (1 Chronicles 29:6–9)

The leaders of the people give willingly and generously. Their open-hearted and openhanded responses bring great joy. Giving always does that, especially when it is lavish and comes from deep in the soul. And David? He is so happy! What a way to leave this earth, knowing your example has inspired others to give sacrificially to build a temple that will honor the Lord, inspire God's people, and endure for centuries! Fellow warriors, may you and I do the same!

But David gives more than his money. He gives his knowledge, wisdom, and expertise:

> Then David gave his son Solomon the plans for the portico of the temple, its buildings, its storerooms, its upper parts, its inner rooms and the place of atonement. He gave him the plans of all that the Spirit had put in his mind for the courts of the temple of the LORD and all the surrounding rooms, for the treasuries of the temple of God and for the treasuries for the dedicated things. He gave him instructions for the divisions of the priests and Levites, and for all the work of serving in the temple of the LORD, as well as for all the articles to be used in its service. . . .
>
> "All this," David said, "I have in writing from the hand of the LORD upon me, and he gave me understanding in all the details of the plan." (1 Chronicles 28:11–13, 19)

What knowledge has God imparted to you over the course of your life? What do you know? What are your skills? What has the Spirit of God taught you that you can leave behind?

I was once in a group of "empty nesters," and together we were studying Romans 12:3–8, a passage about spiritual gifts. We were seeking to discover what we had to offer God and others at this stage of life. This passage clearly teaches that God gifts every Christian in a special way. We went around the circle, asking each person what his or her gifts were. The responses were quite revealing. Several said, "I just don't know." One or two said, "I don't think I have any gifts." Others put it this way: "Well, whatever I may have, I don't believe it amounts to very much." Over and over again, people valued themselves and their abilities at a very low level. Each time someone spoke, the group would erupt in gasps of surprise and laughter that anyone could sell himself or herself so short—*until it was their turn to tell what their own gifts were!*

Men, we do God no honor when we act as if we have nothing to give. We are denying our Lord's work in shaping our lives when we think this way. You have immense stores of wisdom, experience, and skill. It is a tragedy when seasoned warriors like us begin to feel that we have lost our usefulness, that we can no longer make a difference in this world. That is a lie from the Enemy. Don't believe it! Rise up and put on your armor. Even if you don't lead the charge, you can help younger warriors learn how to fight. Teach them what you know. You will be fulfilled, and they will rejoice that you have given them gifts of wisdom, knowledge, and experience that are worth more than gold!

Grow powerful in prayer, praise, and faith

David praised the LORD in the presence of the whole assembly, saying,

"Praise be to you, O LORD,
God of our father Israel,
from everlasting to everlasting.
Yours, O LORD, is the greatness and the power
and the glory and the majesty and the splendor,
for everything in heaven and earth is yours.
Yours, O LORD, is the kingdom;
you are exalted as head over all.
Wealth and honor come from you;
you are the ruler of all things.
In your hands are strength and power

to exalt and give strength to all.
Now, our God, we give you thanks,
  and praise your glorious name." (1 Chronicles 29:10–13)

David here sets an example of powerful prayer.

Once we become seasoned warriors, we may no longer be *leading* the fight, but we are still *in the fight.* Even if our bodies fail, we can still fight the good fight in prayer. David is getting up in years here, but what does he do now? *He leads the people in faithful prayer.* As we age, our faith should keep increasing. Like Joshua in his golden years, we can share our testimony of God's faithfulness: "Now I am about to go the way of all the earth. You know with all your heart and soul that not one of all the good promises the LORD your God gave you has failed. Every promise has been fulfilled; not one has failed" (Joshua 23:14).

Don't you think that Joshua's testimony inspired the generation coming behind him? Can we not also share how God has been faithful to us, and recount for younger warriors the amazing answers to prayer we have seen? Yes, we can! And when we do, we will inspire their trust in God, and leave a legacy of faith. My brother, go out and do it! Even though your body may weaken with age, you can continue to be a man of faith, and a warrior in prayer.

Then David said to the whole assembly, "Praise the LORD your God." So they all praised the LORD, the God of their fathers; they bowed low and fell prostrate before the LORD and the king. (1 Chronicles 29:20)

We close our charge to seasoned warriors with David, the great warrior of worship, leading the people in praises to God. What a fitting way for him to end his time on earth. As he lived—in praise, thanksgiving, and worship—so now he ends. One of the last pictures we have of David in this life is of the great king leading his people not only in prayer, but also in praise. Look at how they respond: They bow low; they fall prostrate before God; they all worship the Lord. Seasoned warriors, we need to lead the people around us to praise God!

A final charge

David has one last charge for Solomon.

"When the time drew near for David to die, he gave a charge to Solomon his son: 'I am about to go the way of all the earth,' he said. 'So be strong, show yourself a man, and observe what the LORD your God requires: Walk in his ways, and keep his decrees and commands, his laws and requirements, as written in the Law of Moses, so that you may prosper in all you do and wherever you go.' " (1 Kings 2:1–3)

Brothers, may we pass on words like these to our sons and sons in the faith! *Come on, son—be strong! Be a man! Lead God's people with integrity, courage, righteousness, and perseverance. Do the job God has given you to do.* Don't you love those words? Don't they just flat-out light you up? May we as older warriors leave this kind of legacy of manhood for the younger men around us!

A victorious departure

My brothers, we above all people—we who have lived long and fought hard—need to be filled with gratitude, and eagerly await the joys that God has in store for us in heaven. I don't plan to die any day soon... seasoned warrior that I am, I hope the Lord grants me many years left to fight. But the day will come when my time draws near. And that day will come for you, too, brother warrior.

When at last it is our time to prepare to leave this world and join the angels and the redeemed in heaven, may we praise God more and more!

As the aging Psalmist says,

> *Do not cast me away when I am old;*
>   *do not forsake me when my strength is gone. ....*
>
> *But as for me, I will always have hope;*
>   ***I will praise you more and more.*** (Psalm 71:9,14, emphasis added).

May we, like David, end our years on earth in praise and celebration. May we leave behind all the faith, wisdom, and experiences that God has given us as our gifts—our legacy—for others to inherit. May we march triumphantly through these final years into a glorious sunset, praising our God all the way home to glory!

Chapter Eighteen

Dealing with Defeat

David said to Nathan, "I have sinned against the LORD."
2 Samuel 12:13

For though a righteous man falls seven times,
he rises again,
but the wicked are brought down by calamity.
Proverbs 24:16

Failure is the warrior's truest test. We all lose some battles. What we don't want to do is lose the *war*.

A victorious fighter is not the man who is never beaten; a victorious fighter is the man who rises from defeat and emerges triumphant. He suffers loss but rises again—forgiven, recovered, restored.

A warrior is defined not only by the battles he wins, but by the losses he overcomes.

A warrior is defined not by the fall, but by how he gets up.

Has Satan knocked you down, brother warrior? Have you suffered defeat? Are you haunted by a sense of guilt, paralyzed by self-doubt? Are you afraid to fight again?

It's time to rise again. It's time to run back to battle.

The only warrior who was never defeated—even once—was Jesus. He faced every enemy we face and, by the power of God and because of his surrender to God, won every battle. The rest of us, including the greatest men and women of the Bible, have all had our losses. What made our Bible heroes ultimately victorious was the way they fought their way back to their feet. And so it will be for us as well. Let us now learn from David how to rise up after we have suffered defeat in the great battles of life.

David's greatest defeat

David's most famous defeat occurred in his relationship with Bathsheba (you can read the story in 2 Samuel 11–12). This episode was not a single failure, but a series of them. That is how defeat works. If we are not humble and vigilant, we can quickly plummet from one loss to another. At first, David makes a selfish choice to stay home instead of engaging with the enemy on the battlefield. Then he develops a wandering, lustful eye. Next he makes a foolish inquiry, which leads to adultery with the wife of a loyal friend and fellow warrior. From there he descends even deeper, into a deceitful, manipulative cover-up. The whole debacle ends with murder.

Brothers, we want to avoid any defeat by Satan. But when we do stumble, we don't want to stay down; we want to recover as quickly as possible. We want to defeat to be an exception, we don't want to allow compromise and sin to become a life pattern. Once Satan knocks us down, he wants to pound us into discouragement, unconsciousness and death. Don't let it happen—get back up and fight again!

David fell as hard as a man can fall. When Saul died in disgrace, David lamented and sang, "How the mighty have fallen" (2 Samuel 1:19), but now, some time later, we find that David himself —the man after God's own heart- -has descended into sin. Laziness, lust, selfishness, deceit, and murder have brought him down and imperiled his soul. His honor, his reputation among his men, and even his walk with God—all are at risk.

Most men would not be able recover from such a fall, but David does. When confronted with his sin by the prophet Nathan, David humbles himself. He mourns, confesses, and repents. Psalm 51 is the prayer that tells the story of David's recovery from the terrible defeat of his sin with Bathsheba. We will explore the lessons we can glean from this great psalm of recovery to help us in times of defeat—those times when we need to repent and find the will and strength fight again. If David's victory over Goliath can teach us how to win, his defeat with Bathsheba can teach us how to rise from crushing loss.

How did David recover? How can we? Here is the song he wrote that tells us how.

Appeal for mercy

> *Have mercy on me, O God,*
> > *according to your great compassion*
> > *blot out my transgressions.*
> *Wash away all my iniquity*
> > *and cleanse me from my sin.* (Psalm 51:1–2)

David appeals to God for forgiveness, but not on the basis of his own goodness, not on the basis of how humble he is, or even how sorry he is. He comes before the Lord completely depending upon God's grace and mercy. Note carefully how he pleads with God: "Have mercy on me according to your unfailing love; according to your great compassion" (v. 1, emphasis added).

Warriors, when we are defeated by sin we can only cast ourselves completely upon God's mercy. We have no hope other than God's grace, given us through Jesus. If we try to base our forgiveness upon our goodness—even upon the depth of our sorrow and repentance—we will fall short. We can never pay God back for our sin with anything we have to offer. We can only humble ourselves totally under the cross of Christ.

Make no excuses

> *For I know my transgressions,*
> > *and my sin is always before me.*
> *Against you, you only, have I sinned*
> > *and done what is evil in your sight,*
> *so that you are proved right when you speak*
> > *and justified when you judge.* (Psalm 51:3–4)

David offers no rationale for his actions. He does not try to make himself look better. No blaming Bathsheba. No blaming his years of suffering while running from Saul. No excuses of any kind. He simply says, in effect, "I sinned. I was wrong. This is all my fault." And when he says to God, "Against you and you only have I sinned," he is not discounting that he has sinned against Bathsheba or her husband Uriah; he is simply recognizing that all sin is ultimately sin against God. Yes, we sin against others (and in so doing we may harm them terribly), but the bottom line is that when we sin against another person, we sin against someone else, too—we sin against our God. All sin crucified God's Son, Christ; he bore it all. Every sin we have done or will ever do was carried by Jesus to the cross. When we face that truth, we stop making excuses and start taking responsibility.

Do you remember the lessons we learned from Saul's response to his failures? Instead of owning up to his mistakes, he rationalized, minimized, and blamed others. He lied himself for so long that he may have begun to believe his own lies (see 1 Samuel 15). And brothers, that is one of the most dangerous things about making excuses: we start believing Satan's falsehoods and end up deceiving ourselves. Until we take full ownership of our own mistakes, we will not change; we will never recover from defeat.

Ask tor truthful insight into yourself

Surely you desire truth in the inner parts;
you teach me wisdom in the inmost place. (Psalm 51:6)

If we are to be mighty men of God, we must be men of truthfulness and absolute integrity. There can be no deceit in us—none. If we want to be men of character, we must see and admit the full truth about who we are and the things we have done. As long as we live with illusions—viewing ourselves as better than we are, or making excuses for sin in our lives—we are vulnerable to repeated spiritual defeat.

As we have noted, all sin has somewhere in it the element of deceit, and especially of self-deception. Before he came to repentance, David rationalized his sins in his own mind (see Psalm 32:1–5). You may be wondering, "But David was the man after the heart of God! How could he do such a thing? How could he excuse such a clear-cut case of disobedience?" Brothers, the fact that a man like David could justify such egregiously sinful behavior should cause all of us to understand and heed Paul's admonition to "work out your salvation *with fear and trembling*" (Philippians 2:12, emphasis added). When we deceive ourselves, we mess up our insides; we lose our moral compass. As Paul puts it, we "suppress [choke] the truth" (Romans 1:18). Let's be honest with ourselves, with our brothers, and with our God!

Seek a deeply broken heart

> *The sacrifices of God are a broken spirit;*
> *a broken and contrite heart,*
> *O God, you will not despise.* (Psalm 51:17)

David did not want to just make a superficial apology to God. He longed for deep, profound brokenness and conviction.

If we are to come through a defeat into full recovery, we need to beg God for a deeply humble and broken heart. When we succumb to sin, we do so by hardening our heart, by searing and numbing our conscience. When we repent, we need to get our heart and sensitivity back.

Do you remember what we said back in the chapter on heart? *A good heart means knowing you don't have a good heart.* That may sound a little strange, but it means that we can have a good heart only by *asking God to help us have one*. We need to pursue having a good heart with all of our heart. A good heart is something we must fervently seek, but it is also a gift from God. God can put a tender heart of flesh back into us when our heart has turned to stone (Ezekiel 36:26–27). We are so needy that we can't even get our attitude right without God's grace to help us! (Hang with me through the next couple of sentences, my brothers!) If you are like me, sometimes you just have to pray, "God, I don't really want to do the right thing right now. But deep down, I want to want to obey you. Help me to *want to want to*!"

As I mentioned in an earlier chapter, my wife has helped me better understand how to make the journey to a broken heart before God. Here is what she says: "When I am not doing well spiritually and when my heart and attitude are not right, I have a 'Gethsemane prayer.' I go to God as Jesus did in the garden and beg him for a good attitude. I get my heart as far as I can get it, then ask God to please, please get my heart the rest of the way there." That makes sense to me!

I think this is what Paul had in mind as he contemplated that he was not yet where he wanted to be:

> *Not that I have already obtained all this, or have already been made perfect, but I press on to take hold of that for which Christ Jesus took hold of me. Brothers, I do not consider myself yet to have taken hold of it. But one thing I do: Forgetting what is behind and straining toward what is ahead, I press on toward the goal to win the prize for which God has called me heavenward in Christ Jesus.*
>
> *All of us who are mature should take such a view of things. **And if on some point you think differently, that too God will make clear to you.*** (Philippians 3:12–15, emphasis added)

Get your heart as far along as you can get it. Then go to God and ask him in his mercy to get you the whole way there. Ask him to humble you, to discipline you, to open your mind, and to teach you the truth of what you need to learn. Pray this prayer with David:

> *O LORD, I call to you; come quickly to me.*
> *Hear my voice when I call to you.*
> *May my prayer be set before you like incense;*
> *may the lifting up of my hands be like the evening sacrifice.*
>
> *Set a guard over my mouth, O LORD;*
> *keep watch over the door of my lips.*
> *Let not my heart be drawn to what is evil,*
> *to take part in wicked deeds*
> *with men who are evildoers;*
> *let me not eat of their delicacies.*
>
> *Let a righteous man strike me—it is a kindness;*
> *let him rebuke me—it is oil on my head.*
> *My head will not refuse it.* (Psalm 141:1–5)

My version of the prayer in Psalm 141 goes something like this: "God, I am not where I need to be. I must be blind to some things I need to see. Please, Father, do whatever it takes to get me where you want me to be, to teach me the truths I need to see."

And then, my brothers, I get ready for some convicting, challenging, life-changing conversations and moments to come my way!

Ask for—and accept—a thorough, complete cleansing

Cleanse me with hyssop, and I will be clean;
wash me, and I will be whiter than snow....
Hide your face from my sins
and blot out all my iniquity. (Psalm 51:7,9)

David pleads for complete forgiveness. That, of course, is the only kind that God gives. But if we are to recover from defeat, we cannot live the rest of our lives *feeling* only partially forgiven. We need to know and sense in our deepest souls that we are completely, thoroughly, totally washed clean. David wants to be—and to feel—as pure and clean as freshly fallen snow, with no scarlet stain of sin upon his soul (Isaiah 1:18). He wants God to hide his face from his sin—to not look upon it or see it anymore. David does not want to define his life by the sin he has committed, but by the purity and righteousness the Lord graciously gives him.

We all received grace when we were born again in baptism and washed in the blood of Christ. We are no longer defined by our sin, but by the righteousness of Jesus himself. When we have moments when we are defeated by sin later down the road, we need to return to our Lord and receive his mercy once again. And we need to know and believe that when God forgives us after a defeat, we remain his beloved sons. There may be consequences to our actions, and we may have to earn the trust of some of the people around us, but we are not forever damaged in our relationship with our Father. We don't have to work out in the back with the hired men as if we are no longer in the family (Luke 15:17–24). When we falter, our Father does not place us on spiritual probation. When we fall, he does not treat us as second-class citizens in his kingdom—no!

No matter how ugly, selfish, and hurtful our sin has been, we need to go to God and seek full forgiveness and restoration of our relationship with him. If we continue to feel somehow devalued as his child after a failure, then we are far more likely to one day be completely defeated by Satan. And why is that? It is because the Accuser knows if he can make us feel distanced and degraded before God, then he is far more likely to finally win the war. A warrior who continually feels guilty and ashamed is greatly weakened in battle. Duty to our God without a close relationship to him as our Father can only take us so far. The man who lives burdened by an unending sense of condemnation and shame is simply unable to be the mighty warrior he should be. My brothers, claim the full forgiveness of God through the cross and the blood of your older brother Jesus, and the grace of your Father in heaven!

Bring back the joy

> *Let me hear joy and gladness;*
> *let the bones you have crushed rejoice.* (Psalm 51:8)

> *Restore to me the joy of your salvation*
> *and grant me a willing spirit, to sustain me.* (Psalm 51:12)

It is a great thing to *be* forgiven, but brothers, God wants his warriors to *enjoy* being forgiven! Many of us carry continual shame and sadness in our hearts and consciences because we struggle with sin, or because of a past defeat.

David wanted to not just be pardoned; he wanted to enjoy his life again. Think about that for a minute. This man committed adultery with another man's wife and got her pregnant. He then had this man—his friend and fellow warrior!—murdered to cover it up. Does David deserve to have a happy life in the future? Doesn't he instead deserve to live in spiritual misery the rest of his days? Isn't it arrogant and presumptuous for him to even ask for such a blessing?

I do not think David is being arrogant in his request. After all, this is a Spirit-inspired psalm that God has left us in the Bible to teach us how to repent and be made right with him when we have sinned. What God is saying to us through this prayer of David is this: no matter how terrible our sin has been, when we have sincerely and deeply repented, when we are depending on the blood of Christ to forgive us, we can indeed long for, ask for, and even hope and expect to be joyful once again. We can have the same joy we had the day of our baptism into Christ. We can have the same sense of purity, of being cleansed, that we felt when we were first born again.

If not, what do we believe? What are we saying to God? Are we saying that the grace of God was enough to forgive us initially, but that after that, we are back to earning our own way? *No messing up! If you do, you are stained and flawed forever. You are now a second-class citizen in the kingdom. Prepare to live the rest of your life with a sense of disqualification. You can never really be happy again. No more real joy and fun for you! Sorry, bro, you'll just never be really happy again or feel good about yourself deep down inside.*

We put ourselves on "spiritual probation," much like the rebellious but repentant son tried to do in Luke 15. We tell our Father that we are willing to live out back with the hired servants, no longer in the warm embrace of our Father's love. We think we can never feel like a forgiven son again. "I'll just be a hireling now, thank you. I will live under my Father's protection, but not under his roof or within his love. I have forever lost my closeness as a son because of my sin." Well, fellow warrior, the father in Luke 15 wouldn't hear it! He interrupted his son's confession to give him a ring, a robe, new shoes, and a party! And he defended him to his accusing older brother. *So he will do for you and me.*

Have you fallen, my brother warrior? Have you faced defeat? Have you woken up in the pigpen? Then please repent, come to your senses, come home to your Father, and come join your repentance party! Jesus tells us that there is "more rejoicing in heaven over one sinner who repents than over ninety-nine who do not need to repent" (Luke 15:7; see also vv. 11–24).

Live your life to the full again. It's time to trust in the grace of God. It's time to let God forgive you, and then forgive yourself. We are free; we can take ourselves off our self-imposed spiritual probation. *Our Father wants us to be happy again!*

Did you notice what David says in the last part of the psalm? "Grant me a willing spirit, to sustain me" (Psalm 51:12). You can't get your "willing spirit" back if you are plagued with guilt the rest of your life. Love is the greatest and most powerful motivator of all. Fear is "the beginning of wisdom," to be sure (Psalm 111:10); without it, we become arrogant and hard-hearted. But fear is not the *end* of wisdom; God finishes with love. We need to know and feel and embrace his love, acceptance, grace, and forgiveness—way down deep—or we just won't get past defeat. To fully overcome, we have to feel that God actually *likes* us and is smiling upon us once again!

Let God restore you to service

Then I will teach transgressors your ways,
and sinners will turn back to you.
Save me from bloodguilt, O God,
the God who saves me,
and my tongue will sing of your righteousness.
O Lord, open my lips,
and my mouth will declare your praise.
You do not delight in sacrifice, or I would bring it;
you do not take pleasure in burnt offerings. (Psalm 51:13–16)

David wants to be useful once more. He wants to help and teach others again. He wants his life to make a difference.

One of the hardest things for some warriors to do when we have failed God is to get back out on the battlefield. And not just out on the battlefield, out on the front lines.

After a fall, some of us think we are supposed to stay in the background from now on. We have squandered our glory days. We have destroyed our reputation and honor. We may have repented, but now we think we need to just sit quietly and try to stay faithful. Our place is no longer out on the frontlines where we can serve and fight courageously and effectively.

No, brother warrior, you've got that all wrong! God wants you to suit up, shine up your weapons, and run back to battle! Yes, you fell, but that doesn't make you a permanent casualty. You can be healed. You can fight again. That is God's plan.

Brothers, we are not just pardoned, we are restored to victorious service for God. Like David, we can be warriors again.

This is your call back to battle, my brother. Unsheathe your sword. Pick up your shield. Put on your helmet. Run back to battle.

Help other Mighty Men to rise up

In your good pleasure make Zion prosper;
build up the walls of Jerusalem.
Then there will be righteous sacrifices,

whole burnt offerings to delight you;
then bulls will be offered on your altar. (Psalm 51:18–19)

Maybe you aren't in the middle of a crushing personal defeat right now, but how is your battalion—your local church—faring? Are all of you engaged in an inspiring mission? And how are the men around you doing? Are they zealous warriors for God, or have they gone flat? Are they lukewarm? It can be terribly demoralizing for warriors when we see that the men around us have lost their fighting spirit.

Sometimes all of us suffer a defeat together. Sometimes our unit, or the whole army of God, suffers a loss all at the same time. Ever been a part of one of those terrible moments? What happens then? Can we all come back?

Think about the condition of the army of Israel in Saul's time. Things got so bad that on one occasion their enemies taunted Jonathan, saying, " 'The Hebrews are crawling out of the holes they were hiding in'" (1 Samuel 14:11). And later, Goliath mocks the army of God: " 'This day I defy the ranks of Israel! Give me a man and let us fight each other.' On hearing the Philistine's words, Saul and all the Israelites were dismayed and terrified" (1 Samuel 17:10-11). The Mighty Men of Israel are cowering—even Saul and the courageous Jonathan are frightened!

Sometimes this can happen in a church. The men grow dull, fearful, and timid.

Well, my brother, all it takes is *one warrior* to step up and step out and inspire the rest. That's just what David did when he took on Goliath. And when he won that fight, here's what happened:

David ran and stood over him. He took hold of the Philistine's sword and drew it from the scabbard. After he killed him, he cut off his head with the sword.
When the Philistines saw that their hero was dead, they turned and ran. Then the men of Israel and Judah surged forward with a shout. (1 Samuel 17:51-52)

Cowards turned into heroes in about fifteen seconds! A group of men—a whole brotherhood, a whole church—can be roused from defeat, dismay, and discouragement because one warrior steps out in humility, courage, and faith.

My brother, *you can be that warrior*. You can turn the tide of battle. You can inspire your brothers. You can save the day. Do it for God. Do it for your family. Do it for your church. Do it for our brotherhood.

You and I are the descendants of David. We, like David, are men after the heart of God, men who long to be God's warriors. The Bible is a story of redemption. It is the story of men who failed and came back, turning their lives around by God's mercy. We all suffer defeat. I have. You have. And one day we will suffer it again. But that does not mean that defeat has to define who we are. It does not mean that defeat is a way of life. Let us rise up again, and by the grace of God and the power of his Spirit, go forth to war!

> *The cords of the grave coiled around me;*
> *the snares of death confronted me.*
> *In my distress I called to the LORD;*
> *I cried to my God for help.*
> *From his temple he heard my voice;*
> *my cry came before him, into his ears.*
>
> *He reached down from on high and took hold of me;*
> *he drew me out of deep waters.*
> *He rescued me from my powerful enemy,*
> *from my foes, who were too strong for me.*
> *They confronted me in the day of my disaster,*
> *but the LORD was my support.*
> *He brought me out into a spacious place;*
> *he rescued me because he delighted in me.*
> (Psalm 18:5-6, 16-19)

Chapter Nineteen

The Battle Is the Lord's

David said to the Philistine, "You come against me with sword and spear and javelin, but I come against you in the name of the LORD Almighty, the God of the armies of Israel, whom you have defied. This day the LORD will hand you over to me. . . . and the whole world will know that there is a God in Israel. All those gathered here will know that it is not by sword or spear that the LORD saves; for the battle is the LORD'S, and he will give all of you into our hands."

1 Samuel 17: 45–47, emphasis added

The battle we have to fight does not *belong* to us. It is not *about* us. It is about God—his honor, his glory, his people, his truth.

This changes everything for us as warriors—and it changes it *in our favor*. We go into battle and wage this war knowing that we are soldiers in the most righteous cause for which any warrior has ever fought. And because God is with us, we have the assurance of victory. What are our battles? They are different for each warrior. They may be battles of puri- or finances, the conquest of a career or the challenge of childrearing, struggle of strengthening a church or saving one soul. Each warrior is own battles to fight, his own Goliaths to slay.

d's people have never lost a single battle when they fought ac- to God's will and were faithful and righteous. *Not one.*

stepped up to meet Goliath because he knew that evil needed

to be defeated that day. Goliath had defied the armies of Israel, but the One he had really insulted was God himself. Nobody else saw it that way but David. Everyone else saw the situation from a human point of view. Everyone else saw a nine-foot giant who was unbeatable by any living man. David saw a man who had "defied the armies of the living God." And that was unacceptable.

God's honor was at stake. David was not trying to prove himself, his courage, or his manhood. It wasn't about him, or Saul, or Jonathan, or even Goliath. It wasn't about David proving that he was worthy to become king.

Brothers, this book is not a call for us to make a name for ourselves. True, in one sense, we do need to prove ourselves to be faithful warriors. We do need to rise up and go to battle, and inspire others to do the same. But what we are proving is not ourselves but our loyalty to *God*: our faith in him, our commitment to his honor. And when we succeed on his behalf, the power has come from him and all glory goes to him.

The victory has already been won

Satan is a defeated foe.

He lost the war long ago in heaven (Revelation 12:7–9). He and his angels rebelled against God, were defeated, and lost their place with God. He was cast down to earth, and he is enraged against us. He still has power and can bring great harm to God's people and God's cause. *But he has lost the war.* Any victories he may claim are temporary. He will ultimately be consigned to an existence of misery and darkness.

Jesus continued the war, and defeated Satan during his days on earth. Every power of darkness was unleashed against him, but Jesus stood firm. When Jesus went to the cross he led Satan behind him in triumphal procession as a defeated foe (Colossians 2:14–15). "Come down from the cross and we will believe in you" was the message Satan shouted at Jesus (Matthew 27:40–42), but the Lord refused to come down, and in so doing he sealed the fate of Satan and his demons. Jesus could have called twelve legions of angels from heaven to stop the crucifixion and wipe out the Romans and the unbelieving Jewish leaders that day, but he refused to do so (Matthew 26:53). He knew the way to defeat Sata. was by going to the cross and paying the debt of our sin, forever tak: away the hold and authority Satan had over our lives. When he crie "It is finished," *Satan* was finished. No longer did he have a hold

No longer were we under condemnation. For those who would believe, repent, and be baptized, forgiveness was now theirs, and the yoke of the oppressor was broken! The cross, followed by the resurrection, was the greatest loss Satan ever suffered. It broke his hold upon the world.

And yet Satan still has power. He is defeated, undermined, and dethroned, but he is still active and alive. He can still win some battles. If we as warriors choose to serve God, if we choose to go by the word of God, Satan will resist us. He will seek to deceive us and he will tempt us, but he does not have to win. As a matter of fact, when we stand up to him, he is doomed to defeat: "Resist the devil, and he will flee from you" (James 4:7).

What confidence it gives a warrior, going into battle knowing that if he follows the orders of his commander, he is guaranteed to win. There will be intense moments. There will be some losses. But if he remains faithful, all will be well in the end. Such is the confidence we have.

Have you ever recorded a sporting event that your team won, and then watched it later, already knowing the final score? Knowing your team would win in the end? When we watch the recording, our attitude throughout the game is totally different. No matter how bad things may seem to be going, no matter what the score may be at any point, no matter how poorly our team plays along the way, we can view the game in peace knowing that in the end, our team wins.

We can have a similar confidence in living our lives and fighting our battles as warriors. No, we do not have the recorded full story. But we do have the promise of our God that if we remain faithful to him, victory is assured. Let us live our lives with the same confidence that David did when he went out to face Goliath. God is with us, and even though we have not yet slung our stone, God will direct our efforts to a victorious end!

We fight from a position of victory

In any battle, the armies struggle to gain the positional advantage. We want the enemy to be in a vulnerable position. What is our position 'n this battle?

Here is what the Bible says:

Or don't you know that all of us who were baptized into Christ Jesus were baptized to his death? We were therefore buried with him through baptism into death in order that, just as Christ was raised from the dead through the glory of the Father, we too may live a new life. (Romans 6:3–4)

What is our position on the battlefield?

First, we are *in Christ*. In baptism we entered into union with Jesus. We were spiritually placed "in him." That means we are within his righteousness. We are within his goodness. It means that all of his perfection surrounds us. When God looks at us, he sees us through a filter—the perfect life of his Son. That righteousness filters out all of our sin. We are in the safe and untouchable place where the attacks of Satan cannot harm us. Yes, we still have to fight. Yes, the flaming arrows will slam into our shield of faith and the blows of Satan may rain down upon our breastplate of righteousness and strike the helmet of our salvation. But they cannot destroy us. We will take some hits, but we can and will recover. All we need to do is keep fighting!

Secondly, *we are raised with Christ*. We are now, in a spiritual sense, already raised up with Christ: victorious, exalted, outside the reach of Satan's power. It may be hard for us to grasp, but the Bible says that we are, in a spiritual sense, already raised from the dead. Let us understand and believe in our deepest hearts this amazing declaration of God:

> But because of his great love for us, God, who is rich in mercy, made us alive with Christ even when we were dead in transgressions—it is by grace you have been saved. **And God raised us up with Christ and seated us with him in the heavenly realms in Christ Jesus**, in order that in the coming ages he might show the incomparable riches of his grace, expressed in his kindness to us in Christ Jesus.
> (Ephesians 2:4–7, emphasis added)

Fellow warriors, in our baptism, we were not only united with Christ; we not only died with him (thus receiving the benefit of his bearing our sin); we were not only raised with him . . . we were also seated with him in the heavenly realms! The Bible teaches us that when Jesus completed the work of purification for sins and returned to heaven, sat down at the right hand of God (Hebrews 1:3). He was exalted place of authority and victory. He is seated because his work is done now rules as the Lord of heaven and earth.

Of course the Bible is not teaching us that we have a like that of Jesus— he alone is Lord. But there is a vital me amazing promise: we are already seated with Christ in a spiritual sense, and we therefore share in the glorious victory that he has won for us. If Satan wants to come after us, he has to fight uphill! We are seated in glory with Christ!

Brothers, if we are already victorious, if we share in the victory of the death, burial and resurrection of Christ, if we are seated with him, then *let's live like it.* Let's have the confidence of a warrior who knows that he has been promised victory by God himself. Let's go into battle just as young David did, telling Goliath, "You will be defeated. I am going to win, because God is with me, and I can't lose. You are going down. You don't have a chance against God."

Brothers, we can go into the battles before us knowing that we already have the victory. We can only lose if we choose to allow Satan into our lives. If we resist him, the battle may be intense—we will take some blows, we may stumble and even have some defeats—but ultimately we will get back up and go on to victory.

The promise and power of victory

This is love for God: to obey his commands. And his commands are not burdensome, for everyone born of God overcomes the world. This is the victory that has overcome the world, even our faith. Who is it that overcomes the world? Only he who believes that Jesus is the Son of God. (1 John 5:3–5)

The power comes from God. It does not come from us. But we access that power through our faith. Many people in Jesus' day were right there with him, but their lives were not changed. They were not healed of their diseases. They did not overcome their sinful ways. Why not? What was the thing that separated them from those who were healed and transformed? You know the answer: *faith.* "Your faith has healed you. Go in peace" (Luke 8:48). Jesus said words like these over and over again—and this time, he said them to a bleeding woman. Many people touched Jesus that day as he was walking through the crowds, but only the woman who touched him *with faith* was healed (see Luke 8:40–56). In what? Faith in the power and love of God.

We must believe that our God is *able.* When Jesus is approached by blind men who beg him to give them their sight, he asks them an important question: "Do you believe that I am able to do this?" When they reply that they do indeed believe, Jesus says to them, "According to your faith will it be done to you," and he touches them and gives them their sight (Matthew 9:27–29).

Whatever battle we have to fight, whatever Satan throws at us, our *God is able!* If the battle is dependent upon our own power, we cannot win, but if we rely on God's power we cannot lose.

We must believe that God is willing. Sometimes our challenge is more about believing in God's *attitude* than in his *power*. Here is where we as warriors must learn to depend upon God's grace, and not upon our own goodness and perfection. Certainly we must not be living a self-willed or double life. That just won't work. But even the most dedicated warrior among us has his flaws, his weaknesses, and his sins. We need to be totally aware of who we are, and what our failings are. But stumbling and falling and making mistakes will not make God bail out on us.

David wrote in one of his great Psalms, "As a father has compassion on his children, so the LORD has compassion on those who fear him; for he knows how we are formed, he remembers that we are dust" (Psalm 103:13–14). Human fathers who love their sons do not give up on them when they struggle to be strong. When we are being tempted, when Satan is attacking, we must believe that God is willing to come to our aid, and give us the strength and the victory we need.

Brothers, we need to boldly claim God's power in times of battle. When Saul expressed doubt that David could defeat Goliath, listen to the confident words of faith David spoke in reply:

> *"Your servant has been keeping his father's sheep. When a lion or a bear came and carried off a sheep from the flock, I went after it, struck it and rescued the sheep from its mouth. When it turned on me, I seized it by its hair, struck it and killed it. Your servant has killed both the lion and the bear; this uncircumcised Philistine will be like one of them, because he has defied the armies of the living God. The LORD who delivered me from the paw of the lion and the paw of the bear will deliver me from the hand of this Philistine."* (1 Samuel 17:34–37)

But he is not done yet! Listen to these words he spoken to Goliath during their confrontation:

> *"You come against me with sword and spear and javelin, but I come against you in the name of the LORD Almighty, the God of the armies of Israel, whom you ha*

defied. This day the LORD will hand you over to me, and I'll strike you down and cut off your head. Today I will give the carcasses of the Philistine army to the birds of the air and the beasts of the earth, and the whole world will know that there is a God in Israel. All those gathered here will know that it is not by sword or spear that the LORD saves; for the battle is the LORD's, and he will give all of you into our hands." (1 Samuel 17:45–47)

Brothers, in the midst of trial, of battle, of temptation and fear, we need to speak words of faith. We need to reaffirm our trust in God, our confidence that he will give the victory, that he is with us, that his promises are true, and that we believe them! When God sees our faith, he will respond. The victory will be ours.

The patience of victory

We are in a lifelong battle. Our Lord has declared us victorious. He will be with us all the way home. We will not face any person or any situation that is too much for us. God has set limits on Satan—he cannot tempt us beyond our ability, through Christ, to resist (1 Corinthians 10:13). But that also indicates that we *will* have battles to fight. There will be hours, days, weeks—and even months or years—when it may seem that Satan is relentlessly attacking. And indeed that may be true.

What we need to know and claim during these times is that if we endure, if we keep fighting, if we depend on God, if we daily humble ourselves, then God will give us the victory. Some battles, like David's battle with Goliath, are fought and won in a day. Others, like David's struggle against Saul, may drag on for years. That does not mean we do not have the victory. That does not mean God is not with us. It simply means that God has other purposes and plans in place that we do not understand. We simply need to suit up every day and keep on fighting. One day, just as David finally ascended to the throne of Israel, we will claim the promised victory.

Remember, brother warriors: Victory may be a long time coming. But when God has promised the victory, it will come as sure as the dawn!

The victory has been won by what God has done in the *past*.

The victory has been *promised*.

The victory comes by the *power* of God.

The victory will take *patience*.

Brothers, the battle is the Lord's. Let us go forth to war, knowing that by the grace, power, and faithfulness of God, we are more than conquerors.

May it be said of us:

They were brave warriors, ready for battle. Their faces were the faces of lions,
*   and they were as swift as gazelles in the mountains.* (1 Chronicles 12:8)

And may we one day say, as David did:

The LORD lives! Praise be to my Rock!
*   Exalted be God my Savior!*
He is the God who avenges me,
*   who subdues nations under me,*
*   who saves me from my enemies.*
You exalted me above my foes;
*   from violent men you rescued me.*
*   I will sing praises to your name.*

He gives his king great victories;
*   he shows unfailing kindness to his anointed,*
*   to David and his descendants forever.* (Psalm 18:46–50)

Vignette: The Reunion
Based on 1 Chronicles 27–29

David summoned all the officials of Israel to assemble at Jerusalem: the officers over the tribes, the commanders of the divisions in the service of the king, the commanders of thousands and commanders of hundreds, and the officials in charge of all the property and livestock belonging to the king and his sons, together with the palace officials, the mighty men and all the brave warriors.

1 Chronicles 28:1

David's reign as king is nearing an end. The Mighty Men have returned to Jerusalem for one final mission, one final celebration, as David commissions his son Solomon with the task of building a temple for God.

The roads were crammed with men. Great warriors. Mighty Men. David, our aging king, had urgently summoned us to Jerusalem: rumor had it he planned to build a temple for our Lord, and maybe even hand over the kingdom to his son Solomon. We all knew one thing for sure: that we needed to go, without fail. The men were arriving by the hundreds. So many of my old friends were there, Mighty Men beside whom I had fought in battle after battle. I found myself laughing, shouting, and weeping all at once, my heart and mind full of memory.

Then I saw him—Shammah. His hair was graying, but still golden. He still wore his bright red tunic, and his bow was, as always, strapped across his back. He looked as if he was ready to go to war—again. I had not seen him since he left the army after David's sin with Bathsheba. My heart racing with joy, I spurred my mount forward. Shammah saw me, reined in his stallion and rode toward me at a gallop. He leapt off his steed while it was still running, landed effortlessly on the ground, graceful as ever, and ran up to me. I dismounted, and we clasped each other's shoulders and embraced, our eyes filled with tears.

"Well, Eleazar, my old friend, this meeting is a bit more joyous than our original encounter," Shammah said, swiping at his eyes.

"No donkey or donkey dung this time," I said, and we both broke ‚ laughter.

"So why are you not the commander of one of the twelve divisions the king has appointed to guard the city?" Shammah asked. "Surely you are worthy to lead 24,000 men! And David trusts you completely."

"David offered me the position, but I need to be home with my wife and children—I have spent too many years away. I told David there was a better man for the job anyway—my father, Dodai! When I told David of my father's exploits in the early days, he agreed to appoint Father to lead the Guard Division assigned to the second month of each year, right behind Jashobeam's unit that serves the first month. It's more of an honorary position for Father—he provides wisdom and inspiration, but Mikloth will lead the division day to day."[4]

"You must be proud," said Shammah.

I nodded. "No son could be prouder. Father is in his eighties, but he is like a young man again. He and Mother and my sisters and their families have moved here permanently to Jerusalem. I have never seen them happier."

Shammah was silent for a long moment. "I respect what you have done, and I respect your loyalty, but you know how I feel about King David," he said, his eyes darkening. "He has fallen too many times for me to follow him any more. He is no better than Saul."

"Shammah, you left us too quickly! You stepped aside too soon after the Bathsheba and Uriah horror. David has changed—truly changed. His example of repentance has shown me that men can face their God and their friends and make things right. Even great men sin—but the greatest men find their way back to God again. Saul sinned, but he never saw himself or what he did. David has come back to God. He is once again the man we came to trust, admire and follow."

Shammah looked down at the dusty ground, shaking his head. "He stole another man's wife. He ordered the men to abandon Uriah on the battlefield—that's murder, Eleazar! One of his own Mighty Men! Uriah was my friend, and yours too, I thought. . ." Shammah's voice was tight with old anger. "And then what happened within David's own family—rape, murder, rebellion . . . clearly, he lost the favor of God. How can you follow him now? How can you trust him?"

I grasped Shammah by the shoulders. "After you left, David assembled the Mighty Men together. Nathan the prophet was by his side. David got on his knees before us. He said he had failed us, and his God. He

---

4. 1 Chronicles 27:1-15

offered no excuse, only begged our forgiveness. He reminded us of the time when we were all ready to stone him back in Ziklag. He said he had been wrong then, but that God—and we—had mercy on him and let him lead us to rescue our wives and children. He said he had deserved to die then, as he did now. He said if we wanted to stone him right there, he would submit—he would willingly perish at the hands of the people he had harmed."

Shammah looked at me incredulously.

"Shammah, if you had only stayed, you could have seen what I saw that day. Jashobeam was so angry he actually picked up a rock when David offered to let us stone him. If I had not grabbed Jash's arm he may have thrown it—you know him. He does not give his trust or loyalty easily. I have never seen him angrier. But David kept talking, and Jash kept listening. I kept listening.

"Nathan the prophet spoke to us. He told us how he had confronted David with his sin, and how God had taken the life of David's young child. Nathan told us that he had advised David to take Bathsheba as his wife since she would be regarded as an adulteress with no family, no future, and possibly a death sentence if she did not live under David's protection. Nathan assured us that David had a broken heart before God, and that God had forgiven him.

"Nathan called us all to be humble. He said that we needed to remember our own sins, to know we had all failed at different times. He reminded us that we were not in the place of God—that vengeance belonged to God, and God alone. He reminded us that if God were to treat us all as our sins deserved, not one of us would live to see tomorrow. He called us all to forgive David and to repent of our own sins. All this time, David stood beside Nathan, weeping.

"Tell me, Shammah, what king has ever done such a thing? What leader has ever admitted before his followers that he was wrong, and asked their forgiveness?"

Shammah did not respond, but I could see a slight softening in his eyes.

"David pulled me and Jash aside afterwards. He begged our forgiveness. He—he asked for you by name, too, wanting to seek your forgiveness as well." Shammah's eyes widened at this, but I kept speaking. "David thanked us for standing by him, and for standing up for our God.

Jash listened and his anger relented, as did mine. Shammah, give David a chance. Come with me today, see and hear your king. See if my words are true. Open your heart. Please, my friend. Hear me."

After a long silence, Shammah said, "If you lead the way, I will follow behind." We mounted up and rode toward the Horse Gate.

Just inside the gate, we heard a familiar shout. "Eleazar! Can that be you?"

Jashobeam was standing next to my father on a platform with the other division commanders, welcoming the leaders who were arriving from all over Israel. Father held a polished cane in one hand, supporting his bad leg, but he stood straight and tall—ever a soldier. My heart surged with mingled pride and joy, seeing my father standing in a place of honor beside my old friend. Father winked down at me, a small smile playing at his lips.

Jashobeam waved me forward. "Hello old friend! And I do mean old friend—how your hair color has changed!" Jash laughed, loud and long. How well I remembered that laugh.

"It's the crown of the aged," I called, reining in my horse beside the platform. "I see you are growing one, too!"

Jashobeam's jaw dropped, and he suddenly fell to his knees, so close to the edge I thought he might topple off the platform. "Shammah, is that you? Have you returned to us at last? It has been too long, my friend! Where have you been? Thank God you are back! Come up here with me, my brothers." Jash beckoned wildly with his arms. "I want you both beside me today when the king makes his presentation."

Later that day all of us—the Mighty Men of old, the army officers, the officials, the leaders of our nation—gathered in the center of Jerusalem. King David and his son Solomon stepped out onto a balcony high above us. Solomon, young man that he was—surely not far into his twenties—stood a head taller than his father, and bore a hint of David's ruddy complexion. David leaned a little on his son's arm, but his steps were sure and steady. The crowed greeted them with cheers. Below the balcony, a large group of soldiers tended multiple wagons laden with what looked like plunder from the battlefield. I remembered the sight, having seen the spoils of victory many times in my life as a soldier.

David spoke. Even now his familiar baritone voice rang out strong. Confident. Clear. Almost musical. "Fellow warriors, Mighty Men, and friends: Long ago I began to dream of building a temple for the worship of our God—to build a home for the ark of the covenant of the LORD, which has never in all its years had a proper dwelling."

Scattered cheers called out from the crowd.

David waited for quiet and began again. "But that was not God's plan for me. Through the prophet Nathan, God told me that because I am a warrior with blood on my hands, the privilege was to be given to another—to my son Solomon." David turned to Solomon, a proud smile lighting his face. Solomon gave his father a nod.

David placed hands upon his son's shoulders: "Son, now I charge you in the sight of all Israel and of the assembly of the LORD, and in the hearing of our God: Be careful to follow all the commands of the LORD your God, that you may possess this good land and pass it on as an inheritance to your descendants forever.

"And you, my son Solomon, acknowledge the God of your father, and serve him with wholehearted devotion and with a willing mind, for the LORD searches every heart and understands every motive behind the thoughts. If you seek him, he will be found by you; but if you forsake him, he will reject you forever. Consider now, for the LORD has chosen you to build a temple as a sanctuary. Be strong and do the work."[5]

Solomon fell to his knees. The crowd murmured its approval. David kissed the top of his son's head and whispered something in his ear. Solomon nodded. Then David clasped his son's hands, pulled him to his feet, and presented him with scrolls bearing the plans for the temple that God had revealed to him.

David turned back to the crowd and gestured toward the multiple wagons on the street below. "I myself am supplying the gold, silver, bronze, iron, jewels, and all of the materials needed for the construction of the temple. From my personal treasure I give three thousand talents of gold and seven thousand talents of silver, all to be used for building a temple to the glory of God."

We all shouted and stamped, a riot of excitement. "And now, my brothers, it is your turn. I call on you to give of your resources as you feel moved in your heart."

The crowd parted down the middle, a break in the sea of warriors, and men streamed forward. Man after man came forward bearing gifts,

---

5. 1 Chronicles 28:8-10

placing them in a growing, glittering heap beneath the balcony. David nodded to each one. I had little with me, but gave all the coin I had. As I tossed it in, David beamed down at me, his eyes as bright as ever. I saluted.

At first, the giving was loud, joyous—but gradually the laughter and shouts turned to prayer and tears. David stood above us, arms raised in praise to God, tears streaming down his aged cheeks, and his emotion swept across the crowd. Gratitude and joy caught us up in a wondrous tide, and we wept. Beside me, Shammah wept loudest of all.

In all my days of serving my God and my king, I had never seen the hearts of the people or the Mighty Men so moved. This moment was as great as the victory over Goliath, as emotional as the day we had saved our wives and children from the hands of the Amalekites, as exciting as any of our greatest exploits, as joyous as the day David was anointed king. In some ways, it was even greater.

David led us in prayer, as he had done so many times before—before battles, in dark caves, after victories. He lifted his hands in praise. We all fell to our knees.

"Praise be to you, O LORD,
     God of our father Israel,
     from everlasting to everlasting.
Yours, O LORD, is the greatness and the power
     and the glory and the majesty and the splendor,
     for everything in heaven and earth is yours.
Yours, O LORD, is the kingdom;
     you are exalted as head over all.
Wealth and honor come from you;
     you are the ruler of all things.
In your hands are strength and power
     to exalt and give strength to all.
Now, our God, we give you thanks
     and praise your glorious name.

"But who am I, and who are my people, that we should be able to give as generously as this? Everything comes from you, and we have given you only what comes from your hand."[6]

---

6. 1 Chronicles 29:10-14

Then David said to us all, "Praise the LORD your God."

So we all praised the LORD, the God of our fathers; we bowed low and fell prostrate before the LORD.

Later that night, my friends and I found a moment alone, sitting around a fire behind my father's house. How many campfires had we huddled around together over the years—fleeing from Saul, preparing a meal, or preparing for battle?

"Our God was honored today," I said to Shammah and Jashobeam. The flames reached for the sky and lit my friend's faces in a golden glow. "Warriors, what we have fought and suffered for is now coming to pass. It has taken years, but God is faithful. His promises of blessing, protection and victory have come true. I am so grateful he has allowed me to serve him in his army. I am so honored that he has allowed me to fight beside brothers"—my throat tightened around the word, and I swallowed hard—"like you both. I am glad to have known the shepherd boy who became our earthly king. But as David always says, God is the true King of his people. He is our God, and we are his flock. My brothers, we pledged to serve our God. Let us exalt his name all the days of our lives."

"My brothers, I feel as if my own heart is restored to God today," said Shammah. Fire danced in his eyes. "I had become embittered and faithless. This day has shown me that if any one of us loses our faith, God yet remains faithful. Our king has returned to God. I can see it in his eyes. I hear it in his voice. I, too, am returning to my God—and to you, my friends." He gripped my shoulder with one strong hand, and Jashobeam's shoulder with the other. "I will go home to get my family and come back here to serve alongside you both, for the rest of my days."

"And I will do the same," I said. "My father is here, leading God's warriors. I will stand by my father, my friends, my king, and my God for the rest of my life."

Jashobeam stood and drew his sword. It flashed red and gold in the firelight. He held it before us and studied it with a half-smile, as if remembering all the battles he had fought with it in his hand, and us by his side. "Brothers, when we were young, we all left our homes to become warriors in Saul's army. Then after we had joined, we wanted to become mighty warriors. But when we met David, everything changed. He showed us there is a different way—a better way than any of us knew."

Jash sheathed his sword. "Through all of his defeats and victories,

David showed us then, and is still showing us here at the end of his days, how to be men after the heart of God. He taught us to seek the face of our God with all of our hearts through defeat, through victory, and through long seasons of waiting. David led the way for us, but it was really our God who was behind it all, seeking us. God brought us through the valley of the shadow of death to this season of glorious victory. And what is more, our sons are following after us! Now I think we can all say that we have become more than we ever dreamed we would be. We are indeed mighty warriors for—but brothers, we are far more than that. We are mighty warriors for **God.**"

When Jashobeam finished speaking, as one man we fell to our knees, lifted our hands, and worshipped our God.

For tools and ideas
about how to
apply the principles found
in this book please visit

www.WarriorfortheLord.com